Time Out 1000
Songs
to change your life

www.timeout.com

Published by Time Out Guides Ltd, a wholly owned subsidiary of Time Out Group Ltd.
Time Out and the Time Out logo are trademarks of Time Out Group Ltd.

© **Time Out Group Ltd 2008**

10 9 8 7 6 5 4 3 2 1

This edition first published in Great Britain in 2008 by Ebury Publishing
A Random House Group Company
20 Vauxhall Bridge Road, London SW1V 2SA

Random House Australia Pty Limited 20 Alfred Street, Milsons Point, Sydney, New South Wales 2061, Australia
Random House New Zealand Limited 18 Poland Road, Glenfield, Auckland 10, New Zealand
Random House South Africa (Pty) Limited Isle of Houghton, Corner Boundary
Road & Carse O'Gowrie, Houghton 2198, South Africa

Random House UK Limited Reg. No. 954009

Distributed in US by Publishers Group West
Distributed in Canada by Publishers Group Canada

For further distribution details, see www.timeout.com

ISBN: 978-1-84670-082-8

A CIP catalogue record for this book is available from the British Library

Printed and bound by Firmengruppe APPL, aprinta druck, Wemding, Germany

The Random House Group Limited supports The Forest Stewardship Council (FSC), the leading international
forest certification organisation. All our titles that are printed on Greenpeace approved FSC certified paper carry
the FSC logo. Our paper procurement policy can be found at www.rbooks.co.uk/environment.

Time Out carbon-offsets all its flights with Trees for Cities (www.treesforcities.org).

Time Out Guides Limited
Universal House
251 Tottenham Court Road
London W1T 7AB
Tel + 44 (0)20 7813 3000
Fax + 44 (0)20 7813 6001
Email guides@timeout.com
www.timeout.com

Editorial
Editor Will Fulford-Jones
Deputy Editor John Lewis
Proofreader John Pym
Indexers Jackie Brind, Cathy Limb

Managing Director Peter Fiennes
Financial Director Gareth Garner
Editorial Director Sarah Guy
Series Editor Cath Phillips
Editorial Manager Holly Pick
Accountant Ija Krasnikova

Design
Art Director Scott Moore
Art Editor Pinelope Kourmouzoglou
Senior Designer Henry Elphick
Graphic Designers Gemma Doyle, Kei Ishimaru
Digital Imaging Simon Foster
Advertising Designer Jodi Sher

Picture Desk
Picture Editor Jael Marschner
Deputy Picture Editor Katie Morris
Picture Researchers Gemma Walters, Helen McFarland
Picture Desk Assistant Marzena Zoladz

Advertising
Commercial Director Mark Phillips
Sales Manager Alison Wallen

Marketing
Head of Marketing Catherine Demajo
Marketing Manager Yvonne Poon
Sales & Marketing Director, North America Lisa Levinson

Production
Group Production Director Mark Lamond
Production Manager Brendan McKeown
Production Controller Caroline Bradford
Production Coordinator Julie Pallot

Time Out Group
Chairman Tony Elliott
Financial Director Richard Waterlow
Group General Manager/Director Nichola Coulthard
Time Out Magazine Ltd MD Richard Waterlow
Time Out Communications Ltd MD David Pepper
Time Out International MD Cathy Runciman
Group IT Director Simon Chappell

The editor would like to thank Jeremy Brill at Brill (27 Exmouth Market, London EC1R 4QL).

Illustrations Elliot Elam.

Cover photography Rob Greig.

Photography pages 3, 6 Ming Tang-Evans; 8 Andrew Brackenbury; 12 Tony Russell/Redferns; 14 Mischa Haller; 15 Echoes Archive/Redferns; 17 Richard E Aaron/Redferns; 19 Ellis Parrinder; 21 Stephanie Chernikowski/Redferns; 22 Gemma Day; 24 Andrew Lepley/Redferns; 29, 79, 155 BBC Photo Library/Redferns; 30 Herman Leonard/Redferns; 31 Simon Songhurst; 32, 50, 72, 81, 116, 128, 147, 164, 180, 197, 247, 251 Rob Grieg; 35 Stephen Wright/Redferns; 40, 171, 179, 184, 234 David Redfern/Redferns; 43, 172 Charlie Gillett Archive/Redferns; 44, 49, 59, 105, 112, 152 Ebet/Redferns; 46 Magnus Anderson; 53 Stephen Booth; 55, 82, 100, 143 RB/Redferns; 56, 124 Will Fulford-Jones; 62, 63 AFP/Getty Images; 68 Gered Mankowitz/Redferns; 71, 161, 174, 201, 216 GAB Archives/Redferns; 75 JM International/Redferns; 85, 144 Gilles Petard Collection/Redferns; 86 Bob King/Redferns; 92 Des Willie/Redferns; 95 David Corio/Redferns; 97 Janette Beckman/Redferns; 102 Dick Barnatt/Redferns; 107, 130, 154, 243 Mick Hutson/Redferns; 108 Anna Schori; 115 the Estate of Garry Winogrand, courtesy Fraenkel Gallery, San Francisco; 120 Rob Verhorst/Redferns; 123 Su Ingle; 127 Tim Roney/Redferns; 136 Amber Brooks/Redferns; 140 Tom Hanley/Redferns; 149 PALM/RSCH/Redferns; 160 Ron Howard/Redferns; 163 Virginia Turbett/Redferns; 168 Graham Lowe/Redferns; 175 Chuck Stewart/Redferns; 176 ABC/RA/Lebrecht Music & Arts; 183 Brian Shuel/Redferns; 188 Fin Costello/Redferns; 191 Max Redfern/Redferns; 193 PA Photos/AP; 195 Adam Ritchie/Redferns; 196 Dave Swindells; 200, 210 Hulton Archive/Getty Images; 206 France 3 Cinema/Photofest; 208 Barry J Holmes; 209 Warner Bros/Photofest; 214 S&G/Redferns; 217 Mamma Mia! London cast 2008 by Brinkoff/Mögenburg; 219, 220 Ron Scheri/Redferns; 221 Bohdan Cap; 223 Paramount Pictures/Ronald Grant Archive; 224 Gems/Redferns; 231 Gai Terrell/Redferns; 239 Leee Black Childers/Redferns; 240 Jan Persson/Redferns; 246 Franc Collection/Redferns; 249 Scott Wishart; 252 Brigitte Engl/Redferns. The following images were provided by representatives of the featured artists: pages 25, 36, 60 (top and bottom), 64, 103, 131, 132, 156, 182, 248.

Contents

Introduction

Be honest – did you turn here first? Or did you head straight for the index? It's both the blessing and the curse of music books such as these: to some readers, they're only as good as the records featured within their pages. Include some long-lost gem of a B-side that's been forgotten by all but the writer and the reader, and you've made a friend for life. Miss out the casual bookshop browser's favourite single, and you run the risk of being left on the shelves forever.

If that sounds defensive, it's not meant to be. It's simply an acknowledgment that, perhaps more than any other art form, music arouses in us extraordinary passions. It moves us in ways we both can and can't explain: lifting us skywards or filling us with rage, leaving us grinning or plunging us into a deep and inexplicable melancholy. But it also inspires immense loyalties to songs, albums and musicians with whom we've forged some sort of a connection. We feel as though we understand the records we love in a way that no one, perhaps not even the musicians who created them, will ever quite appreciate. We *get* it.

Some of these records will, in some way, have changed our lives. Others will have changed the lives of others. But even so, we can't honestly claim that this book quite matches its title. For one thing, these 280 pages actually hold a total of 1,577 individual recordings – how about *that* for bonus tracks? And for another, it'd be foolhardy of us to pretend that every song mentioned in the pages that follow has the potential to alter your existence in some profoundly meaningful way. During its ascent to number five in the UK singles charts during summer 1975, for instance, 'Funky Moped' by Jasper Carrott probably didn't change anyone's life. Unless, of course, your name is Jasper Carrott. (Hello, Jasper.)

That, in a nutshell, is the aim of the book: not every song mentioned in here will connect with you, but they'll all connect with somebody. *1000 Songs* contains chart hits and operatic arias, folk songs and hip hop cuts, canonical favourites and mysterious obscurities: most musical life is here, represented to some degree or other. And on that subject, please be assured that it's not out of contrariness that, for example, 'Weird Al' Yankovic outnumbers Van Morrison by eight songs to one, or that the book mentions as many recordings by the Chipmunks as by Jerry Lee Lewis. It's simply what happens when you invite more than 30 writers, who between them maintain a huge variety of specialities, interests and perspectives, to write about music.

While there are a few lists contained within these pages, the bulk of the book is comprised of 36 essays, with the aforementioned writers discussing, debating, pondering and praising music of more or less every stripe. These features are sheltered by the umbrella themes

offered by ten separate sections: each offers a different slant on some aspect of music, each contains three or four individual essays, and each is named after an album:

Kind of Blue discusses misery and sadness, romantic and otherwise, while Born to Run contains a trio of essays that are all essentially about escape. The four pieces in For Your Pleasure all relate loosely to entertainment and indulgence; set against it, There's a Riot Goin' On is concerned with anger and dissidence. Being There relates music to a sense of place; Court & Spark takes care of love and sex. Fear of Music encompasses entry-level musicology, covering everything from traditional folk song to the working methods of pop songwriters. Countdown to Ecstasy deals with euphoria and bliss, whether religious or drug-induced. Finally, Talking Book throws the spotlight on songs of stage and screen, and The Real McCoy covers issues of authenticity and quote-unquote keeping it real.

The ten essays that introduce these ten sections each come with a list of 20 additional songs, expanding on the theme of the piece. These supplementary, complementary lists were compiled by the editors, as were the dozen 'Top ten' boxes that are scattered around the book and that take in everything from dance crazes to smoking, songs about the moon to tunes with awkward time signatures.

Also dotted around the book are a series of 40 interviews. Roughly half of them, headlined 'On the record', feature musicians, singers and songwriters discussing a particular piece of music that means something to them. A song that changed their life? In many cases, yes. The remainder of the interviews are extracted or excerpted from the 40-year archives of *Time Out London*: hiding under the theme 'Rewind', they feature everyone from the Beastie Boys to Ravi Shankar lending their own perspectives to the subjects discussed in the essays.

At this point, it probably goes without saying that you won't agree with everything in here. Not to worry: the writers don't always agree with each other. Nick Coleman's combative, convincing essay in favour of the musical human touch, for instance, stands several poles apart from Philip Sherburne's fascinating discourse on the links between electronic music and the city. While Stephen Troussé speaks up for pop's role in modern cinema, Geoff Carter argues in favour of the bespoke movie score. And Mike Shallcross's mind-expanding trip into music's druggier pastures is directly followed by Robert Darden's hymn in praise of American gospel music, the two essays eyeing each other with respectful but wary suspicion.

Some of these essays, lists and interviews are deeply frivolous, while others verge on the academic. A handful concentrate on a single genre, while many others lurch around like Shane MacGowan in a dodgem. What matters, ultimately, is the variety and quality of the music and, we hope, the variety and quality of the writing. Almost by definition, all anthologies of this nature inspire argument. More simply, we hope this one inspires.

All of which brings us back to the where we started. If we may toot our own trumpet for a moment, we're fairly sure that this is the only music book on the shelves with an index that finds romantic composer Franz Schubert nestling next to proto-gangsta rapper Schoolly D, latter-day hip hopper Chamillionaire sitting snugly alongside country-folk songstress Mary Chapin Carpenter, and, perhaps best of all, techno wizard Jeff Mills rubbing shoulders with '30s close-harmony singers the Mills Brothers. These aren't the only 1,000… Sorry. Let's start that again. These aren't the only *1,577* songs that could change your life. But they're a start. Happy listening.

Kind of Blue

TO CHANGE YOUR LIFE

Love
hurts

Douglas Wolk on the inextricable bond between pop and heartbreak.

'You broke my heart,' sings Becky Stark. Behind her on the stage at the Crystal Ballroom in Portland, Oregon, the other members of the California group Lavender Diamond are playing a stately march rhythm, but Stark isn't looking at them as she sings: she's pointing directly at members of the audience, one by one, singing the song's title over and over again. '*You* broke my heart. *You* broke my heart. *You* broke my heart.' It's one of the oldest tricks in popular music, and one of the most reliable: singing about heartbreak.

Emotional complaints aren't necessarily what pop does best. There aren't as many great songs about heartbreak as you might think, and surprisingly few have made it to the top of the charts. But for all that, no kind of art expresses heartbreak better than popular music. That's because a pop song is more than just its words: it's the sound of those words, and the singer singing them, and the melody to which they're set, and usually much more besides. Every aspect has an emotional impact of its own.

The usual definition of lyric poetry is, in a nutshell, verse that aims to express a character's emotional state. But *lyrikos*, the Greek word from which the term 'lyric poetry' is derived, originally referred to verse that was performed to the accompaniment of a lyre. One surviving fragment written by the Greek lyric poet Sappho, who lived around 600 BCE, runs '*mete moi meli mete melissa*': 'for me, neither the honey nor the honeybee' – or, as Cleveland group band My Dad Is Dead put it in the title of a 1997 album, 'everyone wants the honey but not the sting'. Now *that's* a hook.

But Sappho's words aren't Sappho's song, even if you hear them in their original alliterative Greek, because we don't know the music that went with them. After all, the meaning of the words isn't quite the same thing as the meaning of the song. Read aloud the lyrics of a good pop song, and they might not be all that powerful. Start singing, and the blood rushes into them.

That goes double for songs concerned with desolation. Despite a few neat little compositional tricks, the 1963 song 'It's My Party' is pure teeny-bopper stuff, a girl in tears at her own party because her boyfriend's

Al Green is blue.

making a show of his new squeeze. As such, the killer moment in Lesley Gore's performance belongs not to the song but to the singer: in one snapped-off phoneme ('Judy's wearing his ring-*uh*'), Gore conveys a world of furious humiliation. Likewise, Tony Asher's lyrics to the Beach Boys' 'Caroline, No' are basically doggerel. But coupled with Brian Wilson's melody for them, spiking up to stifled-sob high notes before cascading down like just-cut hair on the last word of each line, they become more poignant, even crushing.

Leaving aside what the lyre (or guitar, or piano, or Pro Tools track) is doing in the background, a singer doesn't just pronounce a

song but *interpret* it. Bob Dylan's take on his own 'Just Like Tom Thumb's Blues' is sneering, even hectoring, a borderline-sympathetic portrait of a fool. But when Nina Simone sings the same song, it becomes a first-person account of illusions crushed into dust one by one, of emotional agony so intense that it's stripped away everything from her soul. After the first five verses, she takes a breath and announces, 'Well, that's it, folks – that's it,' before settling, exhausted, into a final verse in which the lyric moves conclusively into the first person. Her tone is broken, helpless in the hands of fate.

Music and performance can play against the ostensible message of a lyric, a trick used over and over by the producers and singers of the classic Motown singles of the 1960s. The Supremes' confectionery 'Where Did Our Love Go' is nominally about a terrible moment, but Diana Ross purrs the whole thing like a come-on: when she sings 'and it hurts so bad', the lyrics might as well be 'and it feels so good' (and she even follows it up with a near-orgasmic little 'ooh-hoo'). Likewise, the Temptations' version of 'I Can't Get Next to You' is less about heartsick helplessness and more about acrobatic power, with the 'I' of the song title distributed between five singers. And when Al Green sings the same song, it's even further removed from its words. In his hands, it's a seduction and a prayer: Green's always been so focused on the balance between erotic love and divine love that whenever he sings the word 'you', even in a secular context, he might as well be capitalising it.

The emotional core of a song, the thing that communicates the singer's state of mind, may not even be sung. Take, for instance, Soho's 'Hippychick', a 1990 one-hit wonder that's remembered chiefly, if at all, for setting the opening riff from the Smiths' 'How Soon Is Now?' to a dance beat. A conversation between a pacifist and her policeman ex-boyfriend, it's actually a sharp little song in its own right: two verses, a refrain and a terrific first line, 'It's hard to tell you how I feel without hurting you.' Singers Jacqui and Pauline Cuff stretch out the 'hard' so it sounds as if the song is going to be about the difficulty of personal experience rather than the difficulty of interpersonal communication. But that wobbling Johnny Marr guitar riff says more than they do: everyone who recognises it from its earlier incarnation associates it with another kind of heartbreak.

No matter how you sing a song, in fact, you're always *singing* it, and this inherent artifice has been addressed by much pop about heartbreak and desolation. Speaking of the Smiths, 'Heaven Knows I'm Miserable Now' is an incredibly sad song, but it isn't overtly miserable: its title is a joking allusion to Sandie Shaw's late-'60s single 'Heaven Knows I'm Missing Him Now', and Morrissey works overtime at ironising pain through the gigantic quotation marks of The Popular Song rather than expressing it directly. Indeed, many of the Smiths' most emotional songs are, on examination, really about the process of declaring the broken state of one's

'At a time when authenticity is a valued commodity in pop music and any performer's biographical details are a few keystrokes away, it's hard not to hear sung heartbreak as the singer's own.'

heart in song. Think of Joan of Arc's melting Walkman in 'Bigmouth Strikes Again', the music out there in 'There Is a Light that Never Goes Out', the acoustic guitar in 'Shakespeare's Sister', the sad singer in 'Sheila Take a Bow'…

A number of the finest heartbroken songs are meta-pop, addressing music's ability to comfort the listener by speaking for their heart: George Jackson's 'Aretha, Sing One for Me', say, or Elton John's 'I Guess That's Why They Call It the Blues'. The Magnetic Fields' *69 Love Songs* is one long examination of what the experience of emotion and the artifice of popular song have to do with each other. But an earlier song of theirs, 'With Whom to Dance?', is a particularly brilliant distillation of the conundrum. To a gentle introductory-waltz-lesson rhythm, Stephin Merritt rhymes 'rings' with 'strings' and 'arms' with 'charms', the magnetically snapped-together language of love songs. Harry Nilsson made one of his sharpest jokes about the same kind of received language in 'You're Breakin' My Heart', continuing its title phrase with 'You're tearin' it apart/So fuck you'.

For all pop's catalogue of songs about heartbreak, it's celebration, another pop speciality, that's usually found at the top of the charts: the songs people love best tend to promise or deliver pleasure, movement and emotional connection. In all its various incarnations from Gloria Gaynor onwards, the disco-era classic 'I Will Survive' is about transcending pain rather than understanding it. And the Human League's 'Don't You Want

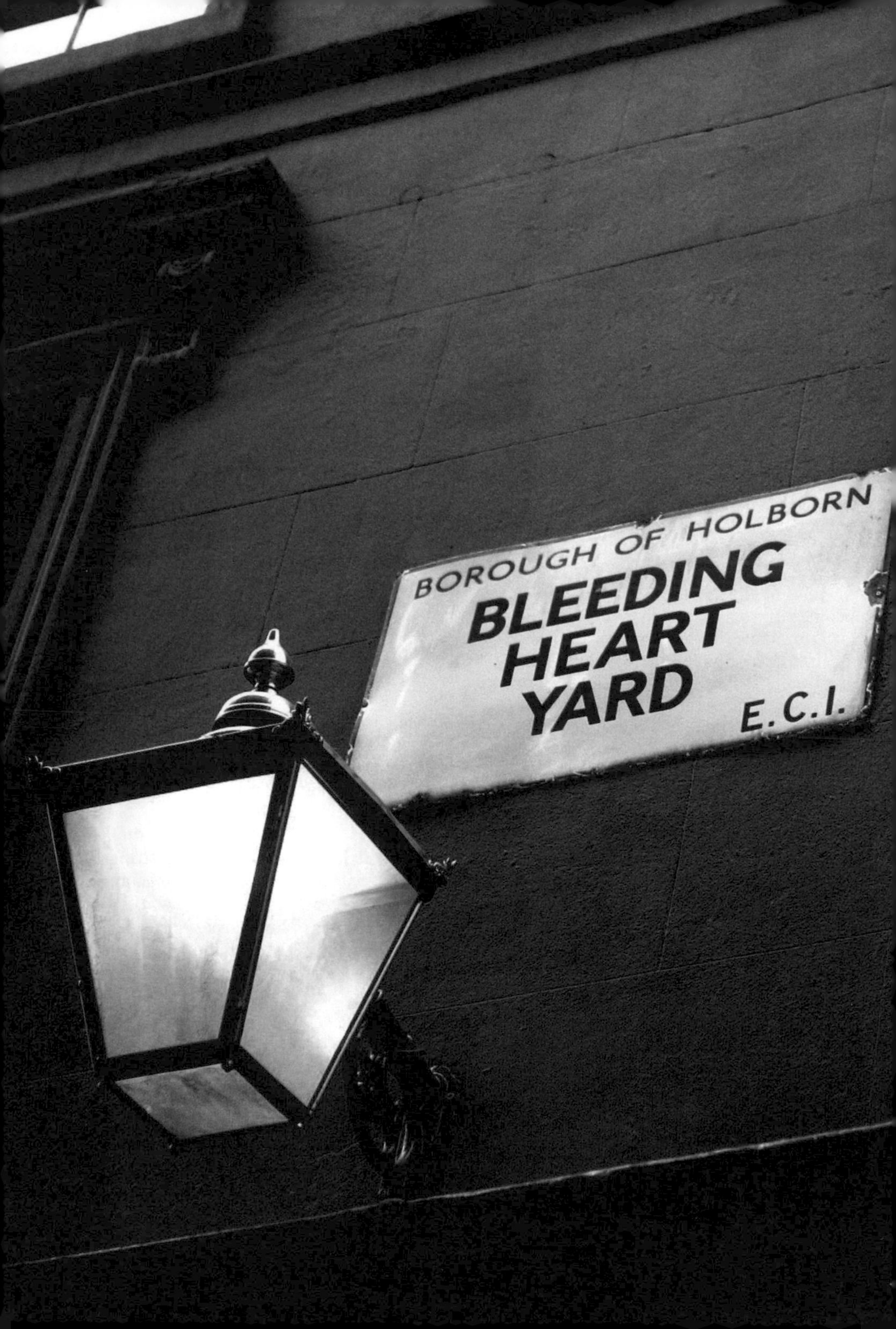
BOROUGH OF HOLBORN
BLEEDING
HEART
YARD
E.C.I.

Me', one of the very few new wave hits to address romantic distress, is effectively a variation on the same theme, with Philip Oakey playing the role of the bad mentor/lover (whose heartbreak we're supposed to understand as well-merited) and Susanne Sulley getting in the final word as the liberated ex-girlfriend.

Plenty of vintage R&B finds the protagonists pleading with or berating a lover, but rarely do they admit to failure or resign themselves to introspection. 'Bloodshot Eyes' was written and first released in 1950 by Western swing pioneer Hank Penny, but Wynonie Harris's jump-blues cover is far crazier and funnier. When Harris sings, he's so indignant at his hard-partying, crocodile-tear-crying girlfriend that he almost doesn't get across how hurt *he* is. 'You should join the *soi-kus*,' he snaps. 'You'd make a real good clown.'

Punk was famously averse to the lyric poet's naked, abject 'I'; the music's sexuality was too guarded and angry to be sad. Still, Buzzcocks zoomed into the gravitational field of heartbreak a few times. On 'Ever Fallen in Love (With Someone You Shouldn't've)', Pete Shelley's verses are nakedly needy, even if they're covered up with the ironic flip of his voice and his Buddy Holly hiccup. The chorus makes an intellectual abstraction of his desire, before the final chord changes stick a big ironic music-hall flourish around the whole thing.

Naturally, there was eventually a counter-revolution against the emotional armour of punk: in the US, with the emo movement that began in earnest during the 1980s with Rites of Spring crying on stage, and in the UK, where do-it-yourself pop bands made their music deliberately wimpy. The apotheosis of the latter approach is Another Sunny Day's 'You Should All Be Murdered', in which Harvey Williams, singing in a little voice that seems to be crouching in on itself, runs off a list of the people that he declares don't deserve to live. There's no menace at all to his delivery; the key phrase, 'the people who broke my heart', is slipped into the middle of the song. A few seconds later, Williams stops singing and lets his guitar cry for him.

Well, maybe it's not exactly for *him*. Some literary critics like to assume that the artist, in the words of Rimbaud that 'made perfect sense' to Bob Dylan, '*je est un autre*': literally, 'I is an other', but translated by Dylan in *Chronicles*:

On the record
Daryl Hall

'Ain't Too Proud to Beg'

The Temptations

If you talk to any black musicians that were around in those days, the Temptations were the black Beatles: they had the same kind of effect on the black community as the Beatles had on the white community at the same time. They were the heroes: they invented a style of singing, they influenced a style of dressing, the way people did all those steps, musical styles… They really had a giant impact on other groups, more impact than people realise. When I was a teenager, I sang in a kind of tribute band called the Temptones, and later we became friends with them.

Anyway, 'Ain't Too Proud to Beg' is probably their best single, something with all the hallmarks – those heavenly harmonies, that choppy guitar on the downbeat, the congas. A great single has to be something that grabs you from the first note and holds you until the last second. This is certainly one.

Daryl Hall performs solo and with Hall & Oates, who recorded 'Ain't Too Proud to Beg' with former Temptations David Ruffin and Eddie Kendrick on Live at the Apollo *(RCA)*

Volume One as 'I is someone else'. The artist's first right, and perhaps also their first responsibility, is to lie, and it's often an error to confuse the singer with the song.

It was easier to keep the division straight in the pre-Beatles era, when the singer had probably never even met the person who'd written the song they were singing. Nobody seriously believed that Elvis Presley was so lonely he could die, or even that 'Heartbreak Hotel' was a metaphor for his own emotions; instead, he conjured up Lonely Street as a spectral scene within a crystal ball, and made it almost real through the conviction in his voice. And even the Beatles themselves rarely implied that they were singing about their own lives. 'Yesterday' isn't an expression of Paul McCartney's sadness; indeed, most of the thousands of singers who've covered it have erred by trying to put themselves into the song. It's just a sad melody, and heartbreak is a more formally appropriate subject for a sad melody than, say, scrambled eggs. Which was McCartney's original working title for the song.

But at a time when realness and authenticity are valued commodities in pop music and any public performer's biographical details are a few keystrokes away, it's hard not to hear sung heartbreak as the singer's own. In particular, it's almost impossible not to extend life into art when you're listening to music by former couples whose collaboration as artists has outlasted their intimate relationship. To hear the vicious irony of Quasi's 'Our Happiness Is Guaranteed', an artificially cheerful rocker about a utopian future in which pain has been wiped away by science ('Love was a problem for our ancestors/It's not such a problem any more'), and to hear the aching spin Sam Coomes and Janet Weiss put on the lyrics, is one thing; to realise that it was recorded after Coomes and Weiss divorced is quite another.

Similarly, much of the frisson of Fleetwood Mac's *Rumours* comes from the two intra-band break-ups that were happening as it was made. Stevie Nicks's 'Silver Springs', a B-side that was later appended to the album, goes beyond the oblique romantic turbulence of the album proper to deliver a direct attack on her bandmate Lindsay Buckingham. On a similar level, Richard and Linda Thompson's 'For Shame of Doing Wrong', a song about a couple longing for a reconciliation they know they

can't have, has become a near-standard. The two of them stayed married for years after they recorded it, yet their subsequent split has retroactively become the subtext of everything they did together. 'For Shame of Doing Wrong' has been covered any number of times, but when it's a man and woman singing 'I wish I was a fool for you again' to each other, it almost always connects.

The best songwriters don't just make us feel their characters' heartbreak – they can pinpoint the exact type of heartbreak they're addressing. Carole King's 'It's Too Late' isn't only a break-up song but a mature, cool-headed assessment of how the break-up came on slowly. Amy Winehouse's 'You Know I'm No Good' is a rageful song, but her bitterness is directed entirely at herself and built through a gradual pile-up of observations. Even better is the remix featuring Ghostface Killah, in which his verse builds to a peak of betrayed indignation that he tries to channel into red-clawed wisecracks.

Working in an altogether different medium, Brett Sparks of the Handsome Family sings his wife Rennie's lyrics to 'Weightless Again' in the measured baritone of a '50s country crooner. The song concerns a sexually alienated couple travelling together, one of them longing to rekindle the spark with the other but no longer able to do so. And while Liz Phair's comparable 'Divorce Song' doesn't mention divorce anywhere in its lyrics, it's clearly about the particular instant where a marriage seizes up and dies: an apology, an explanation, a plea, a sorting-out of emotional details. The song is one long verse with basically no chorus, and starts in the middle of a monologue ('And when I asked for a separate room…'). It could end right there and it'd still burn.

Elvis Costello's *Blood and Chocolate*, the secret jewel of his discography, is pretty much a catalogue of heartbreak-song styles – vindictive ('Uncomplicated'), seething ('I Want You'), gnomic ('Tokyo Storm Warning') – but it's smartest on the subject in its stupidest song, 'I Hope You're Happy Now'. Addressed to the loved one, the lyrics are a withering attack on her new boyfriend: jealous, jeering, contemptuous and finally exploding in a fit of sour grapes ('I never loved you anyhow'). The recording on the album is a straight-up rock 'n' roll arrangement that Costello sings with put-on bravado, a nasty, well-rehearsed lie masking

Stevie Nicks, not long after her and Lindsey Buckingham had gone their own ways.

desperate vulnerability. There's another version, which substitutes a quiet acoustic guitar for the band and hushed resignation for the chutzpah of the album take, but it's not nearly as funny.

The darkest songs of all are the ones that speak to their listeners' worst fears about heartbreak: that it will spread and kill the soul that surrounds it. When Agnetha Fältskog sings Abba's 'The Winner Takes It All', its lyrics written for her by ex-husband Björn Ulvaeus, she's already been destroyed. The words are reserved – the song begins with the singer's

assurance that she doesn't want to talk about it, before she spends nearly five minutes doing just that – but it's Fältskog's performance that reveals the reason she's not lapsing into full histrionics: there's nothing left inside her. Mariah Carey, singing Badfinger's wrist-cutter 'Without You', goes over the top in a way that Fältskog doesn't; she may be claiming she can't go on, but her full-throated holler puts the lie to that.

In Garbage's cover of Vic Chesnutt's 'Kick My Ass', another of those emotionally wrecked songs, the singer's partner has taken a swing at her, and she's quietly apologising for 'making' him do it. The protagonist doesn't have to be a woman, but it's more effective when Shirley Manson sings it. And Johnny Cash's interpretation of Nine Inch Nails' 'Hurt' is even more devastating. The recording's pain and power come partly from the frail, quavering shadow of the voice Cash once commanded, but also from the video, in which the singer looks at pictures of himself and his wife in happier times.

The song that shatters me the most, though – the one I imagine, sometimes, being played at a funeral – is Peggy Seeger's 'Lost', written after the death of her partner of many decades, Ewan MacColl. The loss she describes is the final heartbreak, the lover and the heart gone some place from which they can never return. 'Lost' is the sound of absolute despair and a pain that's Seeger's own, which she's shaped into the strange, familiar form of a melody and then given to the world to hear. We can't lighten her burden, but sharing it gives her listeners a hint of the ultimate heartbreak that awaits us, too.

Heartbreak in 20 songs

'How Men Are' Aztec Camera

Roddy Frame's musing on some unspecified romantic catastrophe tackles heartbreak as only an '80s new man could: ruefully and regretfully, with an uneasy mix of self-awareness and self-centredness, forever on the verge of admitting his anguish but ultimately never quite getting to the point. Very much a product of its time, and not only for those tinkly synths and slick, show-me-the-way-to-America production values.

'Please Come Home for Christmas' Charles Brown

It is, according to the title of one old festive chestnut, the most wonderful time of the year. However, as artists as diverse as Mud ('Lonely This Christmas'), the O'Jays ('Christmas Ain't Christmas, New Year's Ain't New Year's Without the One You Love'), Wham! ('Last Christmas') and Brown (this little peach) have been only too eager to point out, it can also be the most miserable.

'Stardust' Clifford Brown

Mitchell Parish's lyrics, added four years after the tune was premiered in 1927, are evocative, but Hoagy Carmichael's beautiful, meandering melody doesn't really need the emphasis they provide. Nat 'King' Cole, Frank Sinatra and Willie Nelson have all delivered beautiful vocal versions; clarinettist Artie Shaw, breathy tenor man Ben Webster and ever-florid pianist Erroll Garner have all nailed it in their various ways. Still, no one's bettered this bell-clear trumpet solo from the peerless *Clifford Brown with Strings*.

'Mrs Bartolozzi' Kate Bush

The title makes it plain that Bush doesn't want us to think of it as autobiographical. However, she nonetheless completely inhabits this first-person character study of a woman desperately clinging to the ghost of her partner, not to say her own emotional stability, by washing his clothes with her own.

'The Stops' Elbow

It doesn't come without regrets ('I can't undo the day,' sighs Guy Garvey in the very first line), but this is otherwise the tenderest of goodbyes.

'Tears All Over Town' A Girl Called Eddy

Richard Hawley's built an impressive solo career with his own brand of widescreen pop nostalgia. However, he's never bettered the production work he did on Erin Moran's debut album: particularly this opening track, on which his orchestra of guitars provide a telling contrast to Moran's broken vocals.

'How Can You Mend a Broken Heart?' Al Green

Sincerity was never the Gibb brothers' forte: the more emotion they attempt to impart, the more unctuous they appear. Leave it to Al Green to imbue this song, originally a Bee Gees single from 1971, with the pleading, trembling desperation it deserves.

'Boulder to Birmingham' Emmylou Harris

During the 31 years that separated her anomalous singer-songwritery debut from 2000's *Red Dirt Girl*, Harris wrote barely a note of the material she chose to sing. However, the death of former lover Gram Parsons in 1974, the year after the two had delivered a longing cover of the old Everly Brothers hit 'Love Hurts', inspired her to scratch out this solemn but indelibly moving tribute.

'Jilted John' Jilted John

Teenage misery has rarely been expressed quite so vividly as it was on this daffy, fractious piece of character comedy by the man who grew up to become John Shuttleworth but who, back in 1978, sounded alarmingly like Buzzcocks frontman Pete Shelley's kid brother. It even spawned an answer record in the dubious shape of 'Gordon's Not a Moron', credited to Julie & Gordon.

'Surabaya Johnny' Lotte Lenya

Lenya recorded this song a number of times, but never more hauntingly than on *Berlin Theatre Songs*, released five years after the death in 1950 of Kurt

Weill, the song's composer and Lenya's husband. Her voice is weathered by age and cigarettes but not yet shot; perfect, in other words, for delivering Bertolt Brecht's character study of a woman crumbling under the weight of her infatuation with an errant sailor.

'I'm 49' Paddy McAloon

After eye surgery left him visually incapacitated for a time during the 1990s, McAloon found himself drawn to radio phone-ins, often taping what he heard and later replaying it to himself. 'Almost against my will,' he wrote, 'I started to edit mentally some of the things I'd heard. Odd words from documentaries would cross-pollinate with melancholy confidences aired on late-night phone-ins.' *I Trawl the Megahertz*, the resulting album, is a world away from the kind of savvy pop McAloon created with Prefab Sprout: take this blend of orchestral atmospherics and taped excerpts from talk shows, which hinges on the broken voice of a man who's '49, divorced… isolated'.

'Born to Be Blue' Helen Merrill

With the help of a band led by Quincy Jones, just 21 when this was recorded in the last days of 1954, Merrill lends this old Mel Tormé tune an air of cracked, tense dejection.

'Go Now' The Moody Blues

On the surface, its arrangement is almost identical to Bessie Banks' long-lost original. However, the gutsy, chin-up reserve that Birmingham's Moody Blues bring to the song suits its sentiment to a tee.

'So This Is Goodbye' Stina Nordenstam

Pop's most fragile voice is reduced still further to a shadow of a shadow as this song starts seeping from the speakers. And while it recovers a little of its poise a couple of minutes in, it ends up lost and lonely on an imperfect cadence, dissipating like smoke in the breeze.

'Dido's Lament' Henry Purcell

Singers as disparate as Basildon belter Alison Moyet and German androgyne Klaus Nomi have tackled this song of suicide brought on by separation, but it's most effective when it's sung straight: devoid of vibrato and unnecessary ornamentation, the indelible melody doing its own work.

'What Becomes of the Brokenhearted' Jimmy Ruffin

Ruffin walks with his heart in his boots but his head held high on this stately, defiant piece of pop from that mid '60s period during which Motown seemed to churn out a classic a week.

'My Young Man' Kate Rusby

The man in question isn't young any more. He's pensionable, crippled and unable to fend for himself;

A Girl Called Eddy.

'Like a child upon my knee,' sings Rusby, her proud but quavering voice anchored by a gentle, muted brass band. It's touching enough even without the knowledge that Rusby wrote it about her grandmother's devotion to her grandfather, wracked with disease after a lifetime spent working in the Yorkshire mines.

'I Just Don't Know What to Do with Myself' Dusty Springfield

Dionne Warwick made it swing just a little, and the White Stripes lent it thunder. But Dusty Springfield made her version of this Bacharach/David gem definitive by simply diving into the melody and letting herself get carried along on its tide.

'Today I Started Loving You Again' Bettye Swann

Merle Haggard's original is a plaintive and gently ebbing piece of honky-tonk sorrow. Bettye Swann's fearsome cover, though, renders the song almost unrecognisable, the singer lurching between sorrow and pride as she's lifted by a hallelujah chorus of backing singers and roaring horns.

'Love Is a Losing Game' Amy Winehouse

Winehouse's anguish is as tangible as ever, but it's her vocal restraint that makes this *Back to Black* cut so breathtaking.

Cry, cry, cry

Kate Mossman sheds a tear over country music's love affair with misery.

In 2002, Johnny Cash cut what was to become his final single: 'Hurt', first recorded by Trent Reznor's industrial rock band Nine Inch Nails. In the accompanying video, the 71-year-old Cash sits at a table piled high with food and, gazing defiantly at the camera, empties his wine glass over his 'empire of dirt'. His Arkansas roots are represented by grainy footage of country roads, his superstar present by images of larger-than-life posters propped up in an office under a blinking strip-light. Later, Technicolor film clips of the Crucifixion are cut against footage of the singer during his drug years.

Effectively, Cash is performing his own obituary, piecing together a legend from the scattered paraphernalia of a messy life. His voice is thick with weariness; as the relentless one-finger piano part builds in volume, the hairs on the back of the listener's neck spring to life. The song triumphs because its emotional impact is self-conscious, dramatic and meticulously constructed.

Country singers have always worn their big, broken hearts on their sleeves. Somebody once joked that if you play a country song backwards, your dog comes to life, you get your job back and your wife falls in love with you once more. Twelve-verse sagas of death by whiskey, rhinestone dolorosas choking over the letters D.I.V.O.R.C.E.: the clichés are familiar to us all. Quite often, it's hard to know where the caricature ends and the real person begins.

Take, for example, Hank Williams. Scrawny as a hobo, with a thin, reedy voice, the singer came to embody songs such as 'I'm So Lonesome I Could Cry' before meeting what, in hindsight, seems an inevitably early grave. Aged just 29, Williams died in the small hours of New Year's Day, 1953, in the back of a powder blue Cadillac somewhere between Knoxville, Tennessee and Oak Hill, West Virginia. Spookily encapsulated within the title of the singer's last single, 'I'll Never Get Out of This World Alive', Williams' troubled life and death were so romantic that they inspired countless ballads, from 'Rollin' and Ramblin' (The Death of Hank Williams)', performed by Emmylou Harris, to David Allan Coe's 'The Ride', in which the singer cadges a lift with the departed Hank.

But even in the 1940s, Nashville hardly had a monopoly on musical melancholy. Emerging at around the same time as Williams was cutting his earliest records, the 'high lonesome' sound of bluegrass is a sonic memento of days gone by, the stories of settlers in and around the Appalachians caught in the strings of banjos, fiddles and mandolins. And precursive old-time folk songs such as 'Shenandoah', recorded by everyone from Bob Dylan to Keith Jarrett, draw heavily on the lilting ballads of Scottish and Irish immigrants, but with lyrics recast to tally with their singers' new-found surroundings. Even 200 years ago, American musicians were already getting nostalgic about home, without necessarily knowing quite where home was.

In 1947, after country music had become a marketable commodity, Merle Travis was commissioned to write something 'traditional-sounding' for Capitol Records. He came up with 'Sixteen Tons', a miner's complaint told with the raw defiance of a 19th-century slave song. It was one of several songs Travis wrote about the mining life, with the ghoulish 'Dark as a Dungeon' the most famous of them, and set the tone for many subsequent attempts at translating the toil and misery of the working life into country music. Many of these songs have a visceral poignancy, swelling with sweat and tears. They speak of a time when, at least in the imagination of the listener, human suffering was something pure and religious, and death was a glorious prize.

Some 25 years later, Mickey Newbury spliced together a pair of Civil War anthems and a spiritual to create Elvis Presley's 'An American Trilogy', and the King crooned old-time Confederate defeat in words that had children everywhere sobbing into their Kellogg's. National destruction became the death of a parent as seen through the eyes of a child, itself a simple fear that lies at the heart of numerous modern country hits. In Conway Twitty's 1987 hit 'That's My Job', a young son wakes in fright after dreaming that his father has died. Verse after verse of the ballad is rendered with a grim determination until, eventually, the child grows up and his nightmare comes true.

Nearly two decades before Ray Burr wrote 'That's My Job', Dolly Parton tackled the same subject in the moving 'Jeannie's Afraid of the Dark'. In Parton's song, a timorous girl breaks her parents' hearts by telling them not to bury her when she dies, but the daughter's fear of the dark foreshadows her demise in the next verse. Like 'That's My Job', 'Jeannie's Afraid of the Dark' combines innocence with horror to powerful effect. Indeed, both songs ultimately come with the timeless, imaginative force of a fairy tale.

Woebetide the bad moms and pops of country music: the contemporary Nashville scene has spawned a strange and unsettling sub-genre of songs about child abuse. Written by Rob Crosby and Stephanie Bentley, Martina McBride's hit 'Concrete Angel' uses the grim rhetorical figure of a child's grave to hammer home its message, while 'Alyssa Lies' by Jason Michael Carroll cranks up the grief in its final verse as a father tries to tell his young daughter that her classmate has been murdered. Heavy-handed modern fables such as these have become a Southern conservative phenomenon: they aim to show listeners what goes wrong if they neglect their own family

Tammy and George in happier times.

values, while simultaneously encouraging them to thank God that their own kids have everything they need.

Yet not all country songs are quite so mawkish. Others achieve a greater emotional thrust by withholding the gory details and leaving moral judgment hanging in the air. Dolly Parton's 'dirt-poor' childhood in the Smoky Mountains was a saga of love and suffering, at least the way she tells it in interviews. But in her song 'Family', she shrugs her shoulders and sings, simply, that all you can do is your best. And a few years later, Alison Krauss was moved to tears the first time she heard Sarah Siskind's 'Simple Love', detecting in its lyric the trace of a poisoned relationship between a father and his daughter. The nature of the suffering isn't revealed, as Siskind's words focus on the happier bond between her mother and her grandfather. But eventually, the listener is invited to fill in the blanks.

Back in the bar, meanwhile, the long-suffering men of country music continue to clutch their bottles of Jack and hit the spittoon. And yet for all the barroom misery heard in tracks such as George Jones's 'If Drinkin' Don't Kill Me (Her Memory Will)' and Merle Haggard's 'The Bottle Let Me Down', the funniest thing about country music's slew of miserable drinking songs is the way in which, with dogged persistence, the singers labour over the stories they're trying to forget. Occasionally, the drunks achieve their desired oblivion: Brad Paisley's 'Whiskey Lullaby' tells the tale of a man who drinks himself to death (in verse two, his ex-girlfriend follows him to the grave in much the same way). But on the whole, the poor guys are caught in a kind of drinkers' purgatory in which, as Travis Tritt puts it, 'The Whiskey Ain't Workin'': no matter how much they knock back, the pain won't quite go away.

In 'If Drinkin' Don't Kill Me', Jones enjoys the performative aspect of his own drunken wretchedness when, after driving home from a night in the bar (not, presumably, on the lawn mower he once rode to a liquor store after desperate wife Shirley Corley had hidden his car keys), his head slumps on the steering wheel, setting off the horn and waking up the neighbourhood. Indeed, songs of addiction, like songs of regret, often function as country

'In "Wichita Lineman", songwriter Jimmy Webb took an iconic image, the lone figure on a journey through America's heartland, and placed it in a context that was modern, sparse and strange.'

confessionals, themselves a sizeable genre in their own right. The laid-back libretto of Kenny Chesney's 'A Lot of Things Different', written by Bill Anderson and Dean Dillon, is full of such confessions, from romantic wistfulness to regrets about having skipped an Elvis concert. And Chesney's earlier hit 'That's Why I'm Here' is sung in character as an older and wearier man, allowing the then 29-year-old singer to explore the dramatic potential of a life longer and more tragic than his own.

It's one thing to lose your lover and lament it in a slurred soliloquy, but the 1970s also saw a wave of dual-gender duets about separation. The year after they split, George Jones and Tammy Wynette recorded and released 'Golden Ring', a tale of divorce as told through the travels of a wedding band from pawn shop to happy couple and back again. Conway Twitty and Loretta Lynn also acted out a tale of busted love in 'Living Together Alone', as did Dolly Parton and Porter Wagoner in 'Home Is Where the Hurt Is'. But it's hard for a divorcing couple to convey the agony of separation when they're smiling at each other over twin microphones. Dan Hicks pre-emptively hit the nail on the head when, in the late 1960s, he wrote a satiric little cut entitled 'How Can I Miss You When You Won't Go Away?'.

Songwriting duo Hank Cochran and Harlan Howard used a kind of baffled emotional realism when they explored separation in 'I Fall to Pieces', a hit for Patsy Cline in 1961 and now a country standard of sorts. At around

Rewind
Johnny Cash

'Rick Rubin encouraged me to just sit down with a guitar in front of a microphone and start singing,' explains Johnny Cash, sitting in his office upstairs at the House of Cash in Hendersonville, Tennessee on one of the hottest days of the year. 'I'd always wanted to record that way; just, y'know, for better or for worse, me and my guitar, one on one, up close and personal. I'd talked for 20, 25 years about doing that kind of album, but no record company was ever interested until Rick came along.' The end result is *American Recordings*; in his deep, weathered drawl, Cash describes it as 'the record I'm most proud of'.

American Recordings was mostly recorded in Rubin's living room in California, apart from two tracks cut live at LA's Viper Room and two taped in Cash's cabin in the Tennessee woods. 'Sometimes we'd have to stop a take because his dogs would make too much noise, or one of them would jump on my lap, or the phone would ring, or someone would come in, but I really enjoyed the informality of it all. It helped me to relax and let things flow naturally. I wanted to get it really personal, and I feel like we brought that off. You can hear every little mistake and flat note, but the performances are right there, painfully honest.' He smiles.

'Working with Rick kind of smacked of the way it was with Sam [Phillips, head of Sun Records] in '55. The first time I went to him, he said, "Show me what you got." It was just me and my guitar for two or three hours. What was most refreshing with Rick, though, like with Sam, was that after being in Nashville for so long, there was no clock in the studio, nobody punching time-cards, and nobody ever talked to me about budget.' He spits out the last word with a sharp, angry venom.

American Recordings is being released at a time when country music is booming, but it owes nothing to the modern-day Nashville. 'I've always been a Nashville outsider, even though, for the most part, I've recorded there. In the last half of the '70s and '80s, there was a lot of apathy on the part of the record company, and I guess on my part too. They didn't really know what to do with me. I mean, I wasn't one of that group of new hot country artists that wear their pants too tight, with their big shows and special effects and smoke and stuff. I just never have done that. I never felt it was important.

'I'm not a big fan of most of what's going around now. I love Trisha Yearwood and I like Dwight Yoakam, but I like to see a country music artist sit down with his guitar and sing a song. I've seen Garth Brooks do that, but I don't think a lot of them can. Too many of them just try to ride a trend. It kind of reminds me now of the urban cowboy craze of 1979, '80, when Nashville was producing records for people in New York and London who thought it was chic to wear cowboy boots. I just like to see an artist cut his own trail and cast his own shadow.'
Ross Fortune; from Time Out, *29 June 1994*

the same time, writing not with Howard but with a young Willie Nelson, Cochran returned to the theme on the arrestingly simple 'Undo the Right', in which a rejected lover begs for a clean break rather than be forced into the doomed cycle of make-up and break-up. The muddled meters of the song, a 1968 hit for Johnny Bush, betray a certain confusion: its questions suggest the singer still harbours some hope, but his willingness to end the relationship for the sake of his own emotional recovery is strangely triumphant. Bonnie Raitt shows a similar kind of resilience on her recording of Mike Reid and Allen Shamblin's 'I Can't Make You Love Me'.

Country is perhaps the most stylised form of popular music in the world, which often renders its emotional world unconvincing. Tragic motifs are terribly easy to caricature, after all, and characters laden with woes of their own making tend to be a bit of a turn-off. The genre's well-known rhetorical structures cry out for fresh treatment; if a song is to stand out from the parade of affected sadness, it needs an element of surprise.

Gretchen Peters uses a well-worn road-trip motif in 'On a Bus to St Cloud' (later a hit for Trisha Yearwood), searching for a lover who's somehow slipped out of sight. Only halfway through the song does the singer intimate that the lover might have committed suicide; but even then, it's by no means explicit. As Peters told an interviewer in 2007, 'I think songs are better when they're a little bit more murky, or fuzzy around the edges.' So much so, in fact, that Yearwood was 'completely surprised' when Peters explained to the singer what she had in mind when she wrote the song.

While songs such as 'Golden Ring' use familiar items as metaphorical vessels to carry their stories, Hugh Prestwood's 'The Suit', recorded by Jerry Douglas with James Taylor, focuses on a more mundane object in order to tell a tale that's both gripping and tragic. At first, the listener is unsure what kind of formal occasion is being described in the song, until Taylor adds that, for a coat, the main character is wearing the state of Nebraska. Simple structures shot through with lyrics of an unexpected finality and vivid moments of imagination popping up in otherwise well-known stories: country music's surprise turns can be powerful.

In 'Wichita Lineman', songwriter Jimmy Webb took an iconic image, the lone figure on a journey through America's heartland, and placed it in a context that was modern, sparse and strange. With no name and no history, his character asks for neither sympathy nor sadness as singer Glen Campbell moves from verse to verse with the quiet determination of a driver pushing on with his journey. But the song's final chorus, its simplest and most straightforward lines, get to the heart of the matter.

'I was driving my car through the panhandle of Oklahoma,' explained Webb in an interview with country singer and TV presenter Bobby Bare in 1984, 'and it's so flat out there, and stark. Driving along this seemingly endless road with a series of telephone poles going into the distance, I passed a man perched on the top of one pole with his earphones on. He was a picture of loneliness, and I wondered what he was really listening for. "Wichita Lineman" was no more complicated, and no simpler, than that.'

Kenny Chesney, the former Mr Zellweger.

Top ten
The wee small hours

'Gimme! Gimme! Gimme! (A Man After Midnight)' Abba

Agnetha protests that she's miserable about spending every evening watching TV alone in her flat. However, Björn and Benny's pulsating music tells a different story, painting their protagonist as a terrifying minx set on prowling the streets in a never-sated search for company.

'Walkin' After Midnight' Patsy Cline

While Abba's Agnetha seems to go about her manhunt in aggressive fashion, Cline takes her moonlit stroll more out of desperation than with any genuine hope that it might reunite her with the partner who's left her behind.

'Thriller' Michael Jackson

Not for Jackson (and writer Rod Temperton) the world-weary misery that pervades many of the songs on this list: their own witching hour is a Halloween pantomime of bloodthirsty demons, grave-defying ghouls and the inimitably camp Vincent Price.

'Closing Time' Lyle Lovett

'The night's all that's left behind,' offers Lovett towards the end of this beautiful miniature of chair-stacking and cash-counting, seemingly written from the perspective of a bar owner who's lived through a thousand Friday evenings from the other side of the counter. No song better captures that moment when the tills go dark, the lights go up and everyone's just got to find their coat, their date and their ride home.

''Round Midnight' Thelonious Monk

Bernie Hanighen later added some fairly prosaic lyrics (even rhyming 'sad' with 'bad'), but Monk's agreeably wonky melody is best heard without them. Covered by more or less everyone, the tune later lent its name to a beautiful movie directed by Bertrand Tavernier and starring saxophonist Dexter Gordon, a contemporary of the pianist.

'Midnight at the Oasis' Maria Muldaur

The giddiness in Muldaur's voice, which always seems to sound one breath away from laughter or collapse, is perfect for this agreeably ridiculous tale of love in the desert, complete with camels, cacti and romps in the sand dunes.

'One for My Baby (And One More for the Road)' Frank Sinatra

In *The Sky's the Limit*, the 1943 movie for which Johnny Mercer and Harold Arlen wrote this evocative and melancholy monologue, Fred Astaire follows his gently swinging rendition by mock-drunkenly tap-dancing along the bar, kicking over a table of empties and hurling a barstool through the back-bar mirror. If he'd done that anywhere near Ol' Blue Eyes, you fancy he might never have drunk again.

'Starless and Bible Black' Stan Tracey Quartet

Bobby Wellins' plangent tenor saxophone solo tumbles over Tracey's impressionistic piano work and the distant thunder of Jack Dougan's drumming in this evocative four minutes, recorded for the quartet's renowned re-imagining of Dylan Thomas' 'Under Milk Wood'. Perhaps *the* landmark recording in British jazz.

'Harlem Nocturne' The Viscounts

This was originally titled 'Duke's Soup' in homage to Duke Ellington and his saxophonist Johnny Hodges, who inspired Earle Hagen (bizarrely, a trombonist) to write it back in 1939. However, Hagen's publishers suggested he might want to give it a snappier name, at which point the tune started to grow into a big-band standard. Johnny Otis' early recording carries with it a little brooding menace, but not as much as this definitively sleazy version, cut in 1959 by an otherwise unknown New Jersey beat group and a strip-club staple more or less ever since.

'Three Hours Past Midnight' Johnny 'Guitar' Watson

Watson's ferocious, foot-to-the-floor guitar technique has had countless imitators but few equals. There's not really much of a song here: recorded in 1956, it's just a by-the-book, slow-burn 12-bar blues. But by the sheer aggressive force of his personality, Watson turns it into something utterly desperate. 'Look out!' he cries midway through a frenzied, demented guitar solo that sounds like it's played on an instrument strung with barbed wire, with a brick for a pick.

KIND OF BLUE

Sunday bloody Sunday

Dave Rimmer charts the hideous history of the Hungarian Suicide Song.

Songs may change lives, but few have been reputed to change them quite so decisively as 'Gloomy Sunday', known throughout its long and (urban-)legendary history as 'the suicide song'. It acquired its ghoulish reputation not just for a gnawingly sorrowful melody and a lyric drenched in dejection and self-pity, but for its association with a 1930s suicide cult in Budapest, the city in which it was written. Established as a jazz standard by Billie Holiday's 1941 version (still the best known recording), 'Gloomy Sunday' has also proved irresistible to divas and crooners, goths and gloom merchants, plus the odd plain old pop star taking a mid-career tilt at the jazz canon or looking for a little dally-with-the-dark-side cred.

The world's most mournful ballad was composed sometime in the late 1920s or early '30s by Rezső Seress, the self-taught pianist at the Kulács restaurant in Budapest's District VII. (It's still there, on the corner of Osvát utac and Dohány utca; so is the nearby Kispipa, where Seress was later in residence.) It was the follow-up to his 1925 hit 'Még egy éjszakát' ('Still Another Night'); somewhere between the pancakes and the third plum brandy, Kulács diners would often hear him play it.

The basic melody, traditionally described as 'haunting', was there from the off, but the words Seress first growled over his moody minor-key structure were completely different from the song we know today: more apocalyptic than gloomy, imagery of war and devastation rather than heartbreak and suicide. The second stanza's last line was the title under which it was first published: 'Vége a világnak', or 'The World Has Ended'.

It was also in Budapest that, just after World War I, psychoanalyst and Freud disciple Sándor Ferenczi identified a disorder he called *Sonntagsneurose*, or 'Sunday neurosis'. Otherwise healthy professionals would experience distress on the Sabbath, typically bouts of depression. Ferenczi theorised that, deprived of their usual busy routines, his patients were having trouble controlling normally repressed fears and impulses.

Perhaps a dose of *Sonntagsneurose* was afflicting László Jávor, the police reporter on a Budapest daily, when he sat down to write one Sunday in spring 1933. Some say he was lovelorn, others that he was merely broke and hungover after a Saturday night out in Pest. Whatever the inspiration, Jávor banged out new lyrics for Seress's song, transforming the lurid nightmare vision into a florid suicide note. His new version was called 'Szomorú vásarnap', or 'Gloomy Sunday'.

Budapest, of course, is the capital of self-pity. The first line of the Hungarian national anthem suggests, 'We have suffered enough for all our past and future sins.' Suicide is almost a tradition, and until recently Hungary had the highest rate in the world. The man revered as 'the greatest Hungarian', 19th-century moderniser István Széchenyi, blew his own brains out; wartime prime minister Pál Teleki followed suit in 1941. Attila József, the nation's finest poet, hurled himself in front of a train, as did the actor Zoltán Latinovits (from a spot nearby). Even Miss Hungary 1985 necked a lethal dose of lidocaine.

When the Seress/Jávor version of 'Szomorú vásarnap' was published in 1933, it became an instant hit, but it was also instantly credited with provoking a suicide cult. Jilted lovers were said to have left the sheet music on their pillow before sipping poison, or to have leapt from Danube bridges with the lyrics pinned to their clothes – and always, of course, on a Sunday. Others just heard the melody and promptly hanged themselves from the rafters. In 1930s Budapest, up to 17 suicides were supposedly linked, in one way or another, to the song.

There's no such thing as bad publicity. Even as Hungarians were still leaping from tall buildings, 'Szomorú vásarnap' was being translated into English both by the Englishman Desmond Carter and by the American Sam M Lewis. In 1935, the great singer, actor and civil rights activist Paul Robeson, who probably first heard the song on an April 1929 visit to Budapest, recorded the Carter translation in London. To this day, Robeson's remains the gloomiest 'Gloomy Sunday'. His true bass voice, honed on spirituals and as weighty as a ball and chain, follows the beat like the tread of a funeral procession. It's a dirge, in the literal rather than pejorative sense.

In March 1936, on a wave of hype about 'the Hungarian suicide song', no fewer than five versions were released in the USA. One was Robeson's; the other four, including recordings by Hal Kemp and Paul Whiteman, were takes on Lewis's lyrics. Lighter and less rigid than Carter's, the Lewis translation sharpened the suicide angle but also unshackled the words from the structure, allowing what was essentially a funereal folk tune to be interpreted as jazz.

The definitive big-band version was Artie Shaw's 1940 take, with its sweet clarinet dawdling around the melody. But the song's canonisation wasn't truly achieved until Billie Holiday recorded it the following year. Fears that it would prove too morbid for the public led to yet another version of the song: a middle eight was added in an uplifting major key, with text that framed the suicide as a dream sequence. Holiday's restrained but confidently melancholy reading completed the translation of 'Gloomy Sunday' into a jazz idiom and established this version (essentially, the Lewis lyrics with added optimism) as definitive. Later performers would occasionally ditch the 'dreaming' passage, but only Diamanda Galás, in a typically pretentious 1992 version, ever returned to Desmond Carter.

'Gloomy Sunday' slipped through the next few decades as a jazz and R&B standard. Mel Tormé took it to Vegas; Johnny Griffin introduced it to bop; and Ray Charles, Herbie Mann, Sarah Vaughan, Jimmy Smith, Jimmy Witherspoon and Big Maybelle, among others, all adapted it to their particular styles. Big Maybelle's huge, raunchy R&B version was recorded in 1972 for an album called *The Last of Big Maybelle* that was released the following year. Posthumously.

The song-related body count had actually dropped by this time, but morbid myths still swirled around it: typists gassing themselves after requesting 'Gloomy Sunday' for their funerals, for example, or errand boys leaping to their doom after hearing a gypsy busker play the tune. Anxiety about its malign influence supposedly led to bans on a host of radio stations. This may be urban legend, but the BBC does seem to have excluded all

On the record
Vini Reilly

'Alone Again (Naturally)'

Gilbert O'Sullivan

It's not a fashionable choice, but this is a seven-inch single you'll find in my collection and it's one that I still find fascinating and beautiful and depressing in equal measure. It is the saddest song you'll ever hear, all about suicide and bereavement and death. It's astonishing that kids were bopping about to it on *Top of the Pops*, even more amazing that it topped the charts in Britain and in America. Gilbert O'Sullivan did several other great mournful, elegiac, bittersweet, hilarious songs in this vein – 'We Will', 'Nothing Rhymed' – but this is the daddy. I'm sure that Morrissey was taking note.

Vini Reilly has made more than a dozen albums as the leader of the Durutti Column

but instrumental versions from its playlists until as recently as 2002.

It wasn't until post-punk pop acquired an interest in the pre-rock past that 'Gloomy Sunday' ventured out of the jazz world. In 1982, the Associates transformed it into synth-pop melodrama just as Elvis Costello reworked it for acoustic guitar. Its transgressive aura has lured the likes of Marc Almond, Marianne Faithfull, Lydia Lunch and, later, both Christian Death and Satan's Cheerleaders. The creepiest cover on the goth side of town was recorded by Anton LaVey, founder of the Church of Satan, and came complete with chiming bell and ceremonial effects. But German screen star Ben Becker took it the furthest with is growling, glowering 'Trauriger Sonntag', set to the creaking of a boatman's oars (presumably

'In the end, the best versions are the simplest ones. Sung with conviction, the song's nagging melody and heart-rending lyric are harrowing enough without ornament or bombast.'

Paul Robeson cut the song in 1935...

... and **Billie Holiday** followed suit six years later.

while crossing the Styx). It's a world away, at least, from the lavishly mundane orchestral arrangements by Sinéad O'Connor, Björk and Sarah Brightman.

Back in Budapest, 'Szomorú vasárnap' never left the repertoire of every last Roma fiddler and restaurant band (for a typical gypsy orchestra arrangement, try the Tata Mirando version). It's been reclaimed for Central Europe by world-ish artists such as the Czech Republic's Iva Bittová and Slovenia's Vlado Kreslin, and reworked by the Kronos Quartet on *Caravan*. Intriguingly, the Transylvanians, a German-Hungarian folk-rock band, recorded two versions on their recent *Fél és Egész* album. The first uses the original Rezső Seress lyrics, while the second mixes those of Jávor, Lewis and the German translation heard in the 1999 German-Hungarian feature film *Gloomy Sunday: Ein Lied von Liebe und Tod*, which died everywhere except New Zealand.

In the end, the best versions are the simplest ones. Sung with conviction, the song's nagging melody and heart-rending lyric are harrowing enough without ornament or bombast. After Billie Holiday, no 'Gloomy Sunday' collection is complete without Costello's delicate transposition, Tormé's languid lounge-jazz reading or Ricky Nelson's sweetly sparse and surprisingly world-weary take, recorded in 1958 when the teen idol was just 18, but unreleased until 15 years after he died in a 1985 plane crash.

Billy MacKenzie of the Associates, who in 1997 overdosed on prescription drugs in his father's garden shed, was the most recent famous suicide to be associated with the song. But its most notable victim was Rezső Seress himself. In 1968, penniless in communist Hungary while millions of dollars of his royalties languished in a New York bank, he threw himself from the fourth-floor window of his Budapest apartment. He was 69.

Top ten
Smoking

'Deep in a Dream' Chet Baker

The time it takes to smoke a fag is spent in blissful romantic reverie for a lost lover, before the cigarette burns to its butt and the heartache returns. Sinatra delivers a lovely version on *In the Wee Small Hours*.

'Smokin' in the Boys Room' Brownsville Station

Fabulously basic boogie in which a cluster of teens celebrate the end of double physics by popping to the gents for a well-earned gasper. Hey, teacher! Leave those kids alone!

'Three Cigarettes in an Ashtray' Patsy Cline

Less a song about smoking and more a resigned meditation on having your lover leave you for another, but the lyrical device effectively tells its own story.

'When I Get Low, I Get High' Ella Fitzgerald

During the 1950s and '60s, Fitzgerald turned her talents towards sophisticated songs by the likes of Jerome Kern and Cole Porter. Back in the 1930s, though, she was trilling girlishly through entertaining rubbish like this paean to reefer, which remains conspicuous by its absence from the Great American Songbook.

'The Cowboy Serenade (While I'm Rolling My Last Cigarette)' Glenn Miller & His Orchestra with Ray Eberle

Not all cowboys are Marlboro men: while watching twilight fall beyond the hills, the chap in this gentle little canter prefers to roll his own.

'Smoke Rings' The Mills Brothers

Wholly stately, briefly playful but ultimately very touching melancholia; even when the quartet suggest that we should try and 'puff, puff, puff, puff [our] cares away', you can tell they don't really buy it. Les Paul and Mary Ford recorded an equally wistful version, as did KD Lang.

'Smokin' Cigarettes and Drinkin' Coffee Blues' Marty Robbins

Tobacco and caffeine go together like country music and misery; here we get the full house of all four at once. Smoking has also been linked to coffee by such disparate singers as Peggy Lee ('Black Coffee'), Johnny Ray ('Coffee and Cigarettes') and Otis Redding (the awesome 'Cigarettes and Coffee'), but Oasis, inevitably, preferred theirs with alcohol.

'Don't Smoke in Bed' Nina Simone

Unarguably sound advice, written on a note as a tender, even dewy-eyed kiss-off to the husband she's about to leave.

'Legalise It' Peter Tosh

On this suitably slumbersome pro-spliff rumble, erstwhile Wailer and full-time Rastafarian Tosh argues that ganja should be decriminalised because his lawyer likes an occasional doobie, it's good for asthma and tuberculosis (um, always consult your doctor), and, most convincingly of all, 'goats like to play around in it'. The Jamaican government remained unmoved.

'Smoke! Smoke! Smoke! (That Cigarette)' Tex Williams & His Western Caravan

'I've smoked 'em all my life and I ain't dead yet,' winked Western swing pioneer Williams on this fizzy little 1947 hit. He'd apparently cut back to a pack a day by 1985 when, at the age of 78, he succumbed to lung cancer.

A dirty job

Peter Watts ponders the musical misery of the working man.

'Work is a Four-Letter Word', trilled Morrissey by way of Cilla Black on the universally panned B-side to the Smiths' 1987 single 'Girlfriend in a Coma'. In the process, he pretty much summed up the average English rock band's attitude to employment. Even groups that excel at poring over the minutiae of English cultural life – Pulp, Blur, the Kinks, the Jam, XTC – tend to shy away from the topic unless they're using it as a frankly insulting comparison for the music industry (the Kinks' 'Working at the Factory') or to mock middle-class convention (the Jam's 'Smithers-Jones').

Morrissey's fascination with the working classes, especially as described in the realist-prole novels of Alan Sillitoe and Keith Waterhouse, informed much of his early output. However, he drew the line at actually identifying with the jobs they do. Where Sillitoe depicted the monotony of a Nottingham bicycle factory production line in *Saturday Night and Sunday Morning*, the singer boasted that shyness always kept him from finding work ('You've Got Everything Now'). And where Waterhouse nailed the pen-pushing tedium of life as a junior clerk in a small Yorkshire town with *Billy Liar*, Mancunian dilettante Morrissey instead claimed simply that England owed him a living ('Still Ill').

One explanation for this thematic black hole could be that English songwriters embrace a career in music as a means of escaping conventional employment and therefore have nothing much of interest to say about it, an attitude exemplified by the Clash's rejectionist anthem 'Career Opportunities' and 'Dead End Job' by the Police. But another possible reason is that there simply doesn't exist in England any genuine romantic blue-collar cultural tradition, and certainly not one to compare with American country and blues. Both of these genres have their roots in the poor communities of the American agricultural South, with blues emerging directly from the work songs and field hollers of the plantations and railroads.

In 1963, Johnny Cash released *Blood, Sweat and Tears*, an entire album devoted to the working man. The record opens with 'The Legend of John Henry's Hammer', Cash's take on the defining American working-class story-myth of the legendary figure who was said to have worked the Alabama railways in the 1880s before dying of exhaustion when competing in a steel-driving contest against a steam-driven machine. The tale was once taken as a tribute to black defiance – Henry 'Ragtime Texas' Thomas cut 'John Henry' in 1927 and Mississippi John Hurt sang 'Spike Driver Blues' a year later – but the subject proved malleable enough to reflect the concerns of Woody Guthrie, Bill Monroe and Cash, and became a celebration of the working man's spirit in the face of industrialisation and greed. The tale lives on among the self-consciously blue-collared: Southern rockers Drive-By Truckers released 'The Day John Henry Died' in 2004, and Bruce Springsteen included 'John Henry' on his 2006 folk album *We Shall Overcome*.

Rewind
Leonard Cohen

Leonard Cohen, who is 53, stares into his coffee and sucks on a cigarette. 'I was reading in the *International Herald Tribune* that as you get older, certain brain cells die, and the brain cells that die are those associated with anxiety. Maybe that's the way to do it – just wait for the anxiety brain cells to die.'

I can't pretend, Leonard, that I'm not surprised at you taking such a scientific line on feeling bad.

'Sophocles said that every man must meet his fate: either you do it standing up or crawling like a wretch. At certain points in your life, you just have to stand up. As William Henley, the English poet, said:

'In the fell clutch of circumstance
I have not winced nor cried aloud.
Under the bludgeonings of chance
My head is bloody, but unbowed.'
[from 'Invictus']

Cohen is a delightful man. No, seriously. For a poet, he is unflamboyant; for a million-selling pop star he is, shall we say, rather grown-up. He does everything at a philosophical pace; he even looks at you slowly. And that remarkable face is not particularly ashen. It's dark and furrowed with wear, corrugated in complex folds like a prune, its jovian twinkle an ironic overtone to the absurd saturnine gravel-grind of his voice. When I mention that *I'm Your Man* evinces an ironic detachment that might confuse his older disciples, the prune rumples into a smile.

'People use the word irony, but I'd prefer to use the word "realistic". Not the 20 per cent meaning of realism; y'know, that things are just lousy. Realism in the sense that this is a butcher's shop around us, but in spite of that there's tenderness; that the whole thing's a scam, but there's integrity; that all the conflicts in the world are not, never will be reconciled, but at least they're taken into account. In other words, there's a man's experience in each song and you can believe in it.'

Cohen isn't the least bit disturbed by the fact that I'm a 1988-vintage Cohen fan only. 'That's legitimate,' he throbs, like a Thames dredger. In fact, he seems to rather like the idea.

'The old records have a certain vulnerability in them, but I guess I've turned a corner in my recent life that's enabled me to develop a perspective that includes strength with the vulnerability.'

I babble on about how my favourite jazz musicians all speak of strength through vulnerability. Cohen waits patiently for me to finish and picks up the baton.

'Of course, the soup in which these things float is the soup of virtuosity and a high, high visionary creativity. There have to be hours of discipline before these guys will stand up and display their vulnerability as well as their strength. The devotion to that craft develops character. Yes, that's how the character of an artist is refined: through *work*.

'You just learn how to do something. You never master it. The song manifests the life of the heart, but nobody ever masters the heart – we *suffer* the life of the heart. Your devotion to your craft is your response to the thing you can't master.' After two novels, eight anthologies and ten albums of songs since 1956, Cohen still writes every day.

He comes from a 'conservative Jewish community' in Montreal which had no more than a 'leaning towards orthodoxy'. They were, he says, 'decent people, not so much theological as communal, with a live-and-let-live attitude. No one was expected to be without sin.'

He continues. 'I think there's a deep insight in that story in Genesis when Adam and Eve were compelled to leave the garden and they heard the voice of the Almighty saying: "By the sweat of thy brow shalt thou earn thy bread." Sure, it's a nice idea, those Utopian writers who've spoken of a society where there's no work, but I can't imagine it myself. Just on the maintenance level, this world needs a lot of work: you've got to keep yourself clean, you've got to find somewhere to put the garbage and the shit, you've got to find someone to mend the traffic lights.'

But don't you think, surely, that we'll ever escape the feeling of needing to be redeemed from work?

'I think that toil itself is the redemption. There's no ethic or cosmic realm that you suddenly penetrate where you're nourished by these, er, abstract forces of honour or truth or whatever. It's in the thing itself, like there's no life outside this body.'

Nick Coleman; from Time Out, *25 May 1988*

The Smiths. You won't find a job hanging round there, lads.

Springsteen's previous study of work was the mournful 'Factory' from 1978's *Darkness on the Edge of Town*, a sparse and unsentimental look at his father's life as a labourer. However, it's nothing compared with Patti Smith's splenetic 1974 potboiler 'Piss Factory', in which the singer trashes her fellow workers, her boss and the notion of work in general before promising that she'll some day leave and move to New York City to make it big. Contrast Smith's somewhat pessimistic outlook with 'She Works Hard for the Money', Donna Summer's cheerily patronising tribute to the working woman, and you might uncover some of the key ideological, demographical and cultural differences between punk and disco.

Covering similar ground to Smith but with more country panache, Johnny Paycheck scored a 1977 smash with 'Take this Job and Shove It', written by David Allan Coe and later covered by the Dead Kennedys, while George Thorogood's not dissimilar 'Get a Haircut' is a blues-rock take on 'Career Opportunities'. Before them both, Woody Guthrie's 'Talking Hard Work' took a rather more tongue-in-cheek look at work than his own romantic 'John Henry': in it, the singer regales the listener with shaggy dog tales of toil, even adding a sly, witty dig at the integrity of the unions. And at the opposite end of the spectrum is Bobby Bare's discomforting 1975 album *Hard Time Hungrys*, which combines songs

On the record
Billy Bragg

'Scarborough Fair'
Simon & Garfunkel

I've written a book about Englishness and belonging, and this song plays a pivotal role. There's an essential irony that it took these two Jewish American guys from New York City to introduce me to English folk music, to introduce me to a sense of Englishness I'd never felt before. I first heard two girls perform this in a school assembly in Barking. It fires off so many connections for me. There's a very English sensibility in Paul Simon's writing: he wrote a lot when he was here in '65 and '66, and he learned a lot from guys like Martin Carthy, who taught him this version of 'Scarborough Fair'. Hearing this when I was 12 or 13 brought to me a whole emotional landscape that had nothing to do with my parents at all. It was all mine.
Billy Bragg's most recent album is Mr Love & Justice *(Cooking Vinyl)*

about recession and unemployment with spoken-word contributions from men and women struggling for work below the poverty line. It's not really a party album.

But here, at least, the English can contribute; indeed, songs about unions and unemployment are not unknown in the English pop tradition. Billy Bragg's 'There Is Power in a Union', which sounded like a throwback to the 1970s when it was released in 1986 and now comes across like something from the '20s, was actually adapted and reworked from a pro-Union song written during the American Civil War. However, Bragg's lyric really has its origins in the strong socialist bent of English folk, as the singer manfully pretends that the unions, already smashed beyond repair by ten years of Thatcherism, could still defend the common man.

Nearly 30 years previously, the Kinks, led by the rarely idealistic Ray Davies, took a far more jaundiced look at the power of the union in 1970's 'Get Back in Line'. Fitting firmly into the same tradition as John Boulting's 1959 union-baiting film *I'm All Right Jack*, it paints a picture of a normal worker whose day can be made or broken by his self-interested, power-hungry union boss. And by the end of the '70s, English musicians were beginning to reflect the riding uncmployment in the country. Workaday punks Chelsea kicked things off with 'Right to Work' in 1977; a year later, UB40 chose to name themselves after the official form that was then used to claim unemployment benefit (and later titled their 1980 debut album *Signing Off*, presumably as a nod to their own status).

The lack of job opportunities in Britain went on to become a key undercurrent to the music of the 1980s: in songs such as the Specials' 'Ghost Town'; in bands such as Dexys Midnight Runners, who formed after meeting at the benefits office; and even in movements such as the New Romantics, Madchester and rave, all of which emerged as a direct or indirect reaction to growing unemployment. It's a trend epitomised by Elvis Costello and Clive Langer's song 'Shipbuilding': a minor hit for Robert Wyatt, it's a very English take on the American blue-collar tradition that's as much a mournful epitaph for a failing industrial heritage as it is about the Falklands War. After all, work might be a four-letter word, but so is 'dole'.

Born to Run

Trains and boats and planes

David Hutcheon packs his bags and follows music's march around the globe.

In the spring of 1944, the Merry Macs' recording of 'Mairzy Doats' hit number one on the American pop charts, its seemingly nonsensical lyrics ('Mairzy doats and dozy doats and liddle lamzy divey') providing relief from the war. Inspired by an English nursery rhyme, its place in military history is perhaps more assured than its position in the pop pantheon. Like 'The Colonel Bogey March', immortalised in David Lean's *The Bridge on the River Kwai*, 'Mairzy Doats' became an irreverent signifier of membership of the Allied forces.

As American servicemen exported 'Mairzy Doats' around the world, it became another indicator of how all-pervasive popular music can be. Admittedly, it helps if you're backed by an army of well-drilled, heavily armed troops, but 'Mairzy Doats' isn't alone in crossing oceans and influencing global cultures despite being unintelligible to anyone who heard it. The influence of American foreign policy on the world's musical culture cannot be overestimated: with no need for passports or visas, and unable to recognise barriers such as skin colour, music could do the job of war, colonising territories and appropriating hearts and minds. How was General Noriega ousted? He was blasted out of his hideout in the Vatican diplomatic mission in Panama City by Van Halen's 'Panama' played at unbearable volume. It's only rock 'n' roll.

In the hundred or so years leading up to the start of the 20th century and our concept of rock 'n' roll being born somewhere around the Mississippi, African Americans had learned 'western' instruments such as the fiddle and the banjo, and developed unique forms of gospel music that seemed half-indebted to Hebridean and Orcadian traditions and half-drawn from their own continent's diverse cultures. Those with less distant or distorted ties to Africa were able to pass on unadulterated dances and tunes.

But it's important to recognise how much movement there was before that. It didn't just start with slavery, though it had a significant effect. No: with the movement west of the Celts and gypsies, the southern raids of the Vikings, the trading missions of the Chinese, the Arabs and the Indians, and the imperial spread of the Romans, trumpets, drums and stringed instruments took hold across the known world.

As minstrels travelled with European armies, so griots spread the history of West African leaders from the 13th century. When Spain emptied itself of Moors and Jews in the 15th century, North Africa and the Mediterranean Middle East benefited. Yet some things surely remain coincidences. Compare 'Brown Phalla' by Kong Nay, Cambodia's maestro of the long-necked guitar, with 'La Drogue', one of the earliest recordings by king of the Sahara blues Ali Farka Touré, and 'Cross Road Blues' by Robert Johnson, then decide for yourself whether the blues began in the Mekong, Niger or the Mississippi delta.

Somehow, here we are at the start of the 21st century arguing over whether the internet's ability to instantly globalise anything will kill the music industry. Never forget that music has always been carried in the air, and the idea that it could be owned is relatively new. If Vikings were pillaging your village, would it not have been mean of them to insist that you also paid for the chance to listen to their drums and horns? Slavery stole percussion away from West Africa, so why should countries on that continent be asked to recognise Americans' intellectual property rights when their music is returned to them in the form of bootleg CDs? Rap has been an African tradition for centuries, so when Senegal's Didier Awadi sings about *Présidents d'Afrique*, why should we compare him to Kanye West or Jay-Z?

Undoubtedly, America's status in the 20th century has distorted all perspective. How did

Cuba libre: **Mongo Santamaria**.

the banjo get to Africa? Its nearest ancestor is the *ngoni*, a gourd with four strings and a thin neck. The instrument features heavily in the music of Mali, where Bassekou Kouyaté is considered the master thanks to tunes such as 'Jonkoloni'. His reputation is such that he's even appeared at banjo festivals in the US. Yet the banjo itself arrived in Africa via strategic ports, such as Algiers, and American sailors. That's hegemony.

From the start of the media age, pop music moved: it traversed the Delta, it drove up Highway 61 from New Orleans through Clarksdale, where it met Highway 49, and delivered itself to the electric north. It travelled with those who had licence or inclination to move, primarily merchants and the armed services, at a time when most people did not. It hitched itself to radio waves that crossed oceans, serviced overseas personnel and influenced musicians on every continent. In the land of opportunity, music hinted at escape and was seen as the truth and a lie, a reality and a fantasy, freedom and danger.

The truth?

The first pop song to go global was Cuban: 'El Manisero' ('The Peanut Vendor'), a rumba made popular in Havana by Rita Montaner and later recorded for a Hollywood movie by the expatriates Don Azpiazu and Antonio Machin. That was 80 years ago; you've probably never heard either version, though you'll certainly know the tune. The song's popularity in the 1930s was similar to that of the tulip mania in Europe 300 years earlier, yet the Latin bubble never burst.

The lie?

Carmen Miranda's belief that 'bananas is my business' suggested Tinseltown's interest in Brazilian samba was as an exotic side dish rather than a revolutionary folk music. In Los Angeles in 1943, American sailors took it upon themselves to re-educate Latinos for whom the jazz age was the key to improving their lot but who, in the sailors' eyes, had simply forgotten their place in society. The notorious Zoot Suit Riots resulted in hundreds of non-whites being beaten up in attacks that the press would claim helped 'cleanse' the streets.

But the ideas engendered to the Latino community by the zoot suit still appeal to anybody with an ounce of moxie. Dressing up and showing out to threaten society runs

> 'If it hadn't been for the migrants who quit their homeland only to spend the rest of their lives singing about how much they miss the damned place, then the folk and country libraries would be empty shells.'

deep in youth culture, from the low-slung denim of rap to the Tuareg rude boys whose headscarves need to be just so. Malcolm X (then known as Detroit Red) was a zoot-suit wearer; Cab Calloway, of 'Minnie the Moocher' fame, had been wearing one for a decade before the riots; the Who, as the High Numbers, recorded a song by that name as their first B-side. Hell, even Tom was known to wear one when not chasing Jerry. ZZ Top were right: everybody's crazy 'bout a 'Sharp Dressed Man'.

If the mix of cultures in the south-east corner of North America was important, it was even more dynamic in the islands of the Caribbean, and Cuba was the most obvious beneficiary. Its slave population was primarily Yoruban, from what is now Nigeria and Benin. However, the landowners included French nationals (who had fled Haiti) and Spanish natives (Basques, Catalans and former residents of the Canaries), while Chinese labourers had been shipped in to mine and build the railway. In the Havana docks, poor black Cubans played impromptu concerts using tea chests and packing cases as percussion; in the east, roving military bands spread tunes played primarily by guitarists.

Out of this mix came one tune that went around the world more often than any other and is still sung in football stadiums week after week. The words to 'Guajira Guantanamera' were adapted from a verse by the nationalist leader José Marti, shot dead in 1895 during a vainglorious attack on a Spanish army base. That a nationalist poem can become an anthem

Rewind
Ravi Shankar

'I like many rock musicians, and certainly my friendship with the Beatles helped to attract young people to my music. I'm very grateful. George no longer plays the sitar, but we are still good friends and he continues to study the religious philosophies of my country. But I had been building a following among the young for a long time before I met George in 1966.

'I enjoyed some of the pop festivals in which I participated. The Monterey festival [in 1967] was my greatest experience with a young audience. I played for more than four hours and the communication was complete. But now, [the festivals'] atmosphere has changed. The audience neck and smoke pot and roll around, and do not pay attention to the music as they should. I have to explain that our music is as serious as, say, Bach, and deserves the same concentration. In India, musicians can play all night and never lose the audience's attention, but in the west, I have to plan my programmes carefully.

'I realise that westerners may find Indian music difficult because it's primarily melodic, and concentrates on one mood or emotion. This is established in the first movement of a raga, the *alap*, a solo exposition that provides the basis for improvisation. Audiences here usually prefer the next section, the *jor*, as the element of rhythm is added by the tabla drum. In the last section, the *jhala*, we build speed and excitement to the climax. A raga is an aesthetic projection of the artist's inner spirit: he breathes life into the notes through embellishment and ornamentation.

'There was a period of about two years, after the Beatle business, that everywhere I went I was mobbed. I even had what you call groupies. My God, I like women very much, but I did not like these: they were so forced, so artificial.

'Now the hysteria has died away and only the people with a serious interest in Indian music are left. I'm very happy about this. I was criticised harshly in India when my popularity became great: it was said that I had sold out, that my playing had become vulgarised. If you knew how much this hurt me! I've worked so hard to create new audiences for our wonderful traditions, to bring young people to some understanding of them.'
Jan Murray; from Time Out, *20 October 1972*

across the world, using a melody written 34 years after Marti's death, says much about the way music bends to suit all tastes. And if you think the power of that melody has been dimmed by familiarity, check the version by Estrellas de Areito.

Latin Americans moved from the Caribbean and Central America, arriving in the great cities of the North looking for work during the post-war boom. New York's dancehalls reverberated to rumbas, mambos and cha-chas. Surfing the wave was another Cuban, Dámaso Pérez Prado, whose 'Mambo No.5' had a second life thanks to Lou Bega in 1999. With his outrageous costumes and suggestive grunts, Prado was a crossover giant whose 'Cherry Pink and Apple Blossom White' occupied the top spot in the American charts for ten weeks in 1956, just before rock 'n' roll blitzed the nation.

Latin music never lost its appeal. There were hits during the boogaloo years, a trend epitomised by Mongo Santamaria's 'Watermelon Man' and Ray Barretto's 'El Watusi'; during the salsa phenomenon, Tito Puente and Celia Cruz became household names even though their music was too hardcore truly to cross over and gain mainstream acceptance; and then, only a decade ago, a *son* revival made Compay Segundo a star in his nineties and introduced the world to his composition 'Chan Chan' via the Buena Vista Social Club. However, the arrival of rock 'n' roll in America sent Latin music in search of new markets.

Africa fell under its spell immediately. In the newly independent countries, leaders were determined to throw off the yoke of colonialism and develop a new African culture that could unite the continent. In West and East Africa, Cuban music was adopted like a prodigal son by people who immediately recognised its roots. A Cuban ensemble such as Orquesta Aragón, formed in 1939, inventors of the *cha-cha-chá* and still able to fill concert halls in Britain with 'El Bodeguero', found a new audience and toured constantly around countries favoured by Havana's communists.

In Senegal, Orchestra Baobab dominated the 1970s with Latin-flavoured tunes such as 'Utru Horas', their mock-Spanish lyrics phonetically transcribed by the wife of one of the singers so they sounded authentic. In Congo, Cuban music's piano solos were adapted for guitarists; the result was the creation of Congolese rumba

Elvis Presley appears on *The Milton Berle Show* in 1956. Shitstorm ensues.

(also known as soukous) played by great orchestras such as African Jazz, whose 'Independence Cha Cha Cha' celebrated the coming of a new hope for the continent. All the while, governments sponsored musicians in the hope of building a positive, optimistic, pan-African culture. It wasn't until the 1980s, when a new generation of Africans decided to add a further layer of 'Africanness', that Cuban music began to drift out of fashion. Among the chief architects of this development was Youssou N'Dour, whose *mbalax* sound used the sabar drums that were previously regarded as 'too street' for progressive Senegal, but whose hits, such as 'Immigrés', appealed directly to African youth.

Back in America, the rock age was a revolution that was as much about the move into the mainstream of cultural and geographical outsiders as it was about the sexualisation of straight society. Race music and hillbilly music, two sides of the same coin, were no longer recorded in the hotel rooms and radio stations that had been satisfactory for earlier performers. The music was now coming out of New Orleans and the Appalachians and arriving in New York and Los Angeles, putting its feet on the table and being beamed around the planet.

There has probably never been another shitstorm to compare with the one stirred up by the Establishment in reaction to the rise of Elvis Presley after a bump 'n' grind performance of 'Hound Dog' on *The Milton Berle Show* in June 1956. Elvis removed the Cuban influence that was so apparent in Big Mama Thornton's original, but made public the fact that white people thought about sex. Jazz was acceptable on Beale Street in New Orleans just as Little Richard was able to sing about the joys of unbiblical sexual congress on 'Tutti Frutti', but these threats could be eviscerated and bowdlerised. Presley, who even covered 'Tutti Frutti' himself, brought another America to the doorsteps of those who had no intention of travelling down Highway 61.

The religious attacked him, parents were appalled, the press had a field day (the *New York Daily News* said popular culture had reached its nadir in his 'grunt and groin' antics) and fellow musicians nailed their flags to the mast: 'His kind of music is deplorable, a rancid-smelling aphrodisiac,' announced Frank Sinatra. What killed Presley was not his stint in the army but the fact that immediately after he was discharged from it in 1960, he appeared on television with Sinatra, duetting on 'Witchcraft' and 'Love Me Tender', before heading to the recording studio to mimic Caruso and record Italian songs in a mock-operatic style ('O Sole Mio' as 'It's Now or Never', 'Torno a Sorrento' as 'Surrender'). So that's what he'd been doing in Europe…

Yet the backwaters of America, where Presley's music was born, had for centuries silently accepted the immigrant musical forms that would combine to create rock 'n' roll and soul. If it hadn't been for the migrants who quit their homeland only to spend the rest of their lives singing about how much they miss the damned place, then the folk and country libraries would be empty shells. No 'Fields of Athenry', no 'Letter from America', no Charlie Rich's 'Feel Like Going Home'. And no call-and-response gospel traditions, which eventually informed the birth of soul from Ray Charles's 'What'd I Say' to James Brown's 'Please, Please, Please'.

Nigerian pioneer **Fela Kuti**.

And when African musicians discovered this latter development, they took to it with enthusiasm. The Nigerian Fela Kuti was introduced to funk and black militancy in the States at the end of the 1960s: when he returned home, he added African rhythms to the sound he had heard being made by Brown and developed Afrobeat, arguably the most rebellious music ever to come out of the continent. 'Zombie', his masterpiece, was a bare-faced attack on martial law in which he laid into soldiers who blindly do their leaders' bidding. Shortly after its release, 1,000 soldiers smashed up Kuti's compound, attacked his family, raped his singers and beat up his friends and musicians.

Rock 'n' roll, of course, survived. It caught the ships sailing east and wound up in ports on the other side of the Atlantic, in Liverpool, in Hamburg, in Algiers. It caught the planes flying west and found itself entrenched in south-east

Asia. It took the bus to Marrakech, Kabul and Goa. And everywhere it went, it mutated and changed the landscape. In Algeria, it inspired singers to search out the freedom to give air to their opinions in rai, and came up against an Islamic backlash. Extremists murdered stars such as Cheb Hasni for singing pop songs that went against fundamentalists' beliefs. It's no coincidence that Rachid Taha's interpretation of the exile's song 'Ya Rayah' has become a rallying point and an anthem for people unable to return to their homeland.

Hiding under the pseudonym Henry Cording, *chansonnier* Henri Salvador recorded 'Rock and Roll Mops', the first French rock 'n' roll song, in 1956. But a year later, he'd returned to his own boulevardier persona, and his song 'Dans Mon Île' had inadvertently inspired the invention of bossa nova in Brazil. So it was more than a little ironic when, a decade later, the leaders of Brazil's Tropicália movement came under fire for introducing non-indigenous elements to bossa nova. Caetano Veloso and Gilberto Gil, the creator of the ridiculous 'Bat Macumba', were both sent into exile from a country ruled by a repressive military junta.

During the Vietnam War, American servicemen on R&R were entertained in the fleshpots of Saigon, Bangkok and Phnom Penh by local musicians who could copy a current hit faster than the tailor upstairs could copy the latest threads. Creedence Clearwater Revival's 'Have You Ever Seen the Rain?' is still played on the radio in Cambodia, a country in which singers such as Huoy Meas, Sinn Sisamouth and Ros Sereysothea (whose 'Wait Ten Months' is the greatest psychedelic garage-band classic never to make it on to a *Nuggets* compilation) were executed by the Khmer Rouge for participating in the corruption of society.

The former Soviet Republic of Tuva is a landlocked state surrounded by Siberia and Mongolia, yet even here rock music was seen as the key to freedom. Sailors and students returned home as smugglers, bringing contraband LPs in their luggage. Party members put these treasured artefacts on the mantelpiece next to their busts of Lenin and then tried to create a music that matched what they heard, using local musical traditions but not falling foul of Soviet censorship. The result? Yat-Kha's 'Come Along', a seamless blend of heavy metal and throat singing. (The authorities objected to the band's 'spiky strings'.)

In 1987, the Icicle Works released an album entitled *If You Want to Defeat Your Enemy, Sing His Song*. Perhaps if the Axis had adopted 'Mairzy Doats', the story of D-Day might have been one of defeat for the Allies. Yet, as the likes of 'Mairzy Doats' and 'Bat Macumba' demonstrate, it's the songs nobody understands that spread the widest and the fastest, perhaps because fewer people feel left out when they know everybody should be. Perhaps Britain should consider singing its next Eurovision entry in a language that might appeal to more voters. Does anybody know the Polish for 'mares eat oats and does eat oats'?

Around the world in 20 songs

'Your Eyes Are Like a Cup of Tea'
The Master Musicians of Joujouka
Championed in the 1960s and '70s by hippy guru Timothy Leary, the Rolling Stones' Brian Jones and jazz saxophonist Ornette Coleman, the Master Musicians and their predecessors have been making hypnotic, rhythmically complex trance music like this for centuries.

'Mustt Mustt (Lost in His Work)'
Nusrat Fateh Ali Khan
More Sufi music from the other side of the Muslim world. A Massive Attack mix of this signature track became a huge dancefloor hit in western clubs.

'Bombay Theme' AR Rahman
Another Sufi Muslim, Rahman started out playing in jazz groups with the likes of L Shankar and Zakir Hussain. This gorgeously orchestrated piece, featuring a sighing, slurring string section from Madras, is the track that made his name.

'Traveller' Talvin Singh
This 11-minute epic unashamedly takes its cue from AR Rahman, even using the same Madras-based string section and similar orchestral techniques. Singh's Mercury Music Prize-winning album *OK* also features musicians from Japan and China, and integrates techno and drum 'n' bass into traditional Eastern music.

'Mama Tian Na' Sa Dingding
The half-Chinese, half-Mongolian singer and multi-instrumentalist adopts a similar stylistic approach to Singh on her breakthrough 2007 album *Alive*.

'In a Gadda Da Vida'
Albert Kuvezin & Yat-Kha

More music of Mongolian descent, this time from the Tuvan region on the borders of Mongolia and Russia. Like their compatriots Huun-Huur-Tu, Yat-Kha are rebellious Tuvan cowboys: they tout a distorted brand of rockabilly that uses the eerie, overblown sound of throat singing, and a lead vocalist who sings so low that he often sounds like he's delivering a series of low-pitched burps. This version of the old Iron Butterfly number is from *Re-Covers*, a 2005 novelty album of rock songs.

'Cler Achel' Tinariwen

Another gang of outlaw desert rockers, but this time from across the world: specifically, the rebel camps on the borders of Libya and Mali in Saharan Africa. Tinariwen are thought to be the first Tuareg band to use electric guitars.

'Tuareg' Gal Costa

An exotic tribute to the Tuareg tribes of North Africa from the Brazilian pop and Tropicália singer Gal Costa, a long-term creative partner of...

'O Samba e o Tango' Caetano Veloso

The founding father of Brazil's Tropicália movement makes an explicit connection between Brazilian samba and Argentine tango, two folk forms that have been refined into high art, in this, the opening track from his live album *Fina Estampa ao Vivo*.

'Viejo Smoking' Carlos Gardel

Moving across the River Plate (and rewinding six decades), we reach legendary Argentine crooner Gardel, the king of traditional tango and the man described by Bing Crosby as the greatest singer on earth. Gardel is actually thought to have been born in the south of France, as was his fellow accordionist...

'Escualo' Richard Galliano

French-Italian accordionist Galliano has paid tribute to Argentine tango many times, most brilliantly in this album of works by the progressive tango composer Ástor Piazzolla. Galliano has also collaborated with numerous jazz and gypsy musicians, including...

'Les Yeux Noirs' Biréli Lagrène

A version of a Russian gypsy tune made famous by Django Reinhardt, here played by one of the world's greatest guitarists. Lagrène has also worked with other gypsy musicians, among them...

'Schindler's List' Roby Lakatos

Hungarian Lakatos has collaborated with dozens of jazz, classical and gypsy musicians around the world. Here, he plays a haunting version of the theme to Steven Spielberg's film.

'A la Turk' Taraf de Haïdouks

Take some Roby Lakatos-style gypsy violin, add some frenetic cimbalom, flute and double bass, put your foot down on the accelerator until you're going about twice the speed limit and you've got Taraf de Haïdouks, the best known outfit from the Wallachia region of Romania and a ramshackle collective that Johnny Depp famously described as 'the greatest fuckin' rock 'n' roll band in the world'.

'Saturday Nite Special'
The Sundown Playboys

More thrilling accordion madness, this time from across the Atlantic in south-east Louisiana. 'Saturday Nite Special' is full-on Cajun music, first released on the Beatles' Apple label and, unexpectedly, one of Morrissey's favourite records.

'Okete (The Squirrel)'
IK Dairo MBE & His Blue Spots

And yet more fantastic accordion music, all the way from Nigeria (albeit, in this particular case, recorded in Seattle): this uplifting squeezebox classic became a signature tune for the late godfather of Nigerian *juju*. In 1963, Dairo became the first African musician to be made an honorary Member of the British Empire.

'Sunny Ti De' King Sunny Adé &
His Green Spots

From the godfather of *juju* to its most famous proponent, who's on top form on this hypnotic slice of guitar music recorded in the late '60s.

'Puleng' The Boyoyo Boys

More spangly African guitar, but from elsewhere on the continent. This exciting slice of South African township jive features some slinky arpeggiated guitars and shuffling rhythms that were famously borrowed by Malcolm McLaren and Trevor Horn for their 1983 single...

'Double Dutch' Malcolm McLaren

A stand-out track from *Duck Rock*, McLaren's unorthodox meltdown of folk dances from around the world, 'Double Dutch' is an irresistible blend of hip hop, American skipping songs and South African township jive.

'Live at Real World'
The Drummers of Burundi

A few years before *Duck Rock*, Malcolm McLaren had flirted with African music, encouraging Bow Wow Wow (and, more famously, influencing Adam Ant) to recreate the clattering rhythms from the central African nation of Burundi. This 30-minute blast, from a group who played the first ever WOMAD festival in 1982, shows how it should be done.

BORN TO RUN

No place like home

So why, wonders **Will Fulford-Jones**, is everyone leaving?

Songs about home? Simplest, perhaps, to list the songs that aren't. Home is the engine that drives popular song: the most universal of subjects, and one that more or less every artist has, at some point, explicitly or implicitly addressed. And yet, for all that, there's never been any consensus on whether home itself is A Good Thing. 'Should I Stay or Should I Go?' wondered the Clash. Fair question, and one that pop hasn't ever really managed to answer. The singers who find themselves stranded far from their comfort zones often sound desperate to turn right around and return to what they've left behind. But those who are stuck at home are frequently itching to get away from it all and start a new life somewhere, anywhere else. No wonder there's always so much bloody traffic.

From Phil Daniels' *awwright-mate* narration on Blur's 'Parklife' to the imaginary superstar praising 'My Simple Humble Neighborhood' in Maurice Sendak's animated special *Really Rosie*, from Dion's cocksure 'King of the New York Streets' to Randy Newman's unconditional 'I Love LA', pop's always had its share of musicians who are keen to pay tribute to their origins. Similarly, it's never been short of songs in which home is the only place that the singer feels at, er, home. Neither Jellyfish ('I Wanna Stay Home') nor Duke Ellington ('Don't Get Around Much Anymore', lyrics by Bob Russell) are really in the mood for painting the town red; the Drifters get away from the bustle of city life not by leaving town but simply by wandering 'Up on the Roof'; and the Beach Boys sit tight on the angst-packed 'In My Room', a sentiment later echoed 40 years later by power-popper Ben Kweller as he hides in 'My Apartment'.

But in truth, these eulogies to home-set happiness are exceptions rather than the rule. Pop music is an escapist art form, so it follows that much of it should be about escaping: from failed love affairs, of course, but also from schools and jobs, from friends and relatives, from small towns to big cities and big cities to wide open spaces. After all, aren't we all looking to transcend our origins, even if only for the three minutes that a song plays on the radio while we're waiting for the lights to change?

Bruce Springsteen has more or less built his career on the dichotomies of staying and leaving, coming and going. On his first couple of albums, songs such as 'Rosalita (Come Out Tonight)' and '4th of July, Asbury Park (Sandy)' offer a fleeting hope that there might be life beyond the comforts of the New Jersey shoreline, but they're ultimately rooted in the apparently unremarkable towns in which they're set. And, as such, they're effectively based on the idea that if you're stuck in just such an unremarkable town, you need to build up your own romance and mythology. Because unless you live in Asbury Park, no one else is going to do it for you.

Although *Greetings from Asbury Park, NJ* and *The Wild, the Innocent and the E Street Shuffle* won him fans, Springsteen's real commercial breakthrough came with the first record on which he explicitly set his lyrical sights far beyond his immediate surroundings. Writer

Bruce Springsteen.

Top ten
The moon

'Shine On, Harvest Moon'
Milton Brown & His Musical Brownies

Highlighted by a wonderful, Grappelli-esque fiddle solo by Cecil Brower, Brown's 1935 recording of this old chestnut is a good'un. However, like most recordings both before and since, it cuts off the first verse, which reveals that the narrator is a lusty lad frustrated by the clouds that cover the moonlight and send his frightened girlfriend running from his arms and back indoors.

'Bad Moon Rising'
Creedence Clearwater Revival

John Fogerty's biggest hit paints the moon as a portent of doom and despair. See also Echo & the Bunnymen's 'The Killing Moon' and Nick Drake's 'Pink Moon'.

'An Ending (Ascent)'
Brian Eno with Daniel Lanois & Roger Eno

This ethereal reverie was written and recorded for a documentary about NASA's Apollo missions to the moon. The whole album is just as lush.

'Blue Moon'
The Marcels

From Elvis Presley's spooky little stroll to Bob Dylan's grouchy ramble, from Peggy Lee's gentle rendition to Arthur Briggs's trumpet solo (on a gorgeous 1935 take that also features pre-bop saxophonist Coleman Hawkins and gypsy guitarist Django Reinhardt), virtually every other recording of this old Rodgers and Hart tune captures its lonesome flavour better than this preposterously upbeat piece of doo-wop. But, really, who cares? All together now: 'Bomp-baba-bomp, ba-bomp ba-bomp-bomp, baba-bomp baba-bomp, ba-dang di-dang dang, ba-ding bi-dong ding…'

'Moondance' Van Morrison

See him in concert these days and he'll absolutely murder it. But the original is Van at his most convincingly charming.

'Back Side of the Moon' The Orb

The title appears to be a mocking nod to Pink Floyd's *The Dark Side of the Moon*. The music, though, is mysterious and transporting.

'How High the Moon'
Les Paul & Mary Ford

It bears repeating that Les Paul is more than just a model of guitar made by Gibson. Back in the '30s and '40s, the Wisconsin-born musician pioneered the development of the solid-bodied electric guitar after building one from a piece of fence post. And soon after, he pretty much invented multi-tracking, painstakingly layering numerous guitar and vocal tracks in a series of recordings that, more than 50 years on, still sound breathtaking. Best of the bunch? This dazzling take on an old Broadway tune, much covered but never bettered.

'Fly Me to the Moon (In Other Words)'
Frank Sinatra

Sinatra's recording swings as only a band led by Count Basie ever could. Tony Bennett, though, takes a different approach in concert: he puts aside his mic, asks the sound man to switch off the PA and sings the song with just an unamplified piano for company, a show-stopping trick that works just as well in the Royal Albert Hall as it does in a 200-seat Las Vegas showroom.

'Paper Moon' Whiskeytown

This fabulously unexpected blend of country romanticism and little Cuban rhythms is one of countless songs that uses the moon as a harbinger of, or metaphor for, romantic bliss; others include 'Moonlight in Vermont', 'It's Only a Paper Moon' and Brandy's 'Full Moon'.

'Harvest Moon' Neil Young

Beautiful romantic whimsy from the album of the same name. That gentle *psssssh* in the background is apparently the sound of an uncredited percussionist pushing an old straw broom across the studio floor.

Patrick Humphries has made the point that, for a while in the early '70s, some music industry folk wondered whether Springsteen or Tom Waits would be the first to break into the mainstream. Their respective third albums soon solved that conundrum. Waits's was a rambling 75-minute musical monologue recorded in a mocked-up nightclub and scattered with anecdotes about warm beer, inedible diner breakfasts and masturbation. Springsteen's was *Born to Run*.

When it's set next to the Boss's first couple of albums, it's little wonder that *Born to Run* hit such a nerve. More than any record he's made before or since, it's buzzing with enthusiasm for what might lie ahead in a life that hasn't yet moved out of second gear. The optimism in the songs is possibly misguided and certainly exaggerated, but it's optimism nonetheless, and the verve with which Springsteen and band communicated it proved impossible to resist. 'Born to Be Wild' for grown-ups, the album's outlandishly romantic title track remains a radio perennial more than three decades after its release. However, a similar sense of exhilaration courses through the rest of the record: witness the booming excitability of 'Night', say, or the perpetually wide open, traffic-free 'Thunder Road'.

But while it's revealing that Springsteen's career-making album was his first to explore the idea that home is wherever one parks one's car, it's just as telling that he chose to follow it with *Darkness on the Edge of Town*. Gone, for the most part, is the confidence of its predecessor: by contrast, *Darkness…* trades ambition for resignation, the open road for Main Street, the great unknown for the familiarity of home. Like 'Thunder Road', 'The Promised Land' is built on the idea that there's got to be something better than *this*, but it's immediately shot down by the world-weary acquiescence of 'Factory' and is otherwise ringed by songs in which the narrators seem unable or unwilling to let go of their surroundings. It's as if the souped-up motors of 'Born to Run' broke down before they crossed the city limits, or 'Thunder Road' turned out to be a cul-de-sac. You don't choose your home after all, reckons Springsteen. It chooses you.

Ever since *Darkness on the Edge of Town*, Springsteen has constantly returned to the theme of home and what it means to break away from it. *Born in the USA* is full of such

'Jimmy Webb's "By the Time I Get to Phoenix" paints the departing partner as a romantic man of mystery. But the song is really an amazingly callow kiss-off, the narrator an indecisive schmuck who didn't have the balls to say goodbye.'

songs: the ill-fated escapees to 'Darlington County'; the stasis and desolation implicit in 'My Hometown', in which a family ponders shipping out of the only life they've ever known; and, for that matter, the title track, which has a few things of its own to say about what it means to leave home and then return to it as something other than a conquering hero. But nothing in Springsteen's armoury nails the subject quite like 'Hungry Heart', in which a footloose narrator flees one home only to admit that he ultimately needs another to replace it. As with 'Born in the USA', a triumphal musical setting hides a story with a bleaker message.

Like Springsteen, Mary Chapin Carpenter was raised in New Jersey. And also like Springsteen, Carpenter started out with her feet planted firmly on home turf. When, on her early records, someone decides to make a dart for the door, it's usually with no great sense of excitement. 'A Road Is Just a Road' even offers the opinion that what lies between her and her departed partner is 'only dust and dirt', a dreary stretch on which 'the signs all look the same'. But when Carpenter and her characters eventually got itchy feet, her songs started to get considerably more interesting. Her lyrics are full of hellos and goodbyes, but with rather more of the former than the latter.

On the Cajun-inflected 'Down at the Twist and Shout', Carpenter makes her escape to Louisiana, where a blast of Beausoleil is enough to blow the blues away. On 'I Feel Lucky', an $11 million lottery jackpot buys her a way out of the job to which she's just called in sick (not to mention, she winks, the affections of Dwight Yoakam and Lyle Lovett). 'I Am a Town' is a thousand-mile road-trip in five minutes, two dozen snapshots of an America seen from the driver's side in a car without brakes. And 'He Thinks He'll Keep Her', perhaps the most striking of all her songs, struck a nerve with listeners as it climbed the country charts in 1993, despite going against country orthodoxy by explicitly damning the sacred dullness of family life. 'Everything is so benign,' sings Carpenter in the first chorus, before packing her husband's suitcase and breaking up the formerly happy home. So much for 'Stand By Your Man'.

It's an elder sibling who departs in Carpenter's 'Only a Dream', upping sticks at the dawn's early light and leaving the singer 'no sign of someone who expects to be back'. Essentially, it's the Beatles' parental lament 'She's Leaving Home' rewritten from the perspective of a younger sister: not angry or bitter, like the parents in McCartney's ballad, but sad, confused and more than a little sentimental. However, most songs about a child spreading its wings come from the perspective of the person doing the leaving rather than that of the folk they're leaving behind.

On the surface, Madness's 'Our House' is a jaunty ode to childhood in a happy family home until Suggs, at the one point in his song where his voice seems to strain just a little, admits that 'Something tells you that you've got to move away from it'. It's the key moment in a lyric that, with no great fuss or sentiment, eventually slides into the past tense. Still, at least Suggs' memories of his formative years are positive: compare and contrast 'Our House' with the experiences of the Pet Shop Boys ('This Must Be the Place I Waited Years to Leave') and Steely Dan (the acutely acerbic 'My Old School'), neither of whom seem in any great hurry to join Friends Reunited. Or, for that matter, Bronski Beat's 'Smalltown Boy', a compelling tale of a gay teenager forced to wave goodbye to his home as he searches for acceptance and affirmation of his own identity.

When he tackles the subject on 'There Goes My Life', country singer Kenny Chesney, as country singers are generally wont to do, tries to cram a generation's worth of life and incident into three minutes. At the start, the character is a bumbling, immature adult for whom fatherhood has arrived too soon, regretting his foolishness and the opportunities he'll miss as he moves in with his girlfriend to help raise the child he doesn't want. But after 18 years (compressed, without undue complication, into two verses), he's become a proud parent, gutted to see his daughter load up the car and head off in search of the independence he never got to experience for himself and now has no interest in pursuing.

'There Goes My Life' is a virtual microcosm of the bipolar relationship with home that country singers have long maintained. Country doesn't really do ambivalence: at least in the Nashville mainstream, the music deals not in ambiguities but extremes. Characters spend three minutes falling head over heels in love or collapsing out of it, jumping for joy or crying into their adult beverages. Translate that to home life, and it usually means that they're either happy to be tied to the apron strings or desperate to escape them. In the former camp rest such songs as the Carter Family's incalculably influential 1929 recording of 'My Clinch Mountain Home', the archetype of down-home country sentimentality. And in the latter, there's the immense catalogue of songs about hitting the road and staying on it in perpetuity, from the roving romancer narrating the choruses of the Prairie Ramblers' 1939 boastathon 'I Got a Gal in Every State' to the more recent likes of Dierks Bentley's 'Modern Day Drifter' and 'Lot of Leavin' Left to Do'.

Still, country music is hardly the only genre to have gloried in this ideal of the rootless outsider, the vagabond leaving behind nothing but footprints and broken hearts. Sure, Hank Williams set the standard with his eerie, howling 'Ramblin' Man', pseudonymously credited to Luke the Drifter when it was first released in 1953. But the title Williams introduced was later expanded by Dickey Betts of the blues-rocking Allman Brothers, whose song of the same name is basically an uptempo rewrite of Williams' piece, and electro-pop jokers Lemon Jelly, whose own

'Ramblin' Man' is a carefree travelogue that lurches without rhyme or reason from Kyoto to Fingringhoe, Harlem to Dakar.

Others, too, proved no less interested in lying back and watching the world go by. Jazz singer Helen Merrill's breathtaking 1955 recording of 'Any Place I Hang My Hat Is Home', written a decade earlier by Johnny Mercer and Harold Arlen for the movie *St Louis Woman*, transposes the action from the perspective of a rootless female. Similarly, Marvin Gaye picked up his fedora and ran with it on 'Wherever I Lay My Hat (That's My Home)'. The lengthy list of blues songs about hitting the road or the rails is best epitomised by the much-covered 'Key to the Highway'. And, of course, there's Lee Marvin's preposterous take on 'Wand'rin' Star', which the actor mumbles gruffly into his moustache during the almost unwatchable *Paint Your Wagon*. 'Hell is in "hello",' he announces at one point, strolling along a road that, like the movie, seems to go on for ever.

Very occasionally, a roaming singer admits that behind the bravado, he retains an attachment to or weakness for home. Most famous in Glen Campbell's subsequent cover, folkie John Hartford's fluid and appropriately rambling 'Gentle on My Mind' presents the image of a man who's happy to have it both ways: his stuff parked under a girlfriend's sofa, but his heart and his feet forever on the road. The song's message is reminiscent of author Jack Kerouac, an outwardly rootless individual who nonetheless carried with him a deep-seated yearning to settle down. However, for all the song's echoes of *On the Road*, Hartford later admitted that he was inspired to write 'Gentle on My Mind' after a trip to the cinema to watch *Dr Zhivago*.

For every four or five singers who get out of town without much more than a sentimental, three-minute wave goodbye, there's at least one who comes crawling back with tail between legs. The narrator of 'Do You Know the Way to San Jose' has headed south to Los Angeles in a bid to secure fame and fortune. But when she finds neither and her dreams blow away in the breeze, she makes the long trek back whence she came rather than end up pumping gas in the sprawl. Bobby Bare isn't looking for Motortown to make him a star in 'Detroit City' (a lyric later delivered, with surprisingly convincing pathos, by Dean Martin). However,

On the record
Robert Forster

'The Whole of the Law'
The Only Ones

I heard this in 1978, I guess, in the middle of punk rock. It's a ballad, which immediately sets it apart from what was going on at the time. They were a band that were very much championed by the great Nick Kent, who used to write for the *NME* – I followed and respected his taste. It was a great era for import record shops in Australia: people were getting the records in very quickly, and I sought this one out.

They were a little bit of an old-fashioned rock band, really, in the middle of punk: especially on this album, which had 'Another Girl, Another Planet' on it. But it's almost like, to me, the whole album exists around this song. It captures a time at the beginning of my songwriting career, six or maybe eight months after I started writing songs, which is probably why it resonates with me. And when I was 20 or 21, when I heard it for the first time, it seemed like a perfect love song. It's a really liquid, really emotive ballad that sort of just rolls along: very, very romantic, and very longing.

The most recent solo album by Robert Forster, formerly of the Go-Betweens, is The Evangelist *(Lo-Max)*

Rewind
Paul Simon

'My way of working changed when I went to Jamaica to record "Mother and Child Reunion", which was originally a ska song but which the local guys said I had to do in this new reggae style. That's when I decided to leave the studio environment I'd been in during the Simon & Garfunkel period and started to travel.

'You asked about *Graceland*. I don't think a single bad, negative thing came out of that whole business. Sure, there are factions in Soweto and there were debates, but the tour actually got the ANC to change its policy about the boycotts. Obviously, that was important for Hugh [Masakela] and Miriam [Makeba], who were being victimised by the past policy. Their moral support was vital.

'As for the accusations of "cultural tourism", or whatever... Well, it's basically complete bullshit. I've been dipping in all my life. There was a Peruvian folk ballad on *Bridge Over Troubled Water* ["El Cóndor Pasa"]; "Me and Julio Down By the Schoolyard" was very Latin-influenced; then there was "Loves Me Like a Rock", which was gospel. When I did "Scarborough Fair", I got the tune from Martin Carthy; and I used to imitate Bert Jansch's "Angie" [written by Davy Graham as "Anji"], which was the folk instrumental standard when I was in England during the '60s.

'What is culture? It's a limitless thing. It's all around. It doesn't belong to anyone and there are no walls around it. When I'm asked, I often say, "You don't have to be Italian to open a pizza joint," and I stick by that. You know, I use a lot of good musicians and virtually all of them like working with me: I make it fun, I pay them well, I look after them and it's interesting work. That's all I can say.'

But does the globetrotting imply a contempt for contemporary music?

'Not at all. As a musician, I admire George Michael, say, but it just doesn't sound like the popular music I or my generation would make. I feel that what I'm doing is more connected to where I come from: to the '50s, to rock 'n' roll. And when I hear the guitars and the drummers with their incredible custom-made instruments, or all the percussionists on the album [*The Rhythm of the Saints*], then it's just like listening to Elvis sing "That's All Right (Mama)" again.'
Steve Grant; from Time Out, *24 October 1999*

he doesn't find whatever it is he's seeking. Homesick for Ma and Pa, he packs his bags and heads south.

Paul Simon reputedly started writing 'Homeward Bound' while waiting for a train in the unremarkable Cheshire town of Widnes. A succession of plaques commemorating the song's composition have adorned the station's platform: very generously, since the lyric's essentially about the singer's desperation to get away from the place as fast as possible. It's just one of several Simon songs that seem torn between stasis and movement, between familiarity and surprise: perhaps the most famous is 'America', in which the singer takes a bus in search of the American dream but ends up 'empty and aching', homesick in all but name. As Simon sings in 'Train in the Distance', it's all down to the nagging idea that the grass is – or, at least, might be – just a little bit greener on the other side.

There are, reckoned Simon, 50 ways to leave your lover. If you're Jimmie Rodgers ('Train Whistle Blues'), Hank Williams ('I'm a Long-Gone Daddy') or Morrissey's nameless Mancunian evacuee ('London' by the Smiths), you take the train. If you're Roger Miller ('I've Been a Long Time Leavin' (But I'll Be a Long Time Gone)'), you stick out your thumb in the hopes of flagging down a truck. If you're country singer Randy Travis ('No Place Like Home'), you empty the wardrobe but don't quite close the door. And if you've been shacked up with Louis Jordan or Ray Charles, you get your man to do the leaving for you. On 'Someone Done Changed the Lock On My Door', poor Louis is left out in the cold by a girlfriend who's enjoying the company of another man, while Ray's turfed out of his own home and told never to return on 'Hit the Road, Jack'.

Still, at least Jimmie, Roger, Hank and the rest bothered to say goodbye. A number of singers (the vast majority, it should be said, male) simply prefer to steal away in the middle of the night and avoid any confrontation. Glen Campbell's take on Jimmy Webb's 'By the Time I Get to Phoenix' paints the departing partner as a romantic man of mystery, a prisoner of circumstance unable to get through to a woman blind to the folly of her own failings. Those swelling strings don't exactly argue with him, either. But the song is really an amazingly callow kiss-off, the narrator an

Paul Simon and friends, a long way from home back in 1965.

indecisive schmuck who didn't have the balls to say goodbye (or, for that matter, leave a note), and who, midway through the song, even appears to have a little chuckle at the thought that his ex will be calling a phone number that he won't be around to answer. At least when Tom Waits ducks out before the alarm clock rings in 'Ruby's Arms', taking with him only the clothes on his back, he has the decency to express a little remorse.

Of course, it's not always the singer who does the departing: often, they're left behind by a lover who's decided to make their own break for freedom. Ever since the beleagured brakeman's wife began beckoning her errant husband in 'Bill Bailey, Won't You Please Come Home', pop's had a pretty good handle on misery and self-pity: witness Darlene Love's melancholic 'Christmas (Baby Please Come Home)', Al Green's 'Call Me (Come Back Home)' and Bacharach/David's 'A House Is Not a Home', perhaps best heard in Dionne Warwick's 1964 recording.

But, as usual, country music goes the extra mile, and empty homes become big fat symbols

of the singers' now-empty lives. In Willie Nelson's song 'Hello Walls', a deflated Faron Young ends up not just staring at the ceiling but talking to it as he pines desperately for the return of the woman who's left him. In 'Wall to Wall Heartaches', unjustly forgotten Bakersfield country singer Wynn Stewart insists that his room – 'and everything in it' – has been in tears since his woman walked out the door. When a teary-eyed George Jones gives listeners 'The Grand Tour' of his own deserted love shack, he ends up in an uninhabited nursery: Mrs Jones, it seems, has even taken his beloved kid. Caitlin Cary doesn't tug at the heartstrings quite so vigorously, but 'Empty Rooms' makes the same point.

And while another girlfriend leaves another country singer home alone, the cycle continues elsewhere. On they go: from Puerto Rico to Manhattan ('America' from *West Side Story*), from the desert to the ocean (Lyle Lovett's 'If I Had a Boat'), from more or less anywhere to the exciting new horizons of California (Chuck Berry trekking from Virginia by bus, train and plane in 'Promised Land', Eddi Reader dreaming of a new life in a song named for the state, Nat 'King' Cole following the Mother Road in the first recording of Bobby Troup's '(Get Your Kicks on) Route 66'). And, just as

inevitably, back they come: to the home towns they left behind (Elbow's 'Station Approach', at first miserable but ultimately euphoric), to the bars and the clubs they used to favour (Thin Lizzy's 'The Boys Are Back in Town') and, yes, from more or less anywhere back to their good old home in California (Joni Mitchell returning from Europe on track six of *Blue*). Pop would be nothing without this perpetual cycle of arrivals and departures.

But maybe the greatest truth about the nature of making the break is tucked away in the middle of It's Immaterial's 'Driving Away from Home (Jim's Tune)', a noble if inevitably doomed attempt to relocate Kerouac's *On the Road* to north-west England and a novelty hit of sorts in 1986. It's essentially a one-way conversation: a passenger talks to a driver about the possibilities that lie ahead as they pull out of Liverpool, passing suburbs and shops as the road opens and the horizon grows wider. Manchester, it turns out, is only 45 minutes away. Adds John Campbell, almost as an afterthought: 'That's my birthplace, you know.'

And that, in a nutshell, is why songs about leaving home, rather like the act itself, are never quite as straightforward as they might first appear. You can leave home as often as you like, but it never quite leaves you.

South of the border

Chuck Eddy goes down Mexico way... via Nashville.

When Jimmy Buffett released the Parrothead national anthem in 1977, his lyrics didn't place 'Margaritaville' on a map. They did, though, offer a clue about the utopia's location, even if Jimmy hadn't a clue how the clue – his brand-new tattoo of that Mexican cutie – got there. In the decades since, beginning with Brooks & Dunn's 'Mexican Minutes' in 1993 and Tim McGraw's 'Refried Dreams' in 1994, a deluge of modern-day male country singers have taken that tattoo to heart. When they want to flee the fast-paced life above the border (where 'every minute has a heart attack in it', as Brooks & Dunn put it) and waste away a weekend or a season blowing their paychecks on exotic tropical drinks and exotic Latin beauties, they visit Mexico. As Jimmy Buffett postulated in the title of the single that followed his most famous song: 'Changes in Latitudes, Changes in Attitudes'.

But Jimmy Buffett's tattoo didn't invent Mexico. Nor did James Taylor's 1975 'Mexico', which talks about sleepy señoritas with fiery eyes, and how life is so mellow down there that you need a reason to move (the song is even quoted in 'Mexican Minutes'). Nope: in country music, the template goes back all the way at least to Gene Autry in 1939, telling 'Mexicali Rose' to dry her big brown eyes because he'd be back some sunny day, or to Bob Wills & His Texas Playboys in 'New Spanish Two-Step' in 1946, leaving the señorita who held his hand, the one whose 'eyes told me more than words could say', down near the old Rio Grande. You could draw a line from Wills's song all the way

to Gary Allan's easily swinging 2001 country-jazz waltz 'Adobe Walls', as Allan confesses he doesn't understand a word but allows that 'your brown eyes tell me all I need to know'.

Country's fascination with North America's southern frontier has picked up steam at a time when Hispanics are the fastest growing ethnic group in the US – and, not coincidentally, are a demographic to which Nashville's music industry has been slowly reaching out of late. And what makes Music Row's most recent obsession with Mexico even more intriguing is that it's coincided with a renewed nationalist hysteria about immigration: increased border security and vigilante patrols, congressional calls for barricades, conservative radio talk shows. So perhaps it's no surprise that, in country lyrics, Mexico is a place you can't really trust, a nation where innocence gets corrupted.

The narrator of hard-boiled duo Montgomery Gentry's expansive, ominous 2004 'All I Know About Mexico', for instance, loses his girl to a biker 'all hopped up on that marijuana'; she's sunning with him on a blanket in the Mexican sand while the singer's back home trying not to think about scary Tijuana jails. 'There's things down here the devil himself wouldn't do,' Toby Keith tells us atop a clave rhythm in 2004's 'Stays in Mexico', wherein insurance salesman Steve from Sioux Falls and grade school teacher Gina from Phoenix hook up over tequila at Sammy Hagar's Cabo Wabo Cantina. They feel guilty about it, but not guilty enough to keep from repeating their indiscretions before Steve returns to his wife and kids.

The Latin counter-rhythms in 'Stays in Mexico' – and the ones in Toby's 'Good to Go to Mexico' from two years before, in which a less deceitful couple escape the cold November wind but want to avoid establishments overrun with 'gringos and *turistas*' other than themselves – are bolder than in most of Nashville's recent Mexico moves. Whatever you can say about Toby's foreign affairs policy, and you can say plenty, there's nothing timid about the guy. Great singer, too. But even if few of them match Toby's, Mexico songs tend to rank among the liveliest tracks on male country singers' albums, across the board. Invariably, they're sexier and dancier than the Nashville norm. And why not? American musicians of European descent allowing their beats to move with more energy when they're condescending to darker-skinned ethnic groups, and opening up to an erotic physicality they've attached to stereotypes of those cultures, is a phenomenon dating back at least as far as minstrel shows.

At the turn of the '60s, the era of banana-boat calypso and bachelor-pad luaus and girls from Ipanema, American popular music's fetishisation of exotic foreigners hit full force. Pat Boone probably never rocked or rolled like he did in his 1962 novelty hit 'Speedy Gonzales', featuring the peerless voice actor Mel Blanc as a sex addicted, alcoholic Mexican cartoon mouse with more *cucarachas* than enchiladas beneath his leaky adobe. Irreverent Latin acts such as Charo and the Mexican TV clown Cepellin covered the song in the '70s; by 1967, Blanc was offering similarly questionable stereotypes in TV commercials as the Frito Bandito.

Presumably reaching a more collegiate crowd of Anglos, folk revivalists the Kingston Trio made jokes in both Mexican and Japanese accents in their 1958 recording of 'Coplas' and presciently shuffled Gulf geography in a calypso called 'Bay of Mexico' the same year. The liner notes to *Watch Out!* (1966), the highest charting album from ethnic instrumental explorers the Baja Marimba Band (led by a sideman from Herb Alpert's immensely popular Tijuana Brass), raved about their 'lazy Latin sound' and 'horsehair moustaches, fuming cigars, and ill-fitting haberdashery (reminiscent of Wallace Beery as Pancho Villa)'. The current stereotypists of country music tend more toward political correctness, though the Kentucky Headhunters'

rambunctiously *ay-yi-yi*-ing 1991 'Big Mexican Dinner' (which should have been spelled 'Beeeg Mexican Deeenner') was certainly a throwback.

But ethnic stereotypes can come from all directions. In 1965, a Mexican American navy vet from Dallas named Domingo Samudio hit big with 'Wooly Bully', one of rock 'n' roll's woolliest and bulliest moments. Masquerading as Sam the Sham & the Pharaohs, Samudio and his group offered a singular gimmick: counting off the song 'Uno, dos! One, two, tres, cuatro!', Samudio wore a turban, while the Pharaohs dressed as Arabs. 'Juimonos (Let's Went)', a whooping *areeeba*-rock instrumental, featured this enticing bit of border-crossing dialogue: 'You like to travel?' 'Si!' 'Where you like to go?' 'Juimonos, Baja California!'

Crazy stuff; you can bet longtime Texas Mexicanophiles ZZ Top, who've released albums entitled *Rio Grande Mud*, *Tres Hombres*, *Tejas*, *El Loco* and *Mescalero*, were paying attention. On 'Heard It on the X', Billy Gibbons says he learned to play guitar while listening to 'country Jesus hillbilly blues' on Mexican outlaw border radio in 1966. The theme was updated in LA singer-songwriter Warren Zevon's 'Carmelita' ('mariachi static on my radio'), LA rockabilly band the Blasters' 'Border Radio' ('50,000 watts out of Mexico') and LA new wave weirdos Wall of Voodoo's 'Mexican Radio' (*no comprende*, it's a riddle'). Later, the Butthole Surfers took Sam the Sham's and ZZ's insanity a step further into the asylum with 'Mexican Caravan', a seriously stoned garage rocker in which front-nut Gibby Haynes squeals like a javelina in heat about heading down to Miguel to score brown heroin.

That's territory on which Nashville wouldn't dare to tread – though Nashville's weirdest, funniest, most creative '00s act, Big & Rich, just might try some day. 'Jalapeno' opens by echoing Sam the Sham's Spanish count-off from 'Wooly Bully', turns into a shouted, intermittently disco-percussioned boogie about a spicy two-stepping señorita named Maria, then segues into a wacky number – part Tex-Mex polka, part hoedown, part jug-band swing – called '20 Margaritas' about a chef named José who cooks up some mean guacamole and tamales. Modern Nashville has rarely sounded so unhinged.

Still, Big & Rich – and Toby Keith, too – are far from alone in their race to become Nashville's current leading chroniclers of stereotyped Latin culture. Tim McGraw had a go with 'Refried Dreams' and, from 1999, 'Señorita Margarita', the former skirting the issue of Montezuma's revenge, the latter featuring a mariachi break, and both of them quite cleverly punned and catchy. On his 2004 debut album, teen phenom Blaine Larsen offered 'I've Been to Mexico', a good-natured tune with the same moral as Brooks & Dunn's 'Mexican Minutes' – namely, that people in the US need to learn to slow down like their southern neighbours. And in 2006, Larsen's mock-mariachi 'I Don't Know What She Said'

took the gringo-mistranslating-Spanish concept to a ludicrous extreme, as the singer follows a brown-eyed girl down the hall and she tells him '*muy guapo* and something about ho-hos'.

Garth Brooks 'set sail with Captain Morgan' (and made his big calypsofied Buffett move, though he left Mexico out of it) on 1997's 'Two Piña Coladas', but he was faced with a difficult choice on 2001's rowdy 'Rodeo or Mexico', eventually letting yet another pair of dark brown eyes help his decision along (at least until her knife-wielding husband walks in). Best joke: 'Does anybody know the Spanish word for wife?'

BORN TO RUN

When the red, white and blue meets the green, white and red: **Toby Keith**.

Rewind
ZZ Top

Though ZZ Top are now based in Houston, guitarist Billy Gibbons is the sole member to hail from the now recession-hit, oil-refining town close to the Gulf of Mexico. Gibbons' father was a prominent pianist and part-time conductor with the Houston Philharmonic, which explains Gibbons's passionate interest in Schoenberg and Stockhausen. But it was Stella Matthews, the family maid, who introduced him to the blues: to Little Richard, Larry Williams, Jimmy Reed, T-Bone Walker et al. As she did so, the local radio stations in the music-mad state and beyond zipped out mariachi from Mexico, country and western, jazz, soul, rock 'n' roll, and hard blues through the dial and through the night.

'Blues was the quickest way into the three-chord trick,' explains Gibbons. 'It was the easiest thing to get into: they played it a lot on the radio, and you could *get* a lot of it. And I guess it was actually when the Stones started making it available, popularising the blues for the next generation. That helped us.'

Dusty Hill, the bass player, and Frank Beard, the beardless drummer, were both poor boys from Dallas, where the musicians are reputedly much tougher than in Houston. Beard

sat in with Freddie King, who had a habit of kicking errant drummers offstage.

'Boy, he would whup your ass, old Freddie,' recalls Hill, who, much to the annoyance of his mother, was playing black clubs while still a high-school teenager. 'He was an imposing man. If he said, "Don't do that," you didn't. Jimmy Reed never said anything about the music; he just assumed you could play it. He was more interested in finding where we'd hidden his booze.

And Lightnin' Hopkins would never play the same song the same way twice...'

'I recall,' says Gibbons, 'that just before we formed as a trio, Dusty was working at the Old Quarter in Houston. I came down and Lightnin' was talking to him about one of the numbers. Dusty said, "Lightnin', weren't you supposed to go to the second change there?" And Lightnin' said, "Listen: Lightnin' change when Lightnin' wanna change..."'
Steve Grant; from Time Out, *15 October 1986*

In the age of Martina McBride and Sara Evans and Faith Hill and Carrie Underwood and the Dixie Chicks (all of whom, by the way, have recorded excellent songs about hitting the highway in search of a more exciting life), it's worth noting that Nashville seems to present its Mexico myths as an exclusively male fantasy. Unless you count the three albums of traditional Mexican and Spanish songs that Linda Ronstadt recorded between 1987 and 1992, you'd have to bend the perimeters beyond their breaking point – maybe to Nicolette Larsen's bittersweet country-rock version of the Drifters' 'Mexican Divorce', or urban-sophisticate country chart alumnus KT Oslin's doubly horny girls-night-out ditty 'Mexico Road' (which probably isn't about the nation at all), or New Orleans teen fiddle prodigy Amanda Shaw's sweet 'Chirmolito', an ode to the Chicano construction workers who rebuilt her home post-Katrina – to find a song by a woman that ventures anywhere near Garth and Toby and Tim's travel brochures.

But maybe that's got something to do with how women fit into the myth – which, again, is a very old story. If you don't mind stretching a bit in terms of both geography and genre, and meanwhile maybe speculating why so many country songs about visiting Mexico sound more faux-calypso than faux-*norteño*, you could do worse than revisit 'Rum and Coca-Cola', in which the Andrews Sisters got all triumphant about colonialism (after all, it was 1944 and they were winning the war) while discoursing on two generations of Trinidadian women 'working for the Yankee dollar'. If the Andrews Sisters never explicitly spelled out what that 'working' may have entailed, they at least acknowledged that an economic transaction was taking place.

Perhaps the tasks were related to the mysterious dance that rock 'n' roll jokesters the Coasters watched a fishnetted castanet player perform in 'Down in Mexico' a dozen years later in a hep jazz bar. In 1975, in ZZ Top's comparably comical and typically rampaging 'Mexican Blackbird', Billy Gibbons advised in a mock hillbilly accent that when one drives one's Chrysler below the border, one's money is best spent on a certain cantina employee known profanely as 'Puta', since 'dancin' and lovin' is her trade'. Another decade down the line, a long-haired señorita made

'Immigrants from Germany and what became Czechoslovakia brought their accordions to Texas; their waltzes and schottisches soon cross-bred with Mexico's boleros and *rancheras*.'

her intentions perfectly clear when she led neo-trad country drawler John Anderson by the hand up a tavern's stairs in his flamenco-embellished 'Old Mexico'. John's initially impressed by the exchange rate, but the next thing he knows, his money's all gone.

Those jezebels can be treacherous, see. In Merle Haggard's 'The Seashores of Old Mexico', revived into a country hit for George Strait in 2005, a young cowpoke runs from the law in Tucson, and eventually gets a lift from farm workers after losing his bankroll in Juarez when 'one bad señorita makes use of one innocent lad'. Years before, in their 1964 US hit 'Come a Little Bit Closer', New York pop band Jay & the Americans put Latin rhythms swiped from the Drifters and Richie Valens beneath a border-café temptress who makes Jay's mouth water with her beckoning eyes. But then, you guessed it, her boyfriend José shows up, and the guitar player tells Jay to vamoose.

Events of a similar nature no doubt happened in too many old western movies to name. But I'll make room for Marty Robbins' kindred 1959 US chart-topper 'El Paso', a western in four minutes. As its title suggests, it doesn't take place in Mexico per se, but it does involve the obligatory date at Rose's Cantina with a Mexican siren who casts evil spells with eyes blacker than night until a cowhand with no manners cuts in on the dancefloor. At which point Marty steals a horse and hightails it to the badlands of New Mexico, where he's eventually shot dead.

'El Paso' came from an album called *Gunfighter Ballads and Trail Songs*, which probably wasn't so outlandish a title back when country was more western and less exurban than it is now. Or even back in 1983, when Willie Nelson and Merle Haggard topped the country chart with their own western mini-movie 'Pancho and Lefty', about a gunslinger who grows old and cold in a cheap Ohio hotel after murdering a bandit in the Mexican desert and the Federales let him slip away. But give or take Strait's cover of Haggard's vintage seashore ode, most of country's recent Mexican sojourns revolve around being an affluent gentleman of leisure, not a desperate fugitive from justice. Surprising, given the debt that recent country owes to old-school corporate rock, and given that '70s and '80s rock radio had its own outlaws running for the border on ubiquitous hits such as Eddie Money's 'Gimme Some Water' and Christopher Cross's 'Ride Like the Wind'.

Hip hop has thrived on similar felonious themes for years as well, of course, but even hard rock (Sammy Hagar's drunken toga party 'Mas Tequila') squeezes its lemons in Cabo San Lucas these days. Recording for a microscopic indie label in 2005, veteran hard country journeyman Billy Don Burns rip-roared through a song called 'Running Drugs Out of Mexico' (one notable line had AK-47s filling bastards full of holes), but Music Row seems terrified of such stuff. We're a long way from 'Wanted Man', Johnny Cash's geographical catalogue of all the towns (and women) trailing him. On his *At San Quentin* album, which spent four weeks atop the US charts in 1969, the line that draws by far the loudest applause from prisoners is the one in which Johnny gets sidetracked while map-shopping in El Paso then goes 'the wrong way in Juarez with Juanita on my lap'.

Back in 'El Paso', the way Marty Robbins' voice keens up on the high notes – sounding 'wild as the West Texas wind', like his cowboy nemesis in the song – owes something to the fancy, super-emotional filigrees of boleros. It's a technique that's weaved in and out of country music over the years; Roy Orbison was famous for it. But the country crooner who really made Latin music's rococo vocal embellishments work was Mexican American. Raised in a family of migrant farm laborers, the man born Baldemar Huerta in Texas picked up his stage moniker Freddie Fender in the late '50s, he says in the liner notes to his album *Before the*

Next Teardrop Falls, as a way to sell his music to gringos, 'but now I like the name'. And the title of his ornately quivering hit 'Wasted Days and Wasted Nights' (first recorded as a rockabilly track) sums up the theme of the '90s-to-'00s country-goes-to-Mexico wave as perfectly as 'Margaritaville' does. Wasting days and wasting nights is the expressed mission of songs such as 'Beer in Mexico' by Kenny Chesney, who's been known to jam in Cabo with Hagar, and who's such a latter-day Parrothead that he called his summer 2007 concert trek the 'Flip-Flop Tour' (presumably in homage to Jimmy Buffett rather than John Kerry).

Freddie Fender isn't the only Mexican-American ever to hit country radio. In 1973, Johnny Rodriguez hitch-hiked to the top of the US country chart with 'Ridin' My Thumb to Mexico'; he had plenty of other, less memorable hits along the way, and even once did jail time for stealing a goat. Conjunto legend Flaco Jiminez has lent his accordion to lovely border

polkas by clear-singing country hipsters the Mavericks and Dwight Yoakam; in the mid '90s, Tejano singers Rick Trevino and Emilio made successful crossover moves; and more recently, blues-based bar-band brother-trio and Willie Nelson cronies Los Lonely Boys climbed to number 46 on the country charts with 'Heaven'.

But when it comes to country interacting with the styles now lumped together as 'regional Mexican' (which, after all, is a music where bands dress up like cowboys, and often sing about them), that's only the tip of the iceberg. In the 19th century, immigrants from Germany and what eventually became Czechoslovakia brought their accordions to Texas; within decades, their waltzes and schottisches were cross-breeding with Mexico's boleros and *rancheras*. As recently as 1985, you could find a tuba oompah combo of central European descent, such as Leroy Rybak's Swinging Orchestra in Halletsville, Texas, covering the Mexican traditional 'El Rancho Grande'.

Even so, there's more than one way to cross over. In 1982, Freddy Fender recorded a number called 'Across the Borderline', written by Jim Dickinson, John Hiatt and Ry Cooder for the Jack Nicholson movie *The Border*. The lyrics talked about believing the streets on the other side are paved with gold, but once you get there your dreams are shattered. Domingo Samudio, the former Sam the Sham, also contributed to the soundtrack. In 1985, comedy duo Cheech & Chong reached number 48 on the US pop charts with 'Born in East LA', a Bruce Springsteen parody about a US-born Chicano carted off to Tijuana by a redneck immigration agent. And in 2007, cowboy-hatted Houston Chicano comedy rapper Chingo Bling, who sometimes spoofs hillbilly music in songs such as 'Pop Tailgate... Wooooooooooooo!!!', charted with an album called *They Can't Deport Us All*.

Toby Keith, for his part, has toured the US with Ted Nugent, a vocal advocate of stepped-up border security who's been known to spout

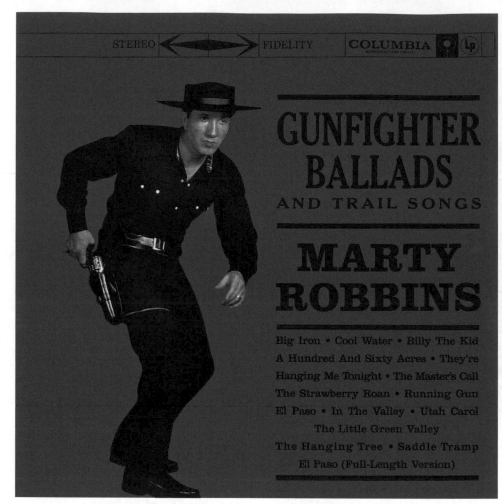

STEREO FIDELITY COLUMBIA

GUNFIGHTER BALLADS
AND TRAIL SONGS

MARTY ROBBINS

Big Iron • Cool Water • Billy The Kid
A Hundred And Sixty Acres • They're
Hanging Me Tonight • The Master's Call
The Strawberry Roan • Running Gun
El Paso • In The Valley • Utah Carol
The Little Green Valley
The Hanging Tree • Saddle Tramp
El Paso (Full-Length Version)

'If you can't speak English, get the fuck out of America' from the stage. And in the comments section beneath Keith's 'Stays in Mexico' video on youtube.com, an internet ignoramus calling himself troak12 babbles, 'To bad Mexicans don't stay in Mexico. Instead they come to America cause they are to fucking lazy to fight for freedom in there own country.'

Country songs themselves, however, wilfully circumvent the controversy, though at least one – Chris Young's 'I'm Headed Your Way, Jose', in which the rookie singer good-naturedly decides to trade places with a Mexican immigrant, slapping him five at the border and telling him he better pack a poncho because northern weather's so bad 'you'll freeze your ass off' – takes current events into account. And then there's Texas songster Robert Earl Keen's eggnog-spiked 'Merry Christmas from the Family', covered by Montgomery Gentry in 2000, in which little sister brings home a new Mexican boyfriend and the relatives get suspicious until he sings 'Feliz Navidad'. Country music is frequently years behind the curve when it comes to commenting on front-page news, but don't be shocked if, at some point, lyrics about immigration become commonplace. For now, though, Nashville's stars are still mostly content to lounge lazily with their margaritas in a mysterious land they envision as one big siesta, searching for that lost shaker of salt.

For Your Pleasure

Desk
jobs

Marcello Carlin praises the musical alchemists behind 30 years of British pop.

It is one of the most remarkable incidences of the passing of the flame from a dying candle to a new one in British pop music. As Ian Curtis extinguished his own life in the spring of 1980, he unknowingly gave birth to the thing that would eventually become known, and periodically resuscitate itself, as new pop. That is to say, a design for pop music was proposed that would be capable of entering both minds and charts but with its philosophies and ideals still soundly embedded in the punk and post-punk that had preceded it. That post-punk couldn't continue as it had been, even if Curtis had opted to sort his mess of a life out and live, was evident: it was already chafing against its inbuilt limitations, and many of its most articulate proponents were getting weary. Curtis's suicide seemed to insert an unanswerable developmental full stop.

Initially hailed and christened by the music press, new pop facilitated what, for many, remains the most creative and exciting era in pop music, all the more valuable for being so visible on the screen, on the radio and in the charts. Just take a look at the UK's top 40 singles lists in the 12-month period from July 1981 to June 1982 and try suggesting that we ever had it better. The hitherto unimaginable likes of Laurie Anderson, Pigbag and the Associates managed to score major hits, while relative long-servers such as Adam & the Ants, Japan and Simple Minds seemed able to find their true voices. In what other era could an eight-minute piece of minimalist performance art (Anderson's 'O Superman') have been kept off number one by a distended, demented reshaping of a 1960s song by an avant-garde jazz/rock keyboardist (Dave Stewart and Barbara Gaskin's 'It's My Party')?

But the same music press rapidly turned against new pop. Suddenly, it was not Authentic; it lacked Soul, Passion and Honesty (note those branding capital letters); it converted Noble Black into Exploiting White. Principal among the critics' complaints was the apparent return of the producer as dominant figure: the familiar post-Spector gargoyle of the tyrannical face of authority, squashing honest post-punk youths with his jackboot of Fairlight sampling technology.

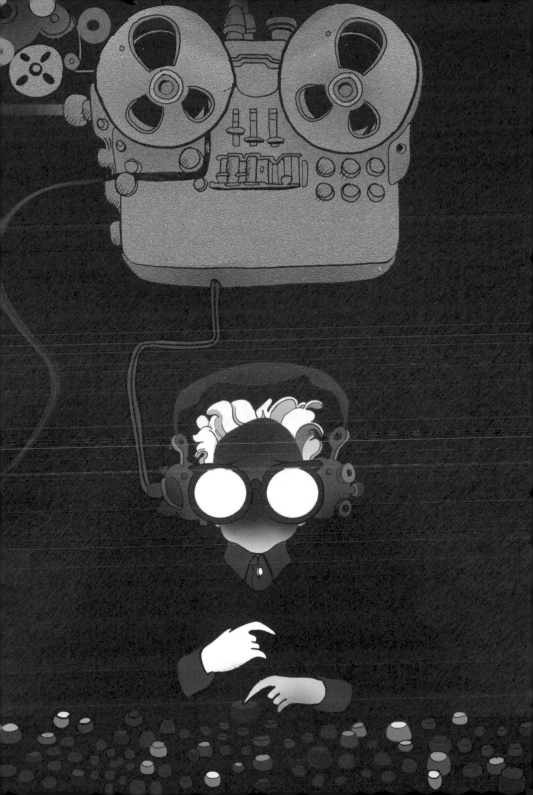

Two years after this photo was taken, **ABC**'s Martin Fry flushed that suit down the toilet.

If the subsequent and constant regeneration of new pop has taught us anything, it's that the best artist-producer relationships are necessarily symbiotic. Thus, it's entirely accurate for Girls Aloud to point out that Brian Higgins and his Xenomania team do not dictate terms and conditions to them; rather, Higgins et al write and tailor their songs and productions with specific focus on the Girls' own personalities. This is why their records – as disparate as the up-yours-dad smirk of 'No Good Advice' and the sublimely, subtly radical 'Biology', which spends two and a half minutes demolishing real rock and girl group

clichés before letting us know how the chorus goes and in doing so turning itself into a manifesto – work so well: because you cannot imagine anyone else singing them. And, by the same token, this is why Girls Aloud fail so spectacularly when attempting to cover songs written by and for others.

Likewise, this is why the producer Trevor Horn found his best soulmate in ABC's Martin Fry. Horn was the part-time member of Yes whose underlying ambition was to make all pop sound like side four of *Tales from Topographic Oceans* (see, for instance, his production work on 'Give Me Back My Heart', in which scampi-and-chips cabaret duo Dollar are made to sound like deities); Fry, meanwhile, was an Eng Lit graduate from Sheffield, knowing his Barthes and Derrida if not as convinced by them as he was by Lydon or Smokey. They found each other and realised, as Horn said, that they were using the disco beat in the same way that Dylan used his acoustic guitar: as a means to a wider and less expected end.

The toweringly ambiguous architecture of ABC's 'Poison Arrow', a single so immaculately constructed and emotionally raw that even Noel Edmonds was moved to a step-by-step analysis of how and why the record worked, confirmed the brilliance and aptness of Fry and Horn's union. And the shattering 'All of My Heart' – when Fry, too late, finally realises that all he needs is love rather than just the look of it, and as he turns into his shoulder to sob quietly, Anne Dudley's elegy of strings seems to embrace him like a hug from God as the camera pans out to reveal a ruined city – kisses the fabric of greatness. This was not a quality Horn was able to derive from avant-garde performance artist Philip Jap, nor Xenomania from all-girl quartet Frank. The importance of the artist is paramount.

Then again, how far is the artist prepared to go to meet the ambitions of the producer? Horn is a particularly interesting case: according to the needs of the specific project, he was willing to submit his inherent extravagance towards the services of a greater good, as happened with Malcolm McLaren on *Duck Rock*, but he was equally capable of imposing his vision without any questions being asked in the belief that his magnification of the artist's qualities is in itself the greater good, as was unquestionably the case with Frankie Goes to Hollywood. Even the most cursory listen to the Radio One session versions of their future hits that Frankie cranked out during 1982 and 1983 confirms that had it not been for Horn's vision – and Paul Morley's anti-marketing – they would have died the same early, ignominious passing that befell dozens of Liverpool indie bands of the period.

In its original form, 'Two Tribes' was simply another in an elongating line of scrawny, ho-hum punk-funk rave-ups about nuclear war. A year or so later, Peter Powell on Radio One gave the first play to the original 12-inch mix of the Horn/ZTT 'Two Tribes' on his Thursday teatime show and the results were sonically terrifying. What Horn did here was merely a more expansive and better funded variant on what the likes of Joe Meek, Shadow Morton and George Martin had been doing a generation before: grasping the central point of the artist and magnifying it to such an extent that they defy ignoring. Nine weeks at number one in a pop world otherwise comprised of such un-pop faces as Nik Kershaw, Lionel Richie and Howard Jones, at one stage reputedly outselling the rest of the top 40 put together: the work was done, inescapable and magical.

By contrast, McLaren was very much in charge of the *Duck Rock* project. Sensing that Horn was getting a little too comfortable and looking for adventure, he persuaded him out of producing the new Spandau Ballet album (not that he needed much persuading; Gary Kemp was quoted at the time as finding Horn's 'schoolmaster' style difficult to handle). Thus Horn expertly mucked up his own perfection, and helped McLaren rein in this scratching he'd been told about. And at the death of 1982, when new pop seemed all but dead, 'Buffalo Gals' suddenly offered an escape route, unquestionably streetwise but manipulated under Sarm Studios' anaesthetic. Horn's team of musicians and engineers went on to construct their own abstract remixes of voices and samples left over from the *Duck Rock* sessions initially for their own amusement, but it eventually coagulated into what became Art of Noise (without the subsequent, Horn-less definite article) and pop time began again.

Horn, of course, was not the only producer intent on making his acts breathe differently. It is unlikely that the Human League of *Dare*, routinely hailed at the time as the most audacious reinvention in pop since Marc Bolan plugged in his amplifier, would have worked so marvellously without Martin Rushent's oddly retro-nuevo production. Key tracks such as 'The Things That Dreams Are Made Of' and 'Don't You Want Me' show Rushent's combination of spotless synthesizer and rhythm programming and those trademark Linn drums, ricocheting from channel to channel just like Ringo or Keith used to do. Rushent was also easily able to grasp the teasing spirit inherent in Altered Images' Clare Grogan: his 12-inch mix of 'I Could Be Happy' is something of a tantric masterpiece, continually delaying her entry by every deceptive means imaginable.

FOR YOUR PLEASURE

Once new pop had fallen out of critical favour and 'reality' had been restored, Ian Curtis's passing was repeatedly referenced as a symbol of the times when things were 'pure'. And in the quarter-century or so in which new pop has risen, fallen and flourished again, every presumed antidote to producer-dominated inauthenticity has been offered, from Big Country to Einstürzende Neubauten, from Wiley to Animal Collective. The fundamental problem with this line of knowingly disingenuous argument is that Joy Division themselves were a group who took on a substantially different guise in live performance than they did on record, and moreover complained bitterly about the edge of their music being lost in the prog dreams of their producer Martin Hannett, yet their two studio albums and three studio singles are the presumed palaces of artifice that have cemented their worshipful reputation.

The argument was in any case detonated by New Order themselves. Though they had been developing and paring their approach for some time before 'Blue Monday', this remains a single that really does stand at one of the most important crossroads of pop, the aching of grief still redolent and palpable three springs later but with a percussive propulsion and new sense of determination that turns their tragedy into the building blocks of the future. Its slow-building but cumulatively phenomenal impact would not have been so considerable had it not been for the expert understanding of beat placement (and displacement) demonstrated by the American producer/mixer John Robie, a partner in innovation of the American hip hop desk-jockey Arthur Baker. Indeed, some accounts have suggested the direct involvement of Baker himself in the creation of 'Blue Monday'.

The record hit especially hard on the hi-NRG circuit and was undoubtedly noticed by the emergent production team of novices Mike Stock and Matt Aitken and the veteran Pete Waterman, since they deployed and reshaped some of New Order's drum programming tricks on many of their early productions. It has been said, lazily, that the near-total dominance of the SAW team in the charts of the mid to late 1980s was an indictment of the poverty of pop at that period; and yet this was the time of house, acieed and nascent techno. As all astute pop operatives do, SAW noted the trends of the day and incorporated them to a greater or lesser extent in their own productions, which were essentially based on a combination of hi-NRG and bubblegum tropes. If they had few competitors, the Pet Shop Boys, the Smiths and New Order themselves being the most prominent, they can hardly be blamed for capitalising on circumstance.

Their real breakthrough came with 'You Spin Me Round (Like a Record)' by bored Liverpool indie band Dead or Alive. Pretty much 'Blue Monday' sung by Tom Jones in RuPaul's cast-offs, the record was tinnily insistent and eventually irresistible, slowly rising to the top of an early 1985 singles chart mostly devoid of anything resembling life. Then came SAW's flood of hits with Princess, Bananarama and others, though Mel and Kim's 'Showing Out (Get Fresh at the Weekend)' from 1986 may be their most extreme production: SAW noticeably pushed some extra buttons whenever the Appleby sisters were involved, and 'Showing Out' became the first credible major mainstream pop hit to take house music into account.

SAW also exploited their own perceived artificiality to their own benefit. 'Roadblock' was a masked rebuke to those intent on Keeping Things Real: it was available as a 12-inch white label for months and widely believed to be an obscure rare groove track from the early '70s, but the purists were obliged to swallow their own mouths when the truth emerged. Then the soap stars came, and if Kylie's work with SAW has proved the most enduring of their mainstream adventures, then again this is down to Kylie herself. Rick Astley could never have captured the same innocence in the face of overwhelming cynicism, the Melbourne sunshine hastily recreated in a Bermondsey basement, as Kylie did on 'I Should Be So Lucky'; and Jason Donovan was wise to retreat to Rocky Horror Dreamcoat territory, as the gleeful stutters of 'What Do I Have to Do?' would have been beyond his well-meaning self.

As dance, Madchester and Britpop took consecutive hold, there appeared to be less need for the role of the producer as an active creative force, or at least not in the same huge neon type: Stephen Street, Owen Morris and Steve Jervier were respectively indispensable to Blur, Oasis and Take That throughout the early to mid

1990s, but were not especially lauded or even noticed for doing so. Only with the second wave of new pop, which in British terms began with the onset of the Spice Girls, did the concept of pop producer as avatar return to visibility. 'Wannabe' will forever be considered a Spice Girls record first, a Stannard and Rowe record second. But its kick-starting importance cannot be overemphasised.

The most immediate beneficiaries of Girl Power were All Saints, who in a different form had even briefly been on the books of Trevor Horn's ZTT earlier in the 1990s. In their run of hits, which have arguably proved more durable than the Spices' (because they were ostensibly less overexposed), we get the first major evidence of influence stemming from the Bristol sound. Neneh Cherry's 1989 top five hit 'Manchild', one of the most elegantly feisty of all girl pop hits, gave early exposure to what would become Massive Attack (with her husband Cameron McVey acting as crucial middleman), and that influence in turn slowly trickled through the pores of pop as the 1990s wound down.

McVey was involved in All Saints' 'Never Ever', the nonchalance of the Shangri-Las brilliantly tranposed to dusk-dotted W11: the shrugged shoulders, the combat trousers, the final derailment into broken beats. Their Nellee Hooper-produced re-reading of 'Under the Bridge' is more a reflection on the original Red Hot Chili Peppers song than a cover of it: loneliness dissolving into a dazzlingly blinding urban twinkle of tin stars, rolls of vibraharp to prevent the singer from drowning. And when they eventually encountered William Orbit, most devastatingly on 2000's 'Black Coffee' – a record that reflects an uneasy seashore peace with the vague threat of abrupt termination in the air (it might be the last piece of music the couple hear on the beach in Jim Crace's *Being Dead*) – they display their ability to get the creative best out of any producer and better themselves in the process.

McVey was also the midhusband to the Sugababes, a trio that may yet prove to be Britain's Menudo: a group capable of consistent existence even as their personnel regularly changes (are they pop's Soft Machine, and is

Aitken, Waterman and Stock, photographed before they learned to sit in the right order.

On the record
Trevor Horn

'That's me playing the bass there,' says Trevor Horn, with a grin. The record producer is sitting at the console of his lavish Notting Hill studio, isolating individual instruments on a master tape. A distorted rockabilly guitar blares out. 'That's me, too.'

He isolates the drums to reveal a hypnotic hip hop loop. It sounds like something from a different song, as do the spooky synth sounds. He clicks some more buttons and everything plays at once: 'All the Things She Said' by Tatu. It sounds nothing like its constituent parts, but every fragment slots perfectly into place. 'It's like a geometric puzzle.'

Horn has been performing this kind of musical alchemy for 25 years. Indeed, many still associate his name with those bombastic orchestrations that were as much a part of the 1980s as shoulder pads, bad hair and monetarism. But that's to ignore the complexity of Horn's studio perfection: the painstakingly assembled layers of sound, the dizzying sonic futurism, the razor-sharp beats, the stunning use of space. 'Most producers think in terms of obstacles,' says Martin Fry of ABC. 'Trevor thinks in terms of possibilities.'

In person, he's endearingly fidgety. A vestigial Geordie accent is softened by a transatlantic rock-biz drawl. Disappointingly, his smart-casual threads are topped with steel-rimmed specs, not the giant plastic ones that became his trademark after Buggles reached number one in 1979 with 'Video Killed the Radio Star'. Heard on Horn's original 24-track master without its synths, it sounds a bit like Steely Dan.

'It does a bit,' he agrees. 'We were all massive Steely Dan fans. Big musos.'

It's easy to forget Horn's muso side. Like his father, Trevor paid his dues as a session bassist. By the age of 21, he was backing everyone from Gene Pitney to Tommy Cooper at a Leicester nightclub. In the mid '70s, he joined the 12-piece house band at the Hammersmith Palais.

'We played four times a week; everything from foxtrots to *Saturday Night Fever*. It was my apprenticeship: it taught me the dynamics of the dancefloor, and I soon learned how hit songs needed simple, catchy basslines.'

His rise as a producer coincided with the development of the studio as an instrument. 'In the '80s, the studio was changing every

week. Some new gizmo would come out and alter how we did everything.' Having always embraced new recording technology, Horn is puzzled by lo-fi, back-to-basics studios such as Toerag in Hackney, where the cache of vintage analogue equipment has attracted groups as renowned as the White Stripes.

'I love the idea of Toerag, but there were so many crap things about that system. Things broke down; desks were noisy; it took ages to set up. I don't want to go back there. I never want the process to get in the way of the song. The great thing about this,' he says, dismissively sweeping his hand across his studio set-up, 'is that you can forget about it a lot of the time. You can just press "record", just as Bob Johnson used to do with Dylan.'

Horn maintains the anti-rockist vibe that defined ZTT, his avant-pop label that, during the '80s, was home to Frankie Goes to Hollywood, Propaganda and the producer's own Art of Noise. 'Rock, harmonically, has a tendency to become a bit of a cliché, one that's set in aspic. But there's still something about the energy of a live band that I love. I still go to a lot of gigs. I look at them playing and think: Wow.'

You like them?

'No, I think: Wow, why did you play it like *that*? I could do it better...'

John Lewis; from Time Out, *3 November 2004*

Keisha Buchanan the Girl Power equivalent of Mike Ratledge?). As with most new pop mark II acts, they work with a rotating cast of producers. On the downside, this leads to the annoying tendency of Sugababes albums to be, by turns, brilliantly adventurous and blandly sterile, but on the upside, it leads to the avant-garde being catapulted directly back into the number one slot. Take Richard X, aka Girls on Top, whose proto-bootleg cut-ups were previously the exclusive province of the centre pages of *The Wire* and limited-edition seven-inches in the Rough Trade shop.

The Sugababes picked up on X's Gary Numan/Adina Howard mash-up entitled 'We Don't Give a Damn About Our Friends' (or someone picked it up for them), retooled it and renamed it 'Freak Like Me', a glittering, era-defining pop masterpiece. Shortly thereafter, the Sugababes again hit number one, this time with the aid of Xenomania. 'Round, Round' remains a thrilling thing, all rattling Bananarama feedback and Velvets guitar drone undertow with a slow 3/4 middle eight that appears to arrive from and disappear into nowhere. Brian Higgins and his Kentish town of helpers understand the architecture necessary for great pop, even if the building is improvised on the spot.

An engineering presence on Saint Etienne records of the mid 1990s, Higgins seems to have taken that group's understanding of the fallibility, artifice and transcendence inherent in pop and tried to make it apply in the larger world. He got his chance when he became involved in writing and producing Cher's 1998 global smash 'Believe', which popularised the Auto-Tune device and justified its existence as a creative tool rather than a lazy prop-up for dull singers. His share of the profits from that record's estimated 20 million sales financed the building of the Xenomania empire, though it's increasingly noticeable that Girls Aloud have become the main focus of their operation: Xenomania don't seem quite able to facilitate the same degree of symbiosis with other artists.

Both manifestations of new pop have also enabled veterans of a different stripe to re-enter the orchards of creativity. Just as Trevor Horn was once the bass player for Tina Charles, so Cathy Dennis was remembered, if at all, for a brief, strained career as a singer and sometime songwriter, a sort of Norfolk Debbie

'Was Kylie always a grinning but blank template? Or was she a woman trying to prosper without being forced into wardrobes built for her by men of differing stripes?'

Gibson, and Rob Davis was the semi-strange guitarist out of Mud with earrings, perm and dresses who still looked anything but androgynous. And yet they gradually – and virtually invisibly – worked their way back towards the core of pop, becoming more integral and central to it. Davis's 'I Said Never Again (But Here We Are)', written for and performed by Rachel Stevens, was derided in some quarters as bogus Antmusic, but close perusal of Mud's initial run of hits reveals that Davis was simply closing a circle of influence, subtly reminding everyone of one of the sources from which Adam got it in the first place.

Stevens, however, showed little discernible interest in being a pop star. Clearly, Dennis and Davis required monuments with which to produce their best work, and so it was that Dennis furnished Britney Spears with one of her best singles. 'Toxic' is a record so futuristic that it still sounds like the ninth biggest-selling single on Jupiter in 2147, all angular swoops and static cut-offs, and yet is also a record you could with some effort picture a Joe Meek-produced Petula Clark singing in 1967. (Significantly, Tony Hatch, Clark's most important producer, was very complimentary about 'Toxic'.) Past meets future to give pop a present. And when Dennis and Davis collided and then colluded, they came up with the pop record that serves, in its smilingly guilty way, both to ask and to answer all others.

Was Kylie always a grinning but blank template? Or was she just a woman trying to get along and prosper, or return to prosperity, without being forced to fit into wardrobes manufactured for her by men of differing stripes? According to Waterman, she was a model pro, or a model of a pro – straight into the studio, guide vocal quickly followed by final vocal, job done in half an hour – but with a slightly impatient aura, as though she was already aware that SAW were providing her access only to the third or fourth step of the ladder and she remained keen to climb higher. Still, her records are identifiably hers, regardless of what Nick Cave or the Manic Street Preachers or Towa Tei or the Pet Shop Boys wanted to do with (or to) her.

So with Kylie, we have the phenomenon of the pop star whose point largely needs to be justified by her writers or producers, but who is fleet enough to jump from ship to productive ship as and when required. That's a less common occurrence than you might think (does anyone think of Elvis's records, for example, as 'produced'?): in popular music, perhaps only Sinatra has managed the same trick with approximately the same amount of astuteness. And like Sinatra, Kylie has mastered the trick of breathing the sweetest of nothings into our ears, offering the illusion of closeness but giving away nothing of herself with a clever, adamant wink. At the centre point of her greatest hit, she sings that there's a secret about her. You're never going to know it, but isn't guessing half the fun?

Apart from Dennis's carefully shadowing backing vocal, nothing gives 'Can't Get You Out of My Head' away as a Dennis/Davis production. The touches are individual, but the overall intention is to facilitate the Kylie record of all Kylie records. And it's in the guessing – the contrast between the sprightly trot of the rhythm and the floating insecurity of the half-tempo backing vocals and winsome synthesizers that do indeed recall similarly titled songs by Mike Westbrook and ELO – that the esteemed critic Paul Morley can consider the record worthy of the greater part of a quarter of a million words, that it can bring the hitherto see-sawing career of Kylie into the antechamber of immortality, and that, in bootleg terms, it could even be fused at the BRIT Awards with 'Blue Monday'. It seems Ian Curtis's candle can never truly be snuffed out.

The producer's art in 20 songs

'Ain't No Other Man' Christina Aguilera produced by DJ Premier

In which the legendary Gang Starr producer lumbers out of retirement to create a thumping pop gem by slicing up an old 1969 Latin-funk track by the Mighty Show-Stoppers.

'A Day in the Life' The Beatles produced by George Martin

His early Beatles productions, such as 'Please Please Me' and 'She Loves You', still sound clean, ageless and shockingly raw, but Martin's best remembered for the ambitious, symphonic scope of the signature track from *Sgt Pepper's*, on which he welded together two distinct songs by Lennon and McCartney using freak-out orchestrations, overdubs and tape-echo.

'Ashes to Ashes' David Bowie produced by Tony Visconti

Visconti's production essentially invented the 1980s: lush synths, slap bass and bleeps of electronic percussion, marshalled brilliantly with Bowie's mumbling backing vocals to produce three and a half minutes of pop perfection.

'Just Out of Reach (Of My Two Open Arms)' Solomon Burke produced by Jerry Wexler

'We didn't know shit about making records,' said Wexler about his early days at Atlantic Records in the 1950s, 'but we were having fun.' He'd figured out what he was doing by the time he hooked a 21-year-old soul singer with an old country tune, setting the stage for the rise of Atlantic in the '60s.

'Crazy' Patsy Cline produced by Owen Bradley

Bradley was as responsible as anyone for taking country music out of the honky-tonks and towards the mainstream during the '50s and '60s, and there's no better example of his cultured sound than this.

'Fisherman' The Congos produced by Lee 'Scratch' Perry

The opening track from the seminal 1977 album *Heart of the Congos* finds Perry in masterful form, sculpting a delicately bouncy dub symphony from this Rastafarian vocal group, backed by a veritable supergroup of Jamaica's finest session men.

'Shhh/Peaceful' Miles Davis produced by Teo Macero

Macero's work behind the desk for Davis would grow more adventurous in the 1970s, especially on the cut-and-paste experimentalism of 1972's *On the*

Kylie Minogue reinvents New Order at the BRIT Awards in 2002.

Corner. But his most effective collaboration with the trumpeter may be the mesmeric 18-minute track that constitutes side one of 1969's *In a Silent Way*.

'99 Problems' Danger Mouse
produced by Danger Mouse

The man behind Gnarls Barkley and the second Gorillaz album made his name with his seditious *Grey Album*, a mash-up of Jay-Z's *Black Album* with the Beatles' *White Album*. This thrilling hybrid of 'Helter Skelter' and '99 Problems' is a highlight.

'Nuthin' But a "G" Thang' Dr Dre
produced by Dr Dre

Dre's first solo album after leaving NWA was more than just a revelation of his own skills. The lazy, '70s-influenced G-funk of *The Chronic* set the tone for the next half-decade, and started a production career that's taken in for the likes of Eminem and Jay-Z.

'Requiem pour un con' Serge Gainsbourg
produced by Serge Gainsbourg

One of Gainsbourg's most hypnotic productions is based on a skittery drum beat, a minimal congo pattern, a one-note bass line and a scratchy guitar riff. Cut in 1968, it predated trip hop by nearly 30 years.

'Wanna Be Startin' Somethin''
Michael Jackson
produced by Quincy Jones

Jones started out scoring for big bands, but he's best known for his work on the album that's sold more copies than any other. All bubbling rhythms, juddering guitars and silly lyrics, 'Wanna Be Startin' Somethin'' simply fizzes from the speakers.

'Transmission' Joy Division
produced by Martin Hannett

All Hannett's usual tricks are here – the gated reverb on the drums, the brittle bass, the chiming guitars buried deep in the mix – as Curtis's melancholy baritone voice is brought to the fore.

'Milkshake' Kelis
produced by the Neptunes

The archetypal Chad Hugo/Pharrell Williams production uses booming, digital bass drums, a playground chant, shards of wobbly percussion and the unmistakeable sound of a Korg Triton synth. At around this time, it felt as if 20 per cent of all songs played on BBC Radio 1 were produced by the duo.

'Bad Penny Blues'
Humphrey Lyttelton & His Band
produced by Joe Meek

'Telstar' invented synth pop, 'Valley of the Sioux' invented Adam & the Ants and 'Johnny Remember Me' invented Marc Almond. However, Meek's work on this deliciously clunky trad-meets-boogie stomper effectively served as the Year Zero for British rock 'n' roll.

'Bat Out of Hell' Meat Loaf
produced by Todd Rundgren

Even more Wagnerian than Phil Spector, Rundgren and right-hand man Jim Steinman erected a wall of sound for Meat Loaf's dystopian rock-opera that was bombastic and ridiculous in equal measure.

'You've Lost That Lovin' Feelin''
The Righteous Brothers
produced by Phil Spector

Spector's fabled wall of sound at its absolute best, with a delicately reverbed tambourine, lots of big tom-toms and what sounds like a huge gothic choir. On hearing Bill Medley's baritone vocals, co-writer Barry Mann thought the record was being played at the wrong speed.

'I Wanna Be Your Dog' The Stooges
produced by John Cale

The former Velvet Underground man – who also produced Squeeze, Siouxsie & the Banshees, the Happy Mondays and Patti Smith, among others – has said that his aim was to 'bring out the essence' of bands he produces. But here, his avant-garde instincts had him beating out a big, dumb, single-note piano line throughout this immutably basic song.

'Papa Was a Rollin' Stone' The Temptations
produced by Norman Whitfield

A house producer at Motown, Whitfield spent his twenties ('I Heard It Through the Grapevine', 'War') building up to this taut, thrilling piece of post-pop. It's a sign of his sonic invention that the song always seems to be going somewhere but, harmonically, doesn't move an inch.

'Sexyback' Justin Timberlake
produced by Timbaland

JT described his comeback single as being 'like David Bowie and David Byrne covering a James Brown song', but thanks to Timbaland, the reality was weirder: Duke Ellington's 'Caravan' covered by Soft Cell and produced by Spank Rock.

'Man! I Feel Like a Woman!' Shania Twain
produced by Mutt Lange

For much of his long and lucrative career, Lange specialised in hard and hard-ish rock: AC/DC's world-conquering *Back in Black*, both of Def Leppard's '80s smashes. However, he never made a more radical record than Shania Twain's *Come on Over*, which hauled country music out of Nashville and all over the world. Worldwide sales: 40 million.

Make 'em laugh

Heard the one about the comedy songs, wonders **David Cavanagh**?

Let's write a comedy song. You and me. I'll write the lyrics (which will be wonderfully clever and howlingly funny) while you compose a tune that's catchy and memorable. Our comedy song will delight the world, spreading hilarity eternal. It cannot fail.

O catastrophe! O wretched affliction! Our comedy song has failed. My lyrics came out horribly misjudged (puerile rather than satirical, with witticisms that fell on deaf ears) while your so-called catchy tune sounded smug and banal. Our comedy song 'sucks all the hope out of life' (*NME*) and 'will no doubt embarrass these two idiots forever' (*The Independent*).

We've learned an important lesson. The comedy song, unlike music that seeks to be serious, will never win points for profundity, let alone originality, yet the comedy songwriter faces obligations as tough as any in show business. A successful comedy song relies on a 'medicinal compound', to borrow a phrase from the Scaffold's 'Lily the Pink': a careful balancing of weights, measurements and dosages. Part of the skill lies in giving the illusion that the comedy is the dominant half of the partnership, even though the melody is what ultimately sticks in our head.

Whichever comic route one takes (urbane, profane, mock-solemn, spoof), it's essential to get the song's internal logic established straight away. Flanders & Swann, the much-loved West End theatre doyens of the 1950s, chose an endearingly silly premise for 'The Gnu Song': a proud gnu taking umbrage at being mistaken for other animals. The foundation thus laid, Flanders' verbose wit ('call me bison or okapi and I'll sue') can savour every rhyming opportunity that the concept of a snobbish gnu allows. Similarly, the Depression-era song 'Jollity Farm', recorded by the Bonzo Dog Doo-Dah Band in 1967, places its central idea up front (a farm where all the animals are insanely happy), enabling the anarchic Bonzos to spiral off into surrealism and whimsy ('Grunt! Howl! Grunt! Howl!') as each creature is introduced.

The late Jake Thackray, so often the lugubrious exception to the rule, takes his time revealing the premise of 'On Again! On Again!', opting for a devastating opening line ('I love a good hum on a woman') followed by a discursive lead-up to the main topic (women who won't stop talking). Once we realise where he's taking us, Thackray's circuitous methods become funnier and funnier; moreover, with no repeated choruses to slow them down, his syllable-packed stanzas seem like tumbling waterfalls of ever-increasing ingenuity.

The road to satire is paved with good intentions, but having a supercilious loathing of your subject is always an advantage. Stan Freberg and Frank Zappa, two brilliant Americans who abhorred rock 'n' roll and flower power respectively, are not often twinned as kindred spirits. But there are clear satirical parallels between Freberg's 1954 hit 'Sh-Boom (Life Could Be a Dream)' and Zappa's 1968 album track 'Flower Punk', not least in the way they expose a fundamental crassness in their target genre. Freberg, parodying a contemporary doo-wop single by the Crew Cuts,

Rewind
Randy Newman

Unlike other writers of the rock generation, Randy Newman has always seemed reluctant to bare his soul in song. Instead, he's given us a wryly comic commentary on the American way, charting the darkest corners of human experience with a wit as accurate as it is terse but always in penny-plain English. As the man says, 'I like to be understood.'

It's ironic, then, that understanding sometimes seems in short supply when it comes to public appreciation of his outlook. There's often a tantalising ambiguity to his songs that derives from devil's advocacy: slyly appearing to defend Southern racism and apartheid in 'Rednecks' and 'Christmas in Capetown', launching a tasteless onslaught in 'Short People'.

'What happens in the songs,' he explains, 'is that you take these awful characters and you don't agree with 'em but you make 'em a little human. After all, they are people. You can't just set up some guy to knock him down. You've gotta let him make the best argument he can, even when he's got no argument.

'It's a risk you take. Sometimes when I'm writing, I do get scared, but I do nothing about it. The only thing I regret is "The Blues" on the last record [*Trouble in Paradise*]. I was making fun of the sensitive singer-songwriter type, and there's a line about this kid who has a bad life and so he runs to his piano for solace. That was a mistake; it has an edge. I mean, I never play the piano to cheer myself up, but there are people who do. Still, no one was offended by it except me.'

His contribution to the John Landis comedy *¡Three Amigos!* is something else entirely: three beautifully deadpan ditties in the cornball Western tradition of Tex Ritter, and even a hand in the script.

'It is a very different kinda humour, 'cause it's aimed at a very different audience. The audience for my songs wouldn't have been a drop in a bucket for these guys. I'm generally pleased with it, though it's akin to when people used to record my songs before they got too weird. I was never happy with it; I mean, *never*. But I'm not ashamed of the film. In fact, some of the least sophisticated stuff was my idea. I kinda like that custard pies thing.'

Geoff Andrew; from Time Out, *20 May 1987*

makes his singers put rags in their mouths to get the moronic slurs and mumbles he desires ('I distinctly understood a word that time,' he warns them at one point), while Zappa heaps ridicule on San Francisco's psychedelic hippie community with the aid of a wannabe Haight-Ashbury dropout and comically speeded-up voices spouting cretinous hippie platitudes. Zappa and Freberg demonstrably relish their sly touches of smirking accuracy.

As Zappa knew, profanity and scatology can be a winning formula. But again, the balance must be right. Derek & Clive's faux-sombre 'Jump', sung by Dudley Moore at the piano, is laugh-out-loud funny for three crucial reasons. We are not expecting the words 'you fucker' to occur in such a doleful-sounding piece; the witnesses to the house fire are not, as they claim, holding a blanket; and, in conclusion, Moore lends an almost hymnal melody to the unforgettable line 'We are miserable sinners, filthy fuckers'. A song that should have been pathetic ends up providing uncontrolled mirth every time.

Upping the ante for a harder-to-shock generation, 'Uncle Fucka' from the movie *South Park: Bigger, Longer & Uncut* enthusiastically combines torrents of profanity, a grotesque premise (the 'amusing' side of incest) and bravura sequences of high-speed flatulence, all to stunning effect. The accompanying tune is full of infectious energy, reminiscent of a show-stopper from *Oliver!* or *Smike*.

In the history of the comedy song, the week ending 15 September 1973 has a special place. That week, at the height of glam-rock and David Cassidy fever, the UK's top 50 included not one but three comedy songs that have all assumed legendary status. Curiously, none of them was a new release. 'The Ying Tong Song' by the Goons was the oldest: dating back to their BBC wireless broadcasts of the '50s, it's a breakneck recording of an absurdly funny song with manic interludes seemingly every few seconds. If that was an anachronism to Radio 1 listeners waiting patiently for Suzi Quatro, so were the clanking chains and bubbling potions of Bobby 'Boris' Pickett & the Crypt Kickers' 'Monster Mash', a delicious Boris Karloff homage from the 1962 American hit parade that was bizarrely disinterred 11 years later. And finally, there was 'The Laughing Gnome' by glam superstar David Bowie, a flop 45 from 1967 released by his former record company to capitalise on his new-found fame. One can imagine how the perky ditty's re-emergence must have mortified the wan creator of *Aladdin Sane*. But note the speeded-up voices of those gnomes. Even in '67, Bowie knew all the comedy tricks.

The 1970s were a golden decade for the comedy song, even if one of the most renowned actually came from the '30s. Laurel & Hardy's 'The Trail of the Lonesome Pine', a highlight of their 1937 feature *Way Out West*, operates in not dissimilar territory to 'The Ying Tong Song' (formality interrupted by slapstick; someone being hit over the head), and in 1975 the loveable tale of the Blue Ridge Mountains struck such a chord with the British public that it only narrowly missed being the Christmas number one. In the event, a rather sillier song called 'Bohemian Rhapsody' won the race.

Neither Benny Hill's 1971 chart-topper 'Ernie (The Fastest Milkman in the West)' nor Jasper Carrott's 'Funky Moped', from four years later, could have existed without the inspiration of American culture, yet in their concept and execution, both are wholly and colloquially English. There's perfect union between pathos and bathos in Carrott's Black Country lad whose moped will be a surefire babe-magnet as soon as he gets the front mudguard fixed. And while his own comedy, like Carrott's, was overtaken by fashion, Hill's celebrated milkman saga remains an extremely impressive piece of writing. The song's internal logic is faultless, its narrative a life-and-death struggle involving bitter love rivals. The saucy double entendres are typical of Hill, of course, as is the notion of a humble milkman being a secret Lothario, but there's also a linguistic flair worthy of Chuck Berry at work.

By contrast, Berry's own chart-topping comedy song, 'My Ding-a-Ling' from 1972, sees the great man use an innuendo-heavy sledgehammer to crack a puny, one-joke nut. Usually regarded as Berry's artistic nadir, this trite penile singalong outsold every other record he ever made. That's the problem with comedy songs. There's simply no accounting for taste.

Michael Flanders and, at the piano, **Donald Swann**. Gnu not pictured.

Here comes the sun

Dan Epstein settles down by the pool with a glass of something cold.

While I haven't crunched the numbers, tallied the totals or, frankly, done any real research on the subject, I'm completely confident in asserting that summer has inspired more great songs than any other season. Sure, there's been a whole pile of memorable tunes waxed in honour of Christmas, but I'm hereby disqualifying them from consideration due to their inherently limited listening context. Much as everyone loves a festive Yuletide jingle, it's impossible to hear one between New Year's Eve and late November without peppermint-flavoured bile rising to the back of one's throat. A good summer song, however, can last all year long.

Just ask the Beach Boys, who turned the concept of *Keepin' the Summer Alive* (the title of one of their less successful albums) into a cottage industry that's still going strong nearly 50 years after 'Surfin'', their first single, shot the curl into the lower levels of the American pop charts. Initially focused on the celebration of Southern California surf culture, head Beach Boy Brian Wilson soon came to the conclusion that summer wasn't just a handy backdrop for his many songs about drag racing, woody-waxing and teen romance, but also a temporal and conceptual standard by which one's very existence could be marked and measured. In Wilson's pre-LSD world, everything pretty much boiled down to Summer Past, Summer Present or Summer Future, or some combination or gradation thereof. Summer, in other words, as a permanent state of mind.

But although the 1975 compilation that kick-started the group's US revival was titled *Endless Summer*, many of the summer songs in the Beach Boys' catalogue are imbued with the melancholy knowledge that the season – and, by extension, youth – isn't quite so endless after all. 'Girl Don't Tell Me', appropriately found on 1965's *Summer Days (And Summer Nights!!)*, takes a pragmatic, even jaded approach to summer romance. In the song, the singer (Carl Wilson, though Brian wrote it) is reunited with the girl he romanced last summer. During the intervening months, the girl never replied to any of his love letters, and his mind seethes with jealous visions of all the guys she must have been banging while he was away at school. However, since her hair is even longer than he remembered and her ass looks great in a tight pair of shorts, he resigns himself to another summer fling with her, but with one difference: this time, it comes with the understanding that it means nothing.

If 'Summer Means New Love', as an instrumental track from the same album hopefully posits, it also means *sex*. People wear less clothing, require more alcohol to slake their thirst and generally tend to be more amorously adventurous than they would be in, say, a February blizzard. Or, at least, that's the case made by Reg Presley in the Troggs' 1975 thumper 'Summertime', which has precious little to do with the Gershwin standard of the same name. As the band makes with an uncharacteristically slinky acoustic groove, our Reg apes a slow burn, so excited by all the

Top ten
Clapping

'Tighten Up' Archie Bell & the Drells

'Hi, everybody!' says the voice on the 45. 'I'm Archie Bell and the Drells!' Presumably there was more than one person behind this irresistible piece of fluff, an American chart-topper in 1968 and still a guaranteed floor-filler four decades later. The way the relentless clapping emerges in the middle of the single, and the way it vanishes more or less as soon as it arrives, makes it sound as though a handful of studio onlookers simply decided to give the horn section a round of applause.

'Unsquare Dance' Dave Brubeck

Brubeck's mix of musical erudition and cultural populism resulted in some fabulous little cuts that are often rather more complicated than perhaps they first appear. 'Unsquare Dance' is a straightforward little 12-bar blues in the decidedly un-straightforward meter of 7/4, all held together by handclaps that seem to grow more resolute as the piece progresses.

'Close to Me' The Cure

Robert Smith and chums spent much of the '80s lurching between 16rpm misery and 78rpm jollity. Found on 1985's *The Head on the Door*, 'Close to Me' falls firmly into the latter category, a simple ditty given an unexpected lease of life by a few well-placed handclaps scattered around the off-beats. And, of course, by Tim Pope's still-hilarious closet-bound video.

'The Clapping Song (Clap Pat Clap Slap)' Shirley Ellis

This really isn't much more than a nonsense rhyme set to a Bo Diddley-ish rhythm on the bass, topped off by a horn section apparently getting paid by the note and a singer who sounds like she wishes she'd gone home 15 takes ago. Still, there's a genius of sorts at work in these grooves. The clapping instructions are effectively useless, but you'll be fine if you stick to the twos and fours.

'Hand Clapping Song' The Meters

Typically spartan piece of taut, metronomic funk from the New Orleans quartet, found on their third album *Struttin'*. Tighter than spandex and a whole lot more presentable.

'Hey Ya!' OutKast

Thing is, you'll need a third hand if you also want to shake it like a Polaroid picture.

'Clapping Music' Steve Reich

Reich took the phasing techniques he'd pioneered on tape pieces such as 'It's Gonna Rain' and translated them into this thrillingly primal piece for nothing but two pairs of hands. One person claps a relatively simple rhythm throughout the piece; the other claps the same rhythm, but shifts a half-beat out of sync with his partner every 12 bars. The piece ends when, usually after about five minutes, the second musician has moved back into sync with the first. Sounds complicated? Try *playing* it…

'Car Wash' Rose Royce

The movie's long since been consigned to cult status at best. However, the soundtrack, written and produced by former Motown man Norman Whitfield, remains a disco classic, and the start of the title song contains what's arguably the most famous handclap riff in pop history. Whitfield, incidentally, was also responsible for the propulsive handclaps in another one-chord wonder, the Temptations' 1972 US number-one single 'Papa Was a Rollin' Stone'.

'Cecilia' Simon & Garfunkel

This juddering and agreeably muddled campfire singalong from *Bridge Over Troubled Water* sounds like it was written and recorded in five minutes flat.

'In the Navy' The Village People

They want you as a new recruit…

Keepin' the summer alive:
the **Beach Boys**.

tender female flesh on display in the summer sun that you can practically hear him drooling over the microphone.

Of course, we should probably cut Presley some slack. Nowadays, we barely bat an eyelid when some starlet or other flashes a full beaver while falling out of a limo. But back in the early 1970s, the trend for hot pants blew more than a few male minds, and inspired better men than the Troggs to put pen to paper. On their 1972 album *Whatcha See Is Whatcha Get*, the usually dignified Detroit soul group The Dramatics completely lose their shit when confronted with 'Hot Pants in the Summertime'. By the end of the track, lead singer Ron Banks has been reduced to a mere shell of a man, desperately trying to get the attention of passing 'big-leg' women in order to inform them that they sure look good. Yeah, pal, as if they didn't know *that* already…

Speaking of Gershwin's 'Summertime', there are more than 4,000 studio recordings of the *Porgy and Bess* aria out there somewhere, and you pretty much can't go wrong with any jazz or soul rendition you happen to uncover. My own favourite instrumental take comes courtesy of LA Latin soul combo One G Plus Three, a pulsing, lowrider-worthy version tucked away on the flip of their 1970 single 'Poquito Soul', while Al Green takes the vocal honours for his rendition on 1969's *Green Is Blues*.

Chess Records' soul man Billy Stewart also waxed a memorable version of the song, filled with his trademark chuck-buck-cluck vocal mannerisms, but his recording is simply out-summered by his two 1965 hits, 'I Do Love You' and 'Sitting in the Park'. With their rolling, Latinesque grooves, ringing guitar and piano lines and dreamy backing vocals, both songs sound as if they must have been cut on a warm July day with perfumed purple clouds rolling slowly over the Chicago lakefront. The fact that they were actually recorded in December 1964 takes away none of their glorious summery radiance.

When pressed to make a summer mix disc, I'll inevitably make a beeline for the soul bin. That's not to denigrate cuts such as the Queens of the Stone Age's drug-addled 'Feel Good Hit of the Summer', XTC's pastoral 'Summer's Cauldron' or any of the many versions of Eddie Cochran's deathless 'Summertime Blues', all of which – in very different ways – take a slightly ambivalent attitude to the warmest months. And it's not to downplay the more exuberant likes of Mungo Jerry's goofy 'In the Summertime', Alice Cooper's explosive 'School's Out', Slade's rollicking 'Summer Song (Wishing You Were Here)', T Rex's whimsical 'Celebrate Summer' and the Lovin' Spoonful's gritty 'Summer in the City'. It's just that, for me, getting in the summer groove requires some actual *groove*, which is why Sly & the Family Stone's hazy 'Hot Fun in the Summertime', Kool & the Gang's synth-coated slow-jam 'Summer Madness' and the Commodores' aptly named 'Easy' (a massive US hit in summer 1977) are all required listening.

By the same token, War's cheerfully meandering 1976 hit 'Summer', basically the aural equivalent of sitting on your front porch on a hot day with a 40-ounce bottle of Colt 45 in a brown paper bag, and 'Let's Go (It's Summertime)', a horn- and organ-stoked funk obscurity by James Reese & the Progressions, also hit the spot. The same can be said of just about any jazz version of Marcos Valle's 'Summer Samba', aka 'So Nice' or 'Samba de Verão', which is virtually guaranteed to deliver the goods in a mellow sort of way. And then there's the Isley Brothers' incredible version of Seals & Crofts' 'Summer Breeze', wherein Ernie Isley's sizzling guitar lines rescue the ballad from its drippy post-hippy origins and launch it deep into outer space.

But while the Beach Boys would never admit it, summer doesn't always live up to our expectations. Reflecting our weariness are songs such as Love's bilious 'Bummer in the Summer', the Style Council's faux-soul lament 'Long Hot Summer', Hüsker Dü's bitter 'Celebrated Summer' and 'Weird Summer' by 1990s power-poppers the Velvet Crush, all of which ultimately aim to lessen the sting of our own disappointment.

Still, at least we can always take comfort from the way that the protagonist in the Kinks' immortal 'Sunny Afternoon' handles his predicament. Left on the verge of penury

'But although the Beach Boys would never admit it, summer doesn't always live up to our expectations.'

by a rapacious tax collector, kicked to the kerb by his girlfriend, awaiting the forced sale of his stately manor without any clue as to his next move, and generally just marinating in a mess that's more or less of his own making, the guy simply pops open a cold one and enjoys the remaining rays of a summer day. Ultimately, that's the underlying message of any great summer song: this sunny afternoon is all we have, so we may as well get the fuck outside and enjoy it.

On the record
Noddy Holder
'The Girl Can't Help It'
Little Richard

This simple, two-minute rock 'n' roll song with rubbish lyrics genuinely changed my life. I'd already heard the rock 'n' roll of various people like Elvis and Bill Haley and Fats Domino but this was something else. The very sound of it excited me. Then I saw a movie called *The Girl Can't Help It*, and Little Richard came on and performed the title song. I remember him with his big bouffant hair and his baggy, shiny suit, pounding his piano while his band behind him swung their saxes in unison. It absolutely floored me.

When I finally saw him live, it was just pandemonium. He was jumping on the piano and every time he shook his head the sweat came out into the crowd. He was wearing powder and make-up and he was as camp as custard, but we didn't really understand. The teddy boys were going mental. I thought, this is what I want to do. I want to be a colourful, extrovert, dressing-up rock 'n' roll singer. Little Richard changed my life.
Noddy Holder was the lead singer of Slade

Eat to the beat

Michaelangelo Matos settles down to dinner with four very hungry singers.

It's likely that every artist discussed in this book has at some point sung for his or her supper. Singing about it, though, is a more specialised task. There's something inherently garrulous, bordering on silly, about songs that are explicitly concerned with what the musicians are going to treat themselves to after the gig (or, for recording-studio hounds, during it). Sure, these foodstuffs are often standing in for other types of human delight, whether as cheap metaphor (50 Cent's 'Candy Shop') or in more sophisticated terms (Dusty Springfield's 'Breakfast in Bed', which isn't really about the meal). But what concerns us here are songs in which a bite to eat really is just a bite to eat. So let's say grace and begin.

Three squares and a midnight snack have infiltrated their way into just about every style of pop music, but songs about food tend to be more prevalent in the earthier genres: R&B, pre-bebop jazz, country, folk and our good friend the novelty hit. In particular, African American music has long been tied to food, from the so-called 'chitlin' circuit' of clubs in heavily black cities in the South and the north-eastern US to the metaphoric terms 'jam session' and 'gumbo'. Black music and soul food are connected at a deep level, and it's hardly surprising that of the four artists on whom I'm going to focus, three are African American.

Louis Jordan, the rhythm and blues singer, saxophonist and bandleader, can without hyperbole or errant mythmaking be said to have invented rock 'n' roll. One person who might agree is Chuck Berry, who acknowledges

learning plenty from guitarist Carl Hogan of Jordan's band the Tympany Five (a name they used no matter how many people were actually in the band at any given time). Along with Louis Armstrong, Jordan was the most transcendently popular African American musician of the 1930s and '40s: he regularly crossed over to the lily-white US pop charts, no easy feat for an R&B performer at the time, and even scored a few country hits. Listening to his music, his success isn't surprising: Jordan's driving rhythms, solid melodic sense and ever-present sense of humour have lost none of their brilliance or appeal.

Jordan liked something into which he could sink his teeth. Sometimes he sang about food metaphorically: 'Beans and Corn Bread' took race relations to the table, while the two-part 'Saturday Night Fish Fry' depicted a police bust of a raucous barbecue. But often, Jordan simply revelled in good eats for their own delicious sake, as on 'Cole Slaw', 'Ration Blues' (recorded in 1943, and all about cutting down on food consumption during World War II) and the self-explanatory 'Hungry Man'. Jordan's easy vocal style was perfect for the subject: he was the kind of man with whom you could fall into conversation at a lunch counter without even realising it.

The same can't be said for Slim Gaillard: he was one of jazz's great eccentrics, and that's saying a lot given some of the weirdoes who've played the music. Lots of jazzmen, especially in the bebop era, spoke in loose slang, but Gaillard embellished it with his own personal touches:

the word 'vout' and 'o-rooney' were often thrown in more or less at random. (Upon being introduced to Mickey Rooney, Gaillard is reputed to have asked the actor for his last name.) Gaillard was the hipster's hipster, so respected that, around the time they were remaking jazz in their own image, Charlie Parker and Dizzy Gillespie were happy to play as his sidemen on a couple of 1946 cuts (see 'Slim's Jam').

But Gaillard is included here because he was the most shameless of musical gourmands with the broadest of tastes. He enthusiastically endorsed Jewish fare with 'Matzoh Balls' and 'Dunkin' Bagel' ('Smash! In the coffee'). He loved a snack: see the immortal 'Potato Chips' , with its unforgettable refrain, 'Crunch, crunch, I don't want no lunch'. And he beat Little Richard to the title 'Tutti Frutti' by a good decade; but where Richard never pretended he was singing about ice-cream, Slim scatted away

'James Brown sought the same kind of communal vibe in those grooves as might a family sitting down to Sunday dinner.'

about strawberry and vanilla. That was a mere warm-up for 'When Banana Skins Are Falling', with a bizarre lyric that sends up Tin Pan Alley metaphors over a light Cuban beat. And, of course, there's the smorgasbord that is 'Eatin' with the Boogie', which finds Gaillard raving about everything from candied yams to '*steeeewwwed* tomatoes'.

Slim Gaillard's gustatory passion fits his general image as a wiggy bon vivant. However, anyone familiar with James Brown's

Louis Jordan & His Tympany Five working up an appetite.

'Weird Al' Yankovic sings for his supper.

background can spot that his many food songs are rooted in sheer need. After growing up dirt-poor, Brown drove himself (and his band) harder than just about any musician before or since: staying on the road 300 nights a year, playing multiple concerts per day, and – over a couple of decades, from the ground up – redefining the entire rhythmic structure of popular music. Needless to say, such a task required fuel.

From 1960's '(Do the) Mashed Potatoes' (credited, for contractual reasons, to Nat Kendrick & the Swans) to the flurry of popcorn-related songs he cut in the late '60s, many of Brown's food-oriented records were actually named after dances. But to leave them out of this consideration would be missing the point. A record such as the blistering 'Mother Popcorn' embodies the workings of the foodstuff for which it's named: it sizzles and explodes regularly but never quite predictably, not unlike kernels in a kettle. (Hank Ballard's JB-produced 'Butter Your Popcorn' is, it should go without saying, much smoother.)

What's more, Brown sought the same kind of communal vibe in those grooves as might a family sitting down to Sunday dinner. One of the most illuminating passages in *Living in America: The Soul Saga of James Brown*, Cynthia Rose's superb study, concerns the bandleader's long-standing road habit of ordering late-night barbecue ('He knows every rib joint in the South!' journalist Gerri Hirshey tells Rose). Especially with the early '70s recordings by Brown's band the JBs, food titles connect the musician's life with family: see the likes of 'Breakin' Bread', 'Pass the Peas' and 'Rice 'n Ribs'. And since a musician's life isn't always easy, we also got a classic entitled 'Givin' Up Food for Funk'.

The artist who's done the most to keep food on the charts over the last couple decades, though, isn't an innovator, except in the playground sense of making up new words to hit songs. But if anyone is associated with foodsong in the public mind, it's Lynwood, California's own 'Weird Al' Yankovic. An accordionist from age seven and your classic

Top ten
Drinking

'Pop a Top' Jim Ed Brown
Set next to nostalgic fluff like 'Scarlet Ribbons (For Her Hair)', with which the singer enjoyed success as part of clean-living family group the Browns, 'Pop a Top' comes across like Tom Waits at his most exaggeratedly mashed. Heard on its own, but it's less woozy, but it's become a honky-tonk classic: heralded by the sound of a top being popped, its chorus is an archetypally country mix of remorse and resignation.

'I Belong to Glasgow' Will Fyffe
One night after a concert, music-hall singer Will Fyffe ran into a rather inebriated gentleman at the city's Central Station. The man appeared disoriented, so Fyffe asked him where he called home. 'I belong tae Glasgow,' slurred the man, through a smile. 'And Glasgow belongs tae me.' A satirical yet affectionate look at the joys of hitting the town on a Saturday night, the song has since become the city's unofficial anthem.

'Lay Something on the Bar (Besides Your Elbow)' Louis Jordan & His Tympany Five
Because, like the man says, 'They can't ring up your elbows on the till.'

'I Ain't Drunk' Jimmy Liggins
On 1953's 'Drunk', backed by the fabulously named Drops of Joy, Liggins slouched his way through heroic quantities of moonshine, red wine, gin and whiskey before collapsing in a heap. By the following year, his constitution had improved a little for this rollicking ode to just one more round, but it was just self-denial: the hungover follow-up was 'No More Alcohol'.

'Funky Cold Medina' Tone Loc
Blend vodka with peach liqueur, blue curaçao and cranberry juice, and you'll end up with something that's more or less undrinkable. However, according to Loc's daft novelty, this hideous blend is also the world's most potent aphrodisiac, attracting his dog, a transvestite and a blind date who pitches marriage on the first meeting. White wine for the lady?

'One Scotch, One Bourbon, One Beer' Amos Milburn
In John Lee Hooker's hands, this becomes a pretty aggressive request. However, this swinging 1953 original phrases it in gentler and more plaintive fashion, as Milburn pleads for a little something – okay, three little somethings – to help blot out his romantic misery.

'Streams of Whiskey' The Pogues
A predictably raucous little tribute to the booze that apparently continues to fuel Shane MacGowan, the band's singer and the song's author. The video, apparently shot for a mere £60, finds MacGowan supping whiskey in a deckchair by the side of the Regent's Canal wearing nothing but a pair of red Y-fronts, before the band repair to what's now the Water Rats pub on the Grays Inn Road for a session that appears to take in rather more than the 15 pints of beer detailed in the third verse.

'The Bottle' Gil Scott-Heron & Brian Jackson
The son of a former Celtic footballer, Scott-Heron cut this pulsing anti-alcohol tract in the early 1970s. However, despite his earnest early warnings about the dangers of addiction, the singer developed a rather more serious dependence of his own: his career in freefall, he's spent the last decade in and out of jail on a number of charges relating to the possession of cocaine.

'Two Pints of Lager and a Packet of Crisps Please' Splodgenessabounds
Admirably straightforward piece of oi! idiocy in which Max Splodge (possibly not his real name) struggles to get the beers in before last call. The title was later borrowed by the BBC for a flabbergastingly terrible sitcom.

'The Piano Has Been Drinking (Not Me)' Tom Waits
Waits' spellbinding pantomime of a career has been dotted with references to getting loaded: 'Jockey Full of Bourbon', the saloon-bar pick-up of 'I Never Talk to Strangers', the malt liquor that fuels 'Frank's Wild Years', even the title of debut album *Closing Time*. However, he reached an alcoholic apogee on this 1970s drunk-in-denial track, though the original on *Small Change* pales next to the hysterical rambling live version on *Bounced Checks*. 'Watch me skate across an acre of linoleum,' he offers at one point, alternately enunciating and slurring his words. 'I *know* I can do it.'

Rewind
James Brown

You're playing London in July. Can you tell me what kind of material you'll be performing?

'I'll jus' be doin' James Brown, period. When you come to see James Brown, that's what you come to see. James Brown.'

Are you competitive with other artists?

'I got no competition. It's like Santa Claus. The next guy can come along, but he's still gonna be Santa Claus. I don't worry about that no more. But the main thing I don't understand is: how come I'm more popular today than I was 15 years ago? That's strange.'

Do you think that's partly down to hip hop and how much you've been sampled?

'Yes. And the older people want their kids to hear *real* music. That's another thing. This one-chord vamp thang, y'know? Most people don't make music no more 'cause they don't know how. They never found the structure. They just put a hook in there, a beat in there…'

Are there any current artists that you think are really good?

'I listen mostly to jazz artists. I like Jimmy Smith. Grover Washington: he's nice. And I like Chuck Mangione. Chick Corea.'

So you're more inclined to listen to more mellow music than the music you play?

'Oh *yeah*. I play my own jazz tunes. I'm just developin' this because… my stuff is so dynamite and so *bitin'*. There's no way in the *world* you can rest if you hear my music. You gotta *get up!*'

Is all that stuff about you fining musicians for playing wrong notes true, or just legend?

'I was very tough – *very, very tough* – because they didn't know what to do. When I hired Maceo Parker, I hired him 'cause his brother played drums so good. I taught Maceo by hummin' his solos and showin' him exactly what to play. Now I have a young man named Jeff Watkins, and it's funny, y'know? No one has a monopoly on music. Jeff Watkins is a tall, off-brunette white kid and he has about as much soul as anyone I've ever seen.

'So, Maceo… One time Maceo was working on a garbage truck. I turned him around. Fred Wesley is a tremendous musician, but the musicians I had in those days… I have a better calibre of musician today. Because I'm playing harder stuff, and those musicians had problems doing the simple stuff in those days.'

Garry Mulholland; from Time Out, *22 July 1998*

suburban American geek, Yankovic loved rock 'n' roll and comedy in equal measure, and began fusing them in the late '70s with his unusual instrument.

Yankovic's first single, a send-up of the Knack's 'My Sharona' that he retitled 'My Bologna', set the tone. Although the singer chose other topics for subsequent parodies ('Like a Surgeon', for example), food inspired his greatest work. Not always, of course: 'I Love Rocky Road' has pretty much been forgotten by history, as has 'Fat', his reworking of Michael Jackson's 'Bad'. But 'Eat It', the MJ rip that preceded it, is a minor geek classic – especially the video, which turns Jackson's tense street-gang epic into the goofiest-on-purpose four minutes MTV showed all decade. Less well remembered but just as deliciously stupid is 'Taco Grande': the song targets that most deserving of relics, Spanglish-rap one-hit-wonder Gerardo's 'Rico Suave'.

On 2006's *Straight Outta Lynwood*, the parodist hit paydirt with 'White and Nerdy', a riff on Chamillionaire's 'Ridin' Dirty' that became Yankovic's first top ten hit. But it was his demolition of R Kelly's 'Trapped in the Closet' saga that ranks as Yankovic's all-time masterwork. Eleven minutes long, 'Trapped in the Drive-Thru' utilises Kelly's sing-song melody and slow-build dynamics, not to mention his breathlessly absurd sense of melodrama. But instead of an endlessly twisting storyline with an endlessly mutating cast, Yankovic goes in the other direction. The entire story: the narrator and his wife decide to get fast food to go and tedium ensues. That's why it's the funniest thing Yankovic has ever done: he gets every detail absolutely right, from his wife fuming that she didn't even want to go out for chicken sandwiches and curly fries in the first place to the gnat-like attention span of the kid taking their order.

If you've ever spent time in a Middle American suburb, this is your story writ large… excuse me, writ super-sized. If you haven't, you need nothing more to put you right in the middle of the action; or, as the case may be, the inaction. And if you're fascinated by the way food has written itself into popular music, hearing this ridiculous number will serve as a logical end-point for the whole thing. Or at least that's where I'll leave it, because I have to get going. I'm *starved*.

There's a Riot Goin' On

Uneasy listening

Garry Mulholland sticks up for hip hop's offensive past.

At some point during the last 20 years, even the most feminist and liberal among us began to shrug and accept a fearsome level of misogyny in hip hop. The genre's journey from a Bronx-born underground African American art form of the late '70s to its current status as the world's most commercially successful musical culture has operated like a parallel universe to the political correctness that has entirely transformed the way we're allowed to speak to each other in the western world. While most of us nervously censored ourselves, rappers and their fans revelled in their graphic flagellations of women and gays.

Of course, male-dominated hip hop has produced much of the best music of the last 25 years, and it's the music that remains the foundation for its inexorable rise and rise. But one suspects that the lyrics and the stance of hip hop, and the effect they've had on the walk and talk, clothes and catchphrases, manners and values of our increasingly laddish, apolitical society, is plain obvious. Rappers say the things that we're too scared to say. They're our anti-heroes. At a time when the

world's battleground is an information war, a man who just says what's on his mind without giving a shit what anyone thinks is Robin Hood, Guy Fawkes, Jesse James and Dirty Harry, all rolled into one tidal wave of niggas, bitches, faggots and hos.

But in writing an overview of musically extraordinary but lyrically uncomfortable rap, one has to acknowledge that hip hop is as complex a world as the one it conquered. Ice T's 'The Iceberg' opens up many of those complexities. It's taken from the former Tracy Marrow's third album, *The Iceberg: Freedom of Speech… Just Watch What You Say*, which, apart from boasting a long and clumsy title, established the first West Coast gangsta rapper's favourite theme: censorship. The album even featured some spoken-word contributions from Dead Kennedys frontman Jello Biafra, one of America's most outspoken anarcho-lefties.

The album was a bewildering listen for someone like me, a diehard believer in punk and the pro-women, pro-queer, post-punk world it inspired. One minute you were cheering on

this guy's courageous, educated, multi-racial stand against the American Right and the forces of reaction and repression. The next you were realising that the only thing for which Ice T (who'd named himself after pimp-turned-writer Iceberg Slim) was fighting was the right to rap about assaulting ugly bitches with flashlights.

It wasn't long before Ice T came up with an idea that was incendiary enough to attract the full wrath of the US body politic. In 1992, he decided to form an all-black heavy metal band called Body Count. Their eponymous debut was one of the great satirical albums of its time, juggling the ironies of American racial conflict, censorship and sexual hypocrisy in a hilarious, bad-taste comedy manner that you imagine illuminated light-bulbs above the heads of Eminem and the makers of *South Park*. But therein lay the problem. By using loud guitars and naughty swearing as his Trojan Horse, Ice T had succeeded in his mission to get into the CD players and the heads of middle-class white kids. And a few of those kids' parents heard 'Cop Killer' and got very angry indeed.

A three-chord punk thrash with a chorus designed to be hollered by spotty boys, 'Cop Killer' was issued in the wake of the Rodney King/LAPD furore and took police brutality as its theme. But the theme got lost somewhere amid drum breaks morphing into the sound of gunfire, and Ice T sneering at the grieving family of a dead policeman. Ice T wasn't the first musician to threaten the police in song. But with all the detail about black gloves and guns, and the song's apparent call for murder, he was definitely the most convincing. Time Warner, the rapper's record label, found themselves called into emergency meetings with irate shareholders, among them Charlton Heston, while anonymous callers made death threats to the company's staff.

Within weeks, 'Cop Killer' had been pulled from the album. 'I ain't gonna die over no song,' Ice T explained. But the perceived climbdown wasn't appreciated by hip hop's increasingly rabid fanbase, who deserted the rapper more or less overnight. By this time, the fans were growing increasingly uninterested in the music or the safety of the artists. They wanted rappers to live out their outlaw fantasies so they didn't have to; those that didn't were rejected as fakes, or sell-outs to Whitey. It would be less than four years before they got the martyr's violent death they seemed to crave, the ultimate proof that hip hop was 'keepin' it real'.

But before we get there, we have to ask: how did hip hop come to this? When did its commercial triumph become so inextricably linked with misanthropy and violence? Was its journey from radical black art form to corporate-sponsored nihilism simply an inevitable repeat of the capitalist co-option of rock music and the counterculture? Or is there something deeper

Ice T, unsweetened.

and darker going on here? Lest we forget, this is a book about recommending music, so it's best we look at some of the greatest indefensible hip hop recordings for some answers.

In 1973, when the eras of Blaxploition movies and conscious soul-funk were at their heights, and around the time that a South Bronx DJ called Kool Herc was figuring that parties at which people talked over funk records instead of reggae ones might be a nice idea, a poet called Lightnin' Rod made the first gangsta rap album. What made *Hustlers Convention* different from the work of the Last Poets, the group of radical black spoken-word artists that Rod (aka Jalal Mansur Nuriddin) had formed in 1969, was the change in emphasis from 'you' to 'I'. On rap-poems such as 'Niggers Are Scared of Revolution', the Last Poets hectored the African American about his (they were Muslims; of course, *his*) inability to overturn white power. But on *Hustlers Convention*, Lightnin' Rod became the young street hustler to which so many conscious soul records alluded but held at arm's length, and was too busy fighting other black men to fight The Man.

The album is a short story, backed by a host of A-list funk musos (including, on a number of tracks, Kool & the Gang), about a late '50s street kid gambling and doing drugs while other kids played in the street, and hustling so successfully that he was 'Running through bitches like rags to riches'. He ends up shot and sentenced to death, spending 12 years on Death Row, but any morality in this tale is virtually obliterated by the relish of Lightnin' Rod's delivery and the power-packed cinematic funk that drives one of the finest albums that no one's heard of. Check out the thrilling opening track 'Sport' and you'll understand why the have-your-cake-and-eat-it modus operandi of gangsta was a phenomenon waiting to happen.

When the Sugar Hill Gang's 'Rapper's Delight' helped introduce the planet to hip hop in 1979, it unleashed a slew of chancers great and lousy, talking in corny voices over funk or synthetic beats about money, partying, charming the ladies, break-dancing, getting laid and having cash money. It was cute, with a side order of black self-elevation. But few took the genre seriously until 'The Message', Grandmaster Flash & the Furious Five's

> 'All rap needed was someone smart enough to make the connections between rebellion, misogyny, violence, bad taste and the kind of reckless individualism for which rock 'n' roll appeared to have lost the stomach.'

vivid depiction of ghetto misery. A huge surprise hit, it proved that, in the era of Reaganomics, there was a big audience keen to escape into someone else's nightmare reality.

However, sick humour was always lurking somewhere beneath early hip hop's crossover cuteness, and it had its first popular and influential airing on 'La-Di-Da-Di', the B-side to human beatbox Doug E Fresh's novelty 1985 hit 'The Show'. During it, the cartoonish Ricky D (aka Slick Rick) comes up with a sexist nursery rhyme in which a girl's mother is so keen on Rick's charms that she beats up her own daughter to get him, before being rejected by our debonair hero for having a 'wrinkled pussy'. The song became such a cult hit that Snoop Dogg covered it in tribute on his debut album.

At the time, all rap needed was someone smart enough to make the connections between rebellion, misogyny, violence, bad taste and the kind of reckless individualism for which rock 'n' roll appeared to have lost the stomach. And in the mid 1980s, two very different artists did just that.

The Beastie Boys' 1986 debut album *Licensed to Ill* finally made plain what the early records by Run DMC and LL Cool J had only hinted: that the best way for hip hop to move from novelty dance hits to unit-shifting albums was to court outrage. On the back of a live show that featured girls in cages and a giant

Rewind
Beastie Boys

'I was at this party the other night, and this man went on and on about how the Beatles had ruined western civilisation,' said Hester Diamond, mother of a Beastie Boy, to the *Los Angeles Times* in February. 'I listened for a while and finally said: "If you have problems with them, you should hear my son's band."'

The three Beastie Boys have spent the last four months terrorising America with a colossal caricature of teenage rebellion. A lot of people have taken it seriously. Not, presumably, the two million teens who've bought their album, but the parents and the ministers and the hotels. The group were banned from all Holiday Inns after turning the furniture in one room into wood shavings. And in LA, they flooded their suite after their famous 'shower trick' exploded and caused $25,000 of damage. 'Yeah,' says MCA, 'but we probably make that in a week.'

The highlight of the Beasties' stage show is a whopping great pink phallus that leaps out of a black box; the show also features topless women in a cage. 'Actually, we're not misogynist,' protests MCA. 'I like any girls so long as they've got great big tits.' Adds Adrock, apparently also not a progressive male, 'I don't like homosexuals. I have to live above transvestite prostitutes in my street. It makes me sick.' The band wanted to call their album 'Don't Be a Faggot' but CBS said they'd cut their fingers off.

The Beastie partnership began four years ago, but it was sharpened with the arrival of Rick Rubin, now their label head, producer and co-writer. The result of their endeavours is the ideal mid-'80s crossover: not only the mesh of punk, rap and hard rock, but also the critical gel of black and white. 'The fact that they're white is an opportunity,' says Russell Simmons, Rubin's black partner. He should know. Run-DMC, his brother's band, had to hook up with Aerosmith to guarantee their big break last year.

The Beasties' lyrics don't tackle social or political issues in the style of much black rap. They present a lewd, brattish and spiky cartoon rap: a filthier Monkees, an alco Bash Street Kids. But Adrock's father, playwright Israel Horovitz, isn't impressed. 'He kinda wishes we were more like the Beatles.'
Simon Garfield; from Time Out, *13 May 1987*

inflatable cock, these three middle-class Jewish New Yorkers made a link between ghetto machismo and frat-boy puerility. 'Robbin' and rapin'' ('Rhymin' and Stealin'), 'The girlies I like are under age' ('The New Style') and 'Girls! To do my laundry!' (the deliberately idiotic 'Girls'), they howled in a nasal whine, beating down various fantasy authority figures with baseball bats and guns in an orgy of gleeful liberal-baiting. Among those questioning the amorality of this best-seller were listeners that wondered whether the colour of the artists had anything to do with their commercial triumph. Because the nearest black equivalent barely sold a bean.

Philadelphia's Jesse B Weaver renamed himself Schoolly D and, in 1984, made the first widely acknowledged gangsta rap single, 'Gangster Boogie'. On his first two albums, 1986's *Schoolly D* and 1987's *Saturday Night! – The Album*, Schoolly's flow was an eerie contrast to the declamations of the Beasties et al: he sounded stoned and calmly, happily psychopathic, as his voice worked over dislocated, ghostly beats that sounded like threats echoing off the walls of deserted underpasses. Ice T later acknowledged his debt to the likes of 'PSK What Does It Mean?', 'Saturday Night', and 'Parkside 5-2', which glorified the guns, bitches and drugs lifestyle of a real Philly gang called the Parkside Killers. But there was also art and weirdness to Weaver's work. In 1988's 'Signifying Rapper', the old folk tale of the signifying monkey is given a ghetto reality twist as 'a big, bad faggot' proceeds to hand out a beating to a bullying pimp, all carried out to the accompaniment of a Led Zeppelin sample. Abel Ferrara later used the track for his equally transgressive movie *Bad Lieutenant*.

The next key record in the development of gangsta or 'reality' rap came from hip hop's South Bronx birthplace. Released in early 1987, Boogie Down Productions' first album *Criminal Minded* came with the baggage of a sleeve photo depicting rapper KRS-One and DJ Scott La Rock holding guns, an evocative image that assumed added resonance when La Rock was shot five months after the album was released. In truth, La Rock was a social worker and had died trying to intervene in a street argument. But these details were lost among the apparent authenticity of a brutal, reggae-tinged album about gangs, guns and how 'The pussy is free, but the crack costs money' ('The P is Free', a B-side reworked into 'Remix for P is Free' on *Criminal Minded*) had possibly killed one of its makers. The most controversial track on the album was 'The Bridge Is Over', which went public with a spat between Boogie Down Productions and a hip hop collective from the Queensbridge Housing Projects called the Juice Crew. Taken alongside his friend's murder, KRS-One's lyrics established the vicarious thrill of watching rap beefs get so out of hand that their macho games of dare are played to their ultimate conclusions.

Public Enemy may be rightfully praised as the politicised, articulate and sonically innovative brand leaders in what we now know as the Golden Age of hip hop, a period that lasted roughly from 1987 through to 1991. But even Chuck D's hero status has to be qualified by the misogyny of 'Sophisticated Bitch' and 'She Watch Channel Zero?!', let alone the alleged anti-Semitism of sidekick Professor Griff. As such, it wasn't much of a leap of bad faith to add Public Enemy's anti-establishment anger and wall of noise to the Beasties' liberal-baiting sexism, Ice T's pimp persona, Schoolly D's gang testimonies and a hefty dose of cartoon misanthropy, and make it into the definitive gangsta rap package.

Straight Outta Compton, the 1988 album from Los Angeles rap group NWA (Niggaz with Attitude), featured 'Cop Killer' blueprint 'Fuck Tha Police', the fuck-you thrill of the title track, and a whole lot of fucking everybody and everything moral and progressive that hip hop – that *pop* – had thus far produced. It also introduced the world to the production genius of Dr Dre, the angry young rapper and chubby-cheeked future comedy actor Ice Cube, and, among the album's murderous contempt for women, gays, authority and everyone black that wasn't in the band, some of the funniest lines ever recorded in pop. Leader Eazy E is, according to 'Straight Outta Compton', 'a brother that'll smother your mother and make your sister think I love her', while 'Express Yourself' sees Dre hollering: 'I'm expressin' with my full capabilities, now I'm livin' in correctional facilities'.

There's been plenty of talk lately in the UK about musical 'guilty pleasures'. Not sure what

Philly pioneer **Schoolly D**.

kind of pantywaist needs permission from a DJ before they allow themselves to enjoy 'Escape (The Piña Colada Song)', but I do know that jumping round the room to *Straight Outta Compton* involves suspending every bit of peace-loving liberal virtue I have. Still, that's what I do, from time to time, and the pleasure isn't innocent. I'm dancing to a musical caricature of other people's hell. And that's the secret of gangsta rap's success. If you live in a beaten, violent place, you can use NWA and their musical children as rebellion and defiance. If you don't, it's instant porn and horror with a funky-ass beat.

Straight Outta Compton split hip hop into East versus West, NY versus LA, conscious versus gangsta, art versus commerce. And suddenly, rap seemed to concern itself with bitter conflict: with somebody, with anybody. Rap groups that weren't explicitly violent and bigoted were written off as 'pop', 'soft' and – the implications were blatant – too white or just plain gay. Authenticity was measured in how 'real' a rapper's gangland back-story was, how willing he was to threaten other artists, how prepared he was to show his violence in public.

The cool, gun-toting misogyny of Dr Dre and Snoop Dogg, the anti-Jewish and Korean rants of 'No Vaseline' and 'Black Korea' from Ice Cube's *Death Certificate* album, the gleeful lust for black-on-black violence on early Cypress Hill records (check out the remarkable 'How I Could Just Kill a Man'), the bizarre macho justifications of the normally fluffy and cuddly A Tribe Called Quest on 'The Infamous Date Rape': all roads seemed to lead to the unsolved 1996 and 1997 murders of Tupac Shakur and Biggie Smalls (aka the Notorious BIG), after a long and bitter public war between their respective LA and New York labels and entourages. Hip hop finally had its martyrs: you can't get realer than dying over music.

Something broke in rap music as it attempted to rein in its worst impulses. While Eminem brilliantly encapsulated all the misanthropic ironies of hip hop, putting misogyny and homophobia in psychological and economic context but quickly burning out in self-parody, great artists such as OutKast and Kanye West became exceptions, rare signs of creative life adrift in a sea of mumbling materialist chancers such as P Diddy, Jay-Z, 50 Cent and DMX. The gun fantasy became the gold fantasy, the music simplified itself into ringtones, and the best rappers – Dizzee Rascal, Roots Manuva, Sway, Plan B – were suddenly British. Hip hop became an African American mirror of country music: a corporate cash cow with little connection to its roots, a simple formula music for simple formula people, a bland din with an underlying message of conservative loathing for those who aren't 'us'.

The strange irony is that you can easily blame the tunes I've mentioned above for rap's decline, but if you made them into a mixtape, it would be just about the most irrationally exciting blast of musical genius and indefensible rebellion that a pile of dead presidents could buy. And that's why, for better or worse, hip hop is the most powerful and influential music in the world. The more it offends, the deeper it reaches inside us. It's the only fitting soundtrack for a fucked-up planet.

Hip hop guilty pleasures in 20 songs

'Spelling BEATNUTS with Lil' Donny' The Beatnuts

This short, filthy blast of unrepentant playground sexism, found on the group's 1999 album *A Musical Massacre*, is an acrostic set to the eight letters that together make up the band's name. It's unforgiveably vile, but it's set to such an infectiously funky beat that it sounds fantastic.

'Ruff Ryders Anthem' DMX

One of DMX's violent hymns to the mafioso lore of the communal rap clan. As ever, DMX sounds like he's preaching a sermon while holding a loaded gun to a member of the congregation.

'Bitches Ain't Shit' Dr Dre featuring Jewell, Lady of Rage, Kurupt & Snoop Doggy Dogg

Guest rapper Snoop Doggy Dogg plays the amoral pimp again on the final track of Dr Dre's landmark 1992 album *The Chronic*, and here manages to endear himself with an invitation for us to 'Lick on deez nutz and suck the dick'.

''97 Bonnie & Clyde' Eminem

This track takes a sample from Will Smith's Bill Withers-inspired buddy song 'Just the Two of Us' and twists it to fit a macabre tale of a psychopathic father cheerfully telling his infant daughter that he's just killed her mother, before asking the traumatised kid to hold the rope while he sinks mom's body in a lake. Later covered, rather more poignantly, by Tori Amos.

'Let a Ho Be a Ho' The Geto Boys

This disgraceful assault on womankind – which suggests that only a 'ho-assed nigga' would hesitate to put a ho in front of a trigger – is, sad to say, brilliantly delivered over a funky, minimal breakbeat that cuts up the bassline from Pink Floyd's 'Money'. It's slightly more palatable than the Geto Boys' 'Mind of a Lunatic', which imagines the thoughts of a psychopath as he rapes and murders a woman.

'6 'n the Morning' Ice T

Sometimes credited as the first ever gangsta rap track, this defiantly old-school cut appeared on the B-side of Ice T's 1986 single 'Dog'n the Wax (You Don't Quit Pt.II)'. It's a lengthy narrative of a young gangsta escaping from an early-morning police raid and bragging about the benefits of crime.

'Da Bitchez' Jeru tha Damaja

Gang Starr's DJ Premier works his magic on a sumptuous piece of jazz-funk from the Crusaders, only for the Damaja to live up to his name and stamp

Straight outta Compton: **NWA**.

his way across the thing with a dunderheaded, half-witted lesson in misogyny. 'Most chicks want minks, Diamonds, a Benz,' he reckons. 'Spend up all your ends. Probably fuck your friends.'

'Aww Skeet Skeet'
Lil Jon & the Eastside Boyz
Found on the 2004 album *Crunk Juice*, this is the finest and filthiest example of crunk, the genre of rap to come out of Atlanta, Georgia. In crunk-speak, 'skeet' means to ejaculate.

'Simon Says' Pharoahe Monch
That compelling, four-note sample, culled from the theme to *Mothra vs Godzilla*, reduced 'Simon Says' to novelty status when it reached the charts in 2000. It also hides a wealth of profoundly offensive lyrics ('girls, rub on your titties') that are rendered oddly compelling by Monch's masterful delivery and his multi-syllabic rhyming schemes. Unfortunately, not everyone agreed: after the owners of the copyright to the Godzilla music complained about the sample, which Monch had neglected to clear, the single and the album were pulled from the stores and remain unavailable to this day.

'The What' The Notorious BIG
Found on Biggie's 1994 album *Ready to Die*, a release acclaimed by no less a musician than Randy Newman, this duet with Method Man is strange and woozy enough for you to forget that it's a brazen celebration of murder. It also, rather delightfully, sees Biggie rhyme 'illest' with 'What you talking about, Willis?'

'Nigga Please' Ol' Dirty Bastard
Dirtier and angrier than Jay-Z's track of the same name, this 1999 cut finds the gruff-voiced Wu-Tang man recite a list of racist clichés and turn them into the vainglorious boasts of a black Superman. Possibly the best use of the N-word in hip hop.

'Throw Ya Gunz' Onyx
On this track, the first single from their 1993 debut album *Bacdafucup*, Onyx described their bleak celebrations of the underclass as 'grimee'. Certainly, their spiky, gruff-voiced, raspy and ragged delivery had more in common with black-metal nihilism than gangsta rap.

'We Luv Deez Hoez' OutKast featuring BackBone & Big Gipp of Goodie Mob
If actor, dandy and psych-rocker André 3000 was the highbrow half of OutKast, then Big Boi, with the dog-breeding business and a lap-dancing club in his basement, was always the proudly stupid one. Still, Big Boi's rhythmic scansion and his flair for a pop hook certainly led to some great tunes, like this ridiculously offensive track from 2000's *Stankonia*.

'You're Gonna Get Yours' Public Enemy
The opening track from Public Enemy's 1987 debut *Yo! Bum Rush the Show* carried none of the urgent militancy of much of their later output: it was just a big, dumb, brilliant song about having a big, dumb, brilliant car. Oddly, it's a lot less offensive than some of the sexist, homophobic and racially separatist tracks on some of their more 'conscious' albums.

'Holla Holla' Ja Rule
Even when bragging about sexual potency, Ja Rule does so with an almost inhuman violence. 'Holla Holla' features an ear-catching mention of 'homo thugs', which possibly inspired Chris Morris's sketch about 'street poofs'.

'Treat Her Like a Prostitute' Slick Rick
A heroically stupid and offensive novelty track from the London-born rapper's 1988 album *The Great Adventures of Slick Rick* that serves as the missing link between gangsta rap and Benny Hill.

'Gin and Juice' Snoop Doggy Dogg
The year after Snoop Doggy Dogg (as he was then) built up an audience by dint of his guest turns on Dre's *The Chronic*, his 1993 debut *Doggystyle* became the fastest-selling rap album in history. Its sales were surpassed several years later by Eminem, but this track remains an irresistibly wobbly deep funk highlight.

'Sweet Talk' Spank Rock
A perfect example of Spank Rock's ability to fuse uptempo European electronica (courtesy of producer Alex Epton) with some of the dumbest and most gleefully sexist areas of American hip hop (courtesy of rapper Naeem Juwan). Thankfully, the group also have a female MC, Amanda Blank, who gives as good as she gets.

'Spoonin Rap' Spoonie Gee
Gabriel 'Spoonie' Jackson brags about his talents as a 'baby-maker' and a 'women-taker', about his low-level criminality and about his spell in prison on this faintly amoral proto-gangsta track from 1979. However, it's his echo-laden voice, the minimal beat and the wonderfully boingy noise from the flexatone percussion that makes 'Spoonin Rap' a classic. Trivia: on the label of the original 12-inch, his name is spelled as 'Spoonin Gee'.

'Indian Flute' Timbaland & Magoo featuring Sebastian & Raje Shwari
This 2004 Timbaland production features an outrageous lyric that finds rapper Melvin 'Magoo' Barcliff inviting the Asian object of his desire to have her womb 'beat up'. It's all made surprisingly palatable by use of a hypnotic beat and a haunting Indian flute sample.

Boys will be girls

Kimberly Chun charts the gender-bending history of pop and drag.

Social conservatives, hard-rock homophobes and dancehall gay-bashers have all done their best to keep it from prominence, but there's no disputing that drag culture has retained a long and storied foothold in pop music. For every dozen leather-jacketed toughs, there's been a flamboyant singer or two who's seemed intent on tweaking public perceptions of rock culture's innate masculinity. And what's more, drag culture has proudly resurfaced of late, flaunting its glitter, glamour and chic in the face of a world otherwise keen on dressing down. Whether proffered by shaven and well-shod beefcakes or by tarted-out faux queens, drag has almost become a spectator sport in the music world: place your bets on who swans more fiercely among the boys who imitate the girls who mime the boys who ape the girls.

Some writers have claimed that drag resides at the sub-basement foundations of rock culture. In *Vested Interests: Cross-Dressing & Cultural Anxiety*, in a chapter titled 'The Transvestite Continuum', Harvard professor Marjorie Garber suggests that Liberace was inspired to ever-camper heights not by Broadway or cabaret but by the cultivated flamboyance of earthy old rock 'n' roll. Suing a British newspaper for libel in 1959 after it had implied he was homosexual (he won the case), the pianist told the court that he needed to 'dress better than the others who were copying me… [including] a young man named Elvis Presley'. Writes Garber, going against critical orthodoxy as she describes the similarities between Liberace and Presley, 'Elvis became a *cause* of feminine virile display'.

Ironic, then, that the King was in turn influenced by the Candelabra Kid's high-camp glitzerati displays: witness Presley giving Liberace a run for his rhinestone flash as he shakily croons 'Suspicious Minds' during his famous Hawaii concert of 1973.

However, rock's relationship with drag really began, as did so many things, with Little Richard. 'I was a drug addict! I was a homosexual! I sang for the devil!' he sermonised in later life, having lost his attitude and found religion. But back in the '50s, at the first commercial stirrings of rock 'n' roll, the mascara-soaked, big-haired and blatantly sexualised Richard Penniman revelled in musical and visual outrage. Were his tastes as 'Tutti Frutti' as the once-obscene tune suggested? Did it matter? Whatever the truth behind the pompadour and face-cake, Penniman dragged drag kicking and screaming into pop orthodoxy, supercharging its ambiguity with an irresistible, youthful excitement on the manic likes of 'Lucille', 'Good Golly, Miss Molly' and 'The Girl Can't Help It'. And it wasn't all about the image. Richard openly taunted all-comers, asking them 'Baby, Don't You Want a Man Like Me?', before flitting back to the church with one last request: 'Baby, Don't You Tear My Clothes'…

Little Richard may have played hard to get, but his admirers were unable to resist the magnetism of the image he created. Ray Davies winkingly spelled out the attraction that dare not speak its name on the celebratory 'Lola', slyly addressing the 'What are you, a girl or a boy?' accusations often fielded by long-hairs

'You want some?' David Johansen and the **New York Dolls**.

of his generation while also playing off his own conflicted feelings about androgyny. Lola is as forbidden a fruit as Nabokov's Lolita, whose own under-age allure is invoked by the song's hook. Too bad that the protagonist pushes the dark brown-voiced man-vixen away.

Other counterculture adventurers were all too happy to echo Davies's confused insistence that 'girls will be boys and boys will be girls'. The Rolling Stones assumed dark, Monty Python-esque drag for the sleeve of 'Have You Seen Your Mother, Baby, Standing in the Shadow?'. David Bowie took every opportunity to up the provocation ante, whether wearing a streamlined frock as he warbled 'Teenage Wildlife' in concert or donning a Poiret-like cardboard gown while backed by German androgyne Klaus Nomi on a 1979 *Saturday Night Live* performance of 'The Man Who Sold the World'. However, they all paled in contrast to the tranny-hustler sass 'n' trash of a stiletto-heeled David Johansen, drawling 'Looking For a Kiss' alongside the New York Dolls. While Johansen's baritone is drenched with manly menace, his feathered hair and femme polka

dots scream coquettish seduction. And that's before we've met the band, who themselves resemble menacing gutter punks hustling both sides of the boulevard: the mean streets *and* the girlie glam-ways.

Paralleling punk but culturally worlds apart from it, the disco scene sprang from New York's gay subculture. And when the underground went overground in the mid '70s, it became inevitable that, sooner or later, an artist would emerge from it into the mainstream and challenge public perceptions of sexuality and gender. Sylvester had been a legend on San Francisco's gay scene since the late '60s, but it wasn't until he remade himself into the first male disco diva that he was introduced to ordinarily conservative audiences who didn't quite know what they were seeing or hearing. Was that a man or a woman that listeners clocked crooning 'You Make Me Feel (Mighty Real)' on their radios in 1978? The accompanying promo clip, in which Sylvester strolled through an array of flamboyant costumes while fluttering an ever-present fan, only confused matters further. This was night fever of a very alien variety.

With only a few exceptions, most notably Wayne (now Jayne) County, the '70s and '80s punks that followed in the wake of the New York Dolls didn't do well by the cross-dressing antics they pioneered. Instead, drag found its fuck-me-heels footing in over-the-top pop, where such blatant artifice was more than accepted by a world otherwise rife with intolerance. The same voters who'd welcomed Reagan and Thatcher also applauded the sweet, self-consciously faux pop of Boy George, who cunningly pleaded for tolerance on 'Do You Really Want to Hurt Me' and toasted the ever-mutable tranny wardrobe with 'Karma Chameleon'. It turned out that America did indeed 'know a good drag queen when it [saw] one', as Boy George quipped while accepting a Grammy in 1984. Later that year, Dead or Alive singer Pete Burns tweaked the male-female fashion mix with his figure-flattering kaftans and cheese-draped guilty pleasure of a hit, 'You Spin Me Round (Like a Record)'.

An even stranger sideshow was provided by the hair-metal scene that emerged around the same time, which bizarrely chose to express its masculinity through a distinctly feminine appearance. Despite their primped perms and painted faces, the likes of Kiss and Twisted Sister chose to dispense with drag's seductively subversive messages and instead framed their appearances with highly heterosexist musical imagery: take WASP's 'Animal (Fuck Like a Beast)', for instance, or Mötley Crüe's cover of 'Smokin' in the Boys Room', delivered from behind effeminate haircuts and made-up faces but apparently without even a dab of irony. Groups such as these may have appropriated the Dolls' desire to cause controversy, but their womanising fronts and neanderthal posturing reassured mainstream audiences that they weren't, god forbid, *fags*.

Post-punk, post-riot grrrl and post-*The Crying Game*, not to mention post-Divine, Rupaul, Lypsinka and drag's other incursions into mainstream pop culture, it's no surprise that the boys who will be girls and the girls who will be bioqueens penetrated even deeper into American musical culture. Nirvana's Kurt Cobain delighted in tweaking rockist convention by frolicking in a dress. Dyke-core combo the Butchies opened the dressing-up box for the Devo-parodying cover of their album *Are We Not Femme?*. And then there's

'For every black T-shirted screamo singer or Western-shirted indie kid, there's a handful of gaudy dandies and full-tilt mandies cavorting in the halcyon fields of gender-blending confusion.'

the extraordinary case of Genesis P-Orridge, who's transformed himself into a pandrogynous cross between himself and Lady Jaye, his late mate/bandmate. These physical changes have paralleled a shift in his music: certainly, it's hard to imagine the P-Orridge of '70s Throbbling Gristle embracing the softer, almost infantile anxiety that's tangible on Thee Majesty's 2007 album *Vitruvian Plan*. 'My name's Fluffy!' yelps P-Orridge from behind a transformative Vocoder on 'Thee Land Ov Do Do (A Cautionary Tale)'.

The continuum has been taken up by a new generation in the 21st century. With a full proud face of paint and plaster, drag is rampant once more, tottering in its Christian Louboutins toward its next pomegranatini and clutch of adoring indie boys. For every black T-shirted screamo singer or Western-shirted indie kid, there's a handful of gaudy dandies and full-tilt mandies cavorting in the halcyon fields of gender-blending confusion. These birds of paradise and angels of light are blithely disregarding the so-called real world's call to war, and all of the heightened butch high-jinks that realm requires. Blissfully throwing glitter, glamour and outrageously hued eyeshadow in the face of religious fundamentalism and codified gender roles, they're reviving the gorgeous, kitchen-table couture corpses of flaming creatures long since gone.

These days, there's little reverence for or knowledge about what might be called traditional drag performance. Still, Devendra

On the record
Thurston Moore

'Hey Joe'

Patti Smith

This is an absolutely pivotal, catalytic song for me. I'd read her journalism in *Creem* magazine; I liked the voice that she wrote in, and the pictures of her were great. So I sent off for this single – it was on her own imprint, MER, and it cost $2, which was quite a lot of cash at the time. It was her doing a piece of classic rock and adding her own recitation to it, so that it had one foot in the great American rock canon and another in this new genre that was later to become punk. And it completely delivered. 'Piss Factory' was on the B-side, which was an even more powerful piece of recitation. I'd never heard anything like that before, that kind of impassioned music. It was perfect.
Thurston Moore is the guitarist and singer with Sonic Youth

Banhart's publicity-shot excursions into exquisitely face-painted and bejewelled bearded drag hark back to the fabulous Hibiscus of the pivotal San Francisco '60s counterculture theatrical collective the Cockettes (who, incidentally, once included the aforementioned Sylvester among their number). The troupe were freaks among freaks: beautiful to behold, almost always stoned, shattering straight norms left and right. As hetero Cockette Martin Worman says in a documentary about the group: 'Did I have the nerve to get on stage in a dress? Yes! It didn't take as much nerve as riding a motorcycle on a wall… But in a different way it seemed very dangerous.' Banhart's photographic homage to the group is, in the words of one of his own songs, truly 'A Sight to Behold'.

On the other side of Banhart's communal freak fest sits the solitary figure of Antony Hegarty. On *I Am a Bird Now*, he rhapsodises fading drag beauty in the high style of transvestite Holly Woodlawn; the album's cover even features Candy Darling, who, like Woodlawn, was one of the Warhol Superstars of the '60s and '70s. Hegarty's is a dark but heavenly vision that dovetails perfectly with the cabaret, piano-(wo)man excursions of Baby Dee, a transgendered singer-songwriter who gathered such indie-rock luminaries as Will Oldham and Andrew WK to help her realise cracked-genius remnants of twisted vaudeville like 'Big Titty Bee Girl (From Dino Town)' for her 2008 album *Safe Inside the Day*.

But perhaps the best embodiment of latter-day high-femme drag comes from back across the tracks, and a performer who looks backwards for her inspiration while remaining a defiantly 21st-century star. Above the neck, with her phallic, jet-black beehive and Cleopatra-style, eyeliner-heavy make-up, Amy Winehouse is all Ronette. But below, in a white wife-beater and super-low-slung jeans, she could be mistaken for the Leader of the Pack. Part Rizzo, part Kenickie, she's a mod greaser's fever dream, slurring out 'Me and Mr Jones' and 'You Know I'm No Good' as her crowds work themselves into a steamy, soused lather. In essence, Winehouse is a study in drag inspiration: adored by gays and straights, boys and girls, and perfectly styled both for diva-loving tributes and camp send-ups. It's hard not to suspect that Little Richard approves.

Devendra Banhart.

Rage hard

Stevie Chick uncovers the anger and fury behind 40 years of hard rock.

Midway through *Here, My Dear*, his double-album treatise on heartbreak that effectively served as his divorce settlement to first wife Anna Gordy, Marvin Gaye poignantly observed that 'anger destroys your soul'. Wise words indeed, but his sentiment isn't typically shared by the more feral purveyors of rock 'n' roll.

Within rock music's lexicon, anger has been defined both as an energy (John Lydon) and a gift (Zach de la Rocha). It's also now the fuel of choice for swarming sub-genres such as hardcore punk, thrash metal and rap rock. However, it wasn't always as prevalent in music as it is today. Adolescent frustration may have been a key part of rock 'n' roll's DNA since its Jurassic era, but Eddie Cochran's grounded-by-pa 'Summertime Blues' hardly qualifies as rage. And even when heavy metal first began to stir with the primordial riffs of Steppenwolf, Led Zeppelin and others, the lyrics typically waffled on about machismo, lust and the wispy cod-spiritualism that characterised the end of the hippy era.

Rock and rage connected convincingly for the first time in late '60s Detroit. Fittingly, the MC5 chose to ally themselves with the Black Panthers over the hippies, calling for 'rock 'n' roll, dope and fucking in the streets' in the White Panther Manifesto drafted in 1968 by their manager John Sinclair. The band's ear-ringing revolutionary assault was powered by a hazily politicised rage, expressed through violent R&B riffs, Rob Tyner's full-throated holler and their impassioned call, on the title track to their unimpeachable 1969 debut album, to 'Kick out the jams, motherfuckers'. These were the early sparks of punk, later to blaze through downtown New York and, with greater impact, the UK.

Although British punk is typically regarded as a reaction against prog rock, it also drew inspiration from the doldrums in which the country found itself during the 1970s. The grey skies, three-day weeks and racial tensions that dogged the country at the time served to build up a smothering claustrophobia that punks sought to puncture before it suffocated them. From the Sex Pistols baiting prurient and prudish society with gleeful spite on 'God Save the Queen', to the Clash's incitement to 'White Riot' and the Slits squarely aiming their bruising, dub-informed clatter at the limp crotch of rock chauvinism (best heard on 'Shoplifting' from their *Peel Sessions* collection), punk was righteous, desperate fury set to noise possessed of a brutish passion that easily redeemed its musical limitations.

America's hardcore scene, which emerged in the early 1980s, further distilled this passion. Mobilised by their rage at the banality of suburban America and the decidedly oppressive tenor of the nascent Reagan presidency, kids across the country – and many of them *were* kids – formed bands that revelled in their anger and their youth, both of which propelled their raucous riffs at a breakneck pace. 'It matched my energy level, my anger level,' remembered Sebadoh's Lou Barlow, then bassist with Massachusetts hardcore group Deep Wound.

Black Flag bring the noise in 1985.

California's Black Flag were the leaders of the pack. With its image of a skinhead punching a mirror with splintering, bloody fury, the sleeve of their epochal 1981 album *Damaged* set the tone for the haywire thrash of tracks such as 'Police Story' and 'Thirsty and Miserable'. But the Flag's music – a blistering, acrid din that drew heavily on Black Sabbath and, towards the end, free jazz – was only one outlet for the group's anarchistic and nihilistic ire. The band ploughed their energy into backbreaking shoestring tours across America; the confrontational shows often ended in three-way pitched battles between the musicians, their fans and the police.

Washington, DC's Minor Threat played to similarly violent crowds, whipped up by the lightning-speed attack of whipcrack songs such as 'Straight Edge' and 'Seeing Red' and the enfranchising lyrics of frontman Ian MacKaye, preaching passionate abstinence and raging against the mainstream. The group idealistically aimed to translate their anger into positive energy; for evidence, see Dischord, the highly independent record label set up by MacKaye that thrives to this day.

Top ten
Thatcher's Britain

'Between the Wars' Billy Bragg

During the 1980s, *Top of the Pops* was awash with unexpected sights. However, few were quite as striking as Billy Bragg standing alone beneath the unforgiving glare of its coloured spotlights in front of an audience of mulleted teenyboppers and singing – not miming! – this self-penned protest song, less than a month after the year-long miners' strike had officially ended and the same week that 'Easy Lover' climbed to number one.

'Loadsamoney (Doin' Up the House)' Harry Enfield

'Shut your mouth and look at my wad,' offers Harry Enfield's cheerfully obnoxious plasterer on this tatty little bodge-job, an absolute stinker even by normal novelty-record standards. By attempting to satirise the greed-is-good capitalism of the '80s with such a cheap little cash-in, it pretty much becomes everything it initially appears to despise. Produced, he won't thank us for reminding you, by William Orbit.

'FLM' Mel & Kim

The cure for what ails you, according to the Appleby sisters by way of Stock, Aitken and Waterman, is just fun, love and money. Would that life were that simple.

'Rent' Pet Shop Boys

Neil Tennant often passed comment on '80s society during the first three Pet Shop Boys albums: sometimes attacking it with a brick, as on the strident anti-privatisation satire of 'Shopping'; sometimes looking on from the shadows, as on 'Suburbia'; and sometimes lending it a beating heat, as on this acutely observed miniature from 1987. It's never made clear whether the protagonist is a wife, a kept woman or even a prostitute, but the ambiguity, and Tennant's fragile but slightly removed delivery, serve the story beautifully.

'Kick Over the Statues' The Redskins

Attacking the walnut of Thatcherism with the sledgehammer of blundering skinhead soul, the Redskins were too left wing even for Red Wedge, the Billy Bragg-led collective that did for Neil Kinnock pretty much what the Springsteen-led Vote for Change tour did for John Kerry in 2004. This comes from their only album, the rather optimistically titled *Neither Washington Nor Moscow... But International Socialism*.

'Ghost Town' The Specials

As Britain dissolved into a mass of riots during the summer of 1981, brought on in the wake of spiralling unemployment, institutional racism and increasing discomfort with a government at its lowest ebb, the eerie 'Ghost Town' crept to the top of the charts, providing newscasters with a ready-made soundtrack for the scenes of destruction they were preparing to screen. More than 25 years later, it still sounds astonishing.

'Come to Milton Keynes' The Style Council

Arguably the strangest single of Weller's 30-year career (and unarguably the strangest video), this deceptively jaunty ditty is a wayward condemnation-by-proxy of middle England in the 1980s, its streets apparently awash with Stanley knife-wielding ten-year-olds and heroin-addicted little girls. It flopped.

'Mother Knows Best' Richard Thompson

Unlike the Beat ('Stand Down Margaret'), Elvis Costello ('Tramp the Dirt Down') and Morrissey ('Margaret on the Guillotine'), Thompson waited until the Milk-Snatcher was out of office before delivering his explicitly personal diatribe against her on 1991's *Rumor and Sigh*. Still, judging by the venom in both his lyrics and his delivery, he'd been planning it for a while.

'One in Ten' UB40

Like the band's name, this dubby skank referred to the unemployment figures that were spiralling at the time of the single's release in 1981. Five years later, they seemed more concerned about the rat in their kitchen.

'Shipbuilding' Robert Wyatt

Set to Clive Langer's beautiful tune, Elvis Costello's lyric is a weary, melancholic but ultimately devastating indictment of the demise of the northern shipyards, the fast-falling British economy and, most of all, the decision to go to war in the Falklands. Costello himself recorded it in 1983 in the company of trumpeter Chet Baker and an awful lot of reverb, but Wyatt's understated version, released the previous year, remains definitive.

Hardcore's speed and aggression eventually found an echo in thrash metal. Metallica, pioneers on the scene, drew inspiration from the late '70s groups dubbed by the music press of the time as the New Wave of British Heavy Metal. But while many of those earlier groups often descended into cock-rock clichés and Dungeons & Dragons-style fantasies (one notable exception was Judas Priest, whose scything hit 'Breaking the Law' was an undetected nod to the then-undisclosed homosexual lifestyle of frontman Rob Halford), Metallica let their bile do the talking on their 1983 album *Kill 'Em All*. On later tracks such as 'Master of Puppets', 'Disposable Heroes' and 'The Shortest Straw', the group directed their galloping spite towards The Man, voicing the rage of the quadriplegic war veteran, the abused child, even the sanatorium prisoner.

Superstardom and creative irrelevancy followed. However, for a while, Metallica's furious, incandescent brilliance was matched only by Slayer, Californian thrashers whose violent, controversial lyrics and imagery (their masterful 'Angel of Death' was named for Nazi sadist Josef Mengele) were calculated acts of aggression towards censorship groups such as Tipper Gore's Parents Music Resource Center. The success enjoyed by Metallica and Slayer proved that even in its most unvarnished form, anger could be lucrative. But in their wake, the metal community ploughed still further into the depths of bad taste and musical extremity – particularly within the black metal scene, where the incipient hostility led to acts of religious desecration and even murder.

As the 1990s dawned, the prevalent musical trend was a bipolar mess of anger and ennui. While a boundless fury certainly informed the howls that Kurt Cobain unleashed across grunge's defining moment, Nirvana's 'Smells Like Teen Spirit', the troubled singer/guitarist aimed his anger, destructively, at himself. At around the time that *Nevermind* was released, the riot grrrl movement was throwing politicised invective and primal clatter back into the rock arena: Bikini Kill's 'Rebel Girl' is a brilliantly polished blast of riot-rock. Former Black Flag frontman Henry Rollins saw out the era expressing his boundless rage via the muscular rock of his Rollins Band (their 1991 album *End of Silence* is breathtaking in its tirelessness) and his own droll spoken-word

Desperately seeking Nirvana: **Kurt Cobain**.

performances. And metal was defined by the crystalline crunch and blunt violence of Pantera. The group's anthemic 'Walk' was an obnoxious, up-for-a-scrap troublemaker of a single, frontman Phil Anselmo's palpable antagonism concentrated into a diamond-cutting bark (and, eventually, bitter, racist on-stage rants).

Rage Against the Machine emerged in the wake of grunge's implosion, inspired by the realisation that the type of hip hop delivered by the likes of NWA and Public Enemy was easily as effective as metal at articulating anger. The group's then-revolutionary fusion of rap vocals with heavy riffs, held together by a guitarist (Tom Morello) whose fret abuse bridged the distance between the two poles, was powered by a blunt approach to politics that found

On the record
Dizzee Rascal

'Smells Like Teen Spirit'
Nirvana

THERE'S A RIOT GOIN' ON

It always annoys me how limited some people are with their influences. You get rappers who only listen to rap, you get garage MCs who only listen to garage. I'm not like that. I listen to pop, soul, classical, heavy metal – anything that can expand my range. I'm extreme when it comes to music. I immerse myself in a genre at the point where most people would stop. And that's what happened with rock: not just Nirvana, but stuff like Sepultura and Soundgarden. I bought the albums, I immersed myself in that scene. I find the passion in this music cleansing. When you're angry, this music cleanses you. The rage is in the music. 'Smells Like Teen Spirit' is like a three-minute bout of anger. It's cathartic.
Dizzee Rascal's most recent album is Maths + English *(XL)*

beauty in a hurled Molotov cocktail. Zach de la Rocha's vocals fused rap's rhythmic rhetoric with hardcore's holler. The delivery was perfect for their polemical approach, which burned brightest on 'Killing in the Name' from their eponymous debut album.

Towards the end of the decade, Rage Against the Machine's blueprint was lifted wholesale by lesser groups such as Linkin Park and Limp Bizkit, aping the sound but lacking the fury and, indeed, the politics. Their rage was that of the bored suburban kid: Limp Bizkit's jockish frontman Fred Durst came off like a teenager throwing a temper tantrum, rewriting 'Summertime Blues' for spoiled frat boys. Briefly a very lucrative flavour of the month and then hideously unfashionable almost immediately afterwards, this impotent nu-metal wave seemed to prove that rock 'n' roll rage is only truly palatable when it's the righteous voice of the oppressed railing at the oppressor – the romantic image of one man 'screaming at a wall… some day it's gonna fall,' in the words of Minor Threat's Ian MacKaye.

Certainly, 21st-century musical anger has been best expressed through bands with just such a level of idealism. The success of System of a Down, Armenian-American rockers whose savagely adventurous riffage backs lyrics of crudite, politicised fury, suggests that anger, when artfully expressed, is still a marketable commodity; see 'BYOB' ('Bring Your Own Bombs'), written in protest at the Iraq war. Meanwhile, hardcore moshpits only get more ferocious: the likes of Converge are greeted with violent 'circle pits' wherever they play.

The cream of this screamo crop were Seattle's Blood Brothers, whose chaotic, eclectic riot peaked on tracks such as 'USA Nails' and 'Six Nightmares at the Pinball Masquerade' from their 2003 album *…Burn, Piano Island, Burn*. The group's fervent distaste for the hypocrisies and injustices of society found expression in thrash-punk of bionic precision, with hyper-inventive twists. The group split in late 2007, but the scene they led, and that survives without them, proves that there's still vivid, vituperative life left in rancorous rock 'n' roll. Maybe, in the end, Marvin was right. But if anger does destroy the soul, what better way to free ourselves from it than by screaming it away over thunderclap guitars and nosebleed-inducing drums?

Being There

City life

Philip Sherburne on electronic music and the urban environment.

Morton Feldman: This weekend, I was on the beach… And on the beach these days are transistor radios… blaring out rock 'n' roll… all over.
John Cage: And you didn't enjoy it?
Feldman: Not particularly. I adjusted to it.
Cage: How?
Feldman: By saying that… Well, I thought of the sun and the sea as a lesser evil.
Cage: You know how I adjusted to that problem very much as the primitive people adjusted to the animals which frightened them… They drew pictures of them on their caves. And so I simply made a piece using radios. Now, whenever I hear radios – even a single one, not just 12 at a time, as you must have heard on the beach – I think: 'Well, they're just playing my piece.'
John Cage and Morton Feldman, in conversation on WBAI, 1966

At 8pm on a Saturday evening, London's Fabric nightclub – a vast, brick-walled labyrinth within a former meat-packing warehouse – is empty but for a few stray employees coiling cables or stocking the bar. It is over-bright and, for a room soon to be packed with heaving bodies and booming bass frequencies, strangely silent. A PR representative from the club is describing the nuances of the sound system; in particular, the subwoofers installed beneath the floorboards that emit not so much sound but vibration, a subtle, ticklish rumble that shoots up through the dancers' bodies like the shocks of a Tesla coil. As if summoned by her words, a gravelly vibration trundles across the room: an echo of the London Underground, en route to the tube station a few blocks away.

Like John Cage's compositions for transistor radios, the 21st-century nightclub has absorbed the sound of the city. And so, too, has the music that animates it, tuning itself to the city's specific resonance and adopting a grammar based upon FT Marinetti's dictum that 'Noise is the language of the new human-mechanical life'. Contemporary electronic dance music is certainly more than simply a kind of noise-cancellation strategy, just as Cage's radio compositions were more than a way to cope

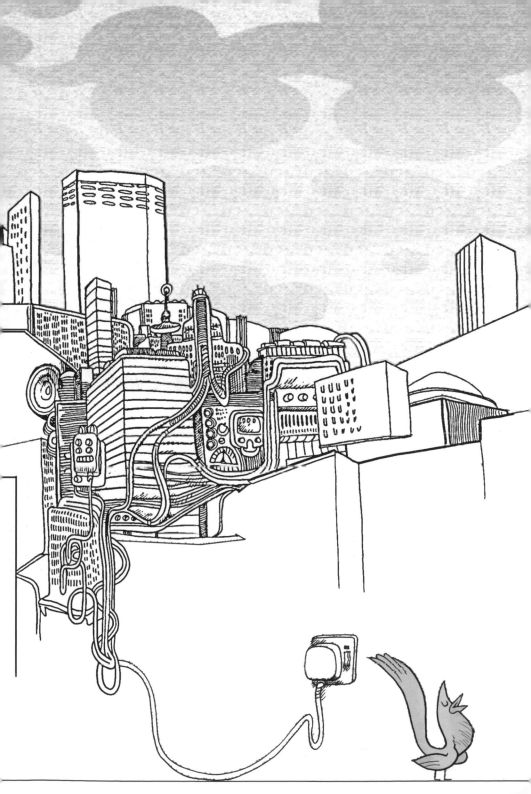

Men-machines: **Kraftwerk**.

with mid-century noise pollution (a term the composer himself almost certainly would have abjured). But it takes its sonic cues from the industrialised world in a way quite unlike steadfastly humanist genres such as rock, pop and jazz.

This isn't to say that earlier musical forms didn't take similar inspiration from industrialism and urbanism. Consider George Antheil's score for Fernand Léger's 1924 film *Ballet Mécanique*, which incorporated player-pianos, electric bells, sirens and even aeroplane propellers. Country, folk and blues would be unthinkable without the rhythms of rail travel and the lonesome wail of the locomotive. Detroit rockers the Stooges, prefacing the *motorik* pulse of both Kraftwerk and Detroit techno, derived their own pistoning garage rock in part from the chug of the local automobile factories. But in contemporary electronic music, Luigi Russolo's Futurist categorisation of noises – roars, whistles, jingles, 'baked earth' sounds and the like – has become the blueprint of a musical form at once mimetic of the industrialised world and transformative of it, determined to transcend the modern city's

shimmering, compromised façades by folding its strata deep within the music itself.

From its origins in musique concrète, Miles Davis and Teo Macero's cut-and-paste jazz compositions and Chicago's spliced-tape disco edits, electronic music has embraced, celebrated and advanced the cause of a post-humanist aesthetic rooted in the Futurists' desired communion with steel and cement. A continuation of the course paved first in gaslight and macadam, later steel girders and glass skin, and finally silicon and fiber optics, electronic music champions the man-made over the naturalistic. Radically disembodied, a showcase of sound divorced from its source (what composer R Murray Schafer has lamented as 'schizophonia'), today's electronic music flowers simultaneously in gardens of circuitry and the jungle of the jumbled, psychedelic mind. But the roots of the music, like those of its social formations, are found in the cities of the late 20th century.

Many of electronic music's fundamental tropes can be read as reflections of the urban, industrialised experience. The music's self-conscious futurism – not just in its alien sounds and impossible sequences, but in its very founding myths, in aliases like Phuture, Cybotron, Inner City and Model 500 – encapsulates what writer Kodwo Eshun has called 'the artificiality that all humans crave'. As Caspar Pound, head of the Rising High record label, enthused in a 1991 interview with *iD*, 'The best thing about [techno subgenre] hardcore is all the soul's been taken out. We've had 200 years of the human element in music and it's about time for a change.' As Eshun puts it, 'Sonic futurism always adopts a cruel, despotic, amoral attitude towards the human species.' But instead of lamenting such apparent amorality, electronic music's most devoted followers embrace it.

Indeed, the music's recombinant aesthetic, in which no single song is ever its own end, might be seen as a reflection of the way cities are perpetually rebuilt, with the unchanging grid below giving way to a mutable skyline above. While Malvina Reynolds and Pete Seeger parodied suburban norms in the folk song 'Little Boxes', house and techno celebrate architectural uniformity by building tracks that take the shape of little boxes themselves: compact rhythmic machines designed to be stacked on top of one another, soldered and cemented together under the hands of the DJ.

Kraftwerk are a virtual archetype of the way in which techno learned from cities and, in turn, cities learned from techno. The Düsseldorf band's name even translates as 'power plant', at once both reflecting the post-war fascination with the trappings of industrial life and prefacing the role that deindustrialisation would play in techno's renegade urban footprint. (Berlin's Berghain, one of the world's most celebrated nightclubs, is itself situated in a remodelled former *kraftwerk*.) And the group's aesthetic, robotic men-machines standing stock-still behind their synthesizers, prefaced a shift from 20th-century Fordist production to the so-called 'knowledge workers' of the 21st century, dirtying their hands only with data.

Again and again, cities have figured as heroic figures and organising forces in techno's development. Detroit is its ground zero, a metaphor that's doubly apt given the way in which Detroit techno found inspiration in the ruins of a city that had been emptied by the riots of the 1970s and the economic failure of the '80s. Inspired by the sophisticated futurism and urbane artifice of Kraftwerk, new wave and Italo-disco, Detroit's black teenagers invented their own music, pounded out on cheap, discontinued Japanese synthesizers and drum machines, to be laid over their own unglamorous urban experiences. Simon Reynolds has written that Cybotron's 'Techno City', one of the genre's founding tracks, 'was inspired by Fritz Lang's vision in *Metropolis* of a future megalopolis divided into privileged sectors high up in the sky and subterranean prole zones.'

Throughout the history of Detroit techno, the scene has been defined by a defiant localism that can't simply be reduced to nostalgia for a once-proud city. 'At Peace with Concrete', a 1998 track by Detroit's Urban Tribe, emphasises the ambivalence felt by its creators for their dilapidated surroundings. And the title of *The Collapse of Modern Culture*, the album on which it's found, can be seen as both a cry of protest and a glumly Romantic paean to decay, a post-industrial 'Ozymandias'. An outlaw genre with its origins in renegade parties, techno needed space in which to develop. With its unused buildings and emptied streets, Detroit provided it.

Berlin provided another such locus of musical and cultural possibility. After the Wall came down, DJs, promoters and dancers recolonised the abandoned warehouses of the blighted former East. And as techno's followers drew new maps to reorder a city whose circulation had so long been stoppered, they served to jump-start both the process of reunification and the real-estate speculation that continues to reshape the city's layout today. The seminal 1992 collection *Tresor II: Berlin & Detroit – A Techno Alliance* cemented a link between the two cities that had already been forged through sound.

For all the stylistic differences between the many strands of contemporary electronic music, they share certain sonic strategies, many of them redolent of the urban environment from which they emerged. The four-to-the-floor kick drum, the common denominator of virtually all house, techno and trance, echoes piledrivers staking out the site of a new high-rise; both literally and metaphorically, it's the music's foundation. The long, clean lines and short, repeated phrases of minimal techno, its parallel lines of hi-hats and snares, are akin to the organising principles of the International Style of architecture; this is as true of mid 1990s tracks such as Jeff Mills's 'The Bells' and Robert Hood's 'Station Rider E' as it is of more recent cuts such as Audion's 'Mouth to Mouth'. And as minimal house and techno have become looser and more liquid, no longer pegged to the rigid quantisation of the MIDI clock, they've taken on the rippling forms of Frank Gehry's complex, computer-aided surfaces. The polymorphous undulations of Ricardo Villalobos's albums *Achso* and *Thé au harem d'Archimède* recall nothing so much as the mercurial forms of Gehry's Guggenheim Bilbao.

Indeed, electronic music's focus on timbre and texture, in which the tonal colour of a given sample or synthesised sound eclipses the more conventionally musical traits of melody and harmony, reflects the play of surfaces that give the city its three-dimensional character: shimmering granite, expanses of plate glass, neon cast across back-alley façades. The three-dimensional vectors shooting through Sun Electric's 1996 track 'Parallax' bring to mind the sort of light-and-shadow-play captured by photographer Garry Winogrand in his sidewalk study 'Los Angeles, California', in which human agents are borne along arrows of sunlight reflected off glass and concrete like tracers of some hidden urban energy currents.

Of course, not all electronic music's urban investments are self-consciously futuristic; there are also pre-industrial echoes deep within techno. The bell tones and tolling syncopations of Superpitcher's 'More Tomorrow' and Efdemin's 'Acid Bells' are rooted in the church bells that have rung over Europe for centuries and become encoded in its citizens' sonic DNA, while the rhythms of house and techno are generally traced back to African drum circles. However, the vertical arrangement of much electronic music evokes skylines every bit as dizzying as *Blade Runner*'s. Taking cues from Steve Reich's 'Music for 18 Musicians', most electronic music stacks element upon element, finding its motion not only in the headlong tumble of a steadily galloping beat but also in the overlay of polyrhythms and the multiplication of overtones.

Less impressionistically, the sound of the city has literally made itself heard in electronic music of all stripes, but particularly that with a multicultural charge. Reich's early tape compositions 'It's Gonna Rain' and 'Come Out'

both find their musical logic in fragments of speech with explicit ties to the urban experience; the former is a looped recording of a preacher holding court in San Francisco's Union Square, while the latter is derived from the testimony of a black youth who had been arrested and beaten by police during the 1964 Harlem riots. Three decades later, Reich extended the idea of folding found sound into music with 'City Life', which wedded a small ensemble of woodwinds, strings and percussion with the sampled sounds of car alarms, piledrivers, police sirens and even recordings of the New York Fire Department's field communications on the day that the World Trade Center was bombed in 1993.

The documentary impulse continues to inform electronic music's bricolage aesthetic. Although she spent part of her childhood in Sri Lanka, MIA's music is animated by the cultural cacophony endemic to the immigrant-dominated London neighbourhoods in which she grew up. On *Kala*, Indian bhangra, Jamaican reggae and black British hip hop collide to echo the sound of her own urban upbringing; the sonic vérité of 'Paper Planes' even extends to gunshots and cash registers punctuating the chorus. It's not simply a question of musical influence: urban British dance music like that made by MIA, or like jungle before her, holds its ground at the site of a hypothetical soundclash, those Jamaican musical duels where victory goes to the loudest sound system and the rudest MC. 'Bombscare' by early hardcore outfit 2 Bad Mice, like so much of hardcore and jungle's grimly apocalyptic output, exorcises urban dread by indulging terror fantasies, exploding breakbeats into atomic particles and filling the sonic spectrum with the long decay of an actual bomb explosion.

Working in a more rarefied sector than the jungle clubs in which dancers cock their fingers in a pantomime of gunplay to the accompaniment of beats born from the cadences of automatic weapons, German sound artist Christina Kubisch approaches the sound of the city as might an archaeologist. Hers, though, is the archaeology of the present. Kubisch's *Electrical Walks*, in which listeners are fitted with headphones designed to capture and amplify the ambient electromagnetic waves being emitted by cash machines, television monitors, anti-theft systems and even electric trams, uncover the hidden wiring of the city. Where Susan Sontag was concerned with the 'ecology of images' threatening to smother viewers in an overgrown mediascape, Kubisch attends to an ecology of sounds, the ubiquitous and possibly pernicious frequencies that bombard us every second of every day.

Instead of forging a straight course down the sidewalk, the participant on a Kubisch walk bobs and weaves, all the better to catch stray electromagnetic waves. The ears are no longer a support system for the body: the body now puts itself entirely at the service of its hearing, with all other senses rendered secondary. It feels not unlike the experience of meandering through the city after an all-night party, with drugs still in one's system and the fabric of consensual reality rendered unusually permeable.

Kubisch's Situationist-influenced urban interventions are more properly the realm of the avant-garde art gallery than the populist dancefloor. However, the sounds she accentuates carry an uncanny similarity to the queasy sine-wave undulations foregrounded by such ultra-minimalists as Carsten Nicolai and Ø (Mika Vainio), whose CD *Mikro Makro*

harnesses the buzz of magnetic resonance imaging systems and radio-telescope recordings and smudges it into an uneasy drone reminiscent of high-voltage power lines. Like many experimental electronic musicians of the '00s, Nicolai and Vainio approach ambient music by turning the principle behind it upside down. Where Brian Eno's *Music for Airports* proposed a music tailored to industrialised environments, 'glitch' artists cut tiny fragments from the world – electromagnetic hum, skipping CDs, failing hard drives – in order to create snapshots of post-industrial frailty.

The Doppler effect – the apparent slowing-down of a sound, such as an ambulance's siren, as it passes the listener – is a reminder of the way in which individuals are continually being sucked into the sound patterns of the city and then spat out again. It's the sound of alienation, of the impossibility of keeping up with the city. The queasy filters of Paperclip People's 'Throw' are brimming with the melting tonalities of the Doppler effect, defamiliarising the good-time stomp of classic disco in the same way that Berlin collective Chain Reaction's reductionist dub techno emphasises urban alienation by simulating the sound of a nightclub as heard

'Los Angeles, California', taken by **Garry Winogrand** in 1969.

from blocks away. The Chain Reaction artist known as Various Artists, whose alias takes techno's facelessness to the point of absurdity, is a prime example of this strategy, smearing sonic details into an indistinct blur and leaving only the kick drum's chugging pulse as a reminder of the music's dancefloor origins.

For all their influence over the urban character of electronic music, from city-minded pioneers such as Cybotron and the subwoofer-bumping hot-rodders of the Miami bass scene through to proud former East Berliner Ellen Allien (her first two albums are called *Stadkind* and *Berlinette*) and Various Artists, Kraftwerk didn't limit themselves to the urban environment. Indeed, with songs such as 'Autobahn' and 'Trans-Europe Express', they led the exodus out of the city into a new, interconnected and borderless space where non-place is the same as every-place. As David Toop has written, 'Kraftwerk's fascination with the endless vanishing points of motorways and railway tracks [provided] the structural model on which their own compositions were based.' That structural model remains the foundation for house and techno today: an endless beat, a continuum-pulse 'without measure or end', to borrow a phrase from an album by the electro-acoustic improvisers AMM. Electronic music may be the last urban music of the 20th century, but it's also the first post-urban music of the 21st.

For electronic music also offers a reminder that cities have lost much of their status as the world's primary creative hubs. Detroit techno arose from the middle-class suburbs of Detroit; its African American originators dressed in fashions found in *GQ*, named their parties after exclusive clothing stores and idolised music imported from Europe. The UK's acid house culture was transplanted from the gay black discos of Chicago and developed in the Balearic resort of Ibiza; the rave movement of the late 1980s and early '90s thrived in the countryside, where space was plentiful and police were not; and Ibiza and Goa continue to reinforce the idea of house music as the soundtrack for island getaways. Cities aren't irrelevant: every week, another well-known musician moves to Berlin to take advantage of its low rents, lax laws and tight-knit musical community. But in the US, where the once-venerable cities of Detroit, Chicago and New York no longer boast particularly vibrant scenes, many listeners' primary interface to the movement is their computer.

In 2004, the artist known as Deadbeat – raised in Kichener, Ontario, then resident in Montreal and latterly in Berlin – performed a concert from the bridge of a tugboat as it circumnavigated the harbour in Valparaiso, Chile. His audience was not on board but scattered across a flotilla of a dozen or so launches, each carrying a dozen life-jacketed listeners tuning in to a sound that seemed to filter Jamaican dub reggae through the lens of contemporary techno. As the tugboat made its way through the harbour, Deadbeat's digital delays and synthesised echo effects were supplemented by naturally occurring reverberation and Dopplering. At one point, with the flotilla bobbing between the tugboat and a massive dry dock, a proliferation of echoes threatened to drown the downbeat in ghost tones.

The aquatic metaphors inherent in the sound couldn't have been clearer. Deeply influenced by African rhythms, Jamaican dub and African American forms, electronic music has been described as a product of what the cultural critic Paul Gilroy calls 'the Black Atlantic'. Detroit techno outfit Drexciya claim to represent an amphibious race spawned from pregnant African women who were thrown overboard during the Middle Passage; Berlin techno veterans and dub enthusiasts Porter Ricks named themselves after a dolphin and regularly nod to the ocean in the titles of tracks such as 'Nautical Dub,' 'Port of Call' and 'Trident'. And as the 21st century barrels onwards, electronic music is becoming ever more liquid. House and techno may be the products of asphalt, but in the 21st century, the city most relevant to electronic music will be a lost one: Atlantis.

The sound of the city in 20 songs

'After Rapidly Circling the Plaza' AMM

AMM's uncompromising aesthetic reflects both the cultural underground from which they emerged and the metropolis that inspired them. This 23-minute blast of improvised noise is as vicious as they got.

'INQB8TR' Bark Psychosis

'INQB8TR' isn't *about* the urban environment per se. There are no direct references to it in title or lyrics, and no lazy sonic signifiers. But its dreamy yet edgy sound world, at once agoraphobic and claustrophobic, seems drawn from the very fabric of London.

'Frankie Machine' Elmer Bernstein

Shorty Rogers' variation on the Bernstein's theme for *The Man with the Golden Arm* perfectly evokes the the urban underbelly to which Frank Sinatra's jazz-drumming, card-dealing junkie returns after a spell in jail, and which was surely his downfall in the first place. The blaring horns grab the attention, but the whole thing lives and dies on the fevered clatter of Shelly Manne's hi-hat.

'City Wakes Up' Biosphere

Geir Jenssen's slow-moving electronica is generally inspired by the natural world, and particularly the Norwegian rurality he calls home. But in 1996, he built a new score for *Man with a Movie Camera*, an essentially narrative-free documentary about urban life in Russia during the 1920s. Driven by a soft but relentless metronomic pulse and awash with distant rattle and echo, 'City Wakes Up' is its highlight.

'The Downtown Lights' The Blue Nile

The first pair of albums from Glasgow's Blue Nile are two sides of the same coin. While *A Walk Across the Rooftops* photographs the city between sun-up and sundown, the warmer, lusher *Hats* soundtracks the same streets after dark. The imagery evoked by Paul Buchanan verges on the hackneyed, but the gleaming music and Buchanan's weary yet yearning voice transcend the clichés to the point where this is essentially wee-small-hours Sinatra with synths.

'Abandoned Cities' Harold Budd

'I'm in love with titles,' writes Budd on the notes to this album, conceived to accompany an art installation in 1983. 'What they say is one thing; what they mean as they whistle through my life is something else.' Listeners are presumably welcome to take this heavy, sullen piece of ambience however they please; we prefer to think of it as a deserted downtown taking a laboured deep breath before the morning arrives and it has to go through the whole damn day all over again.

'Distant Lights' Burial

'When I'm awake all night,' admitted this wilfully anonymous dubstep musician to *The Guardian* in 2007, 'sometimes I see the people and the city waking up around me. I feel a bit moody at them for stepping into my night-time. What I want is that feeling when you're in the rain… It's a shiver at the edge of your mind, an atmosphere of hearing a sad, distant sound, but it seems closer, like it's just for you.'

'First Construction (In Metal)' John Cage

'First Construction (In Metal)' seems to wed Russolo's Futurist aesthetic to Cage's auditory perception of the industrial city. Driven by a perpetual pulse, it's both breakable and unshakeable.

'Alleys of Your Mind' Cybotron

The early '80s singles issued by Juan Atkins and Richard Davis come across as a virtual hybrid of New York electro and Kraftwerk's 'perfection *mekanik*'. However, there's little doubt that the duo were just as driven by the dystopian Detroit they called home.

'Kollaps' Einstürzende Neubauten

What could possibly sound more urban than music made using not only the tools that built the city, but parts of the city itself? Built from the rattle and clash of sheet metal and power tools, the first album from Einstürzende Neubauten (translation: 'Collapsing New Buildings') is an uncompromising statement of intent. More than 25 years on, its title track remains a terrifying blast of noise from the city's core.

'City of Light' Fennesz

A humming, intense, static-soaked miniature; not unlike tuning in to the city's power grid.

'The Grid' Philip Glass

Glass's music for Godfrey Reggio's impressionistic 1983 film *Koyaanisqatsi* both evokes and mimics the action (and, often, the inaction) on screen. 'The Grid' is the urban centrepiece of both movie and soundtrack.

'Herculean' The Good, the Bad & the Queen

Blur's album *Modern Life Is Rubbish* aimed to capture something about London in the early '90s, but it did so entirely through Damon Albarn's lyrics and not through any great sonic invention. The Good, the Bad & the Queen was another matter – never more so than on this rattling, anxious ballad, a kind of 25-years-on reworking of the Clash's 'Ghetto Defendant'.

'Here's Looking at You' Charlie Haden Quartet West

Haden's inspiration is the Los Angeles of the '30s and '40s: Chandler and Fante, chrome and cigarettes. This is deeply nostalgic jazz, soaked in strings and cloaked in smoke. But 60 years after the era to which it's in such thrall, Haden's languid music can still evoke it in a heartbeat or two.

'In the City of Red Dust' Jon Hassell

'The city twitching in delirium tremens,' reckoned writer and musician David Toop about *City: Works of Fiction*. And it's never twitchier than on this fizzing, disorientating collage of polyrhythms, samples and digital manipulation.

'…Of Lights' Jack

Anthony Reynolds' Altman-esque intermingling of several urban snapshots lurches to ragged but compelling life under the tutelage of Scott Walker's producer Peter Walsh, found sound moving in and out of focus above an ever-present bass drone and a group that constantly threatens to explode but always stays in the shadows.

'Neon Lights' Kraftwerk

In typically contrary fashion, the warmest moment in Kraftwerk's catalogue is a blinking, twinkling ode to artificiality, and to the nostalgia and romance it provokes and evokes. See them play it live, and you'll be greeted with a backdrop of Düsseldorf neon shot by the group themselves in the 1970s.

'*' M83

The third album from French act M83 is one record you're safe to judge by its cover. The sleeve of *Before the Dawn Heals Us* pictures a gleaming urban skyline at night, its plugged-in luminescence ebbing away towards a coal-black sky. A fearsome collision between fever-pitch guitar-rock and heady synth-pop, '*' is as close as the record comes to capturing it in sound.

'The Morning Commute' Jerry Martin

Martin has said that this orchestral piece was inspired by the drive into San Francisco, and specifically by the traffic approaching the ever-busy toll-gate that guards the Bay Bridge entrance to the city. As the strings swoop and soar and French horns sound a distant fanfare, trumpets mimic the horns of the jostling cars. Composed for the soundtrack of the computer game *SimCity 4: Rush Hour*.

'Amériques' Edgard Varèse

Written soon after the thirtysomething composer left his native Paris for the United States during World War I, 'Amériques' is the sound of a musician captivated by his new surroundings, of '20s New York City brought vividly to life by a sizeable orchestra and a cacophonous percussion section. It was completed in 1922 but not performed until 1926; in the intervening four years, New York witnessed the premiere of Gershwin's 'Rhapsody in Blue', the work's more civilised cousin.

States of
mind

Sylvie Simmons studies America's myth of itself.

At the end of 2007, I was sent an album called *Song of America*, three CDs (one red, one white, one blue) that purported to tell the history of the USA through 50 of its popular songs. It was curated, oddly, by former US Attorney General Janet Reno, a woman not known for her musical chops. Reportedly, her motivation was to interest the youth of America in their nation's past and, by extension, identity.

There might have been better ways of achieving this ambition than asking a motley collection of artists (John Mellencamp, Martha Wainwright, Take 6, Beth Nielsen Chapman, the Black Crowes and others) to cover songs about liberty, slavery, the Civil War, civil rights, dead Indians and the atom bomb. But, as invariably happens when a themed compilation collides with a music journalist, what it did do was start me thinking about which songs I'd select for my own *Song of America* album.

There's no shortage of material from which to choose. America's myth of itself, like its T-shirts, comes in one size: extra-large. Curiously, though, as my list started growing – Simon & Garfunkel's 'America', Kris Kristofferson's 'Me and Bobby McGee', Roger Miller's 'King of the Road', Little Feat's 'Willin'', Tom Waits's '(Looking for) The Heart of Saturday Night', Tom Petty & the Heartbreakers' 'American Girl', Bruce Springsteen's 'Thunder Road'   it seemed that, in this instance, one size really does fit all. Because once the decorations were removed, the songs I picked were all about much the same thing: movement. Moving to, as you'd expect from a nation of immigrants, and moving on.

For a diversionary few hours, I found myself making lists of American songs that paid homage to towns and cities. Not the obvious ones, the likes of New York, New Orleans, Nashville, Los Angeles, Las Vegas and San Francisco, but the less glamorous spots. Often, the less exotic the place, the more haunting the song: 'Galveston', 'El Paso', 'Do You Know the Way to San José', 'Fort Worth Blues', 'Knoxville Girl' and, of course, 'Wichita Lineman', one of the most evocative songs in all of American pop.

From 'Me and Bobby McGee' to 'Boulder to Birmingham', Emmylou Harris's moving (in both senses) tribute to Gram Parsons, there are plenty more songs that list multiple places. 'I've Been Everywhere', recorded by singers such as Hank Snow and Johnny Cash, namechecks more than 80 towns, while the unquashable truck driver in Little Feat's aforementioned 'Willin'' ticks off half the towns in the 'T' section before taking the traditional American outlaw route to the US–Mexico border and back again. Indeed, movement is one of the characteristics that distinguishes American songs from British songs, especially in relation to cars. Those early songs by the Beach Boys and Springsteen paint cars as almost mythical things, symbols of masculinity, independence and glory. In America, cars mean endless highways, moving on, escaping. In Britain, cars mean traffic jams, the M25, going in circles or going nowhere at all.

And since there's nowhere to go, it stands to reason why the British don't really do those American-style love songs to towns. It's not just that US place names often sound so much

Rewind
Tom Waits

Tom Waits thrums his fingers on the table. Scratches his chin. Casts around the room: piles of CDs, a cased guitar on a couch and a glass coffee pot before him, stained brown.

'My feeling is, to a certain degree, all sounds are music. And of course it's your job to decide what you think's appropriate for the project and what's not. If you realise that when you hit this furnace with the leg of a chair as hard as you can, you get a better sound than you do on your drum set, then you're going hit the furnace with the chair.

'I like my music with a little bit of grind and grime and rind. I like it with the pits and peel. I remember those early Bob Dylan bootlegs that were so difficult to hear. The quality of them was so bad that it actually added to the mythology. It's like when you listen to an old Caruso 78 and you hear the scratches, and it sounds like he's trying to reach you from the bottom of a mine.

'It's important to travel your own path. Conformity is a fool's paradise. I think I'm influenced by people just like everyone else is, but I try to fight the urge to conform. I keep wanting to use turntables and stuff, but my wife says no, she says that's going to be like a ducktail eventually, or a flat-top or a Mohawk. And I struggle with that. I can't really tell.

'I mean, most musicians don't go to school: they listen to records. They sit down next to a record player and put their ear up there and wonder, "What the hell's he doing on that thing?" and try to learn off it. And I assume somebody at some point will do that with my records. It's a natural cycle to the whole experience of evolving as a musician yourself: you hope others evolve. I love slave songs and work songs and jump-rope songs, all those early beginnings, and where it's going and where it is now and where it'll be in ten years.'

And what's he listening to now?

'Well, I really like Wu-Tang Clan. Those guys kill me. And there's this guy named Bob Log III. You ever heard of him? He wears a motorcycle helmet and has a microphone inside of it, puts the glass over the front so you can't see his face, and he plays slide guitar. It's just the loudest, strangest stuff you've ever heard. You don't understand one word he's saying. I like people who glue macaroni on to a piece of cardboard and paint it gold. That's what I aspire to.' He sits back and grins a crooked grin.

Ross Fortune; from Time Out, *24 April 2002*

more seductive than our Anglo-Saxon variety ('Do You Know the Way to Scunthorpe', anyone?); it's that there simply aren't that many cities in the UK that raise a spark in a heart hungry for adventure. The country is just too small. Which is why when the British romanticise a specific geographical place, it tends to be in miniature: a park or a street, such as the still-life 'Penny Lane'.

It's partly context. To me, born and raised in London but now living in the US, British songs feel like real life, whereas American songs have a dreamlike, cinematic quality. Even American songs whose characters or situations come from a gritty reality – pretty much anything from Tom Waits's album *The Heart of Saturday Night*, say, or one of Springsteen's sympathy-for-the-working-stiff songs – feel like they exist in some strangely lit world the other side of a barroom looking-glass.

I was listening to the Kinks's 'Waterloo Sunset' recently when, for the first time, I noticed the effect of the Americana element – the old rolling river – on a song set in the middle of a prosaic inner-London scene: it adds an element of agoraphobia. Londoners are used to rush-hour claustrophobia, so it must be the agoraphobia that sends the lovers scurrying away to a place where they can be safe and sound. America, if you step outside its cities or towns, is not a place for agoraphobics.

I'd been trying to figure out for some time why, though I felt such a strong connection with almost any kind of British music, I loathed traditional British folk. Especially since I'm very fond of American folk, which musicologists will tell you is British and Irish folk brought by emigrants to the US. Part of the anathema doubtless stems from traumatic childhood memories of loud, over-enunciating music teachers warbling 'The Bay of Biscay-O'; or, worse yet, country dancing. But it's more than that. There's something claustrophobic about it. Much British folk seems to stay in one, small, proudly unchanging, pastoral place. But when these old British songs were taken across the water, bumped in wagon trains across wild terrains and hauled up into the Appalachians, they were given movement and space.

Americans would probably say they gave them freedom, same as they gave the immigrants. But, of course, space can feel a lot like freedom, and in America there's a

'The themes of leaving home and missing home stuck around long after the mass displacements of the Depression and the Dust Bowl gave way to prosperity and suburbanisation.'

whole lot of space: not just geographic, but psychological. One thing you notice from those old American songs about hardship and trouble and death is that there's still a sense of confidence, however unfounded in reality, in their hopes of a brighter tomorrow, if not in this world then the next. Actual optimism in the face of adversity, in other words, as opposed to Britain's dark humour, nihilism and stiff upper lips. The other big difference between the US and the UK, besides the space, is that Americans are all about Yes We Can, while the British are Don't Be Fucking Daft. That's what keeps Americans moving on.

Interestingly, though, all the while that the characters in American song have their eye on the future, they have a powerful sense of the past. When they're moving on, there's almost always the presence, whether overt or implied, of what they're moving from. *Home*. Sometimes, this being a nation of immigrants, it's another country; sometimes it's bricks and wood and a chimney. Still, the ghost of home is generally there.

In Tom Petty's 'American Girl', it's in that 'one desperate moment' when the past sneaks up on a woman just as she's planning her getaway. In Simon & Garfunkel's 'America', it's when the boy on the Greyhound bus, the only soul still awake, watches the moon rise over an open field and feels achingly empty and lost. And in Jimmy Webb's 'By the Time I Get to Phoenix', it's how the miles the protagonist puts between himself and his past are constantly measured against thoughts of home and what his wife will be doing there.

BEING THERE

The hungover drifter in Kris Kristofferson's 'Sunday Mornin' Comin' Down' is taken back, by the smell of chicken being fried, to something that he'd left behind 'somewhere along the way'. And in Kristofferson's much-covered 'Me and Bobby McGee', a young couple hitch the enormous distance from Louisiana to California together, until that moment when Bobby takes off alone, 'looking for a home'. This duality between leaving home and feeling homesick is what fuels the extravagant sentimentality and neon-lit nostalgia of those great Tom Waits songs, with their longing for a lost past that never was. It also fuels the mawkishness of a great deal of country music.

Back in the 1920s, when country was still called 'hillbilly' music (and jazz and blues was known as 'race' music), a young New York record executive named Ralph Peer set up a temporary recording studio in Bristol, on the Virginia–Tennessee border, and advertised in newspapers for talent. That summer of 1927, he found 19 acts, two of whom would become major stars. One was Jimmie Rodgers, a hard-living, yodelling white bluesman from Mississippi who'd learned to sing and play from black railroad workers, and who made his way to the audition by hopping the trains. The other was the Carter Family, sober, rural Christians who sang the old church songs and folk songs on which they'd been raised, and who'd driven down from the mountain in a borrowed car, wearing their Sunday best.

The Bristol sessions became known as the Big Bang of country. All country music since has some element of either Jimmie Rodgers' happy-go-lucky, blues-picking, drinking, womanising hobo, who moved on for the simple sake of moving on, or the Carter Family's stark, pious world, in which you left home only to find work or escape catastrophe and with a heart full of sorrow, or if you were carried away from it in a box bound for your heavenly home. Often it had elements of both: Hank Williams, a Rodgers disciple, had a side career recording moralising songs as travelling preacher Luke the Drifter, while Johnny Cash, who toured with and married into the Mark II Carter family, had parallel lives as a gospel singer, a Bible scholar and the amphetamine-stoked Man in Black.

The themes of leaving home and missing home stuck around long after the mass displacements of the Dustbowl and the Depression gave way to prosperity and suburbanisation. So did hedonism and stoicism. When country music was co-opted, along with blues and boogie-woogie, into rock 'n' roll, the motifs all settled happily into their new surroundings. And when rock 'n' roll became rock, the themes coalesced into the form of one great American archetype: the cowboy, an independent spirit, a man's man, rugged and free, at one with the wild landscape, riding into town, hitting the bottle, grabbing the girl, doing what a man's got to do and then moving on.

Historically, the classic cowboy era didn't last long, even in a history as short as America's: 20-odd years in the late 19th century, between the rise of the cattle industry and the bigger rise of the railroads. But the cowboy is tattooed right through the American psyche and culture: in film, of course, but also in literature (Hemingway and Mailer are as much cowboy writers as Cormac McCarthy and Zane Grey), on TV (from the reruns of down-homey *Little House on the Prairie* to reality show *Cowboy Me*, the wannabe Stetson-wearer's equivalent of *The Apprentice*) and even in commercials (those ads in which tank-sized SUVs normally seen drifting through shopping-mall car parks instead race through the wilderness, kicking up dust as they head towards the sunset). It's in religion: that wilderness again, with Jesus taking on the devil *mano a mano*. And it's in their politics: George W Bush's inarticulate Texan machismo is pure cowboy, as, at heart, is California governor Arnold Schwarzenegger, the classic taciturn strongman.

The cowboy, Rousseau's Natural Man fused with a king-size Marlboro Man, does for Americans what the Académie Française tries to do for the French: provide it with an identity based on a pure and impossible ideal. It's impossible because the Académie's obsession with having an 'authentic' French language into which foreign words can't intrude is ultimately as futile as a 21st-century American identifying with a ready-romanticised 19th-century figure altered out of all recognition by 20th-century cinema, literature and song, and somehow finding it authentic.

The country's widespread identification with a harsh rural Southern past is odd, but it's there wherever you look. There was an article in the *New York Times* a while back about a place in the Appalachian foothills of south-east

Kris Kristofferson, live in 1975.

Ohio that had become a popular weekend getaway among stressed-out New York executives. It was a music camp where city slickers could shuck off their suits, sleep in bunk-house cabins, learn to pick tunes on an acoustic guitar or a banjo, and generally channel their inner hillbilly or cowboy.
A quick canter through the internet will throw up any number of dude-ranch vacations aimed at urbanites.

Interestingly, the cowboy hat, that symbol of wide open plains and rugged masculinity, was invented by a sickly urbanite, a milliner from what was then the second largest city in the country. When John B Stetson's doctor in Philadelphia suggested a trip out west for his health, he showed some hunter friends his party trick of turning a dozen beavers into a big, waterproof hat (skin them, dunk the pelts in boiling water, knead them until the fibres interlock, shape into a broad-rimmed bucket and poke a dent in the top). They proved so popular that when he got back to Philadelphia, he started manufacturing them. It was 1865. The United States was just 89 years old.

Real cowboys these days wear caps; Stetsons don't really cut it in trucks. The best place to see a cowboy hat nowadays is on Country Music Television, at the gatherings favoured by the largely suburbanite audiences of neutered Nashville contemporary country, or in gay bars (Ang Lee's *Brokeback Mountain*). Tom Waits may be Stetson-free, but he's arguably a cowboy poet. On *The Heart of Saturday Night*, the guy hopping the trains, gassing up the car and heading for a place

where the clouds are 'like headlines on a new front-page sky' (even if he ends up in a bar) isn't all that different from the solitary man on the horse riding into another sunset.

Similarly, Bruce Springsteen's battered-but-not-completely-broken working-class men on *Born to Run* haven't entirely given up on the Promised Land, aka the American Dream, however far in the distance it may be. The roads leading there may be almost as jammed as they are in Britain, albeit not with commuter traffic but with 'broken heroes on a last-chance power drive' ('Born to 'Run') or the skeletons of abandoned cars and the ghosts of abandoned lovers. But, in big gestures, as if this were a Cinemascope Western and not a blue-collar song, Springsteen's protagonist declares that freedom can be theirs. They may be living in 'a town full of losers' ('Thunder Road'), but there's hope beyond the city limits.

By the time he reached *Nebraska*, Springsteen had soured on the American Dream. Inspired by *Badlands*, Terrence Malick's movie about a killing spree, the 1982 album was populated by desperate people with no use for innocent idealism or the power of rock 'n' roll. Moving on did no good here. Instead of gleaming cars riding through mansions of glory, there's a grey sky and snow weighing down the windscreen wipers, and a grim, unending highway with nowhere to turn off. When, in the album's title track, the judge asks the murderer why he did it, he answers, 'Well, sir, I guess there's just a meanness in this world.'

On his last tour before recording the solo *Nebraska*, Springsteen had been covering 'This Land Is Your Land', Woody Guthrie's ballad of the dispossessed, and the one John Mellencamp tackles on *Song of America*. There's also a Springsteen composition on *Song of America*, covered, in one of the best performances on the album, by soul veteran Bettye LaVette. It's a place-name song, but not a glory song or a cowboy moderne song or an American Dream song or a moving-on song. It's 'Streets of Philadelphia', a song about AIDS.

A quarter century later, getting a handle on America's idea of itself isn't easy. The Bush victory divided the US down the middle, and the internet chopped each half into tiny pieces. Cyberspace isn't like real space: online, you can reinvent yourself over and over in seconds, and you don't need the American identity to do

On the record
Lamont Dozier

'I Can't Make You Love Me'

Bonnie Raitt

This was written by two Nashville guys called Mike Reid and Allen Shamblin. Mike Reid used to play in the NFL for the Cincinnati Bengals – he only ended up writing songs when he was injured and out of the game. And Allen Shamblin wrote a string of country hits in the 1980s and '90s, including 'Don't Laugh at Me' [by Mark Wills]. But 'I Can't Make You Love Me' is their classic.

Apparently, it comes from a real-life news story about a guy who's been harassing his ex-girlfriend – the judge said to him, 'You can't make someone love you.' The song turns that into a heartbreaking tale of unrequited love, about someone who doesn't want to be patronised but knows that the object of her desire will never love her. Bonnie's version is the best known, but it's such a pure song that it can be done with just a piano and a voice. I saw Mike Reid perform it in Nashville and I completely choked up. I was in tears, all over the place. Very embarrassing!

With the Holland brothers, Lamont Dozier wrote and produced countless Motown hits in the '60s, among them 'Where Did Our Love Go' by the Supremes and 'Nowhere to Run' by Martha & the Vandellas

so. And with the record industry gone to the dogs and the number of independent artists increasing daily, it's hard to find a collective identity to which everyone subscribes in the truly popular song. There's talk, with so many people stuck at computers and the cost of gasoline soaring, of America having slowed down: becoming unwilling to move, and growing extremely hostile towards people – immigrants and visitors – who do.

So when an American act that first found success in the UK bring back with them another little bit of England, in tribute to those old British emigrants, the words 'Icky Thump' carry considerably more resonance than they otherwise might. As Jack White puts it: America, 'You're an immigrant, too.'

Forever England

In brief? The English like putting on a show but get easily embarrassed. Sentimentality and earnestness are to be sniggered at. We share an understanding of in-jokes, camp and brickies in make-up, none of which translate abroad unless it involves some or all of the cast of *Monty Python's Flying Circus*. We are always apologetic, and have an appetite for both discipline and anarchy. We're as changeable as the weather, which we love to go on about. It rains and we're melancholy. Or we moan. Losers are venerated; we root for the underdog. Pretty much, the English define passive-aggressive.

Strip away the Celtic influence in British song, try to find the bare bones of Englishness, and you uncover a strange and intoxicating musical catalogue. Let's put the Beatles and the Smiths aside; their own catalogues are well thumbed already. Instead, let's look elsewhere as we try to uncover what we're all about, from the Home Counties to the Humber to Houghton-le-Spring.

Bearing little resemblance to the supreme gentility of PG Wodehouse or David Niven, the performers to whom we're about to bow down share the Masonic handshake of Englishness on a grubbier level. Yet they define the nation's character just *so*. Plough through these songs and you'll find the key not to the England of William Blake, but, perhaps, to the England of William Roache. Harvesters, Adnams Broadside, net curtains. Two nights in and one night out. A nation of sensible jumpers and kebabs before bedtime.

Marie Lloyd had what Colin Macinnes described as a 'friendly, assured impertinence'. She was the girl next door, if you happened to live next door to the Old Bull & Bush. A little like Diana Dors after she'd grown a bit pudgy in the 1970s, Lloyd resembled nothing so much as a barmaid. She first took the stage at the Eagle on City Road, the same one mentioned in 'Pop Goes the Weasel'. Much of her subsequent repertoire predated the recorded music era: 'Don't Dilly Dally', 'A Little of What You Fancy Does You Good', 'Wink the Other Eye', and, the best of the lot, 'She'd Never Had Her Ticket Punched Before'.

Like Morrissey and the Carry On crew, Lloyd was a fan of the double entendre. When the words to her songs were wedded to her winks and gestures, the singer became the target of groups hell-bent on cleaning up music hall, the curtain-twitchers already among us even at the turn of the 20th century. Summoned before a committee, Lloyd showed how the filth was all in their minds by singing 'A Little of What You Fancy' with an aura of sweetness and light, then following it by delivering the drawing-room ballad 'Come into the Garden, Maud' with winks, nudges and all manner of lewd suggestiveness. Lloyd's oeuvre is best summed up not by either of those songs but by her 1912 recording of 'Every Little Movement Has a Meaning of Its Own'. It's saucy and improper but never overtly sexual; such is the English way.

At its best, music hall brought out everything that the Victorians loved to sweep under the carpet. There was a taste for discipline

So sick of easy fashion: **Adam Ant**.

Top ten
London

'Sittin' Here' Dizzee Rascal

Taut, twitchy and uncomfortably redolent of the kind of East Enders whose lives go undocumented by TV soap operas, Dylan Mills's debut album still sounds ahead of the curve.

'Sunny Goodge Street' Donovan

Donovan uses the image of a pot-hound hungry for chocolate and goes off on a dreamy tangent that may or may not have been influenced by that selfsame hash. The song was one of the first mainstream pop numbers in the UK to mention drugs in explicit terms; appropriate, perhaps, that soon after it was released, the singer became the first high-profile UK pop star to be arrested for the possession of marijuana.

'Waterloo Sunset' The Kinks

This was originally and almost unimaginably titled 'Liverpool Sunset', until Ray Davies turned his gaze back to the river that courses through so many of his songs.

'London Is the Place for Me' Lord Kitchener

Some outsiders move to London nursing a deep-seated fear that they might have made a mistake (see 'London' by the Smiths); others find that the romance simply doesn't last (the Kinks' 'Life on the Road', David Bowie's 'The London Boys'). On this little ditty from 1948, Jamaican calypso singer Lord Kitchener expresses nothing but optimism and delight, perhaps because he wrote it before he arrived.

'One Better Day' Madness

Although it's lifted by the 'Dancing Queen' piano in the chorus, Madness's ode to Camden's homeless is a slightly discomfiting contrast to the chirpier way they travel through the same streets while 'Driving in My Car'.

'West End Girls' Pet Shop Boys

When you get down to brass tacks, this is a pretty bleak portrait of London in the 1980s, although that indelible bassline put the listeners who pushed it to number one firmly off the scent.

'Common People' Pulp

The Britpop worm started to turn when Jarvis Cocker's acerbic tale of middle-class students artlessly slumming away their youth in London became a indie-disco anthem for middle-class students artlessly slumming away their youth in London. Unironically.

'Up the Junction' Squeeze

Pairing 'better' with 'tenner', 'took me' with 'bookie' and 'happen' with 'Clapham', Chris Difford's geezerish character confessional is virtually its own dissolute London rhyming dictionary.

SQUEEZE
Produced by SQUEEZE/JOHN WOOD
Original sound recording made by A & M Records Ltd.
SIDE 1
45 RPM
Time: 3.10
A
AMS 7444
AMS 7444 A*
℗ 1979 A & M Records Ltd.
Rondor Music (London) Ltd./ Deptford Songs
UP THE JUNCTION
(Chris Difford/Glenn Tilbrook)
(From the A & M Album "Cool For Cats" AMLH 68503)
A & M

'Ticket Collector' Simon Warner

The funniest track on the sadly forgotten *Waiting Rooms*, which comes off as the original cast recording to a big-budet musical about London that was only ever performed in Warner's bedsit, finds our hero caught at the farthest reaches of the Metropolitan line without the requisite Travelcard. 'What would *I* be doing in Watford,' he asks rhetorically, 'except seeing family?'

'Let's All Go Down the Strand' Charles Whittle

Many music hall songs about London tell us surprisingly little about the city back in the days when all the men wore hats, but this bouncy little singalong is more evocative than most. Later covered, in a career nadir, by Blur.

('Hold Your Hand Out, Naughty Boy', popularised by Melbourne-born singer Florrie Forde) and sexual confusion, courtesy of male impersonators such as Vesta Tilley and Ella Shields ('Burlington Bertie from Bow'). The lugubrious Sam Mayo even made tutting an art form, though he also lampooned the national tick of wailing that fings ain't wot they used to be with 'Things Are Worse in Russia' ('Have you backed a loser or got indigestion, or have you had gin for your tea?'). Known as the Immobile One because of the complete lack of emotion he showed on stage, Mayo even had the smarts to sing about music hall as a dying art.

The demise of music hall was a subject that doubtless concerned Ray Davies, the most celebrated chronicler of English life during the 1960s. 'Autumn Almanac' was the follow-up to 'Waterloo Sunset' in 1967 and another big hit; its jolly knees-up stance doesn't sit quite as neatly with the group's retrospective Britpop reputation as the likes of 'Days' or 'Tired of Waiting for You', but it's every bit as revealing about Davies's Anglophilia. A very conservative rebel here, the singer describes how he prefers his football on Saturdays and his roasts on Sundays, implicitly suggesting that he's none too keen on Sky's relentless tinkering with the fixture list. 'My poor rheumatic back!' he groans a little later, all of 22 years old at the time.

It's easy to see how John Major could have latched on to Davies's view of Albion in his ill-fated 'back to basics' period as PM, but how would he have squared it with a very different Davies song, issued only a year earlier on the B-side to 'Sunny Afternoon'? 'I'm Not Like Everybody Else' is multi-purpose Anglo anarchy, from a whisper to a scream. Some have claimed it as an early gay anthem, but it's more likely to represent the English desire to conform (morning coffee at 11, afternoon tea at four) while simultaneously yearning to break free of routine and become an individual, a naked civil servant. Over ominous chords, Davies suggests that you can ask him to do anything you like – confess his sins, stand in line, doff his cap – while intimating that behind the sly smile, he's a time bomb.

If Davies tended to keep his explosive tendencies out of the public eye, John Lydon assuredly didn't. His facial contortions were Old Man Steptoe, his delivery a pilled-up Norman Wisdom. While the Clash struck poses in any available ghetto, Lydon retained an unstable mix of pride and embarrassment about the Finsbury Park estate on which he was raised. The famous Bill Grundy interview and, especially, a *London Weekend Show* piece by Janet Street-Porter showed the Sex Pistols to be an exacting mix of arrogance, shyness and dirty humour. 'Anarchy in the UK' has everything, really. Rhyming 'anarchist' with 'anti-Christ' is funny, and Lydon's warning about our ambitions for the future being little more than 'a shopping scheme' acted as a national warning that Bluewater Britain failed to heed.

The anarchy that defines the legacy of Coventry group Stavely Makepeace was largely unintentional. Led by Nigel Fletcher and Rob Woodward, the group claimed to be influenced by Joe Meek, Gene Vincent and Elvis, though their catalogue sounds like nothing else. While über-English acts such as the Bonzo Dog Doo-Dah Band and XTC paraded their eccentricities like bling, Stavely Makepeace seemed genuinely confused as to why anyone might consider their music weird. '(I Wanna Love You Like a) Mad Dog', the group's debut, sounded like a one-man oompah band, phased to simulate a psychedelic experience and awash with the kind of nudge-wink filth that had landed Marie Lloyd in hot water. Naturally, it's the unsexiest record imaginable.

Three years later, Fletcher and Woodward penned a woozy pub instrumental called 'Mouldy Old Dough'. It wasn't up to 'serious' attempts on the chart such as 'Mad Dog', they reckoned, so they released it under the pseudonym Lieutenant Pigeon. But if it wasn't for the Makepeace/Pigeon delineation, nobody other than Woodward and Fletcher could tell which of their records were meant to be novelties. A number one single from Belgium to Australia, 'Mouldy Old Dough' took the sound of a country in severe depression around the world. Miners' strikes? Rampant inflation? Crack open a Party Seven and we'll all get sloshed. After all, things are worse in Russia.

Try as Stavely Makepeace occasionally did, Adam Ant proved to be rather more sexually intriguing. Bursting on to the punk scene with a whip in his valise, Ant immediately caused problems by picking the decidedly non-punk

'Young Parisians' as his first single in 1978. Straight away, the twin influences of the dandy's twirling cane and the theatre's velvet drapes were more obvious in his handiwork than the safety pin and the wrap of speed. Two years later, 'Cartrouble' threw revved-up glam into the mix for good measure, and a hero was born.

What no one expected, perhaps apart from Adam himself, was a brief period of superstardom. 'Dog Eat Dog' pushed him into the charts, its minor-chord darkness effectively fusing Gary Glitter's early hits to Burundi drumming, before 'Antmusic', an irresistible call to arms, sealed the deal. Fame brought the opportunity for Ant to involve Diana Dors, Lulu and pantomime in his promotional videos; 'Beat My Guest', the B-side to 'Stand and Deliver' was *Carry on Screaming* for the Roxy crowd. But all the while, amid the frenzied ten-year-olds, the pancake and the rockabilly riffs, the dandy highwayman looked so intense. It was as if this pop lark wasn't just about fun:

it was all Very Important. This is something the Americans really don't get. It was, and remains, hugely appealing.

'The devil take your stereo and your record collection,' snorted Ant on 'Stand and Deliver', providing fresh evidence that performers attacking their contemporaries in song with scything wit can be a beautiful thing. The Pet Shop Boys, pop's own Gilbert and George, decided to burst Bono's pretty balloons when the Irishman started to take REM's 'World Leader Pretend' a little too literally. The English have traditionally deflated pompous tyrants by laughing at them (something the current government would've been wise to remember, but what are you gonna do), and a medley combining the empty roar of U2's 'Where the Streets Have No Name' and Frankie Valli's strip-club campothon 'Can't Take My Eyes off You', released as a double-A side with the Bono-baiting 'How Can You Expect to Be Taken Seriously?', was a perfect retort to the quartet's shameful hauteur. The Irish group licked their wounds and reinvented themselves as a comedy act with an album called *Pop*. How awful.

The sharp tongue of Mark E Smith may not have had quite the same impact on his fellow artistes, but it's not for want of trying. 'The Beat, Wah! Heat – Male slags!' he drawls on 'Slates, Slags Etc'; well, that's them consigned to the dustbin. The Fall's leader – 'lead singer' hardly does his dictatorial style justice – combines a love of MR James's ghost stories and Wyndham Lewis's Vorticist manifesto with an effortless anti-fashion stance and, that fine English ingredient, bloody-mindedness. 'We've repetition in the music and we're never going to lose it,' he sang on their very first single in 1978. Thirty-odd albums later, he's proved his point.

The result of Smith's endeavours is an urban folk of which Ewan MacColl, a fellow Salford native, would never have approved: it's the sound of trashed cotton mills, of placcy bags caught on the branches of stunted trees on Burnley estates. The *Grotesque* album painted a picture of England in 1980: a land of cash and carry, container drivers and, on 'English Scheme', painfully right-on lefties who 'talk of Chile while driving through Haslingden'. After mulling over what's wrong with his country, his conclusion is sharp and abrupt. 'If we was smart, we'd emigrate.'

Mark E Smith: this nation's saving grace.

On the record Linda Thompson

'A Little of What You Fancy Does You Good'

Marie Lloyd

There are hardly any recordings of Marie Lloyd. No film footage; not even many photographs. Yet a century after her heyday, people still know who she is. It's amazing how she touched people's hearts. It wasn't that she was a great singer – it's just that she was a wonderful performer who affected so many different kinds of people.

Lloyd was an emancipated woman at a time when women didn't even have the vote. And she was a rebel, leading a strike demanding better treatment for variety performers. They wouldn't have her play the Royal Command Performance because they thought she'd offend the royal family. Instead, she hired a hall on the same night and said to the audience: 'Every Marie Lloyd show is a performance by command of the British public!' Which I think is fantastic.

My family was steeped in music hall. My father's mother used to sing music hall songs like 'A Little of What You Fancy Does You Good', and everyone loved them. My mother was even a performer for about five minutes: she was 'Vera Love: Speciality Dancer'.

Music hall faded away in the first part of the [20th] century. They shut the theatres and turned them into bingo halls. The working classes have largely forgotten about it, and even folk historians were often snooty about it. Which is odd, because it's very much part of folk culture.

Linda Thompson's most recent album is Versatile Heart (Roundor)

World of Twist, another Manchester group, took Smith's micro-detailed analysis of the nation and its musical deviances to a different place. Their twin influences were the supposedly opposing forces of northern soul and prog rock, sizeable English cults of the 1970s, which the group then allied to the electronic pop of the Human League and Roxy Music. Singer Tony Ogden had the looks of a slightly seedy matinée idol; keyboardist Andy Hobson grinned through every show, while flaxen-haired MC Shells specialised in 'sea noises'. Released in 1991, 'Sons of the Stage' was their high water mark.

When Ogden decided to abandon singing before their second album, half the band mutated into beard-and-lipstick pioneers Earl Brutus and things got very interesting. They also, though, got angry, hilarious, apologetic and tearful. Brutus liked a drink or two and were wont to take the stage in a fairly refreshed state, performing in front of a glittering British Rail logo. The full gamut of pent-up English emotion was eventually bared on 'Come Taste My Mind' ('I wear the clothes that make you cry'), 'Life's Too Long' and 'On Me, Not in Me', replete with a half-whispered 'sorry'.

Pissing on stage would have been frowned upon by Joe Meek, but he embodied every characteristic mentioned so far. Meek's reliance on pills and coffee, his own stimulants of choice, led him towards many of the emotions that were later all too visible at Earl Brutus performances, though the producer supplemented them with a large dose of paranoia. He wanted very much to fit in, but only if he was allowed to do exactly what he wanted, how he wanted.

On the record
Mick Jones

'Pop Goes the Weasel'

Anthony Newley

Around the time that the Clash were recording *London Calling* in Wessex Studios, Highbury, there was a well-stocked jukebox that was a real musical education. We heard loads of old rockabilly, reggae and soul, but we also heard loads of old English stuff like Tommy Steele, Lionel Bart and Vince Taylor. Anthony Newley's version of 'Pop Goes the Weasel' was a particular favourite. The Clash never recorded it, but we used to do it at soundchecks all the time. People thought we were mad. But Newley was hugely important because he sang in an English accent, and that was something we tried to do. He laid down the template for punk – it was a mix of music hall, English eccentricity and rock 'n' roll energy. I still love it today.

Formerly singer and guitarist with the Clash, Mick Jones is now in Carbon/Silicon

Meek's attitude resulted in him being fired from Lansdowne Studios in Holland Park, where he'd built London's first stereo recording set-up, and eventually led to him taking on the major labels (EMI, Decca, Pye) from his own premises above a leather goods shop on Holloway Road. The arrangement suited him and his music: there was no boss to rein him in, the rent was cheap, and, alongside local playwright Joe Orton, he could make promiscuous use of the public toilets on Madras Place. He wanted to paint 'Welcome to Meeksville' on the railway bridge beside the tube station, but the jobsworths at the council wouldn't let him.

The music that came out of the Holloway Road flat was a souped-up notion of pre-Beatles pop, filtered through Meek's love of electro-wizardry and slutty blonde boys. It was the sound of the English seaside, of fairgrounds and sticky-fingered fumbles in the years before Lady Chatterley, but it also reflected his obsession with outer space and the occult. Meek's greatest works – Glenda Collins' 'It's Hard to Believe It', 'Telstar' by the Tornados, the Blue Men's 'The Bublight', 'A Tribute to Buddy Holly' by Mike Berry – channel these wild desires into three-minute vari-speeded masterpieces. Before he shot first his landlady and then himself in 1967, Meek appeared well aware of the pop producer's relatively short mortal life and his own waning popularity. Pushed to the very edge, he produced some of his best records: 'This Too Shall Pass Away' and 'Eyes', both by the Honeycombs, offer just a taste of the fear and loathing in Meeksville.

Quite a lot of anger and misfired emotion, all in all. How we'd love to be more emotionally open as a nation, but we're always likely to spoil a tender moment by making a silly joke and saying 'sorry'. We have a bad tendency to self-destruct. Jake Thackray, the singer and songwriter who subtly dissected the English way of life in songs such as 'Lah-Di-Dah', was eventually destroyed by 'On Again! On Again!', on which he went too far by singing 'I love a good bum on a woman'. The tutters had their day. Thackray's BBC contract wasn't renewed and he became an alcoholic, dying just before a new generation of admirers hailed him as a gentleman and a scholar, the Jerome K Jerome of song. As *The Daily Mail* might say: 'Oh, England...'

Small world

Kim Cooper travels the globe without leaving her immaculate vintage Dansette.

ateline: A cocktail party in a middle American suburb, some time in the late 1950s – The ambrosia chills in the Frigidaire as the gals flit around each other in the sunken living room, the abstractions on their new, crisp frocks adding an unnoticed, surrealist guest list to the event: clowns and poodle dogs, big heads with bigger hairdos, dancing atomic symbols, hula dancers. Out back, Dan and Hank are stacking the grill with neat skewers of pork nuggets, canned pineapple chunks and lurid red cherries. Soon they'll bring the steaming meat inside, where it'll be placed like a pagan offering on a dining table dressed with rattan matting and a whole pineapple as a centrepiece, with green olives floating above the potato salad in slender toothpick orbits.

Every hand clutches a sweating beverage cribbed from the book of some master mixologist toiling away under fishnets, larded with Japanese floats and glazed pufferfish, transforming rum, blue curaçao, canned fruit and sickly sweet tropical juices into something that tastes harmless but packs a monstrous punch. The hostess whips up another pitcher. The kids are at Grandma's. The record changer clunks and drops another platter on the pile; as the needle slides into the groove, it emits a net of sound that transforms this safe suburban space into something like a jungle.

Liberty Records' marketing men called it 'exotica', which was perhaps meant to suggest 'erotica'; there's still no better term with which instantly to evoke the mysteriously lovely, oft-uninhibited American leisure-class soundtrack of the late 1950s and early 1960s. Taking the light-classical traditions popularised by the easy listening cocktail jazz of George Shearing and Earl Gardner and transporting them to idyllic, distant climes where they were fused with blood-stirring percussion, composer-arrangers such as Les Baxter, Martin Denny and Arthur Lyman crafted an evocative genre that neatly straddled the line between background music and foreground fantasy.

Exotica's visibility exploded in 1957 with the release of the Martin Denny LP from which it takes its name, still among the most common discs in American thrift shops. (Tikiphiles, however, consider Les Baxter's 1951 *Ritual of the Savage* to be the genre's masterwork.) Denny's Polynesian-inspired music attracted a broad range of American record buyers, from hi-fi enthusiasts to older folk seeking respite from the twitchy bleat of the rock 'n' roll beat, while his album covers, most featuring sloe-eyed model Sandy Warner, perhaps appealed to more prurient interests.

Ex-Denny sideman Arthur Lyman soon spun off with his own combo, lending a jazzier edge to the style. Soon enough, sonic thrill seekers could scratch their imaginary voyage itches with Frank Hunter's *White Goddess* ('Ritual of the Torch', 'White Goddess'), Yma Sumac's octave-straddling Peruvian Princess pop (try 'Xtabay' and 'Taita Inty' from *Voice of the Xtabay*), Denny protégée Ethel Azama's *Exotic Dreams* ('Friendly Island'), Les Baxter's *The Sacred Idol* ('The Feathered Serpent of the Aztecs', 'Pyramid of the Sun') and Stanley

Top ten
Trains

'Marrakesh Express' Crosby, Stills & Nash

The hippie dream started to go sour not long after this 1969 single, but Graham Nash's jaunty piece of perpetuum-mobile pop about taking the railroad south from Casablanca is awash in optimism, both cultural and romantic. That said, he may have had an ulterior motive for making the trip: certainly, the 'smoke rings' Nash puffs from his lips in verse three may not have come from a common-or-garden Marlboro.

'Train to Skaville' The Ethiopians

By the sounds of it, the Skaville service was hardly an express. Still, no matter: there might be little urgency about this gentle jaunt beneath sunny skies, but the sweetest of horn sections, and the falsetto harmonies that mimic it, ensure it's a wholly pleasant ride.

'Down in the Tube Station at Midnight' The Jam

Three decades after Paul Weller's committed but rather wordy tale of getting beaten up while waiting for the last tube home, you're now more likely to be assaulted by a Transport for London-approved busker playing Weller's 'Wild Wood' on a licensed busking stage at the bottom of an escalator. Some people call this progress.

'Choo Choo Ch'Boogie' Louis Jordan & His Tympany Five

Hard to believe that it took three people to write such an unwitting advertisement for rhyming dictionaries, but the 18 weeks that this toe-tapper spent at the top of the American R&B charts in 1946 meant that the trio probably did all right out of the collaboration.

'Mystery Train' Little Junior's Blue Flames

The Elvis version is better known, but then the Elvis version usually is. The original is a darker, stranger thing, hitched on a rhythm section that never quite seems sure of itself and Parker's lost and lonesome holler. You've heard the song, now read the book (Greil Marcus's cultural history of early rock 'n' roll) and see the movie (Jim Jarmusch's evocative curio).

'Trans-Europe Express' Kraftwerk

This chugger did for the cross-continental TEE rail network what 'Autobahn', released three years earlier in 1974, did for the German motorway system: by attempting to capture its ambience, it elevated a journey from something mundane and workaday to something altogether more other-worldly, even mystical. Five years later, Afrika Bambaataa stole the riff for his electro-defining single 'Planet Rock'.

'Nobody Cares About the Railroad Anymore' Harry Nilsson

Nilsson's gentle tribute to the good old days of American rail travel, set in the years before the construction of the interstate network and the rise of commercial airlines left it an anomalous novelty, is as much a kiss goodbye to youth as to trains, sung from the perspective of a couple growing old while the world around them stays as young as ever.

'Different Trains' Steve Reich

'Different Trains' indeed: the 'crack train from New York' to LA that Reich took during the first few years of his life between his estranged parents; the 'cattle wagons' that shuffled European Jews to concentration camps at the same time; and the transcontinental trains ridden by Holocaust survivors who escaped to America after the war. Reich's score is dotted with train sirens and bells, but it's driven by the ebb and flow of voices taped by the composer: of Holocaust escapees, of train porters, even of the composer's own governess.

'Train Whistle Blues' Jimmie Rodgers

No one did more to cement the train's mythic status in pop than the Singing Brakeman, who spent his life careening between studios, railroads and hospitals before succumbing to tuberculosis in 1933 at the age of 35. Rodgers' contention here that the blues leaves women weeping while men head for the station is a neat precis of John Gray's entire career.

'Down in the Subway' Soft Cell

Marc Almond's most dramatic attempt at career suicide came in 1983, when, following a less than favourable review, the 27-year-old singer turned up at the offices of Record Mirror brandishing a bullwhip and then immediately announced his retirement. He changed his mind in weeks but Soft Cell were toast, signing off with this clattery cover of Jack Hammer's cheery ode to jumping in front of a train.

Wilson's *Pagan Love* (especially 'Ritual of the Fertility Tree'). Soon, earthly exoticism gave way to other-wordly exploration, fuelling a space-age pop genre that incorporated all the creative freedoms of exotica fused with the futuristic potential of electronic instrumentation.

The enduring image of the first-wave exotica listener is of a suburban gentleman or lady, in early middle age and probably highly social. After all, the music's popularity evolved concurrently with the rage for tiki parties, those backyard fantasias packed with leering totems, tight sarongs, strong liquor, loud shirts, flaming torches and lewd remarks about pu-pu platters and getting lei'd.

Many who spent their weekends at these theme parties had personal experience in exotic climes. Anyone who served in the Pacific Theater of Operations during World War II passed through Hawaii, where a decade later Martin Denny would develop his distinctive bird call and frog croak arrangements while playing poolside at the Shell Bar at Honolulu's Kaiser Hawaiian Village Hotel. As such, for Americans, the tropics came to be emotionally charged with sex-and-death associations that lurked barely behind the surface of its romantic symbols. What's more, the region had become deeply enmeshed in the American psyche with the popularity of *South Pacific*, the Broadway play inspired by James A Michener's Pulitzer Prize-winning stories that ran from 1949 to 1954 before spawning the 1958 film and its chart-topping soundtrack. Further encouraging awareness of the South Seas came with the granting of US statehood to Hawaii in 1959.

While mock Hawaiiana was the most visible 'world music' of its day, the appearances of various Latin, African and Asian (or, in the parlance of the times, Oriental) signifiers, in the form of unusual instruments, suggestive song titles, atypical percussion patterns and polyglot lyrical utterances, rendered exotica's psychic space as truly global, if inauthentic. But no savvy musical archaeologist would sniff at the lugubrious organ stylings of LA television personality Korla Pandit, a mysterious 'East Indian' posthumously outed as a black man from Missouri named John Roland Redd, or the frenetic jungle rhythms of 'orphaned African tribesman' Chaino, actually Chicago bongo whiz Leon Johnson. And among the fake personas were some surprisingly authentic artists:

'Slick Italian crooners wrapped their tonsils around Neapolitan airs, cha-cha albums evoked the lost playland of pre-Castro Cuba, and Herb Alpert's Tijuana Brass created a genre of horn-happy *turista* pop.'

recruited by US military intelligence in the 1940s, Ghanaian drummer Guy Warren came to collaborate with American jazz players; Mexico's Juan García Esquivel applied his genius for ping-pong stereo arrangement to traditional Latin folk songs on such recordings as 'Baia' and 'El Negro Zumbon'; and 'Nature Boy' Eden Ahbez really was a vegetarian proto-hippy who lived beneath the Hollywood sign, although his Brooklyn mama named him Alexander Aberle.

Behold the American turntable as cultural melting pot, after Harry Belafonte's *Calypso*, the first ever million-selling album, topped the charts in 1956 and ignited the folk boom. Pretty soon, slick Italian crooners were wrapping their tonsils around Neapolitan airs, cha-cha albums were evoking the lost playland of pre-Castro Cuba, and, well into the rock era, Herb Alpert's Tijuana Brass were creating a genre of horn-happy *turista* pop so successful that it was aped by a list of unlikely combos that reads like a gag from *Mad* magazine: the Guadalajara Brass, the Mariachi Brass (featuring, of all people, Chet Baker), the Border Brass, the Mexicali Brass, the Country Brass, the Juarez Woodwinds, the Erin Go Brass, even Al Tijuana & His Jewish Brass. Chief among the faux-Alperts was the prolific George Garabedian, who produced Tijuana Brass soundalike albums for Taco Bell, Pepsi, Alpha Beta supermarkets, Der Wienerschnitzel and other corporations. The Chipmunks even got into the act with a single called 'Sorry About That, Herb', while Alpert sideman Julius Wechter, a former Denny

THE SOUNDS OF **Martin Denny**

LIBERTY

EXOTICA

Martin Denny seemed strangely reluctant to appear on his own album covers.

collaborator, led the moustachioed and massively sombreroed Baja Marimba Band.

There were also genuine ethnographic recordings available for the purists, among them Folkways' collections of Haitian drums, Mexican mushroom ceremonies, and Pygmy, Maori and Aborigine song. And tucked in the back of many a record cabinet were veil-bedecked belly-dancing albums that simultaneously evoked the mysterious Middle East and encouraged daring wives to undulate for their husbands. The Fax label eventually played upon exotica's linguistic suggestiveness when it issued *Erotica – The Rhythms of Love* (1959), wherein hepped-up LA session cats created manic walls of percussion, squeaking bedsprings included, over which a man and woman panted primitive love calls. That the record is hard to find today is partly due to the fact that the US Postal Service had it declared obscene, a ruling that stood despite an appeal in which the producers introduced

recordings of music by everyone from Les Baxter to Rimsky-Korsakov in the hope of putting their party album into acceptable, shippable context.

Back at the cocktail party, it's grown dark. Sated, the gang gathers around the halogen glow of the slide projector and clicks through one couple's vacation pictures, selecting an appropriate instrumental album to accompany the scenes. Wild drums punctuate an African safari; bird calls permeate the Kodachrome Amazon; winds through the Hawaiian palms need the soft tinkle of wind chimes. With exotica as the backdrop, the world turns at their feet. Before them lie the promise of continued prosperity, well-behaved children, victory over Communism, Americans in space, and the opportunity to explore the distant shores whose imagined soundtrack already thrills their blood. For now, though, they're safe and comfortable in the 'burbs, twirling their paper umbrellas as the lights flicker out all over the country.

Court & Spark

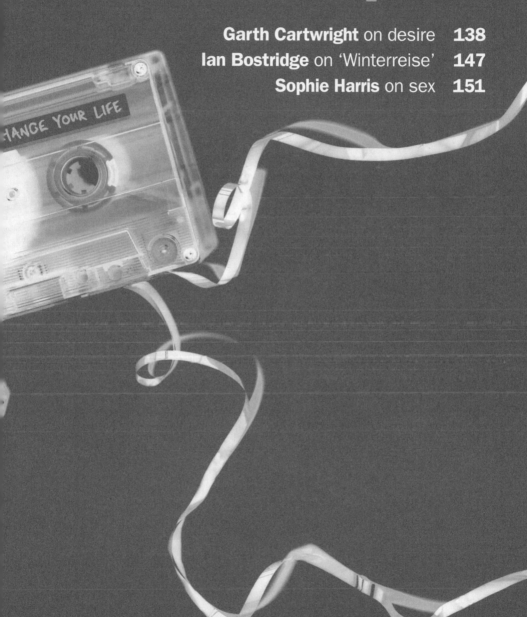

CHANGE YOUR LIFE

Matters

of the heart

Garth Cartwright on the desire and yearning of American music's golden age.

For those of us who use records to map our emotional lives, there's no shortage of music to use as markers. And nor is there any shortage of variety, both within our native cultures and beyond them. Plenty of so-called world music channels our emotional inarticulacy in tongues that we appreciate rather than understand. Listen to Cape Verde's Cesária Évora, who expresses the *morna* with a stoic grace on songs such as 'Mar Azul' and 'Sodade', or to the clear, sad voice of Tex-Mex singer Lydia Mendoza on the likes of 'Mi Problema' and 'Mal Hombre'. But there seems to be just as much universality in the best elemental American music from the 1950s and '60s: in blues and in soul, in country and in rock 'n' roll, and in the earliest stirrings of '60s pop. The one thing that links it all together is the one thing that links us all together: simple human desire.

The origins of much American popular music can be traced back to one man. Thomas Dorsey started out as a barroom pianist, masquerading under the name Georgia Tom when cutting dirty blues such as 'It's Tight Like That' with Tampa Red in the 1920s. However, Dorsey eventually took the skeleton of the blues and reshaped it into gospel music on the likes of 'Take My Hand, Precious Lord', written in 1932. The structure and pitch of Mahalia Jackson's subsequent recording, rooted in the passion of Georgia Tom's blues but applied to the search for Thomas Dorsey's new-found Christian faith, helped turn the song into a standard. On Jackson's version, the composition's brooding melodic majesty stands out, but so does the power and conviction in the singer's voice.

'Take My Hand, Precious Lord' works so well because beneath its religious surface, it seems to yearn for the transcendence offered by justice, love and even sex. Indeed, Jackson could be addressing her man just as much as her God. Presumably well aware of the dangers of entangling religious yearning with physical desire, Martin Luther King, Jr once suggested that 'Take My Hand, Precious Lord' was his favourite song. Jackson repaid the compliment by singing it at King's funeral, Dorsey's words now taking on an aching for a brilliant man slain by vipers.

Although Dorsey deserted his former bedrock in search of salvation, many other blues musicians stayed right where they were. On reputation alone, Robert Johnson has become the music's Byron, shrouded in myth after embodying the live-fast-die-young ethos that's now seemingly demanded by our nihilistic pop culture. Yet for all the legends that surround him, Johnson's music continues to convey an emotional directness that few have matched since his death in 1938. On the implosive 'Love in Vain', for example, every note Johnson pulls out of his guitar suggests a deep, hungry desire, while 'Stop Breakin' Down Blues' sees the singer strut, swagger and generally boast wildly about his sexual prowess. Yet such priapic bragging often seems to mask a certain agony just under Johnson's skin; or, at least, under his breath. On 'Dead Shrimp Blues', an absurd comedy of impotence, he sings with a savage, cynical pleading.

Elmore James was a Mississippi disciple of Johnson, electrifying his precursor's swagger and adding to it a fierce, slashing slide guitar on such tracks as 'Something Inside of Me'. In his book *Deep Blues*, critic and musicologist

Robert Palmer wrote that while James's sound, and particularly the bristling intensity of the instrumental interplay, built much of what we now call 'rock', his contemporary Jimmy Reed emphasised the 'roll', gently shuffling into the listener's ear like a friendly anecdote on a hot summer's evening. Not that Reed was anything less than a consummate bluesman. On 'Ain't That Lovin' You Baby', he slurs out his insistence that he'd turn to crime in order to win his woman back ('Ain't that lovin' you, babe?'), before ultimately realising that the object of his desires doesn't even know his name.

At around the time Reed released 'Ain't That Lovin' You Baby', a decade or so after the end of World War II, gospel and blues were both being pushed forward by musicians keen to stamp their own personality on the sounds that had initially inspired them. But while one went in search of salvation, the other hunted only for sin. A young Ray Charles learned the musical lessons implicitly outlined by 'Take My Hand, Precious Lord' but returned Dorsey's vision from Heaven to the bedroom on 'What'd I Say', in which Charles builds the Southern

Ray Charles.

preacher/gospel choir call-and-response until it practically reaches orgasmic heights. Also recorded in 1959, Charles's 'I Believe to My Soul' offers a different but no less dramatic juxtaposition of emotions: although the singer seems either fearful of or embarrassed about his own cuckoldry in the lyrics, the midnight-blues atmospherics of the accompanying music tell their own story.

After Charles effectively liberated popular post-war American music, a tidal wave of similarly passionate soul and blues followed in his wake, much of it emerging from Memphis, Tennessee. Illiterate gospel veteran Bobby 'Blue' Bland began life as a blues shouter but soon found that his audiences were moved more by his sensual vocal caresses. His 1959 single 'I'll Take Care of You' is as eerie and mesmerising as soul music gets, as Bland offers not just intimacy but protection from the savage world outside. Bland's contemporary OV Wright, meanwhile, possessed perhaps the most cracked and haunted voice in American music. On 'Eight Men, Four Women', which finds the singer being tried by 'a jury of love', Wright makes his desire for sexual and spiritual salvation sound like the most important thing on earth. Was Overton Vertis pleading with a lover, a dealer or his creator?

Of all the black female singers working around the same time as Bland and Wright, none was tougher than Etta James. Starting out at the age of 16 with 1954's hormonal hurricane 'The Wallflower (Roll with Me Henry)', James sang with an almost unhinged passion. Her 1967 classic 'I'd Rather Go Blind' presents infatuation as despair, every vocal inflection fierce and profound. Indeed, during the latter half of the '60s, James's intensity was perhaps matched only by Aretha Franklin. Check 'I Never Loved a Man (The Way I Love You)', on which Franklin wails about a marriage that's left her both physically and emotionally bruised. 'My friends keep telling me you're no good,' she hollers, 'but I'd leave you if I could.'

'I Never Loved a Man (The Way I Love You)' was recorded in January 1967. In December the same year, Franklin cut 'Ain't No Way', a lover's prayer like few others and a virtual Everest in soul music's catalogue of desire. The song finds a male counterpoint of sorts in 'Stay in My Corner', a similarly desperate 1968

'Songs such as "Save the Last Dance for Me" seemed to capture something universal about the nature of desire before wedding it to melodies that were as hummable as they were evocative.'

cut by Chicagoan vocal group the Dells. The Civil Rights struggle of the 1960s seemed to give black singers such as Franklin and the Dells' Marvin Junior an added intensity when they wailed about being mistreated. Sexual freedom and personal relationships may have been the explicit subject matter of songs such as 'Stay in My Corner', but a greater liberty was surely on the minds of both singers and listeners at the time.

Across the tracks, Elvis was the first white American singer to embrace the carnal release offered by the marriage of blues and gospel; revealingly, he even cut his own versions of both Dorsey's 'Take My Hand, Precious Lord' and Charles's 'What'd I Say'. But by the mid '60s, countless white musicians had followed suit and started to base all or part of their repertoire on the blues. Posthumously, Robert Johnson accumulated many white disciples: in the UK, Eric Clapton's Cream covered Johnson's 'Cross Road Blues' (retitled 'Crossroads') in 1968, while Led Zeppelin recorded the singer's 'Traveling Riverside Blues' for the BBC the following year. And back in the US, Janis Joplin fused the blues with bar-band rock on her recordings with Big Brother & the Holding Company. The Texan singer owed huge debts to Etta James and to Bessie Smith, both the despair with which Smith imbues 'Empty Bed Blues' and the more party-hearty passions emphasised by the 1920s blues pioneer on 'Gimme a Pigfoot'. But for all her obvious influences, Joplin later reached deep inside herself to turn the Dan Penn and Spooner Oldham-penned ballad 'A Woman Left Lonely' into a great roar of loneliness and lust.

Ultimately, the Rolling Stones proved to be Robert Johnson's shrewdest white understudies. Mick Jagger has never been one for yearning: on ballads such as 'Wild Horses', he comes across as truculent and insincere, while the Stones' take on Johnson's 'Stop Breakin' Down Blues' (simply retitled 'Stop Breaking Down' on *Exile on Main St*) captures Jagger's leering nature. But on the band's 1969 version of 'Love in Vain', another Johnson original, Jagger is at his most emotionally persuasive.

Country relies on lyrical tropes more than any other music. And though there have been exceptions (Loretta Lynn, for example), the Southern Protestant mentality that guided so much of it tended to draw a veil over lust in favour of a kind of courtly love ideal. But while the means differ, the ends remain the same: like blues and gospel, country music is ultimately all about desire, and often about the ashes left in the wake of its collapse. Just as Robert Johnson became the Lord Byron of the blues, Hank Williams has become country's Johnson: ferociously talented, consumed by music, living fast while apparently all too well aware of his forthcoming doom. On 'Hey Good Lookin'', he's a wolf-whistle on legs, letting the drugstore cowgirls know he's hotwired with desire. But the melody of 'I'm So Lonesome I Could Cry', its polar opposite, almost weeps from the speakers.

George Jones's often lunatic behaviour suggests his records should sound like a honky-tonk maelstrom. And in the beginning, some of them did. But the singer's later, Billy Sherrill-produced hits such as 'A Good Year for the Roses' and 'I Always Get Lucky with You' are extremely eloquent, whether mourning separation or pleading for loving intimacy. Compare Jones with Gram Parsons' strained and cracked vocals on 'A Song for You', a eulogy for those who'd partied too hard and now were paying the price, or the way Gary Stewart's high tenor shrieks at the pleasures yet to unfold on 'Your Place or Mine', which sees a barroom pick-up take on an almost religious sense of ecstasy.

While blues and soul spent the late 1950s and early '60s developing in the wake of Ray Charles's early singles, pop music was simultaneously reinventing itself, still delighting in its own excitable youth. At New York City's Brill Building, where, since the 1930s, songwriters had been shoehorned into tiny offices and ordered to churn out hits, tag teams such as Burt Bacharach and Hal David, Gerry Goffin and Carole King, and Doc Pomus and Mort Shuman effectively rewrote the pop rule book. The hits delivered by the duos placed a sense of unabashedly adolescent longing at the centre of the pop charts, and it's stayed there more or less ever since.

From the pens of these urbane songwriters, a number of them Jewish, came a catalogue of songs that launched the careers of countless young black American singers. And many of these songs succeeded because of the way in which they lent adult gravitas to apparently teenaged scenarios. Dionne Warwick brings elegance and sophistication to Bacharach and David's hurting and even slightly petulant lyric for 'Anyone Who Had a Heart'. The Shirelles sound not desperate but proud as they beg a boyfriend not to leave on the morning after the night before in Goffin and King's 'Will You Love Me Tomorrow'. And the retooled, Ben E King-led Drifters' recordings of two Pomus and Shuman songs, 'This Magic Moment' and 'Save the Last Dance for Me' (apparently written by polio-crippled Pomus for his wife, a Broadway dancer), are majestic and grown-up celebrations of young love. Songs such as these, two of which topped the US charts, seemed to capture something universal about the nature of desire before wedding it to melodies that were as hummable as they were evocative.

As if the music's appeal needed further emphasis, Brill Building veterans King and Neil Diamond both parlayed their early '60s experiences on the teen-pop factory into massive success as singer-songwriters a decade or so later, tempering the intensity of the songs they once penned for other artists as they did so. On her 1971 album *Tapestry*, King turns to several of the hits she'd written for others in her teens and early twenties, and delivers them with a slightly weary air. Her flawed voice clearly made as much of a connection with listeners as did the purer vocals of the pop acts who made her songs famous the first time: in the US alone, *Tapestry* sold more than ten million copies.

Hank Williams.

Guilty! Memphis soul man **OV Wright** in 1967.

While the Brill Building songwriters drove New York's pop industry back in the early '60s, Phil Spector began to pick up where they left off out on the West Coast. Indeed, the Hollywood-based producer even headed east near the start of his career in order to serve a brief apprenticeship in New York, and later relied heavily on material written by or with staff songwriters working in the Brill Building or one of its adjacent commercial hothouses. Much like 'Anyone Who Had a Heart' and 'Will You Love Me Tomorrow', Spector expressed adolescent desire in rich and powerful fashion – never more so than on 'Be My Baby', a teen

opera of Wagnerian intensity written by Spector with Brill Building veterans Jeff Barry and Ellie Greenwich. More than 40 years after it was released, men still hang on Ronnie Spector's lovelorn anguish, hoping to reconnect with themselves at an age when love and sex overwhelmed all else. Martin Scorsese realised as much when he used the song to soundtrack Harvey Keitel's sweaty insomnia in the opening frames of *Mean Streets*.

Although he was effectively raised in New York's CBGB club at around the same time that punk was emerging (and, for that matter, at around the same time Keitel was battling his own psyche in Scorsese's classic), Willie DeVille saw himself as the late '70s heir to the Brill Building tradition. He even co-wrote a few songs with Doc Pomus, the pair joining forces to pen such titles as 'Just to Walk That Little Girl Home' and 'That World Outside'. But the world didn't respond to DeVille's nostalgia for an age when pop's emotions were operatic in their scale and scope. Punk had taught listeners that cynicism and contempt were easier to deal with than desire and yearning, and DeVille's career failed to take off in its wake.

A decade or so later, pop rediscovered its aptitude for passionate sincerity, but the results were very different. While Warwick spoke volumes by saying – or, to be more accurate, singing – very little, the likes of Whitney Houston and Mariah Carey preferred to trowel on emotion like a plasterer applying stucco, their oceanic melisma recalling Shakespeare's dismissal of the *X Factor* kids of his day: all 'sound and fury, signifying nothing'. Best, perhaps, to retreat to another era, a time when American music was a little less full of itself but seemed both confident about what it felt and, more crucially, how it felt about feeling it.

Desire in 20 songs

'Still Take You Home'
Arctic Monkeys

Barry White it ain't, but Alex Turner's nightclub come-on, arch and reluctant at first yet ultimately a prisoner of its own libido, is no less valid for its pent-up urgency.

'Sweet Love' Anita Baker

Scrubbed and polished to a mirror-ball shine in archetypal '80s-soul fashion, Anita Baker's multi-million-selling second album both defines its era and transcends it. Released in 1986, the whole of *Rapture* remains a tour de force, but that extraordinary voice was never as perfectly pitched as on this ballad of rich romantic contentment.

'The Girls on the Beach'
The Beach Boys

Tantalisingly, croon the Wilsons with a wide-eyed mix of innocence and tumescence, these sun-soaked lovelies are all within reach… but only 'if you know what to do'. Nudge, wink. Did they ever sound quite this adolescent before or since?

'Lilac Wine' Jeff Buckley

'Nina does it best,' reckoned Jeff Buckley about this oft-recorded number from the '50s. 'That's the be-all, end-all version.' He wears his modesty well, but it's misplaced. Buckley's own recording, which arrives with a ballerina's balance and an ecstasy that verges on the beatific, is at least its equal.

'The Dark End of the Street' James Carr

Chips Moman and Dan Penn's shadowy song about an illicit love affair has been covered by everyone from Barbara Dickson to Diamanda Galás. However, they're fighting a losing battle if they think they'll top Carr's definitive original, a worried yet defiant insistence that he and his partner can help each other make it through the night.

'My One and Only Love'
John Coltrane & Johnny Hartman

Coltrane pretty much sleepwalks through the first couple of minutes of this much-covered standard. Hartman, though, totally inhabits both words and music, his measured croon perfect for this ode to blissed-out romance.

'I Want You' Elvis Costello &
the Attractions

'The first verse borrows a Japanese folk song tune,' writes Costello on the liner notes to one of about a dozen reissues of *Blood and Chocolate*, 'and then goes somewhere very dark.' Well, quite: this might be the bleakest recording on the bleakest album in the singer's 30-year catalogue. 'I Want You' is sung by a narrator who switches from bilious indignation to wanton desire with every comma, breathy repetitions of the title separating the otherwise agonised lyrics.

'Born to Be with You' Dion

Age had not withered them, exactly, but it had slowed them down. By 1975, Phil Spector was struggling to re-establish himself in the industry after reputedly waving a gun at John Lennon during sessions for the former Beatle's ill-starred *Rock 'n' Roll* album, while Dion DiMucci, having long since cast aside his Belmonts, was desperate for a hit after seven years without one. Their joint response was the dizzyingly grand and typically Spectorian *Born to Be with You*, with the mountaintop proclamation of the title track its finest moment. The record bombed and the pair more or less disowned it.

'Let's Get It On' Marvin Gaye

The singer made his point in slightly more demure terms a couple of years later on 'I Want You', but it's no match for this slippery slice of unbridled fuck-lust. Especially, of course, that indelible opening, with Gaye's desirous howls lent added weight by a rock-solid rhythm section and a guitarist (Melvin Ragin, who performs professionally under the fabulous pseudonym Wah-Wah Watson) plainly struggling to control his instrument. Stop sniggering at the back.

'You're My Thrill' Billie Holiday

Recorded in 1949 with the assistance of Gordon Jenkins, later a favourite arranger of Frank Sinatra, this is Lady Day at her absolute wooziest: dizzied by lust, drunk on desire. It's a lovely little song, but Holiday's helpless, wordless hums in the third verse say more than any of Sidney Clare's lyrics.

'My Sharona' The Knack

Despite Doug Fieger's repeated requests for his beloved girl to make his 'motor run', we're guessing she's not a mechanic.

'A Case of You' Joni Mitchell

If any individual song can be held single-handedly responsible for the last two generations (and counting) of navel-gazing, toe-curling singer-songwriter confessionals at open-mic nights across the world, it's this one. Still, one can't really blame Joni for her imitators. Like pretty much all of *Blue*,

the album on which it's found, 'A Case of You' perfectly treads the line separating romantic desperation and maudlin self-obsession.

'Me and Mrs Jones' Billy Paul

You can't help but wonder whether 'the same place, the same café' at which Philadelphia soul singer Billy Paul arranged to meet his squeeze in 1972 is at the same dark end of the street where James Carr hooked up with his own unnamed date five years earlier. Mr Jones's thoughts on all this shady romantic activity remain unrecorded.

'Earth Angel (Will You Be Mine)' The Penguins

Last dance at the high-school hop. Where's your date?

'Dance Me to the End of Love' Madeleine Peyroux

Many of Leonard Cohen's early songs are oddly impersonal creations: you rarely get the sense that Marianne, Suzanne, Jane and the rest are anything more to the singer than grist to his poetic mill. This one, though, is an altogether more engaged and engaging creation. Cohen's own recording is rather ruined by a musical backing that sounds like it was bought in the summer sale at Argos; best stick to Peyroux's airy, languid cover.

'If I Was Your Girlfriend' Prince

Prince's catalogue is awash with songs of yearning and desire, but this gender bending creation from *Sign 'O' the Times*, a slinky and skeletal funk workout with vocals credited to 'Camille' (Prince's female alter-ego), is certainly the most intriguing and one of the best.

'No Ordinary Love' Sade

Sade's lyrics, pleading and impassioned, suggest that he's gone for good. But the immaculate music, pulsing and sensual from the first bar to the eventual post-coital wind-down, is anything but despairing. *Indecent Proposal* wouldn't have been half as effective without it.

'…Baby One More Time' Britney Spears

She's claiming loneliness and heartbreak. But the confidence in her voice, not to mention that super-slinky musical backdrop, suggests she's going to win her boy back before the bell signals the start of afternoon class.

'I'm on Fire' Bruce Springsteen

Who knew the Boss had it in him? The most explicit and effective come-on in Springsteen's catalogue forgoes the fist-pumping, rabble-rousing blue-collar rock that dominates most of *Born in the USA* and replaces it with a moonlit croon. You certainly wouldn't bet against him getting what he wanted.

On the record
Amy Winehouse

'Moody's Mood for Love'

King Pleasure

When I was at stage school we used to learn showtunes; you know, everything from Cole Porter to Stephen Sondheim. They all sounded a bit corny when we learned them, and it wasn't until I heard jazz musicians performing them that I realised how good these songs were. A great singer like Ella Fitzgerald or Sarah Vaughan or Dinah Washington or Frank Sinatra could transform one of these melodies: make them swing, make them breathe. King Pleasure is an extreme example. He takes showtunes and jazz standards and improvises over songs like a saxophonist playing a solo, making up lyrics as he goes. This one is a classic. He sounds so relaxed, but he's absolutely on the edge here. I did a version of this on my first album *Frank* as a kind of tribute. *Amy Winehouse's most recent album is* Back to Black *(Island)*

Top ten
Caroline

'Caroline, No' Beach Boys
Tony Asher originally wrote the lyrical refrain to Brian Wilson's ethereal melody as 'Oh, Carol, I know'; Wilson misheard him at first, but the pair decided they preferred it that way and reworked the song accordingly. It's the closing track on *Pet Sounds*.

'Oh Caroline' Cheap Trick
A characteristically straightforward if slightly leaden fist-pumper that bursts in without knocking, shouts its piece as loudly as possible and dashes straight out the door again in a hair under three minutes.

'CAE' (Enigma Variations No.1) Edward Elgar
Almost archetypally Elgarian, as a little motif slides in and out of focus above and below an orchestral backdrop that itself curves gently from comforting melancholy to stirring pride and back again. The identities of the people about whom Elgar wrote the *Enigma*'s 14 short musical portraits were disguised behind initials on his score, though the code has long since been cracked: 'CAE' was Caroline Alice Elgar, the composer's wife.

'Sweet Caroline' The Gap Band
Unrelated to Neil Diamond's karaoke perennial, this smooth and awesome chunk of early 1980s synth-soul comes from the Tulsa group that, the previous year, went 'Oops Up Side Your Head' in rather more fidgety fashion.

'Caroline' Kirsty MacColl
MacColl rarely gets the guy in her own songs; when she does, it often triggers some kind of crisis. This particular Caroline is the best mate whose friendship she's probably just lost after quietly stealing her boyfriend. But despite all the guilt, the cheery choir of multi-tracked Kirstys that dominate the relentlessly jolly chorus suggest that she's perfectly happy with the swap.

'O Caroline' Matching Mole
Robert Wyatt's plangent lyric concerns his break-up with artist and writer Caroline Coon; the gorgeous tune is by David Sinclair, keyboard player with blundering Canterbury prog-rock group Caravan.

'Miss Caroline' Eddy Mitchell
Diamond's abovementioned 'Sweet Caroline' translated rather scattily into French, framed by a twangy and slightly out-of-tune guitar, dotted with perfectly ridiculous fluttering piccolos and belted out as if it was the last song on earth. Which, one day, it probably will be.

'Caroline' Harry Nilsson
Depending on which way the wind's blowing, this little delicacy is Nilsson and songwriter Randy Newman either at their gentlest or at their most disarmingly sinister.

'Roses' OutKast
Affection is hard to find on André 3000's fearsome kiss-off to his own Caroline, from the nursery-school scatology of the chorus to the 'punk-ass bitch' pay-off towards the end of this unexpectedly vicious six minutes.

'Pretty in Pink' The Psychedelic Furs
The inspiration for the John Hughes film of the same name, which – naturally enough – didn't feature a single character called Caroline. It also wasn't anything like as dark as Richard Butler's lyric, but at least Molly Ringwald looked lovely in her thrift-store hand-me-downs.

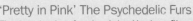

ALL RIGHTS OF THE PRODUCER AND OF THE OWNER OF THE RECORDED WORK RESERVED. UNAUTHORISED COPYING, PUBLIC PERFORMANCE, BROADCASTING, HIRING OR RENTAL OF THIS RECORDING PROHIBITED. MADE IN ENGLAND

PSYCHEDELIC FURS

CBS

(LC) 0149

A 7242
A 7242 A*
CBS Songs Ltd
℗ 1986 CBS
Records
45 RPM
STEREO
MCPS/BIEM

A SIDE

PRETTY IN PINK
(The Psychedelic Furs)
Recorded by: Charles Harrowell
Produced by: Chris Kimsey
Mixed by: Chris Kimsey
Original sound recording
made by CBS Records

CBS AND ⬛ ® CBS INC.

Love's labour's lost

Ian Bostridge unravels Schubert's masterpiece of existential despair.

C lassical music is made up of many jostling, overlapping genres and forms – symphonies and concertos, operas and overtures, oratorios and chamber music. Some of these forms and genres, maybe most, were invented at a particular and easily pinpointed time: opera in the late 16th century; symphony in the mid 18th; oratorio in the mid 16th.

Song, of course, has always existed. Men and women have sung words since human beings were human beings, since language itself was invented, and composers in the classical tradition have always written songs for them to sing. But towards the end of the 18th century, a new type of song came into being in Germany, forming the basis of a genre that, despite the existence of alternative native equivalents such as art song and *mélodie*, we usually call by one of the German words for song: lied.

Today, lieder recitals are a regular part of the diet of music-making in all the main centres of Western classical music (New York, London, Paris, Munich, Vienna, Tokyo and so on). But at the peak of the form's popularity a century ago, the lied was at the cutting edge of musical experimentation, the most famous lieder were as well known as pop songs are today, and a city such as Berlin could support as many as dozen lieder recitals a week. What was special about the lied?

Two things, one technical and the other more purely aesthetic. In the first instance, the development of the piano – with its scope for virtuosity, its range of colour and its quasi-symphonic power – gave new possibilities of liberation and sophistication to the art of keyboard accompaniment. Voice and piano were now able to act as equal partners in a form of chamber music that had the potential to rival the string quartet for its musical daring and opera for its dramatic impact.

The aesthetic development, meanwhile, was down to the immersion of German composers in the Romantic literary and philosophical movements of the day. Franz Schubert, the pre-eminent songwriter of the early 19th century and the composer often credited as the inventor of the lied tradition, wrote songs that spoke of love and death, of nature and the meaning of life, in a way which, through the music, seemed profound and compelling, radical and even urgent. Crucially, most of these songs avoided relying on religion or Greco-Roman mythology, the methods through which composers had traditionally addressed these issues.

Previously, the musical classicism of Haydn and Mozart had held in balance the demands of society and individual, had contained its darker impulses within the balance of classical form. Later, Beethoven created the modern image of the composer at odds with society, a romantic rebel. Schubert's songs, and much of the rest of his chamber and piano music, project a highly private aesthetic, revealing a questing individual whose consciousness resists heroism or social integration. This music was written in the Vienna of Metternich, after the failure of the French Revolution, the stresses of war and the defeat of Napoleon, with a culture policed and restricted by reactionary diktat.

Rewind
Jane Eaglen

The title role of *Turandot* is the Everest of the Italian soprano repertoire. A special voice is needed to hurl out those defiant phrases, as firm as iron girders. Lincoln-born soprano Jane Eaglen has the voice, but does she like the character?

'Not really,' she says cheerfully, 'but I try to make her as sympathetic as I can. There are a couple of moments. I try to think of her as a young girl caught in the royal situation. It's the way she's brought up: she's unhappy, rather than a cow.'

Premiered in 1926, Puccini's final opera tells the story of a Chinese princess who not only refuses to marry, but also ensures her suitors' love remains unrequited by executing them. She finally succumbs, but no one comes out of it well. 'Calàf's not exactly a nice person,' says Eaglen of the mysterious stranger who eventually wins the princess.

As the end of the opera nears, Turandot and Calàf wade through innocent blood towards the happy ending (and a reprise of the climax of 'Nessun Dorma'). However, not all the notes are Puccini's. The composer died before the opera was completed, and it was famously – or notoriously – left to Puccini's pupil Alfano to patch up the score. 'Puccini was infamous for changing [his works] until the last moment,' adds Eaglen. 'You can only imagine how it might have ended.'

Turandot's much-heralded entrance poses dramatic problems of its own. 'You're not even on in the first half. It's an incredible set-up, everyone waiting. People say it's easier just to stand and sing: it's not true. With the aria, you're setting up the whole ceremony. [There's] not much action or movement – just statement. It's like walking on a tightrope.'

Mention of Eaglen's mastery of Brünnhilde underlines her versatility. Wagner and Puccini both need vocal heft, but another favourite role of Eaglen's, the title character in Bellini's *Norma*, is the ultimate touchstone of early 19th-century *bel canto*, the art of spinning a fine, unwavering line with crystalline agility.

'I've always believed that you sing everything with the same technique, Norma the same as Brünnhilde. You need finesse in every role. I put some *piano* notes into Turandot, and each Brünnhilde has trills.'
Martin Hoyle; from Time Out, *21 February 2001*

The greatest result of the collision between these historical circumstances and Schubert's creative endeavours is *Winterreise* ('Winter's Journey'), a song-cycle set to poems by Wilhelm Müller, completed in 1827 and in many ways the first concept album. Unlike *Die schöne Müllerin*, Schubert's first big song-cycle, also set to Müller's poems and written four years earlier, *Winterreise* doesn't really have a plot; and unlike song-cycles that preceded it, it's prodigiously long, coming in at around 70 minutes in a modern, relatively brisk performance.

Over the course of *Winterreise*'s 24 separate songs, we get inside the head of a man who, for some unspecified reason, has split up with his girlfriend; and who then goes out into a snowy landscape and wanders, lost to the world and at times to his own reason, conscious of being alone as a rejected lover, but also, ultimately, as a human being in a meaningless cosmos. He is at turns morose, angry, self-lacerating, self-dramatising, deluded, crazy and funny. Indeed, his mood often changes dramatically within the cycle's individual songs. 'Rückblick' suddenly moves from anger to remembered charm, while 'Frühlingstraum' sees a chocolate-box melody followed by a rude musical awakening before the song ends on a note of dreamy desolation.

Many have seen *Winterreise* as a dark, gloomy work written for a low voice, lugubrious and slow at its worst. In fact, Schubert wrote it for a tenor: it's spiky, capricious and packed with humour (gallows and otherwise), full of twists and turns and contrasts; mania as much as depression, if you like. Schubert uses all sorts of styles – beautiful hymn-like melodies ('Die Nebensonnen'), crackpot waltzes ('Täuschung'), thigh-slapping parodic marches ('Mut') – and mixes them throughout: using different lengths and varied tempi, while also allowing for simple contrasts between high and low musical styles.

The end product is one of the defining moments of Western civilisation: poised on the brink of modernity, Beckettian before Beckett (who loved it), but also full of an incredible wealth of beautiful melody, of boundless consolation in the face of an apparently nihilistic vision. It starts with the protagonist wandering out into the snow ('Gute Nacht') and ends with him confronted by an old man playing cracked old tunes on his hurdy-gurdy in the icy street ('Der Leiermann'), an image at once of hope and desolation.

COURT & SPARK

Let's get it on

Sophie Harris gets jiggy with it.

First off, let's get a couple of things straight. Or, at least, as unrumpled as we're going to get in an essay about sex, that happily messiest of human activities. Songs about sex are as diverse as the people who do it: one person's idea of sexy is another's idea of damp socks. There are even people who rely on Barry White's gloopy 'Love Serenade' to get in the mood.

Songs about sex don't necessarily have to be explicit, but it's language that's chiefly concerned the BBC during its eight decade history. Since its first broadcast in 1922, the corporation has banned dozens of records from its airwaves for fear that they might offend its listeners. Some songs have been deemed too political for broadcast (Wings' 1972 single 'Give Ireland Back to the Irish', for example), while others have been seen as too insensitive at times of conflict (the Cure's 'Killing an Arab' was one of several records that were briefly banned during the Gulf War). However, the Beeb's most memorable bans have been its sex-bans, so sweetly prudish that they've become a cornerstone of British culture.

Even before the Rolling Stones got really filthy (check 'Rocks Off' from the glorious *Exile on Main St*), a rather clean-cut Mick and co were briefly banned – smack! – from the BBC's airwaves with the release of 'Let's Spend the Night Together', on the grounds that the song promoted promiscuity. Across the Atlantic, the Stones were even required to retitle the song 'Let's Spend Some Time Together' for a 1967 appearance on *The Ed Sullivan Show*. Still, the band's musical invitation was put in the shade two years later by Serge Gainsbourg's infinitely muckier 'Je t'aime… moi non plus', so filthy that it was banned twice by the BBC (in 1969 and 1974) and even denounced by the Vatican.

The story behind 'Je t'aime…' is a wonder in itself. After ol' big ears treated Brigitte Bardot to a date that went horribly wrong, Bardot refused to go on another unless he wrote her a mind-blowing song. Gainsbourg duly did so, but cannily insisted that he couldn't complete it without Bardot's participation. However, when Bardot's husband found out about the steamy collaboration, he demanded that the record be withdrawn, leaving the resourceful Gainsbourg to recruit British beauty Jane Birkin for the song's gasps, sighs and even the odd bit of singing. During his career, Serge would return to sex again and again (*Histoire de Melody Nelson* is a key musical knee-trembler), but never to quite such delicious and plausibly sticky effect.

Skipping past the corporation's bans on Cliff Richard's 'Honky Tonk Angel' (Cliff imposed it himself after belatedly discovering that he was singing about a hooker) and Donna Summer's disco heavy-breather 'Love to Love You Baby', the Beeb's most famous no-no was slammed down in January 1984. Halfway through a cheerful spin of Frankie Goes to Hollywood's 'Relax', Radio One breakfast show DJ Mike Read stopped nodding along to its thudding bassline, climactic rhythms and squelching noises and whipped the needle

Prince... and Nikki?

off the record. A blanket BBC ban ensued, whereupon 'Relax' shot to number one and became, at the time, the fourth biggest selling single in UK history.

Of course, songs about sex don't always have to be about The Act itself. It doesn't always take two to tango. Still, most musical odes to masturbation are pretty grim; and, perhaps unsurprisingly, the least sexy of all tend to be British. Take banjolele-toting weed George Formby and his shrill 'With My Little Stick of Blackpool Rock', for example; or, for that matter, Ivor Biggun's gruesome 1978 send-up 'The Winker's Song (Misprint)', in which the

soon-to-be *That's Life* panellist Doc Cox spends the chorus happily chanting that he's a wanker. 'Orgasm Addict', Buzzcocks' grubby hymn to self-abuse, and the Vapors' 1980 alarmingly frenetic hit 'Turning Japanese', apparently inspired by the facial contortions brought on by relentless onanism, aren't really any sexier.

Happily, not all odes to masturbation are sleazy tales of stained jeans and crumpled tissues. Australian combo the Divinyls fare rather better with their cheerily explicit 'I Touch Myself', as do Parliament with the mighty funk skronk of 'Up for the Down Stroke'. But they pale next to Prince: not for such straightahead copulanthems as 'Cream', 'Gett Off' and 'Sexy MF', but for a 1984 album track that thrills to the sight of a girl whiling away time in a hotel lobby by having a wank over a magazine (alas, Prince doesn't reveal which one; *Take a Break*, perhaps?). By verse two, 'Darling Nikki' has dragged Prince back to her rather more private lair, wherein he discovers a Hamley's-scale array of sex toys.

The kings and queens of sex on record, Prince among them, are always explicitly, audibly enthusiastic about getting their rocks off. 'I'm gonna *suck ya!*' hisses Marc Bolan in T Rex's glam-rock stomper 'Jeepster', which does everything but click its glittery heels with glee at the very thought of it. Etta James's steamy recording of Willie Dixon's blues standard 'I Just Want to Make Love to You' is every bit as taut with anticipation, albeit in a rather different way.

But then there are also plenty of songs about sex, and very *specifically* about sex, that just aren't sexy. James Brown's 'Sex Machine' is a furious, feverish record, but it's somehow too frantic, too spitty and ultimately too focused on its star to be a turn-on. It does, after all, take two people to do it *real* good. Madonna's dreadful 'Erotica', with its listless backbeat and its limply gasped chorus, is even less convincing. And even ghoddier still is the say-it's-true-and-people-will-believe-it boasting of ragga buffoon Shabba Ranks on his super-smoove '90s hit 'Mr Loverman'.

No: if you want to distill sex on to a record, it's got to be in the music as well as the words. As the old adage goes, every generation thinks it invented sex, but one only has to skip back several decades to see that in the US, blues and soul musicians have been doing (it) very well for a while now, thank you. Check out John Lee Hooker's 1962 hit 'Boom Boom', later covered in thrusting fashion by Louisiana swamp fox Tony Joe White; Sonny Boy Williamson's 'Good Morning Little School Girl', first recorded back in 1937; and even 'What'd I Say', on which Ray Charles managed to evoke a wild, hair-shakin' world of abandon with his call-and-response chorus. But like all the most potent smells, sights and sensations, the raw power of the blues still endures in the 21st century on the likes of the White Stripes' 'Ball and Biscuit'. Above a squirming mess of pounding drums and explosive guitar, a

'The kind of frizzy hair, spandex leggings and effeminate shrieks favoured by the likes of WASP's Blackie Lawless briefly amounted to the very embodiment of musical masculinity.'

swaggering, cocksure Jack White promises he'll let you see it if you want to, as if 'it' wasn't already clearly visible through his red trousers. Phew.

Music about sex took a change of course in the late 1940s and into the 1950s, as commercial concerns helped usher in a golden era of innuendo. From R&B hits such as the Toppers' 'Baby Let Me Bang Your Box' (was *anyone* fooled into thinking it was about playing the piano?) to Wynonie Harris's 'Keep on Churnin' ('Til the Butter Come)', R&B singers weren't shy about using an ill disguised analogy or two in order to get their point across. And the winking likes of Bull Moose Jackson didn't even bother with double entendres: on the preposterous 'Big Ten Inch Record', a single entendre was plenty.

The calypso backdrop to Lord Kitchener's fabulously rude 'Dr Kitch' is a world removed from the likes of 'Keep on Churnin''. However, Kitchener's lyrics could have come from Harris himself. After the Trinidadian calypso champ warns his female 'patient' that he's not a 'qualified physician', he eventually delivers his 'injection', at which point the poor woman yelps that she can't bear the size of Kitch's 'needle'. Just as well for womankind that during his stay in England, Kitch spent his energy watching cricket.

Aussie rockers AC/DC have built a career on similarly unsubtle innuendo. One such cut, 'Let Me Put My Love into You', even found its way on to the infamous 'Filthy Fifteen', a list of apparently offensive songs drawn up in 1985 by Tipper Gore's Parents Music Resource

Centre (PMRC) as guidance for moms and pops concerned that their sons and daughers were being corrupted by rock music. America's parents took cautious note, but the kids immediately and predictably turned the manifesto into a shopping list and were thus introduced to the delightful likes of Judas Priest's 'Eat Me Alive' and WASP's 'Animal (Fuck Like a Beast)'.

Indeed, for a brief period in the mid 1980s, the kind of frizzy hair, spandex leggings and effeminate shrieks favoured by the likes of WASP singer Blackie Lawless amounted to the very embodiment of musical masculinity. Women (this was a Neanderthally heterosexual art form) swooned and flashed their tits to the likes of Whitesnake's 'Slide It In' and 'Slow an' Easy', while the boys preened and primped their perms in tumescent anticipation. And when, in 1986, Aerosmith teamed up with Run-DMC for 'Walk This Way', it marked a

melding of two of pop's supposedly sexiest genres, wedding the howl and growl of rock to the physical grind of hip hop.

Although blighted by exhaustive lyrical references to bitches and hos, not to mention the more recent conjoining of hip hop with iffy porn thanks to Snoop Dogg, rap has nonetheless produced more than its share of make-out music. And once again, *conveying* sex wins out over *describing* sex, blow by blow. The title track of Kool Keith's *Sex Style* concept album is a veritable catalogue of indecency, but the explicit lyrics and dark aggro backbeat helps make the scenario about as enticing as a date with Grotbags. Contrast it with velveteen-clad hip hop queen Missy Elliott's deliciously sensuous slow jam with Ginuwine on 'Friendly Skies'. This passenger/stewardess scenario doesn't get much filthier than references to turbulence and buckle-belts, but with its whispers, sighs and fluttering R&B backing, it's akin to listening in on something very private indeed.

A stranger take on sex altogether was provided by Digital Underground on their 1990 track 'Sex Packets', a fictional story about a hallucinogenic, non-addictive, non-harmful ghetto drug with the power to transport a man to a world of imagined physical ecstasy. The song even announced that no sex could be safer, but its warm, smooth beats and wayward weirdness found a sinister counterpoint in the depressing reality of ghetto life in the early 1990s, and particularly the rise of AIDS and crack addiction.

Given the gravity and scale of the AIDS epidemic, it's odd that there have been so few successful attempts to make safe sex sexy, at least in the pop arena. George Michael's excruciating instruction to 'explore monogamy' on the promotional video for his drearily sexless 'I Want Your Sex' is surely the nadir; the high point is perhaps gal rap trio Salt 'n' Pepa's buoyant 'Let's Talk About Sex', which packs an important message into a velour-tracksuited singalong. Blur's anthem 'Girls and Boys' is no less catchy, but the song's underlying assertion that modern-day love is rife with paranoia is noticeably less optimistic.

Blur had to set their aesthetic to a disco beat in order to add even a little animal magnetism to their music, which raises the question whether indie boys, traditionally the stuttering,

Oh, do stop it, **Steven Tyler**. You'll go blind.

Rewind
Jane Birkin

'I trusted Serge at all times,' says Birkin when asked about 'Lemon Incest', the duet Gainsbourg wrote and sung with the couple's daughter Charlotte, then 12 years old. 'The thing that people who know very little about Serge won't realise is that he was tremendously shy. The whole reason he changed his name from Lucien to Serge when he started making records is because Serge is a nom de guerre, a mask. And, if anything, his shyness inhibited his relationship with Charlotte.'

In many ways, 'Lemon Incest' was the perfect meeting of immense tenderness and innate contrariness, the two separate sentiments that informed much of Gainsbourg's work. The same can be said of the soul-baring intimacy of the songs he seemed to set aside for his wife even after they separated, such as the poignant 'Baby Alone in Babylone' (taken from the 1983 album of the same name).

'He gave me all the sad songs,' says Birkin. 'Sometimes I'd go to see him in concert and he'd sing songs that he'd written for me, songs that would make him so sad that bubbles would come out of his nose. So perhaps he *wanted* his sadness to be known.'

Gainsbourg never really received much acclaim across the Channel, something that Birkin regrets. But has she never been tempted to move back home and acquaint herself with '90s London?

'I'm not sure. There are certain things I absolutely adore about London: the pubs; the darts; the little seats in taxis where you can talk to the drivers; the parks and the fact that you can eat your sandwiches there. In France, you're not even allowed to touch the statues. Half the joy of statues is touching the bosoms and the bottoms.'

Peter Paphides; from Time Out, *19 March 1997*

Although previous and subsequent marriages to composer John Barry and director Jacques Doillon bookended Jane Birkin's relationship with France's most celebrated singer-songwriter, Serge Gainsbourg has remained the metronome of her life. There were the 12 years they spent married, and the daughter that the union produced. There was *that* single, of course, as well as the numerous other recordings on which they collaborated. And there was even a 1975 movie, directed by Gainsbourg and starring Birkin alongside a truck-driving Joe Dallesandro in the kind of chaotic yet desolate moden romance that typified Gainsbourg's erotic, cliché-gobbling world view.

'When it came out,' recalls Birkin with a clipped London propriety, 'my mother phoned to ask me what my new movie was doing in Soho's Classic Moulin. And I said, "Ma! I don't know! In France, it came out on the Champs-Élysées and Truffaut's gone *crazy* for it!"'

'Je t'aime... moi non plus', the chart-topping single after which the movie was named, is the first thing that most Britons know about Gainsbourg. The second is that he once appeared alongside Whitney Houston on a French talk show and announced, to Houston and the nation, 'I want to fuck her.' And the third thing is the one that leaves most potential Gainsbourg fans slightly uneasy about what they might be getting into.

pasty-faced cardigan-wearers of the musical community, can ever really do sexy on record. Circumstantial evidence would appear to suggest not. Consider the limp guitars, the lame-o drumming and the shy stage mannerisms that typify everything from *C86* to the Kooks; or, post-Oasis, the bragging lads in parkas who seem far more comfortable glassing someone for spilling lager on their shoe than getting down to business.

But for all that, alternative rock has occasionally managed a little spice. In 1988, My Bloody Valentine's Kevin Shields delivered the juddering, ecstatic 'Soft as Snow (But Warm Inside)', a woozily sung paean to girl-on-top grinding. And then there's Pulp's 'Sheffield: Sex City', a breathtakingly seedy nocturne in which keyboardist Candida Doyle recalls a childhood spent being kept awake in her council block by a neighbouring couple having it off… and then another, and another… 'Like some kind of chain reaction,' she says, dourly. 'Within minutes, the whole building was fucking… It's such a happy, exciting sound.' As is so often the case, the song's underlying realness is what makes it sizzle.

On the other side of the tracks, sexy music can be poetic, even delicate. Freak-folk hero Devendra Banhart achieves just such a feat on the lacy, lovely 'The Body Breaks', one of very few songs to combine enduring romantic love with an urge to really get down. 'The body sways like the wind on a swing/The bridge through a hoop or a lake through a ring,' coos Banhart, making Grace Jones's 'Pull Up to the Bumper' seem rather clumsy by comparison.

Banhart's sweet, leftfield poem stands in huge contrast to today's pop hits: the stuff that comes blaring out of schoolkids' mobile phones, gets shouted over in strip-lit supermarkets and is downloaded with non-committal ease. So it's heartening to hear 50 Cent and Justin Timberlake declaring their wish to get back to basics. 'Ayo Technology' pounds and throbs to an electro beat and swirls of synths, but its message is decidedly earthy and even a little old-fashioned. 'I'm tired of using technology,' squeals Timberlake. 'Why don't you come and sit on top of me?' These days, we're never more than a click or a tap or a bleep away from contact of some sort. But it's not fucking, and the very best pop music reminds us that it never will be.

On the record
John Darnielle

'40 Hours'

Sarah Dougher

Sarah Dougher's '40 Hours', from her album *Day One*, changed my life and continues to do so, but what does that even mean? It didn't make me rich; it didn't put food on my table; I was not able to use it as a component of a successful defence strategy at trial. But it did open my eyes to the notion of engaging adult sexuality in song, rather than trying to pretend that the only sex worth having is the adolescent stuff on which rock music has built its church.

Some people spend their lives never learning to love who they are, and most people don't stop to think – because we're busy, because we have our own lives, because we're human – that every person we see may be starving to raise his or her hand and say, 'I'm here, and I am filled with love, and I wish could share it, because it is a tidal force inside of me.' All this sounds like some tie-dyed rainbows-and-ponies stuff when I talk about it, I know. But it's a cold, stone-hard truth, too, I think, which may be why we get defensive or dismissive when we talk about it. Except that you don't get defensive or dismissive when Sarah Dougher sings: 'And I will love whoever I want, love whoever I want, love whoever I want.' Your defences drop. And then you just cry like a child, and wish everyone in the world could sing '40 Hours' at least once in their lives.

John Darnielle's most recent album as leader of the Mountain Goats is Heretic Pride *(4AD); he is also the author of* Master of Reality *(Continuum)*

Fear of Music

1000 SONGS TO CHANGE YOUR LIFE

Write

or wrong

John Lewis hunts down some songwriters to learn the tricks of their trade.

Keep a notebook with you

'All songwriters carry notebooks with them,' says Billy Bragg. 'All the time. You never know when an idea will crop up.'

Pete Waterman concurs. 'You hear little flashes of conversation, little quips, clichés, puns, things like that, all the time. Phrases like "I Should Be so Lucky", "Better the Devil You Know", "Showing Out", "Roadblock" – they were all phrases I heard in conversation. I remember writing them all down. Before you know it, you've triggered off a series of connections and you can work with that.'

In fact, suggests Elvis Costello, you should never let your notebook leave your sight. 'Always keep a notebook and pencil next to the bed. That witty lyric or that brilliant idea that comes fully formed in the middle of the night? You *will not* remember it in the morning. Oh, and practise writing in the dark, too.'

Sing nonsense

You've got your tune, and you've put a few chord changes over the top. Now you need some lyrics. Paul McCartney famously began writing the lyrics to 'Yesterday' with the couplet 'Scrambled eggs/How I love the smell of scambled eggs.' Paul Weller, meanwhile, started 'Going Underground' with a guitar riff and then found certain phrases emerging from it. 'I kept singing "The public gets what the public wants" over the top of the chord changes. That started to dictate the mood of the song.'

Singing gibberish is a popular method used by songwriters. 'I have an old ghetto-blaster above my piano,' says Gilbert O'Sullivan. 'Once I get my chord changes and my tune, I just start singing wordless syllables over the top. I tape it and when I play it back, some of the gibberish I sing will resemble real words and sentences.' Frank Black did this with Pixies; some of the wordless rambles survived into the final recordings.

Lionel Richie takes his incompleted backing tracks and plays them back, putting wordless vocals on top. 'I drive my family mad. In the bath, in the kitchen, in the car, I'll listen to demo recordings of the backing tracks and then play them over and over again, singing along to them, until I find a tune and a lyric that fits.'

Just play…

'If you've got writer's block, it's because you're not fucking playing your instrument,' says Paul Weller, forthrightly. 'You need to get in front of an instrument and just play anything. Ideas will come from that. One riff will lead to a chord, which leads to another chord. Before you know it, you've got the start of a song.'

Jamie Reynolds from the Klaxons operates on a similar principle. 'Get yourself a studio, get a groove going, sing some absolute nonsense over the top, put a breakbeat behind it and you're away. That's what I did! That's genuinely it.'

Lonnie Jordan of '70s hitmakers War says that every one of their songs came from jam sessions. 'Someone would come up with a bassline or a guitar riff or a harmonica line, and we'd all join in. Then someone would start hollering. And before you'd know it, we had the basis for a song.'

… But not necessarily your own instrument

John Lennon found his most productive songwriting period, in the late '60s and early '70s, came when he ditched the guitar and started writing on the piano. Because he wasn't as proficient on the piano, he said, he avoided some of the hackneyed phrases he traditionally played on the guitar.

'Playing your second instrument is a good way out of a creative cul-de-sac,' agrees Weller. 'And being in unchartered territory is often a help. I might play a little chord in the right hand and play a completely different bass note in the left hand, something that would be impossible on the guitar.'

'Often, if you pick up exotic instruments you know nothing about, it forces you to view music differently,' says Fyfe Dangerfield from the Guillemots. 'You start marshalling sound, and you start playing sequences of notes you'd never play on your own instrument. That's why I love going to shops like Man Ray in London, trying out Chinese and Indian instruments. It's a real inspiration.'

Only work with someone else if it feels right

Record companies are always keen to get budding young musicians into rooms with other writers, hoping for lightning to strike as it did with Robbie Williams and Guy Chambers. 'That's what they did at the Brill Building,'

John Lennon works on his scales.

according to Burt Bacharach. 'They'd throw us in these rooms with a piano – remember we were all kids at the time, just out of our teens – and make us bang out songs in a matter of hours. That pressure often worked.'

'Motown was about collaboration, too,' agrees Lamont Dozier. 'With Holland-Dozier-Holland, I played the piano, Eddie Holland wrote the lyrics and Brian would do a bit of both, finishing off our ideas.'

It doesn't always work as well, but even the worst experiences have their advantages. 'Sometimes you get put in a room with an experienced songwriter,' says KT Tunstall. 'Even though nothing might came of it, you'll learn a lot from seeing other people in action.'

Weller, though, disagrees. 'I've never really got into co-writing. With the Style Council, I'd sometimes come in with a set of lyrics and Mick [Talbot] would write the music. But I don't think I could sit in a room with someone and thrash something out, chuntering away on two guitars. I'm a bit too self-conscious for that. Songwriting is quite a personal business for me. Me and Noel [Gallagher] or Bobby G [Gillespie] have occasionally talked about writing together, but it wouldn't be us in the same room. I quite like the idea of long-distance writing: recording a riff or a backing track, sending it off, the other person coming up with ideas, chipping away at it and sending it back. That's what me and Graham Coxon have been doing recently and it works well.'

Work out your own discipline

'Songwriting is a job,' says Pete Waterman. 'You can't expect God to hit you over the head with a fully-formed song. You have to work at it.' Waterman, like Paul McCartney, Gilbert O'Sullivan, Randy Newman and Chris Difford, works from an office. When they're writing songs, they physically leave the house and do a disciplined nine-to-five as songwriters.

Ian Dury liked to work at his ideas late into the night in front of a huge A3 or A2 pad, using the white space to write couplets, plot narratives, character descriptions and general plans. Elvis Costello does a similar thing, using A2 pads to transfer the fragments of notes that he may have accumulated in scrapbooks and Dictaphones. 'The page quickly resembles a mad equation,' says Costello, 'with fluorescent markers connecting one stanza to another.'

On the record
Pete Waterman

'She Loves You'
The Beatles

This is the ultimate pop song. You really can't get any better than this. What I love about it is that it treads a fine line between banality and genius. Great pieces of art often do. A lot of things regarded as masterpieces you have to kid yourself to actually like them – there's a touch of emperor's new clothes – but there's no faking it here. It's on the borderline between kitsch and pure genius.

It's one of the early songs that Lennon and McCartney actually wrote together rather than separately. If you look at the words on paper, they're ridiculous. Try and recite it as a poem and it simply does not work – that's why Peter Sellers had so much fun doing his spoken-word parody. But when you weld it on to that swaggering beat and hear it sung in their excited voices, it takes on a different meaning and makes perfect sense.

They really did reinvent pop music in their own image. Every pop songwriter of the past 40 years has had to contend with that legacy. That's a terrible burden for us all, isn't it? How can we even begin to write songs when we have to compete with Lennon and McCartney? *Pete Waterman wrote and produced countless hits as part of Stock Aitken Waterman*

Public Enemy also used to work visually; lyricist Chuck D and producer Hank Shocklee would map out their samples, lyrics and drum beats on the wall of their studio with Blu-Tac'd pieces of A4 paper and Post-It notes. But others prefer to work in a more haphazard way. Paul Heaton likes to take notes that he's gathered and then fly to a foreign country to work on them in a hotel. 'I write my best lyrics in places where they can't speak English,' he says. 'You're lonely and isolated, which is good for creativity.'

Focus on a story

Smokey Robinson once persuaded Stevie Wonder to construct narrative threads for his songs. 'Stevie's music was always brilliant,' says Smokey, 'but as a teenager, his lyrics were all over the place. You'd have someone standing in the rain, then they'd be in a relationship, then they'd be talking about someone completely different. He told me he was just copying things he got from listening to my songs! But he learned that you have to have an overall story, a narrative thread linking those words together.'

'I used to write every song with this girl called Bernadette in mind,' says Dozier, a former colleague of Robinson's at Motown. 'I'd summon up the emotions that she would bring out in me and then try and recreate them in song. Great songs are about sincerity, things that dominate your heart. If you can find a way of turning those feelings into narrative, you've got the beginnings of a great song.'

'Most of my inspiration comes from my own life,' says Cathy Dennis. 'Stuff that's happening to me, not normally what's happening to someone else. One trick I often use is to turn the roles around so I'm on the receiving end of what I would normally be giving out.'

Write more lyrics than you need

'I always tend to overwrite verses for songs,' says Nick Cave. 'Once I've got a story, I find it easy to write. Then, when I'm in the studio, I quickly edit them down, so the story sometimes jump-cuts from one part to another, leaving gaps in the narrative. But I like that.'

'Overwriting is important,' agrees Elvis Costello. 'Once you edit things, it leaves a sense of mystery. The listener then has to work out the missing connections for themself.'

Carry a tape recorder

'I've got tape recorders everywhere,' confesses Lionel Richie. 'Absolutely everywhere. I carry one with me all the time. It's an unhealthy obsession.'

Richie has an unlikely ally in the Fall's frontman Mark E Smith. 'I used to ring up my phone and leave messages on my answerphone when I had ideas for songs. Then I found a little Dictaphone thing that I can bark into.' Smith, though, is keen to stress that not all Dictaphones are created equal. 'Don't get one with those shitty little tapes. You'll never find them again.'

Neil Tennant uses his mobile phone to record stray ideas, either texting lyrics or singing ideas into it. 'But, in the cold light of day, they're usually rubbish.'

Take a break

David Byrne likes to come up with ideas while cycling. 'I stop off on the sidewalk and sing my ideas into a Dictaphone,' he says. Rufus Wainwright likes to lie in the bath and write lyrics, where 'the acoustics are good'.

Billy Bragg, though, prefers to take a stroll. 'I go for a walk with my imaginary dog. I walk for as long as I need. If I only need two verses, I'll walk for two verses. If I need two verses, a chorus and a middle eight, I might have to walk a bit further. It'll be buzzing around my head and I'll write it down when I get back.'

Use other media

'Virtually every song I've ever written has started while I'm watching a film,' says Daniel Kessler from Interpol. 'I tend to start the day by watching a DVD and playing along with my classical guitar. At that time in the morning, there's something very meditative about getting immersed in a movie, and I find that conducive to creativity. If I come up with any riffs, I record them on my Dictaphone.'

Paddy McAloon often finds characters and settings for songs in novels and short stories; Dozier and Ike Turner have always been inspired by TV. Brian Eno has found that a jaunt around an art gallery can inspire certain soundscapes, while Björk has been inspired by everything from philosophy books to classical composition. Marilyn Manson, meanwhile, has cited Nietzsche, the Satanist writer Anton LaVey and Willy Wonka as key influences.

Use technology, but don't let it use you

There's lots of good advice in *The Manual: How to Have a Number One the Easy Way*, Bill Drummond and Jimmy Cauty's fabled and hilariously cynical 1988 guide to the nuts and bolts of creating a chart-topper. However, it may be a little early to adopt wholeheartedly Drummond's main credo: 'If you're in a band, leave it… If you've got instruments, sell them all,' he writes, before suggesting that anyone wanting to have a number one should just invest in sequencers and sampling technology.

Pete Waterman disagrees. 'Technology should be used as a tool, not a prop,' he says. 'It's handy to work to a drum loop, for instance. That can get you in a mood to write a song,

encourage the flow of ideas. But the problem comes when everyone is using the same technology, the same preset voices. Songwriting programmes, like GarageBand on the Apple Mac, can be useful, but they also encourage everyone to think and structure their songs in the same way. You listen to a lot of music now and you can actually see every key being triggered on the program. It doesn't lead to great songs.'

'I've increasingly got sick of people using hip new beats, like it's this season's new handbag,' admits Björk. 'Sometimes you need a big blast of live drumming, and the noise and the filth and the irregularities that come with that.'

Nick Cave finds inspiration in a rather unlikely source.

Rewind
Burt Bacharach

'I find that I have songs rolling around my head all the time. At night, it's the worst – it's like having this jukebox on while you're trying to sleep. It's taken me a while to realise that this is the price you have to pay for being a songwriter. It means I'm never up first thing in the morning with my kids, as I should be.

'I remember working on "Alfie" and trying to finish it. I went to see a play and I'm watching the play, but I'm still working on "Alfie", so I'm not watching the play. So I lose on both.

'Sometimes it's much easier. The fastest song I ever wrote was "I'll Never Fall In Love Again", because we were out on the road on a Broadway show called *Promises, Promises* and it had to go in the show as quickly as possible. I'd been in a hospital for five days with pneumonia, which is where that line about pneumonia came from. Me and Hal wrote that in one afternoon flat.

'I love hearing other people do my songs, especially jazz musicians. McCoy Tyner did some nice versions; so did Stan Getz. But sometimes I think that my music is a bit restrictive for jazz artists. Partly it's because I don't always write "pure" songs in the old Tin Pan Alley sense. Not like, say, Irving Berlin. A lot of the time, the arrangements are written into the songs. Like with "Walk on By": the string section is embedded in the tune. That's the way I wrote it – you can't separate the melody from the arrangement. So it's sometimes difficult to do cover versions without trying to replicate those arrangements.

'But my work was always different from the Tin Pan Alley stuff. In the early days, when I was writing songs for people in the Brill Building, they'd say, "You've got a bar of 3/4 followed by a bar of 4/4? Make it all straight 4/4 and I'll get you so-and-so to do this song." People didn't understand the complicated time signatures in my songs. I never thought like that. I write things like that because it makes sense to me, because it follows the logic of the melody. "Anyone Who Had a Heart" had a seven-beat bar. And the time signatures on "I Say a Little Prayer" are all over the place, but it still grooves. It kicks ass. You can dance to them. That's because I never consciously make something avant-garde. It's all natural.

'I guess I picked some stuff up when I learned with avant-garde composers like Darius

Milhaud, Henry Cowell and Bohuslav Martinů. But I never do so consciously. I'm like a sponge. I soak up years of influences. Same with Brazilian music: I love guys like Milton Nascimento, João Gilberto, Djavan, Jobim, Ibanez. I've never understood the language. They could be singing something political, but it sounds sexy as hell to me.

'If you ask me to name a great pop song, it's got to be something that you can hang on to melodically. And a song that doesn't beat you up, something that sounds good five or six times in a row. "Ain't No Mountain High Enough" by Diana Ross: that's a killer. So is "Papa Was a Rollin' Stone" by the Temptations, or Earth, Wind and Fire's "After the Love Has Gone", or "What a Fool Believes" by the Doobies. Those are four damn good songs: beautifully structured, fantastic melodies, great arrangements, good grooves. And you can dance to them all. I'd have been proud to write any of them.'

Burt Bacharach was talking to John Lewis

'Don't be dictated to by the machines,' says Lee 'Scratch' Perry. 'They can be little devils. You have to treat them with disrespect. Do things to them that they weren't designed for. Don't read the manuals.'

Your songs aren't yours once you've finished them

'Some people have said that the music I write is different to the stuff I listen to,' says KT Tunstall. 'That's because you have to respect the logic of each song you create. You can't try to turn it into something else. Ultimately, the song takes on a life of its own.'

'When you write a song it almost becomes public domain,' says Weller. 'It's not yours anymore. It becomes a part of other people's lives. I love that. For 30 years, people have been dancing or singing or snogging or fighting or fucking to my songs. Part of me has to surrender ownership. It's kind of humbling.'

Ignore all of the above

The main rule of songwriting is that there are no rules. Napalm Death wrote songs that lasted a matter of seconds. Burt Bacharach and John Lennon couldn't stick to 4/4 time signatures. Some songs only use one chord. Many lyrics are nonsense.

THE MANUAL
(HOW TO HAVE A NUMBER ONE THE EASY WAY)

JIMMY CAUTY   BILL DRUMMOND

FEAR OF MUSIC

Songwriting in 20 songs

'Song for Whoever' The Beautiful South
Paul Heaton is at his most deceptively caustic in this lush, romantic ballad about a cynical songwriter who turns women's grief into glory while excitedly awaiting his PRS cheques.

'These Words' Natasha Bedingfield
This Ivor Novello Award-nominated track describes the creative constipation, lack of harmonic imagination and metrical clumsiness that comes from writer's block, bemoaning how difficult it is to be musically clever before surrendering to a string of lyrical and harmonic clichés.

'Not Another Love Song' Deana Carter
The verses of this song, found on Carter's third album, aren't anything more or anything less than a pretty straightforward woe-is-me slowie, but the chorus, in which she whimpers that she can't write any more love songs until her man returns, transports Carter's personal woes into her professional life. Good thing she's a country singer: break-up songs should do just fine.

'Hallelujah' Leonard Cohen
During the long life of this much-covered epic, Cohen has filed at least a dozen verses for it. Some come and go, depending on the performer and the situation, but 'Hallelujah' usually opens in the same way: with the songwriter explaining the structure of his masterpiece to a listener who's not especially interested.

'Sweet Is the Melody' Iris DeMent
DeMent's musing on the hard graft required to drag a melody into shape, and the rewards that await when the hard work's over and the song is finally done, was a foretaste of the troubles that went on to beset her. Apparently unable to complete a set of songs that meet her own presumably sky-high standards, she's not released an album of self-penned material since 1996.

'Song Sung Blue' Neil Diamond
A counterpoint of sorts to the Scritti Politti track below, perhaps, wherein Diamond interrogates the ways in which one can counteract suffering from the blues by writing and performing a blues song. It ultimately brings to mind the headline in spoof newspaper *The Onion*: 'Affluent White Man Enjoys, Causes the Blues'.

'Classic' Adrian Gurvitz
A much-pilloried slice of would-be self-referentiality, famously rhyming 'classic' with 'attic', from the Stoke Newington-born singer-songwriter.

'Over and Over' Hot Chip

The Fisher-Price-funk five-piece from Putney essay a relentless critique of repetitive dance music that is itself a wonderfully hypnotic example of repetitive dance music.

'Williamsburg Will Oldham Horror' Jeffrey Lewis

En route to a studio, Lewis thinks he spots Bonnie 'Prince' Billy on the subway, and is drawn into an extended reverie about the ins and outs of the creative process, the ego-massaging nature of life in (or, in Lewis's case, just out of) the indie-rock spotlight, and whether it's worth him continuing to write the songs that he's currently off to remaster. Oldham responds by kicking him in the teeth.

'I Write the Songs' Barry Manilow

In which Mr Manilow adopts the role of a transcultural, transhistorical muse responsible for all melody that has ever been created in the history of humankind; songs that, indeed, make the whole world sing.

'Who Put the Bomp (In the Bomp, Bomp, Bomp)' Barry Mann & the Halos

Gerry Goffin and Barry Mann's 1961 creation was, on the surface, a thoroughly disposable piece of bubblegum pop, but it also serves as an eerily self-referential song that draws attention to the primal gibberish that provided the basis for so many doo-wop performances ('ram-a-lam-a-ding-dong', 'bop-she-bop-she-bop' and so on).

'Can't Get You Out of My Head' Kylie Minogue

The lyric, according to co-songwriter Rob Davis (formerly of Mud), is not just a straight song of obsessive love but a reference to the insistently catchy 'ear worm' provided by the 'la la la' chorus, a musical phrase that lodges in your neural paths and won't leave in a hurry.

'Sad Songs and Waltzes' Willie Nelson

The misery of the failed songwriter is brought into sharp focus on this low-key number from *Shotgun Willie*, in which Nelson bemoans the fact that while he'd love to get a measure of revenge on his ex by telling the listening public how poorly she treated him, 'sad songs and waltzes aren't selling this year'.

'I Miss You' Randy Newman

Newman at his most wickedly ambiguous. Is it a love song to his former wife? A thank-you note? An apology? Or simply a rather arch song about the process of writing a song, and how any songwriter would sell their soul – 'and your souls' – for a hit record? Certainly, that foggy, froggy voice isn't giving anything away.

'Tennessee Waltz' Patti Page

Okay, so it's not really a song about songwriting. However, this is perhaps the ultimate song about itself, in which the protagonist finds himself dancing with his partner to a tune in three-quarter time called, er, the 'Tennessee Waltz'. The space-time continuum stubbornly refused to be disrupted.

'My Iron Lung' Radiohead

The iron lung of the title is reputedly 'Creep', the hit that kept them alive in the early '90s while simultaneously overshadowing everything else they were trying to accomplish. In 2001, Thom Yorke was reported to have introduced a live performance of 'My Iron Lung' by describing it as being about 'turning out the same old shit to make money'.

'Mr Songwriter' Vic Reeves

A reflexive tribute to the song craftsman, possibly inspired by Rick Springfield's song of the same name, that also pays tribute to weavers, painters, wood-carvers and nut-gatherers. The version on the album *I Will Cure You* is also notable for the presence of the avant-garde jazz saxophonist Evan Parker, whose freeform solo is interrupted by Reeves shouting, 'Pack it in, Parker!'

'The Word Girl' Scritti Politti

Green Gartside had previously written about the pop song as a lexical conundrum; 'Faithless', from 1982's *Songs to Remember* album, and 'Wood Beez (Pray Like Aretha Franklin)', released three years later, both address the secularisation of soul music. But this single explicitly addresses the way in which the word 'girl' is tossed around throughout pop history as a casual punctuation device. Even by Mr Gartside himself.

'Song About the Moon' Paul Simon

Simon has always seemed acutely aware of the way in which songwriting depends on craft as well as inspiration, even going so far as to teach a songwriting class at New York University during the summer after his split from Art Garfunkel. 'Song About the Moon' isn't quite a syllabus in its own right, but struggling lyricists might benefit from its evocatively delivered advice.

'Piano' Jimmy Webb

As well as *Tunesmith: Inside the Art of Songwriting*, his fascinating book on the subject, Webb's written several songs that refer, acutely or obliquely, to the creative process: 'PF Sloan', his tribute to the lost (but since rediscovered) singer-songwriter; 'Another Lullaby', which is pretty much what it describes; and this little ode to the tools of his trade. 'Self-pitying though it may sound,' he notes in the liner to the *Archive* compilation, 'it's really about my love for the physical object.'

Come on feel the noise

Nick Coleman gets rhythm like you get the blues.

Here is a transcription of one of my favourite song lyrics, a line that transformed my life. Please, if you're not on the bus, read the words out loud. It might help you get into the vibe if you were to imagine beneath your voice a walking bassline that double-bumps on the hump (this is an abstruse technical term; if you don't know what it means, guess). Also, try to hear in your mind's ear a bottleneck electric guitar, flaring like a rocket above your voice.

Right, here it is. Out loud, please: 'I'm a bad, bad, bad, bad, bad, bad, bad, bad, bad, bad, bad, bad boy.' Magic, eh? Conjures all kinds of images. Really takes you someplace other and leaves you there with nothing but a strange-shaped hole in your heart and scratches all over your soul. But there it is. That's the power of song.

And in case you're wondering whether it was the content of the lyrics that jiggered me so, it was not. The song might as well have been concerned with bad, bad smells. I concede that the words 'bad' and 'boy' sound good in songs, being both percussive and highly efficient in the semantic sense. The words might have been designed for use in this context, which is the context of shrill, breast-beating, early '70s hard rock. But what those words might mean made very little difference to how they were taken, in my bedroom, in 1973, as the hormones flared in my 13-year-old body and a new kind of sensibility began to flower in the jungle of my selfhood.

It was the sheer *sound* that held me, both the sound of the words and the bendy effect they appeared to have on the click of time. The repetition, the beat-chopping syncopation, the *hit-hit-hit* of all those identical syllables across the double-bumped humping of the bassline – the overwhelming sense that, at this near-hysterical juncture of what was never a very calm song, neither sense nor meaning mattered very much any more and the only thing left to do with words was to convert them into yet another set of drums on which to beat. No, it assuredly was not what those syllables meant that captured me. It was their rhythm, their *feel*: that thing you get when you start to mess around with meter, and time reveals just how elastic it can be.

In case you're still wondering, the song was 'Bad Bad Boy' by the Scottish band Nazareth. 'Bad Bad Boy' could never stand as rock 'n' roll's most transcendent three minutes (it wouldn't stand even as Nazareth's), but it did once stand, for me, as an epiphany. This was a dull coincidence of hormones and pop history, not divine intervention. Had I turned 13 four years later in 1977, during punk's ideological high tide, I'd have been less occupied by feel than by *energy*. The Damned's 'New Rose', for instance, is an exercise in getting from point A to point B as quickly as possible and with maximum audible muscle-twitch. Equally, had puberty gone thermo in 1988, then it's likely that machine-regulated rhythmic pressure would have been my thing. As it was, half the rock groups a white Fen boy got to hear in 1973 were obsessed with the question of feel (the other half were obsessed with the question of what it meant to be 'progressive', but that's another story). Feel was everything to them. It was the point of the exercise.

Having your own feel meant several things to a band in the early '70s. For one thing, it signalled that you were responding only to the impulses of your own bodies and not to those of commerce: you were being yourself and nobody's tool. At the ethical level, it indicated that you had your priorities right. But, more importantly, it signified that you were hooked up to the motherlode. Feel was the value above all others that made gods out of Muddy Waters ('Mannish Boy'), Howlin' Wolf ('Smokestack Lightnin''), Ray Charles ('What'd I Say, Pt.1'), BB King ('The Thrill Is Gone'), Little Richard ('Tutti Frutti'), Elvis Presley ('That's All Right (Mama)'), Jerry Lee Lewis ('Mean Woman Blues'), Otis Redding ('Respect'), Aretha Franklin ('I Say a Little Prayer'), Motown house bassist James Jamerson, James Brown's drummer Clyde Stubblefield, Miles Davis,

The band that launched a thousand chewing-gum ads: **Free**.

John Coltrane… All the heavenly host of American supernals, in other words, the post-war host that deployed feel – and swing, its prototype – as an infinitely variable expression of creative individuation.

Feel was the difference between Bobby Darin singing 'Mack the Knife' and Ella Fitzgerald singing it. It was the difference between squareness and hipness, between stiffness and elasticity. At a formative stage, it was the difference between black and white. To Englishmen in particular, it was what put a distance between the world as it used to be and how we'd like it to be now, please. Feel was the code that unlocked the ultimate differential: what makes popular music popular, and what makes it popular and *great*.

There was a pressing imperative in the early '70s for hip rock groups to have feel, and they went to some lengths to get it. The prime English exemplars would be Free. Slow to medium in tempo, funky without being *funky*, 'All Right Now' aspires to emulate the articulation of the hips during coition. But better than 'All Right Now', I think, is 'Ride on a Pony', an old-fashioned mutant 12-bar lollop with verse and chorus sprung out of their traditional fixings in the blues structure. Simon Kirke, Free's drummer, thinks so too, on the grounds that it was the moment in the studio when the group expressed itself most cogently as a rhythm beast with four backs. God alone knows what the song is actually about. All that's certain is that 'Ride on a Pony' finds four English chaps tapping into the motherlode for all they're worth with swagger and finesse, every joint and cadence in the thing hinged to the point of unanswerable articulacy.

Sex wasn't the only thing '70s rock groups tried to feel. The Rolling Stones' second coming as the Greatest Rock 'n' Roll Band in the World was entirely predicated on their ability to out-feel all-comers, both live (see 'Little Queenie' on *Get Yer Ya-Ya's Out!*, described by Lester Bangs as 'music whose essential crudeness is so highly refined that it becomes a kind of absolute distillation of raunch') and in the studio. The complete expression of that all-encompassing feeliness is 'Tumbling Dice', as heartless a fugitive sneer as the Stones ever contrived and as rhythmically sophisticated. There's certainly no better place to experience the essentials of the group's sound: the push

Rewind
Keith Richards

'The funny thing about those riffs is that if I'm playing them, it's because I still get the same kick out of it, you know? There're riffs like "Tumbling Dice" where you go [kisses his hands and blows on them]: "Jesus *Christ*, it's a sweet riff. This is the feeling I been looking for for-*ever*. Jesus Christ, *is this me*!? HEY, THAT'S ME, BABY, AND I SOUND LIKE *THIS*!"'

Keith Richards rolls back, hands in the air, and wheezes like a boiler. His gang is his pride and joy. He speaks about them proprietorially, wryly, without sentiment but always with a degree of generosity.

'What it comes down to: the only fun in all this, the only reason I do it, the only way I can get a real *spark* out of anything is by playing with other guys. And it's not what *I'm* playing, either: it's what all of us are doing. I mean, if five guys can work together…'

The geometry of music, indivisible in this case from the geometry of gangs, is how Richards would appear to make sense of the world. He remains a fan, enthusing about his reggae and his blues, keen to talk rock 'n' roll, indefatigable in his search for 'spark'.

'A lot of rock 'n' roll bands are what I call Brabazons: they go down the runway but they never take off. I've been very lucky with the oats I've worked with. Charlie, who's really a jazz drummer, can make that beat take *off*. If you've got a drummer who plays like a concrete boot, you just sink.

'But most of it's done on typewriters these days. If rhythm is concerned with the body, which is what I think it's concerned with, you've got to use your whole body to express it. You can't do it like that [taps an invisible keyboard]. And what most people are interested in nowadays is not rhythm itself but the *sound* of the thing that's creating the beat. They got all these new toys, things that'll go CRASH! and wooo-wooo-wooo, but what is actually lacking is *rhythm*.'

He sighs.

'But since rhythm is as important to people as their own heartbeat, it'll establish itself again. I mean, I'm no Back-to-Mono cat – I don't revere Phil Spector 'cause he's only got one ear – but all this shit don't seduce me. It's like a department store at the moment and nobody can get out of the toy department.'
Nick Coleman; from Time Out, *4 July 1990*

FEAR OF MUSIC

of Charlie Watts's drums, the pull of Keith Richards' guitar. Turn it up and listen to the undertow. That's the Stones at their peak, right there, in that tidal tug. It's harder to hear the debt to James Brown, but 'Tumbling Dice' is on-the-one funk re-contoured for louche hippies on downers. It is, for me, the sound of happiness.

Contrast it with Led Zeppelin's 'For Your Life'. Zeppelin were heavy all right, but they also had feel. It's often overlooked that they swung like the clappers, although few among their audience will concede that they ever felt the need to dance. Nevertheless, in terms of rhythmic animus, Led Zep were kin to the Stones, albeit the Stones turned upside down and inside out. Again, it was the relationship between guitar and drums that defined the group's feel. But whereas secret jazzer Charlie Watts drummed palms-up with a light touch, always lifting the beat up and forward on thermals of swing (against which Richards' thick wodges of guitar plunged and barged), Zeppelin's John Bonham invariably played *behind* the click of time, hitting down, earthing the pulse.

In 'For Your Life', Jimmy Page's layered guitars drag and snap at that pulse, as if trying to tear themselves loose of the drummer's moorings. Bonham rides the chain. It's brilliant and attritional but not happy; you might call it the music of enchainment. 'Tumbling Dice' celebrates the freedoms of the fugitive way of life; 'For Your Life', a draggy, shut-down funk concerned with the effects of cocaine anomie and sexual fakery, laments some of its consequences. Both swing like nothing else you've heard; both say what they have to say through how the music feels.

So what were they really after, rock's 'classicists'? A facile answer is that they were after 'sounding black'. A better answer is that they were after exploring the limits of rock expression using the poetics of black music;

a recapitulation, in many ways, of the impulse that gave rise to rock 'n' roll in the first place. Nevertheless, you can bet your original copy of *Great White Wonder* that the 1970s Stones, Zeppelin and Free were as keen on the Band's first two albums as they were on Muddy Waters' Chess canon. Ever heard 'Up on Cripple Creek' on *The Band*? Or 'Rag Mama Rag'? Here's a bunch of white and mostly Canadian boys swinging the jelly out of a sprung boogie and not sounding like minstrels for a second.

Inevitably, rock groups began to compete, as rock groups will. Played out against a backdraft of mass-market soul music of unremitting feeliness and sophistication (Marvin, Stevie, Curtis et al), the competition was to see who might be the feeliest of them all. Just as the Band defined backwoods riddum for psychedelic refuseniks in the late '60s, so Little Feat did so half a decade later for West Coast sophisticates and rock critics. Little Feat were feel fetishists. Their drummer left gaps like canyons. They had a conga player. Lowell George, their frontal lobe, was coolly laid back to the point of prostration. Take away the subtle pitch, yaw and roll of 'Fat Man in the Bathtub' and what have you got? An exercise in time-signature hopscotch.

And when, another half-decade on, Steely Dan hired Bernard 'Pretty' Purdie to rimshot 'Babylon Sisters' on *Gaucho*, rock feel had been recalibrated to the point where it no longer felt like rock. It felt more like jazz: swinging all right, but as chilled as Miles Davis's 'So What' and almost as subtly spacious, a soft play area for both hips and neurotransmitters. Had it really been only six years since the Faces mistook inebriation for feel and recorded 'Pool Hall Richard' while falling down the stairs?

Now, *there's* a question: what do you get when you sacrifice everything – melody, refinement, songwriting, accuracy, chops – on the altar of feel? Not Ella Fitzgerald or

EARLS COURT ARENA
(OPPOSITE WARWICK ROAD EXIT EARLS COURT TUBE STATION)

HARVEY GOLDSMITH in association with
FIVE ONE PRODUCTIONS presents

The Rolling Stones

IN CONCERT

Friday, May 21st, 1976

(Doors open 6·30)

at 8-0 p.m.
NO ADMISSION AFTER 8-15 p.m.

3rd TIER STALLS £4·00

FOR CONDITIONS OF SALE SEE OVER

BLOCK

18

A 31

TO BE RETAINED

The Rolling Stones play Bristol in 1971.

Miles Davis or Steely Dan, that's for sure.
What you get is the kind of music that gave
rise to rock 'n' roll in the first place: honkin',
bonkin' '50s rhythm and blues, or 'race music'
as it was called in the marketing suites of the
day. The rawest kind of social music.

Want to hear a record that's all feel and no
melody, accuracy, refinement, songwriting or
chops? Let me direct you to Rosco Gordon's
'T-Model Boogie'. It's a 12-bar, naturally, sung
mostly on one note on the subject of motor
cars (you supply the subtext). The thing starts
uncertainly and ends when the wheels come
off. In between, a thumping rhythm section,
a couple of horns and Gordon's piano and
felted voice swing like no one has ever swung,
until, somewhere in the middle of the second
verse, just as Cadillac and DeSoto are failing
to compare with the titular Ford, Rosco loses
the metrical plot and swings himself right
out of the pocket. Er… where are we, fellas?
Fortunately, there's a tenor saxophonist who
keeps barging into the picture like a drunk.
He fills the space with a couple of honks to
cover any embarrassment while Rosco sorts
out where the pocket is again, and away they
go once more until it's time to stop.

There's something very beautiful in the fact
that such a record was ever released, let alone
that it achieved ear-worm status among those
privileged to hear it. The reason Sun released
'T-Model Boogie' is that the record felt so good
– like nothing else, in fact. A swingin' vibe won
out over technical excellence; casual jubilation
triumphed over fussy correctitude. Something
unique came to be, something belonging to its
own moment in (pliable) time that can never be
replicated, no matter how hard you try to make
the same mistakes again.

This sense of uniqueness is vital to grasping
the value of feel. Feel may not change the
landscape, or repopulate it. But it does bring
variety to the landscape, and human richness,
and spontaneity. It describes the singularity
of the natural process. Music with feel is a
garden of earthly delights, a contiguous series
of enclosures rolling from meadow to lawn
to arbour to hidden glade to the canalside
allotment reserved for the Faces, enclosures
in which Rosco Gordon may safely graze next
to Steely Dan while Little Richard's 'Keep
A-Knockin'' gives birth behind the bushes to
Led Zeppelin's 'Rock and Roll'.

In search of the downbeat: **Rosco Gordon**.

In the rock mainstream, though, it all changed,
as it was always going to. Feel was gradually
usurped by utility and disappeared into
unacknowledged obscurity in a dusty wing of
the vibe museum, where the relics of 'Tumbling
Dice' are visited in a spirit of gaudy reverence
every decade or so by Primal Scream. What
caused this unhappy tide of events? A number
of things, not least of them the overweening
sophistication of rock in the mid '70s and the
necessity to sweep all that overweening aside.

The genius of disco lay in its four-to-the-floor
reductiveness: yes, you can have feel, but only
if it's the kind of regular feel that commands
universal gallumphing. Punk, meanwhile,
was against feel for ideological reasons.
Viewed from the Year Zero standpoint, feel
was pretentious, conservative, Americanophilic

and probably crypto-racist. Furthermore, it implied the undemocratic need for technical ability on the part of the players. Any bassist capable of locking in to the kick-drum to swing the bottom end of a song could never be construed as a just-picked-it-up-this-morning amateur, a basic requirement of the punk aesthetic in its early days.

Both punk and disco held ferocious anti-elitism as a core value. In the case of punk, no one was to be disbarred from joining a band simply on the grounds that he or she couldn't play an instrument, while disco was equally determined that no one should be inhibited from taking to the dancefloor by tempos and syncopations too funky for the common herd. But while the social modulations encoded by punk and disco may well have done their bit to depose rhythmic feel as the primary objective of popular music, it was the software sequencer that actually killed it off.

Programmed into mathematically precise sonic helixes by Giorgio Moroder in that well-known haven of down 'n' dirty funk, Munich, Donna Summer's 'Love to Love You Baby' was not the first record to make use of sequencer technology. But it was the first mainstream dance hit to make a virtue of the total absence of human DNA in the mix (apart, of course, from Donna's). And *après* Donna, *le déluge*. The programmed beat, with all its implications for DIY musicianship, portability, manipulability, economy and interface, took off like an aesthetic rocket and came to dominate pop music across the genres for the next 25 years, as the electric guitar and drum kit had dominated the first 25.

You'd be entitled at this juncture to make the point that machine feel is just another kind of feel. And you'd be right; it would be absurd to pretend otherwise. What's more, machine feel is compelling; it brooks no argument. So much so, in fact, that as the sequencer tightened its grip on the imaginations of musicians and consumers alike during the late '70s and 1980s, it became fashionable among certain real-life flesh-and-blood rhythm sections to imitate the spartan snap of the mechanised beat.

Perhaps it shouldn't be lost on us that the most stylish and musically sophisticated disco records were those made by an old-fashioned band masquerading as a socio-aesthetic concept: Chic, either under their own name or that of Sister Sledge ('Le Freak', 'Good

'Feel is a choice we make. It's a decision, not a by-product; a style, not an essential. We hear swing as we do upright basses and the surface noise on vinyl – as a sign of another time, not as a mark of our own.'

Times', 'He's the Greatest Dancer'). The Chic rhythm section were machine-like in their implacability and utterly musicianly in their methods. Yet they had *feel*.

Equally musicianly but still more implacable, the Taxi Gang, aka Sly (Dunbar) and Robbie (Shakespeare), propelled reggae towards its own date with digital destiny by regulating the art of the Jamaican skank into a clipped sequence of pops, whirrs and squelches, as crisply uniform in attack and recoil as the pistons in a high-end German saloon. Only the under-drag of Robbie's bass ever hinted at non-mechanical precision – Sly's wrist action might have been programmed by robots. Listen to Gregory Isaacs' extraordinary 'Oh, What a Feeling' or anything by Black Uhuru, both Island recordings from the early '80s. Then compare them to, say, Isaacs' 'The Border' from 1978, propelled by the GG All-Stars. 'The Border' breathes air. 'Oh, What a Feeling' doesn't appear to breathe at all; it functions, and, in doing so, it looks forward to the atmospheric nullity of cyberspace.

The point I want to make is not that machine feel isn't feel, but that it's a completely standardised feel. It's reliable. It can always be predicted. It will proceed in a manner pre-determined by its programmer to an allotted point of conclusion, then stop. On the journey, nothing will affect it because it doesn't have the ability, the sensorium, to react to anything that might occur on the way. Should a bass player suddenly decide to double-bump on the hump,

Sly (left) **& Robbie.**

the rhythm track will proceed impassively, as if nothing has happened, because in its world nothing *has* happened. Were the singer to get carried away and start hitting the same syllable over and over again, syncopating the words like he's beating a drum, the rhythm track would not be in a position to drag back the two and the four just a fraction, to increase the tension, because it wouldn't be able to hear the singer, because it doesn't have ears. No one in cyberspace can hear you sing. And as for swing…

Well, yes, it is now entirely possible to programme a notional feel into a computer. Good old hip hop and R&B have made fruitful use of the technology that has, over recent years, permitted programmers to map on to a rhythm grid that elasticating thing we call swing. It's now entirely possible to deploy feel in a studio without having to record real-life drummers or sample dead ones. But you do have to do it – that is, dial it in – in advance; feel may only arise spontaneously if you have real bodies listening and interacting together at the same co-ordinates in the space/time continuum. Which only confirms the underlying truth that marks our time: feel is a choice we make.

It's a decision, not a by-product; a style, not an essential. It is no longer the point of the exercise, only a reference point for it. We hear swing as we do upright basses and the surface noise on vinyl and the chug of Model-T Fords – as a sign of another time, not as a mark of our own.

I love Amy Winehouse. She has something to say and the voice with which to say it. But talented writer that she is, I don't think it's the imagery in her lyrics that we really tune in to, any more than it's the rats in her beehive or her bad, bad smell. I think what makes us stare is our ears. She has feel. And we know she has feel because whenever we hear 'Rehab' or 'You Know I'm No Good', and we find ourselves being sucked in by all those phrases hanging off the beat like fags hang off her lower lip, we're dimly aware that we're listening to the echo of someone else singing in another time. Amy is busy in the garden, up to her armpits, digging for the motherlode.

And in case you're interested, it's Ann Peebles we can hear, rasping balefully in Memphis more than 30 years ago: 'I Can't Stand the Rain', 'Come to Mama', 'I'm Gonna Tear Your Playhouse Down', 'I Pity the Fool'…

Making it up

Jack Massarik offers a beginner's guide to jazz improvisation.

Many otherwise bright and capable people enter a state of vertigo when confronted with a jazz solo. What the blue blazes, they wonder, is going on? Is the musician following any rules, or simply playing the first thing that comes into his head? Does he expect us to follow him note for note? Would our pleasure be increased if we did? And, if so, what chance do non-musicians have of sharing it?

Double bassist Charlie Haden raised an interesting point when his Quartet West played during the London Jazz Festival in 2007. 'We just love coming to London,' he smiled, 'because you guys have such great ears.' And as if to put this hypothesis straight to the test, Haden quickly mumbled a dedication to his wife and launched into a bass solo without announcing the song. The changes, which sounded familiar, were picked up by the rest of the group, who took turns to take solos.

Even before the group eventually played the theme, listeners with long memories discerned that this was an aged Broadway ballad called 'My Old Flame', recorded by Charlie Parker on several occasions. But while those who remembered the great alto saxophonist's solo might have been able to identify the piece from Haden's opening chorus, many musicians don't have the bassist's confidence in his listeners. Some agree with the conductor Thomas Beecham's suggestion that most people 'don't really understand music – they just like the noise it makes,' while others have said that many people can't even tell a wrong note from a right one.

A basic understanding of chord sequences can be a great help in appreciating jazz improvisation, and you don't need to read music to attain it. Even for novices, it's a knack that becomes easier with practice, and the basic 12-bar blues is a good place to start. Although blues music itself has its own icons, the venerable old chord sequence behind it has also launched innumerable jazz solos. Louis

John Coltrane.

New York, 1946.

Armstrong, John Coltrane and Charlie Parker were all superb blues soloists; indeed, Parker's solo on 'Parker's Mood' was so beautiful that singer King Pleasure saw fit to set lyrics to it. Hammond organist Jimmy Smith was another 12-bar specialist: albums such as *Midnight Special*, *Back at the Chicken Shack* and *The Cat* are full of tracks that rely on the familiar old chord sequence.

While you're listening, count the beats. There are usually four to a bar; if you count from one to four 12 times, you've completed one chorus and are ready for the next. Counting is a key component of sight-reading and is also crucial when listening to musicians 'swapping fours', in which improvisers exchange four-bar breaks with one another. Sonny Rollins, a master of the art, has been known to play entire numbers in four- or eight-bar breaks with his drummer.

Standards, those high-quality songs that go in and out of fashion but never quite die, are another matter. Vocal albums of the 1950s and '60s, most famously those by the likes of Frank Sinatra, Ella Fitzgerald and Sarah Vaughan, are full of them. Get to know them: written, in some

cases, for Broadway musicals, they were the pop songs of their time, a time that happened to be a golden age for songwriting. The likes of 'Autumn in New York', 'I Got Rhythm', 'Tenderly', 'Summertime', 'Oh, Lady Be Good!', 'The Lady Is a Tramp', 'Stars Fell on Alabama' and 'Sweet Georgia Brown' were crafted in the '20s, '30s and '40s by songsmiths such as Jerome Kern, Cole Porter, Irving Berlin, George Gershwin, Harold Arlen, Johnny Mercer and Richard Rodgers, brilliant composers whose rivalries produced what has become known as the Great American Songbook.

Today, only survivors such as Tony Bennett and preservationists such as Stacey Kent record these songs regularly. But in the decades before rock muscled in, they were whistled by every newsboy, hummed by every office girl and played by every hotel band. They were also learned, their melodies and harmonies, by every jazz musician, almost as soon as they were first published and performed. Among Charlie Parker's first jobs when he got to New York was at a taxi-dance hall, where men paid the girls a dime for each turn around the floor. A

Top ten
Awkward time signatures

'All You Need Is Love' The Beatles

John Lennnon would often compose so recklessly that he'd miss out beats, add beats or jump into other time signatures; for example, the rapid rhythmic shifts in 'Happiness Is a Warm Gun'. Here, it means that most of the verse is in 7/4 time.

'Take Five' Dave Brubeck Quartet

Jazz pianist Brubeck has often employed odd time signatures – 'Unsquare Dance' is in 7/4, while 'Blue Rondo à la Turk' is in a stuttering 9/8 – but his most famous work swings effortlessly despite its wonky 5/4 measure.

'I Say a Little Prayer' Aretha Franklin

Like Lennon, Burt Bacharach often skips or adds beats to the standard rock and pop pulse of 4/4, and sometimes uses arcane time signatures. Unlike Lennon, though, he was well aware what he was doing, having spent time studying the work of composers such as Bartok. On the verse of 'I Say a Little Prayer', Bacharach breaks up six 4/4 measures with a single bar of 2/4; the chorus is further complicated by single measures of 3/4 separating the standard 4/4 bars.

'Hidden Shadows' Herbie Hancock

This slice of hypnotic Afro psych funk from Herbie's bafflingly complex 1973 album *Sextant* sees the short-lived Herbie Hancock Sextet improvising for more than ten minutes in the hilariously outlandish time signature of 19/4. Amazingly, it sometimes gets played in clubs; more amazingly, people dance to it.

'Hey Ya!' OutKast

A deceptively complex rhythm that comprises three bars in 4/4 followed by a measure of 2/4 and two measures of 4/4. Count it at half-speed, and it sounds as if it's in 11 to a bar.

'Overkill' Andy Pask & Charlie Morgan

The jerky, off-kilter feel of 'Overkill', the theme tune to *The Bill*, comes because it alternates bars of 6/8 with bars of 4/4. In a 1998 revamp of the show, the whole thing was rearranged into a more pedestrian four beats to every bar. The comedian Bill Bailey suggested that the change may have come about because TV bosses were worried that the irregular time signatures associated with jazz would associate the police, by proxy, with heavy drug use.

'Money' Pink Floyd

This quartet of maths and science graduates presumably had no problem understanding that the first track on side two of *The Dark Side of the Moon*, with its clanking cash-registers and whirring ticket machines, is in 7/4.

'Mother' The Police

This Arabic-tinged novelty track from *Synchronicity*, featuring the drummer Stewart Copeland howling on vocals, is in the disorienting metre of 7/8.

'15 Step' Radiohead

Trust clever-clever Radiohead to open their originally Internet-only album *In Rainbows* with this, a slice of flippy-floppy drum 'n' bass in the time signature of 5/4.

'Main Title from "The Carpetbaggers"' Jimmy Smith

Best known in the UK as the theme to BBC's *The Money Programme*, this churning, rhythmically complex track in 9/8 time was written by Elmer Bernstein but arranged here for Smith by the great soundtrack writer Lalo Schifrin, who himself had a thing for unusual time signatures. It was Schifrin who scored the theme to *Mission: Impossible* in 5/4, although the dim-witted Limp Bizkit later simplified it to plain old four in a bar.

single chorus of each of three numbers was the ration per dance, so the band got through a lot of standards. With his photographic memory, Parker memorised them and would quote meaningfully from them later in his career. A few notes of 'The Most Beautiful Girl in the World', for instance, would signal the arrival of his girlfriend at the club where he was working.

Standards are usually 32 bars in length, divided into two sections of 16 or, more commonly, four sections of eight. In the latter form, the most common structure can be neatly summarised as A-A-B-A: the first eight is repeated, then the middle eight (or 'bridge') varies the melody line before a final eight that sounds broadly the same as the first pair. 'Cherokee' and 'I Got Rhythm' are two such 32-bar standards. The early Miles Davis quintets also introduced a four-bar 'turnaround' that could be played once or repeated indefinitely. Used at the end of a piece such as 'I Could Write a Book' (a 32-bar standard in A-B-A-C form), it sets up a tension-and-release break in which to introduce the next soloist or give the number an attractive extended finish.

Having learned a few standards, you'll be on firmer ground with some great jazz solos. Take Coleman Hawkins's 1939 version of 'Body and Soul', a famous tenor-sax ride through a difficult and beautiful chord sequence so distinctive that Hawkins never bothers playing the actual theme. Similarly, 'Koko', recorded by Charlie Parker in the early 1940s, glides through the chord changes of 'Cherokee' without Parker once stating the melody. His stunning version of 'Lover Man' also doesn't refer to the tune, while his beautiful ballad 'Bird of Paradise' actually improves the line of 'All the Things You Are'.

This kind of corruption of existing material has been common throughout jazz history. 'Lester Leaps In' is Lester Young's version of 'I Got Rhythm', while 'Lullaby of Birdland', written by Battersea's blind piano master George Shearing, is based on the 1928 hit 'Love Me or Leave Me'. Dizzy Gillespie's 'Groovin' High' uses the chord changes of 'Whispering'; 'Clifford's Axe' by fellow trumpeter Clifford Brown borrows a chord sequence from 'The Man I Love'; and 'Four on Six' by guitarist Wes Montgomery is Gershwin's 'Summertime' with just a bit of tinkering.

John Coltrane's masterpiece 'Giant Steps' is derived from an unusual cadence found in only one standard, the bridge of 'Have You Met Miss Jones?'. Experimenting further, Coltrane applied this principle to 'Body and Soul' (as performed by Dexter Gordon in the movie 'Round Midnight'), 'Tune Up' (a Miles original, renamed 'Countdown'), 'How High the Moon' ('Satellite') and 'Confirmation' (a Parker tune, renamed '26-2'). Recorded during Trane's 'sheets of sound' period, these chord progressions are very complex, but great solos don't have to be difficult. Listen to Miles playing 'Summertime' with the Gil Evans Orchestra: each elegant, perfectly shaped phrase seems to hang in the air like vapour trails from a high-flying plane.

Singers, of course, have lyrics with which to keep us posted of their whereabouts. But a number of vocalists have also taken the time to set famous jazz solos to words. As well as writing lyrics for 'Parker's Mood', the aforementioned King Pleasure immortalised tenorist James Moody's solo on 'I'm in the Mood

On the record
Bruce Forsyth

'Emily'

Bill Evans

I'm a big fan of modern jazz, particularly piano players. 'Emily' is a beautiful piece of music. It's my favourite Bill Evans song, and Bill Evans is probably my favourite jazz pianist, so I guess it's my favourite song. It's a jazz waltz based on a very simple three-note theme – like a playground rhyme, or a song that you might hear in a children's toy box – but he develops it with such clever chord changes. It's everything I like in a jazz song. I like my jazz to be neat and tidy, so that I can follow a chord sequence that sounds good. As one modern jazz musician says, it isn't the notes you play, it's the notes you leave out. And that's when the greats of jazz can be really appreciated. Someone like Bill Evans doesn't play a million notes, but he knows exactly what to leave out. That's genius!
Bruce Forsyth first appeared on TV in 1939 and has recently been hosting Strictly Come Dancing *on BBC1*

Wired for sound: **Jimmy Smith** waits for the organ repair team.

for Love' as 'Moody's Mood for Love'; Georgie Fame does a great version of it. And on a long-unavailable Italian album, the wonderful vocalese singer Jon Hendricks put words to all the solos on 'Freddie Freeloader', a blues from the must-have Miles Davis album *Kind of Blue*. On it, Hendricks asked Al Jarreau to sing the Wynton Kelly piano solo, George Benson to take Miles's trumpet turn and Bobby McFerrin to reprise Cannonball Adderley's alto solo; he saved the hardest one, Coltrane's tenor-sax break, for himself. All four singing stars already knew these instrumental solos by heart, simply through having enjoyed them so many times on record.

During their solos, canny instrumentalists often use tricks to keep listeners in touch.

The great Sonny Rollins inserts little signposts of melody into his solos, usually after a really complex passage. Some players use crazy visual effects to achieve the same ends. Critics sniffed when Jamie Cullum started drumming on the piano-lid during his concerts and leaping on and off the piano stool, but he was at least holding their attention. And a certain modern-day trumpeter tilts his head sharply back at the end of each solo, pointing his trumpet dramatically skykwards and blasting his final notes into the ceiling. 'Wow, that trumpeter's fabulous, isn't he?' will be heard at the foyer bar after the show; much to the annoyance of the piano player, who kept his head down throughout the performance and played twice as well. But that's jazz for you. Better just sit back and enjoy it.

Top ten
Samples

'Mystic Voyage' Roy Ayers Ubiquity

With more than 30 of his tracks in near-constant use, jazz vibist Ayers might the most sampled artist of all time. As used by Coolio, DJ Jazzy Jeff & the Fresh Prince and Adrianna Evans, this is one of his most popular cuts.

'Funky Drummer' James Brown

This loop has been used extensively by Public Enemy (on at least seven tracks), the Beastie Boys (once, if not more), Run-DMC (four times), Ice T (at least three occasions) and LL Cool J (five times), among others. The drummer in question is Clyde Stubblefield.

'Good Times' Chic

The basis for the Sugarhill Gang's era-defining 'Rapper's Delight' is a disco-era bassline that has been used by the likes of De La Soul ('A Roller Skating Jam Named "Saturdays"'), Grandmaster Flash ('The Adventures of Grandmaster Flash on the Wheels of Steel') and Afrika Bambaataa's Time Zone ('The Wildstyle').

'Atomic Dog' George Clinton

This 1982 track by the unhinged Funkadelic/Parliament frontman has been used on multiple occasions by, among others, Public Enemy, Ice Cube, Ice T and Snoop Doggy Dogg.

'Take Me to the Mardi Gras' Bob James

The opening drum-and-bell loop from this Paul Simon cover has been sampled by the Beastie Boys ('Hold It Now, Hit It'), LL Cool J ('Rock the Bells'), Massive Attack ('Unfinished Sympathy') and Run-DMC ('Peter Piper'). James's 'Nautilus' has also been widely borrowed down the years by the likes of Eric B & Rakim and Onyx.

'Trans-Europe Express' Kraftwerk

This 1977 track was famously picked up in 1982 by Afrika Bambaataa on 'Planet Rock', and has since been used by a list of artists that includes 2 Live Crew, De La Soul and even Wyclef Jean.

'I Got the...' Labi Siffre

Famously featuring Chas (Hodges) and Dave (Peacock) on guitar and bass respectively, 'I Got the...' has been used by Jay-Z ('Streets Is Watching'), the Wu-Tang Clan ('Can It Be All So Simple') and the Beatnuts ('Beatnuts Forever'), but made its most famous appearance on Eminem's 'My Name Is'. Siffre made Eminem remove homophobic and sexist slurs from the single before granting him use of the sample.

'Ashley's Roachclip' The Soul Searchers

This proto-go-go track from 1974 was sampled by Eric B & Rakim ('Paid in Full' and 'I Know You Got Soul'), Milli Vanilli ('Girl You Know It's True'), EMF ('Unbelievable') and PM Dawn ('Set Adrift on Memory Bliss'), and has also been lifted by LL Cool J, 2 Live Crew, 3rd Bass and Run-DMC.

'Apache' Michael Viner's Incredible Bongo Band

A 1972 version of the Shadows' song, recorded by a bunch of Hollywood session musicians and orchestrated by a former MGM music executive, 'Apache' has been sampled by everyone from Nas ('Made You Look') to Missy Elliott ('We Run This').

'Amen, Brother' The Winstons

This once-obscure B-side, an instrumental version of 'Amen' by Curtis Mayfield & the Impressions recorded in 1969 by a soul group from Washington, DC, has been sampled innumerable times: NWA ('Straight Outta Compton') and Eric B & Rakim ('Casualties of War') are among those who've used it.

FUNKY DRUMMER (Part 1)
(James Brown)
JAMES BROWN
Playable On STEREO Or MONO
STEREO
KING
A JAMES BROWN PRODUCTION
45-6290
SK-13357 Time: 2-36
Golo-Dynatone (BMI)
Inst.
Distributed By STARDAY KING RECORDS INC.

Death by ballad

Colin Irwin reckons that there's nowt stranger than folk.

Heard the one about the bloke who shags his sister and then murders her when he discovers she's pregnant with his child? Or the guy who goes out hunting one day and shoots an arrow through the heart of a swan, only to discover he's killed the love of his life by mistake? What about the man who goes to the gallows crying 'perjuring little whore' after being convicted of raping a 12-year-old girl? Or the stonemason who, with the help of a dodgy nursemaid, takes his revenge on a double-crossing lord by first brutally murdering his baby and then killing his wife?

Norwegian black metal may think it has the monopoly on bad taste, country music may claim to be the daddy of disaster and hip hop may assume it breaks new ground with its outrageous lyrics about moral depravity, but a cursory glance through the ballad collection put together by American folklorist Francis James Child in the late 19th century proves they're all pussycats compared to the gory horrors and macabre deeds that lurk within traditional folk songs. Who needs mock-goth Marilyn Manson or Eminem's tales of bodies in cars when stories of incest, infanticide, paedophilia, suicide, transvestism, sex with elves, vengeful ghosts and bloody decapitations are so rife in folk music? There's a reason why songs such as 'John Barleycorn', the sinister ode to the cyclical regeneration of life masquerading as a tale of ale, have survived for hundreds of years and continue to fascinate new generations.

Considering that early references to 'John Barleycorn' can be traced back to the middle of the 16th century, and that Robert Burns published a version of it in 1782, it's amazing that Traffic should have been inspired by the Watersons to record the song as the title track of an album while they were at the height of rock cool in 1970. By the time Paul Weller duetted with Martin and Eliza Carthy on another version in 2007, the song seemed to have taken up permanent residence in the repertoires of every younger artist on the scene: Chris Wood, Jim Causley and Tim van Eyken are among the singers who've found new ways to tackle the song amid fresh analysis about its history and deep inner meaning.

The grandmama of the repertoire, though, is a rather less complex ballad with fewer avenues for reinterpretation. 'Barbara Allen' is seemingly a simple if painful love story of such extreme sentiment that it stretches credibility to ludicrous lengths. And yet when the consummate Irish singer Mary McPartlan sings it unaccompanied on her fine 2008 album *Petticoat Loose*, the sincere emotions she evokes go a long way towards explaining the enduring potency of its message of unrequited love.

The first known reference to 'Barbara Allen' – or 'The Bitch and the Wimp', as it's sometimes fondly known – is in Samuel Pepys's diary entry for 2 January 1666. Three and a half centuries after the diarist had heard it delivered by an actress called Mrs Knipp, the song is still sung on a regular basis, albeit in greatly differing styles, and continues to incite animated debate about the reasons for the anti-heroine's cruel rejection of her hapless

On the record
Chris Wood

'Our Captain Calls All Hands'

It was Norma Waterson who led me to this song, like a dog to a bone. It appears as track five on volume one of *The Voice of the People*, released by Topic Records. It's just one of the thousands of boy-meets-girl, boy-has-to-go-away songs that fill the English songbooks but that proliferated at the time of the Napoleonic wars. However, for me, this one is different.

The boy opens with the usual 'Sorry, darlin', but I must be off' verse, but she comes right back at him: 'How can you go abroad fighting for strangers.' Not 'fighting strangers'. 'Fighting *for* strangers.'

Right there, in that three-letter word, you have what I feel to be the real history of the English people. There's no cultural confusion for her. She knows what's going on is not of her making. She knows that she has no more influence over her destiny than we had over Blair's decision to take us into Iraq. The only difference is that, generations later, we've been kidded into thinking that as 'the electorate', we have a say in how things are done here.

If you listen closely as Pop Maynard sings in the Cherry Tree, Copthorne, Sussex in September 1956, you can just about hear him thumping the table with his finger. Is he thumping to keep time, or is there a vehemence

in his performance that needs some kind of physical expression, like a tennis player's grunt?

As Norma and I stood in her kitchen, we listened to Pop Maynard until his voice faded away. When I turned to her, she had tears on her face. I asked her what the rest of the series was like. She said that she didn't know. She couldn't get past track five, volume one.

Chris Wood recorded 'Our Captain Calls All Hands' on his album The Lark Descending; *his latest album is* Trespasser *(Reveal)*

would-be suitor Sweet William (or Sir John Graeme, or Jimmy Grove, or myriad other names, depending on the version) as he lay gravely ill suffering from a broken heart. When Babs hears the bells ringing out the news of his death, she finally does the decent thing and lays down to die of remorse, leaving a million unanswered questions in the jungle of alternative versions that have been handed down through the years.

Pepys referred to the ballad, which he titled 'Barbary Allen', as a 'Scotch' song. But throughout the 90-plus versions, its setting shifts from London to Dublin, Reading to Cambridge and North Town to Scarlett Town, among numerous other locations, planting the suspicion that whoever was singing it at any given time moulded the location accordingly.

Listed by Child as number 84 in his 305-strong collection of *The English and Scottish Popular Ballads* (or, in common shorthand, Child ballad 84), it even made it to Sugar Land prison farm in Texas, where folklorist John Lomax recorded an extraordinary version sung by an old black prisoner called Moses 'Clear Rock' Platt in 1933. Contrast Platt's rendition with Jim Moray's edgy, thoroughly modern treatment, issued on his self-titled 2006 album, and you'll get a sense of the eternal power of this faintly absurd yet constantly arresting song. Most of the leading folk singers have at one time sung it, from Fred Jordan to Shirley Collins to Joan Baez to Bob Dylan to Nic Jones, but my favourite recording is by the young singer Cassie Franklin from the Alabama band Southern Brew, who turns it into a hymnal lament.

Great traditional songs are often defined by the eloquence of the language or, in some cases, by a single line. In 'Barbara Allen', the most devastating verse is the moment when Barbara realises the consequences of her hard heart:

'When he was dead and in his grave
She heard the death bell knelling
And every note did seem to say
Oh, cruel Barbara Allen'

Meanwhile, my favourite line in my favourite ballad runs something like this:

'Get up, get up, Lord Darnell cried
Get up as quick as you can
It'll never be said in fair England
That I slew a naked man'

The song is 'Matty Groves' (Child ballad 81, under the title 'Little Musgrave and Lady Barnard'), and I can still remember the moment when, wandering through Soho, I first heard the voice of Sandy Denny soaring through a record shop doorway singing it amid Fairport Convention's epic arrangement on *Liege & Lief*.

The earliest known published version of the song dates back to 1658, although there's an allusion to it in a play written in 1613. Either

'Victorian song collectors such as Cecil Sharp now often cop flak for sanitising the tradition in order to serve an idyllic view of rural England that never really existed.'

way, the fateful night of passion between Matty and Lady Margaret (or, in other versions, Lady Barnard or Lady Darnell) that ends in bloody retribution for them both beneath the blade of the woman's enraged husband has gone through many incarnations since then. In 1943, Benjamin Britten used it as the setting for a choral piece, but it's still a perennial on the folk circuit. Whether as 'Matty Groves' or in the twin form of 'Little Musgrave' preferred by the likes of Nic Jones, Christy Moore and Martin Simpson, it remains a king among songs.

FEAR OF MUSIC

Sussex singer **Shirley Collins**.

Martin Carthy, live in London during 1975.

The folk tradition is full of these gruesome gems. Victorian song collectors such as Cecil Sharp now often cop flak for sanitising the tradition in order to serve an idyllic view of rural England that never really existed, but plenty of vintage nastiness remains intact. Take, for example, the four ballads outlined in the first paragraph: 'Sheath and Knife', popular with the likes of Tony Rose; 'Polly Vaughan', recorded by Anne Briggs in 1964 and, under the title 'Molly Bawn', by Alasdair Roberts four decades later; 'Fanny Blair', stunningly rendered by Peter Bellamy; and 'Long Lankin', most famous in Steeleye Span's recording.

And let's not forget 'Tam Lin'. The most magical of all magical ballads has become a sort of masterclass for singers, who tell the story of the knight captured by fairies and then rescued by the power of love (or, at least, a girlfriend prepared to hold on for dear life as the queen of the fairies turns the knight

into a series of scary creatures). Child alone annotated 14 different versions of this Scottish song, though even he would have been startled to hear, in 2007, the Rastafarian poet Benjamin Zephaniah updating 'Tam Lin' into a modern morality tale about refugees, sex in cars, club DJs and the British legal system.

By definition, traditional songs have no known authorship, and it's this state of affairs that's spawned much of the intrigue about the ways in which they've crossed continents and changed along the way. The progress of such songs through countries and societies, as with Zephaniah's translation, makes a mockery of the rigid purists who flag so-called 'definitive' versions and feign outrage towards those adopting and adapting the music to their own environment, whether with electric guitars, massed choirs or computers. After all, as Martin Carthy is fond of saying, the worst harm you can do to a traditional song is to ignore it.

Countdown to Ecstasy

Get
happy

Peter Shapiro explores the euphoria and escapism at the heart of disco.

It goes without saying that all popular music is, on some level, about release and ecstasy, but no other genre has wallowed in its pleasure principle quite like disco. Unrepentantly resplendent in rhinestones and a feather boa, disco flaunted its hedonism, wealth and splendour like an arriviste at his first regatta. But no matter how much the music tried to woo you with its luxuriant strings, seduce you with its sashaying exotic percussion or just reach down into your trousers with its vocally simulated orgasms, it seemed like disco never quite got you off. In fact, with the constant throb and the sleazy come-ons, every disco record greeted you like a lap dancer, teasing you and leaving you panting but never delivering what the lowlit massage industry terms a 'happy ending'.

Of course, this was entirely intentional. The disco scene was a by-product of the Stonewall Riot of 1969, in which patrons of a notorious Manhattan gay bar finally got fed up and fought back against the cops after decades of surveillance, shakedowns and the superannuated laws that regulated homosexual

admissions and ratios at New York nightspots. Every underground uprising needs a soundtrack, and disco soon became a clarion call for a generation tired of police raids, Victorian laws and the darkness of the closet. The antithesis of the three-minute foreplay-rising tension-climax pop-rock orthodoxy, disco was a polymorphously perverse trance ritual where pleasure was extended and diffused across several hours with an intensity previously untapped in rock clubs or, for that matter, the earliest discotheques.

At early Manhattan clubs such as the Tenth Floor and the Firehouse, the trance-like experience was enhanced by what DJ Barry Lederer has called 'heady, drug-oriented music': slightly dark and spacey funk records such as Billy Sha-Rae's 'Do It' and Bill Withers' 'Harlem' which, compared to the speaker-shredding intensity and splintered syncopations of a James Brown cut, came with a slow-burn intensity and a whiff of psychedelia. The music wasn't tame, exactly: it was more that it was covered in some kind of patina that prevented it from truly leaping

'OK, OK: I *won't* play "Hot Stuff"!'
Donna Summer.

out at listeners. But if the records themselves didn't necessarily leave dancers in a cold sweat, the way the DJs played them sure did. Implicitly political and explicitly sexual, the way in which the music was delivered to its listeners was every bit as novel as the records themselves and, ultimately, sowed the seeds of a cultural revolution.

The concept of mixing records together had been pioneered by a DJ called Terry Noel, who worked with twin turntables at a Manhattan club called Arthur in the mid '60s. However, the art of blending separate records was honed and eventually perfected by the early disco DJs, and by one man in particular. Francis Grasso seemed to view his turntables as musical instruments in their own right, and saw the DJ as a musician of sorts who could create a greater whole from the sum of the parts he carried in his record box. Working at a string of New York clubs in the late '60s and early '70s, Grasso is widely believed to have been the first DJ to beat-mix, overlapping two records so their rhythms synchronised and thus prolonged the mood on the dancefloor. And in originating

the concept, he simultaneously introduced to nightclubs the technique of slip-cueing: holding in place a record while a turntable span underneath it, then releasing his hold on the disc at just the right moment in order to fuse it with the 45 spinning on the other deck.

Grasso blended the unlikeliest of records in the service of the dancefloor. One famous mix saw him meld the percussion breakdown of Chicago Transit Authority's 'I'm a Man' with the eerie, quasi-orgasmic middle section of Led Zeppelin's 'Whole Lotta Love': a thrillingly visceral piece of aural sculpture, it linked tribal percussion with sexuality, an idea revived by countless DJs who followed in his wake, and helped foster the idea that the dancefloor was a place in which eroticism could be shared among all its participants, not just a couple dancing in tandem. But Grasso also used his beat-mixing techniques to play two copies of the same record on his twin turntables, lengthening the grooves of such crowd favourites as Little Sister's 'You're the One' (a Sly Stone side project that starred Stone's younger sister), Osibisa's conga-dominated 'Music for Gong

Gong', and a 1968 cover of the Frankie Valli & the Four Seasons' 'Beggin'' by British psych-rock group Timebox. These were the days before 12-inch singles: Grasso's desire to extend the length of his three-minute 45s, amplifying the euphoria on the dancefloor, was both radical and immensely influential.

Like all the best DJs who followed his lead, Grasso was a master mood manipulator. Built on his love of overbearing percussion, his DJ sets were rousingly physical, and the viscerality of the music was only enhanced by the sensorium of the club where he really made his name. One of the most outrageous venues in the long and colourful history of New York nightlife, the Sanctuary was housed in a former Baptist church that looked as if it had been taken over by Lucifer: instead of the usual frescoes depicting Bible stories and the beatification of various saints, the room featured a huge mural of the devil surrounded by fornicating angels. (You can catch a very brief glimpse of the club – and Grasso at work, lighting up the club's stained-glass windows in time to the music – in the 1971 Jane Fonda movie *Klute*.) Coupled with Grasso's music, the ambience of the church helped charge the Sanctuary with a heady sense of sexual ecstasy.

While Grasso was creating the notion of disco as spectacle, the scene's other true pioneer set about making disco in the image of the Mad Hatter's tea party from *Alice in Wonderland*. David Mancuso began throwing parties in his illegal loft on Broadway in 1970, the year after Grasso moved to the Sanctuary. But unlike the bacchanalian ambience of Grasso's church, the Loft was a place of childlike wonder, with balloons, streamers, Christmas trees and bowls of candy helping to create a vibe somewhere between a Timothy Leary acid gathering and a kindergartener's birthday party.

Mancuso and Grasso's respective playlists often coincided. However, Mancuso was far less concerned than Grasso with beat-mixing and extending the groove of the music he favoured. At the Loft, he preferred to create a musical narrative by tempering more percussive records (such as Olatunji's 'Jin-Go-Lo-Ba (Drums of Passion)', also favoured by Grasso) with discs that generated warmer textures (the gently insistent surge of Eddie Kendricks' 'Girl, You Need a Change of Mind', for example, which many consider to be the first disco record) and

> 'Disco denizens were prisoners of the night doomed by their lifestyle, which itself was the product of contradictory urges.'

the unlikely likes of Les Troubadours du Roi Baudoin's Congolese reworking of the Missa Luba, a centuries-old choral mass in Latin.

In the mid '70s, when disco began to be codified as its own genre rather than simply being used as an umbrella term to denote the records being played by DJs at the various clubs, the music vacillated between Grasso's sense of spectacle and Mancuso's social spirit, between lush strings swooning in the face of beauty and relentless, piledriving 4/4 rhythms that cared only about getting its rocks off. The two DJs also represented the conflicted spirit of the larger gay scene and the '70s as a whole: the communitarian politics of gay pride versus the self-serving anonymous backroom encounter, the beloved communities of the Civil Rights marchers and Woodstock Nation set against the solipsism and self-absorption of the Me Decade.

Perhaps it was this schizophrenia, this push and pull between two apparently incompatible views of the world, that eventually caused disco to abandon the meaning and portent to which pop had aspired throughout the late '60s and early '70s. Instead, the music came to celebrate texture and drama, sensuality and novelty, and its rejection of rock's straight and narrow status quo led to it becoming the first Anglo American form of pop music to embrace continental Europe. In the early days of disco, this meant endearingly daft and heavily percussive cod-Latin rock tracks such as 'Wild Safari' and 'Woman', cut in 1972 by Spanish group Barrabas, and 'Rain 2000' and 'Sultana', both by Norway's Titanic. But by the mid '70s, Eurodisco's range was wider: the music took in shallow rip-offs of Philadelphia soul such as Silver Convention's 'Get Up and Boogie', the symphonic grandeur of Alec R

Costandinos's corny and overblown 1978 album *The Hunchback of Notre Dame* and, from the previous year, the avant-garde synthesizer minimalism of Kraftwerk's 'Trans-Europe Express'.

While Don Ray's 'Standing in the Rain' epitomised all three of these strains, complete with over-ripe production, over-enunciated vocals and a synth line pilfered from Cerrone's 'Supernature' (presumably with permission, since Cerrone co-produced Ray's track), the most important Eurodisco records were those made by Donna Summer and Giorgio Moroder in Munich. 'Love to Love You Baby', released in 1975, and 'I Feel Love', which emerged two years later, revelled in everything that the solemn worshippers of the rock gods derided: decadence, repetition and the machine. 'Love to Love You Baby' might have been 18 minutes of pure pornography. But unlike, say, Mick Jagger's tales of cocksmanship, it was a celebration of female pleasure, and its utter lack of narrative structure and telos is all about the triumph of surrender and ecstasy, not power. 'I Feel Love' is another ode to surrender, but this time, Summer sounds as if she's abandoning herself not to her orgasm but to the machines with which Moroder surrounds her.

There was more than a touch of the cocaine chill and Bacofoil atmosphere of those famous Fiorucci fashion spreads about 'I Feel Love'. But as the '70s grew into the '80s, synthesised disco became still more clinical, especially the music that emerged from San Francisco. 'Can't Take My Eyes off You' and 'Cruisin' the Streets', both by Bill Motley's Boys Town Gang, and Patrick Cowley's 'Menergy' sounded as if they'd been bathed in antimicrobial soap and then cloaked in hazmat suits. The antiseptic, bloodless and often utterly sexless qualities of these records seemed to play on both the accusations of sterility that the disco-sucks crowd levelled at the scene and on most homophobic notions of biology and 'naturalism'.

However, San Frandisco wasn't all about well-scrubbed clones stiffly marching forth from the mad scientist's laboratory. The remarkable Sylvester first garnered attention at the tail-end of the 1960s as part of the Cockettes, a notorious countercultural cross-dressing theatre troupe, then worked in cabaret and made a number of largely forgotten rock albums. Through this variety of styles, he never completely abandoned his roots in the music of the church. But it wasn't until he combined his gospel-trained, sky-high falsetto with mechanised disco beats in the mid to late '70s, as radical a gesture as any Elvis hip-shake, Dylan sneer or Sex Pistols snarl, that Sylvester really found his voice, creating an otherworldly sound that articulated the exquisite bliss of disco's dancefloor utopia. Far more than merely a fast-paced record to which all the Muscle Marys could flex, Sylvester's 1978 single 'You Make Me Feel (Mighty Real)' is disco's ultimate expression of euphoria and release.

Disco didn't only exorcise its demons through a cleansing wail. Songs of desire and desperation were just as much a part of the music's lexicon as were the expressions of ecstasy, and in their own way were just as pleasurable. The eerie reggae of Sylvester's 'I Need Somebody to Love Tonight' is a perfect example of how a slow evocation of unquenched horniness can create absolute havoc on a dancefloor by deferring release. And perhaps the ultimate expression of this attitude was the Italian scene that grew around DJ Daniele Baldelli during the late '70s at Baia degli Angeli in Gabicce and, especially, at the Cosmic Club in the town of Lazise from around 1980. Forgoing dancefloor orthodoxy, Baldelli created trippy collages of avant-garde electronic music (Roedelius's 'Regenmacher', Yellow Magic Orchestra's 'Insomnia'), Afro-Caribbean grooves spun at the wrong speed (Fela Kuti's 'Zombie' slowed down, Yellowman's 'Zungguzungguguzungguzeng' sped up) and straightforward disco (the Rhythm Makers' 'Zone') while a thousand-strong crowd swayed gently.

Back in Manhattan, though, the sets delivered by the very best DJs – Walter Gibbons at Galaxy 21, Larry Levan at the Paradise Garage, Nicky Siano at the Gallery – were more carnal. The music here mirrored the group gropes in the backrooms of such nefarious pleasure palaces as the Anvil and the Mineshaft: deliciously promiscuous, pulsating with irrepressible energy. While these mixes have largely been lost to history (one sub-par Levan set from 1979 has been issued on *Larry Levan Live at the Paradise Garage*), some of the excitement lives on in a number of still-available edits and remixes.

Serious collectors may be able to track down the acetate of Walter Gibbons's signature mix of Jermaine Jackson's 'Erucu', five intense minutes of the record's percussion break before the track is slowly rebuilt into the 'papa-ooo-mow-mow' from the Trashmen's 'Surfin' Bird'. Mere mortals can recreate the feeling of Gibbons's legendary sessions with his remarkable 1976 remix of Double Exposure's 'Ten Percent', the first commercially available 12-inch single and one of the most giddy and intoxicating records of the disco era. And then there are 'medley' discs such as the Big Apple Productions series, John Morales' 'Deadly Medley I' and the uncredited 'Hollywood 2' mix from 1979 that comes complete with a hilarious juxtaposition of Musique's 'In the Bush' and an advert for antacids. Comedy aside, discs such as these more closely replicate the club DJ experience: rapid-fire mixing between dozens of records, building surging momentum and an almost erotic excitement from the ability to cross borders without care.

In addition to their dice-and-splice methodology, New York City DJs in the late '70s began importing dub techniques from Jamaica in order to create more surprise and to stretch the jouissance on the dancefloor. And ultimately, it's records like Larry Levan's mind-boggling soft-porn mix of Instant Funk's 'I Got My Mind Made Up' that illustrate why disco, oozing with spunk and sweat and amyl nitrite, never quite gets you off in the same way as does funk, which almost always builds up to some kind of money shot, or the masturbatory bleat of hardcore punk. Disco denizens were prisoners of the night doomed by their lifestyle, which itself was the product of contradictory urges. The best disco records seemed to understand this. The Peech Boys' 'Don't Make Me Wait', Chic's 'Good Times' and Dr Buzzard's Original Savannah Band's 'Cherchez la Femme' all celebrated and cursed disco's glitterball sophistry, shaking their groove things while warning about hedonism's limits. Even disco, it seemed, understood the price of its own indulgence.

Mighty real: **Sylvester**.

Disco & bliss in 20 songs

'Dancing Queen' Abba

Disco meets pop and goes to Sweden, with relentlessly unfashionable but timelessly brilliant results. The musical inspiration apparently came from George McCrae's 'Rock Your Baby'.

'Night Fever' The Bee Gees

The bittersweet thrill of living for the weekend. The Gibbs' feverishly excited falsetto voices are brilliantly undercut by graceful strings, hypnotic wah-wah guitar and lyrics that suggest the joy of dancing is only momentary.

'Love in C Minor' Cerrone

This marvellously saucy 17-minute track is sort of an uptempo nudge-wink counterpart to Donna Summer's 'Love to Love You Baby'. Bizarre, then, that its central melody bears a striking resemblance to 'Aqua Marina', the song that played over the end credits of Gerry 'Thunderbirds' Anderson's televisual puppet frolic *Stingray*.

'Dance Dance Dance (Yowsah Yowsah Yowsah)' Chic

The breakthrough single by Nile Rodgers and Bernard Edwards confronts the notion of dancing as a means of counteracting the Great Depression. It's said to be the first mainstream single to feature sub-bass (frequencies below around 80Hz), and reputedly wrecked many hi-fi cabinet woofers belonging to unsuspecting listeners in the weeks and months after its release. The subtitle is Gig Young's catchphrase from Sydney Pollack's 1969 movie *They Shoot Horses, Don't They?*.

'If My Friends Could See Me Now' Linda Clifford

Yes, it's *that* one, first sung by Shirley MacLaine in the Broadway musical *Sweet Charity*. But Clifford's rendition takes it to an entirely different place, transposing Dorothy Fields' lyric so it pays homage to the sense of community in '70s clubland.

'My Love Is Free' Double Exposure

Founded by a trio of brothers in New York during 1974, Salsoul was one of the most important record labels of the disco era, pumping out a series of scintillating singles – 'You're Just the Right Size' by the Salsoul Orchestra, Loleatta Holloway's glorious 'Runaway', Carol Williams' 'Love Is You' (the model for Spiller's 'Groovejet (If This Ain't Love)' – that helped shape the sound of the '70s. The still-thrilling 'Ten Percent' was Double Exposure's first dancefloor hit and the first commercially available 12-inch single. This ten-minute track, less revolutionary but no less joyous, was its follow-up.

'You've Got Me Dancing in My Sleep' Frisky

Produced by veteran soul duo Moses Dillard and Jessie Boyce, 'You've Got Me Dancing in My Sleep' supplements a typical disco sentiment (essentially, 'Help! I can't stop moving!') with dazzling piano, a roaring vocal and some casually brilliant Earth, Wind & Fire-esque horn work. One of the great lost disco singles.

'Last Night a DJ Saved My Life' Indeep

Woman struggles to cope as man goes AWOL – the set-up is hardly euphoric. And the music stays in the pocket: there are no soaring strings or gospel hollers to be found anywhere among these grooves. But the message of this late-disco classic – if you're lost, come clubbing and find yourself – continues to resonate more than 25 years later.

'I'm Caught Up (In a One-Night Love Affair)' Inner Life

A unique combination of catharsis and seduction, the bittersweet feeling of lost love summed up in one larger-than-life wail set against pillow-soft strings and surging bass.

'Love's Theme' The Love Unlimited Orchestra

Barry White's experiment in symphonic soul could hardly have been more successful. Familiar from a thousand dancefloors (and nearly as many TV shows), 'Love's Theme' remains one of only a handful of instrumental tracks to reach number one on the US Hot 100 singles lists.

'Love Is the Message' MFSB

MFSB (Mother Father Sister Brother) were the house band of Gamble and Huff's Philadelphia International label, backing the likes of the Stylistics and the O'Jays on a variety of records. But they carved out their own niche with this slice of proto-disco, which strides out on to the dancefloor with a proudly puffed chest and a mile-wide grin.

'Ain't No Stoppin' Us Now' McFadden & Whitehead

'We've got the groove,' claim the backing singers. Yes, they have.

'Disco Circus' Martin Circus

One of disco's great oddities, 'Disco Circus' was created by veteran French group Martin Circus for a comedy movie in which they starred as a gang of soldiers. The film bombed, but when the track crossed the Atlantic and was remixed by the French-born, New York-based producer and DJ François Kervorkian into eight relentless minutes of proto-electro positivity, it became a clubland smash.

Should auld acquaintance be forgot: clubbers ring in 1978 at New York's **Studio 54**.

'Keep on Jumpin'' Musique

Patrick Adams' follow-up to the innuendo-laden 'In the Bush' didn't raise as many eyebrows as its predecessor. However, this ode to staying out dancing until the sun comes up, with lead vocals by Jocelyn Brown, was just as much of a dancefloor hit.

'Weekend' Phreek

'It's party time tonight,' purrs the uncredited vocalist on this pulsating paean to Saturdays, another Patrick Adams production that found immense favour – and repeated plays – at Larry Levan's Paradise Garage in the late '70s and early '80s.

'The Beat Goes On and On' The Ripple

Originally a funk outfit, Michigan's Ripple rethought their music in the mid '70s and came up with this Salsoul archetype: a never-stand-still bassline, a Lycra-tight rhythm section and some glimmering strings. Still a floor-filler.

'Let the Music Play' Shannon

The fat drum beat resembles something from an old-school hip hop single, the squelchy bass sounds like it's jumped out from an early Human League track, and the Latin cowbell might have been nicked from a Tito Puente salsa album. Somehow, all the pieces interlock to create this dark, ecstatic piece of freestyle Latin-disco.

'Lost in Music' Sister Sledge

The aforementioned Rodgers and Edwards are behind this hymn to the euphoric trance of the dancefloor. Rodgers' chicken-scratch riffs remain definitive examples of funk guitar. Check out the Fall's fierce and hilarious version, on which a bored-sounding Mark E Smith drones out the line 'feel so alive' without a hint of irony.

'Disco Inferno' The Trammps

A militant 1960s chant – 'burn, baby, burn' – is subverted into a joyous expression of dancefloor positivism on this ten-minute epic, with singer Jimmy Ellis providing a strangely gruff commentary on the joys of dancing.

'I Hear Music in the Streets' Unlimited Touch

New York's Unlimited Touch spent several years trying to match their debut single, issued in 1980. They never managed it, but there's no shame in that – this effervescent, funky cut is just about perfect.

Altered
states

Mike Shallcross on drugs. (Not literally, officer.)

*What did the Grateful Dead fan say when
he ran out of spliff?*
'Christ, what's this fucking awful music?'

Do you remember the first records to
which you got stoned? Mine were Grace
Jones's *Island Life* and the Sisterhood's
Gift. On Jones tracks such as 'Private Life', the
mix of dub virtuosity, punk-funk nerviness and
shiny, shiny pop production formed a series
of squeaks and burbles that interlocked like the
cogs of some voluptuous Heath Robinson water
sculpture. *Gift*, meanwhile, was and still is seen
as a joke, a vanity project of Sisters of Mercy
frontman Andrew Eldritch that he recorded to
prevent his erstwhile colleagues from using the
band name themselves. But to me, it sounded
like a steampunk Kraftwerk. The beats were
oaky and tribal in an ordered colonial fashion,
the synths huge and archaic with buzzing
valves like my granny's telly. On the lengthy,
gorgeously monotonous 'Colours', the soaring
coda seemed to stretch out forever, like the
spiral staircase to a cathedral's whispering
gallery. But that's what music can sound like
when you're on drugs.

Of course, I'd been listening to songs about
drugs for years before that. I remember the
chuckles in the playground on the day after
the Stranglers performed 'Golden Brown' on
Top of the Pops, when a friend's big brother
told us it was about heroin. I later found out
that it was simply part of a rich lineage of
sickly sweet whistlepops about smack, along
with Lou Reed's earlier 'Perfect Day' and the

subsequent La's hit 'There She Goes'. I'd also
heard the Gun Club's junk opera 'Bad America',
essentially Neil Young's 'The Needle and the
Damage Done' adapted for the big screen by
Jim Thompson, and the Fall's 'Rowche Rumble',
a furious paean to Valium that was sort of an
angrier, more politicised take on the Stones'
'Mother's Little Helper'.

Then there were the songs I never even
realised were about drugs until years later.
Electropop, for me, had been a fluffy, spangly
and easily eschewed proposition, but from the
slightly off-time beats, punky bassline and
Hammer-horror choral pad, I knew New Order's
'Blue Monday' was a different beast. Only
years later did I read that Bernard Sumner has
described it as 'our pounds, shillings and pence
[LSD] record'. Donna Summer's 'Love to Love
You Baby', meanwhile, launched a wave of
elongated, minimalist dancefloor voyages after
a record company executive commissioned a
17-minute version of the track. Legend has it
that the earlier, shorter version had provided
the soundtrack to the aforementioned exec's
cocaine-fuelled sex sessions, but his young
girlfriend had tired of him interrupting their
fucking to change the record.

For many of us, the first time we unwittingly
encountered a song about drugs is when we
heard the Beatles, who only really started
recording music of any lasting importance in
1965 when they were introduced to LSD. Bill
Hicks once said that you knew when the Beatles
were stoned because they let Ringo sing, but
that's not strictly true. The lyrics for 'Tomorrow

194 **Time Out** 1000 Songs to change your life

to help the protagonist sink into selfless nirvana but an engine that could drive them to leave behind the human race and voyage into their own egos. More than two decades later, Ozzy Osbourne's son Louis became one of the residents at House of God, the Birmingham club that spat in the face of happy house and hippy trance, and spawned the hard, dark techno of Surgeon & Regis, a little worm in that generation's utopian rose.

1990. I'm in the Newcastle bingo hall you see in Get Carter, *dancing to hard, noisy Belgian techno, when control of the decks switches to a tall, lanky kid of about 19 from New York. You can tell he's from out of town: he's wearing a baseball shirt rather than the Moschino jerseys favoured by local DJs. He strips the mix down, playing slower, sparser, harder Chicago stuff such as Edwards & Armani's 'Acid Drill'. Then he drops his own track – deep and funky, based around a warping bassline and a spooky whispered refrain of 'ecstasy, ecstasy'. Eighteen years on, Joey Beltram's 'Energy Flash' can still send a shiver up my spine.*

Acid house: blissed out it was in that dawn to be alive. The old guard was out and everything sounded delirious, decadent, *druggy*. The acid house and the indie dance on its coat-tails you all know, but there was also the Day-Glo hip hop of De La Soul's 'Me, Myself and I', with beats as deliciously loose as a badly rolled joint, and a plethora of lysergically inspired rock bands that included Dinosaur Jr, Mudhoney and Rugby's own Spacemen 3, whose didactic credo, as outlined in the title of one album, was *Taking Drugs to Make Music to Take Drugs to*. Their hazy stop/start muse hit its zenith on 1989's *Playing with Fire* and, particularly, the nagging, spiralling 'Revolution', which turned pharmaceutical excess into a duty of civil disobedience.

For the most part, though, the British acid house movement giggled like naughty children about ecstasy. Madchester was not yet Gunchester. E-Zee Possee's shrill 'Everything Starts With an "E"' set the music on a path that led to abominations such as 'Sesame's Treet', a 1992 hit for Smart E's, and, from people who should have known better, the Shamen's 'Ebeneezer Goode'. Contrast this with what happened when American hip hop got hold of

Never Knows' came from John Lennon's LSD-fuelled readings of *The Tibetan Book of the Dead*, but the track's real peculiarity comes from the tape loops set up by Paul McCartney (who was later credited by the band's most inspiring historian, the great Ian MacDonald, with being the real psychedelic Beatle).

Even when the trip goes bad, drugs can result in great music. Black Sabbath emerged in 1969, the year Charles Manson began his killing spree. But contrary to their Crowleyisms, the band's real black mass was not with Christianity but with flower power. Check the tireless rotoring riff of their majestic 'Supernaut', as acid becomes not a tool used

Rewind
Danny Rampling

'The first real awareness I had of acid house was on holiday in Ibiza. I'd been working my way up the ladder as a DJ in London, playing soul, funk, hip hop and the more commercial end of dance. But I was a struggling apprentice with no particular venue, and I felt that a closed-shop attitude was holding me back.

'The major reason I left was because of the last party I'd gone to in London: a Delirium night at the Astoria, when there was a huge outburst of violence. Things were very moody. There were clubs playing house before the acid boom – Delirium, Black Market, Pyramid. But I was unaware, having decided to sell loads of my rare groove collection and try to inspire myself in the States. As soon as I got back in 1987, I went to Ibiza and heard a DJ called Alfredo. My life changed.

'People overstate the differences between the original house music and acid house. Okay, acid was dominated by the bass sound of the Roland 303 sequencer, while straight house was more vocal-based. But even so, acid house was largely a term invented by the media to describe a new phenomenon. It was such an exciting time.

'There's no doubt that people began taking ecstasy at that time. I think it had a palpable, positive effect on the whole scene: it changed a generation's outlook on things and opened their minds. At least, it did at first. But the growth of house's influence would still have happened even without ecstasy. The drug merely accentuated what was happening.

'My wife Jenni and I started Shoom in November 1987. The idea was to have the best party that we could every week. I've heard criticism recently that there was some sort of elitist door policy going on, but that's not true. The door was open to anybody with the right attitude: people with the right heart and mind, regardless of where they came from. The inspiration and the catalyst was the positive, internationalist vibe I'd experienced in Ibiza.

'The moment I realised how much we'd changed the mainstream was when the enormous Sunrise raves began. Entrepreneurs began to muscle in and take it all in a different direction, towards the superclubs like Cream and the Ministry of Sound. Myself and Jenni could have done that and made an absolute fortune. But that wasn't the direction we were looking for: we wanted to keep to the scene's roots, and our own.

'One of my favourite memories was of a party one Saturday night in a house over a bar in Chapel Market. As the weekend stretched into Sunday, more and more people just kept arriving. When the market opened on Monday morning, the stallholders were greeted by the sight of hundreds of us dancing on the roof, around the stalls, in the streets. It was outrageous. That was a very special weekend.

'The cultural commentators aren't exaggerating: acid house *was* a revolution. For two years, there was a tribal kind of unity, a party every night, a genuine sense of community. The scene soon splintered as money and politics moved in. But that period was, without doubt, the happiest time of my life.'

Garry Mulholland; from Time Out, *11 June 1997*

MDMA ten years later: on tracks such as Missy Elliott's 'X-Tasy' and Twista's 'Girl Tonight', the little pills are the gateway to hotter sex.

But the transatlantic fissure was deeper than that. While British acid house producers painted the drug dealer as a loveable Dickensian rogue, the black American musicians who inspired them saw dealers as more sinister characters. By the late 1980s, the anti-hero of Curtis Mayfield's 'Pusherman' had been replaced by cold-eyed, heavily armed psychopaths along the lines of NWA's chilling 'Dopeman'. Chicago's fabulous Phuture kicked off the acid house scene with 'Acid Tracks' in 1987, but not many people listened to the eerie B-side, 'Your Only Friend', in which the ghost of cocaine taunts a dying user, or the later 'Rise from Your Grave', a rousing call for the black community to reject cocaine. German hardcore wunderkind Alec Empire took up their gauntlet with the Gravediggaz-sampling 'SuEcide', but the last acerbic word on E culture came from Green Velvet's 'La La Land', on which the zombified pill-poppers search for party after party to sate their eternal wakefulness.

Detroit's Richie Hawtin had a more ambiguous take. As FUSE, he redefined acid house, doctoring his Roland 303 to hit ear-splitting highs on tracks such as 'Substance Abuse'. Later, as Plastikman, he set out his stall on the album *Sheet One*, its cover dressed up to look like a sheet of LSD tabs. On tracks such as 'Spastik', he began to perfect an intricate percussive sound with a watchmaker's precision but a tripper's magnified eye for detail. And on the sleeve of *Sheet One*'s follow-up *Musik*, Hawtin put the cryptic case for the defence when it came to drug use. 'Just because you like chocolate cake doesn't mean you eat it every day.'

1993. The comedown. Everyone sat down and skinned up. I remember a heavy metal drummer and part-time dope dealer in Liverpool playing us Cypress Hill. 'It's the future, mate,' he said of the stoned dread of 'Hits from the Bong'.

Although King Tubby, the father of dub, banned spliff from his studios, the link between dope and reggae is inextricable. 'Legalise It'

by Peter Tosh, sure, but also the simple sound of dub itself, the stately rhythms and sweet melodies meshing with the hiss of a Bic lighter melting brown slate into wiry tobacco. For me, the last great record in this vein was the queasy elegia of Portishead's *Dummy*. I fell in and out of love, got drunk, smoked some grass and saw my life in the album's penultimate track, 'Biscuit'.

The flip side of the coin was techstep, a hard, cold trope of drum 'n' bass made by white boys from south-west London while smoking the new, super-strong strains of grass that had emerged in the '90s from the lofts and sheds of hoodlum botanists. This wasn't the voice of the streets, but the privilege into which some of the scene's leading participants were reputedly born makes the paranoia in tracks such as Hydro's 'Tha' Bomb Shit' seem more authentic. Next to this, the so-called intelligent jungle of LTJ Bukem was Starbucks music.

On the record
Lee 'Scratch' Perry

'Breathing'

Kate Bush

The music industry is full of devils. Even the ones who are angels turn into devils. Freddie Mercury: he is a devil. Michael Jackson: he was once my hero, now he is a devil. But Kate Bush is the only angel left. Music must have a pure heart. It must have madness; it must have genius. That is why I love Kate Bush.

I was living in England when I started listening to her music – this must have been in the early 1980s. I think it was a girlfriend in Stanmore who first played me Kate Bush records. You could tell that her music is coming from a pure place. Like an angel, she can be scary at first; but like an angel, her voice is comforting. The music breathes, gently. It is calming. I no longer smoke weed, but you don't need to if you have Kate Bush. Her music is all the high you need.
Lee 'Scratch' Perry ran Kingston, Jamaica's legendary Black Ark studios during the 1970s; his most recent album is End of an American Dream *(Megawave)*

2000. London is post-Cool Britannia, and in love with cheap cash. I'm in the sort of nightclub I used to laugh at. R&B provides the soundtrack as people chat and move on like they're speed dating. The drug of choice is coke. The DJ, or possibly the CD changer, skips to Destiny's Child's 'Independent Women'. The dancefloor fills with whoops of glee as Beyoncé and co sing: 'Charlie, how your angels get down like that?'

As in life, cocaine on record is a dubious experience. Even the best songs are cautionary and vaguely sanctimonious tales. Fleetwood Mac's 'Gold Dust Woman', the cyanide soft centre in *Rumours'* lush melodic confection, and its brother, 'Life in the Fast Lane' by the Eagles, drip with self-loathing. Rock stars have the fun so you don't have to. The drug sometimes makes for great little crime dramas, from Johnny Cash's murder ballad 'Cocaine Blues' to Grandmaster & Melle Mel's 'White Lines (Don't Don't Do It)', a single that served as a virtual prototype for HBO's crime drama *The Wire*, but Cole Porter's infamous second verse of 'I Get a Kick Out of You' captures it better than anything else. Why does no one ever listen?

As the drugs have got stronger, the records have got weaker. The self-fulfilling prophecy of Amy Winehouse's 'Rehab' and the Libertines' mythologising of Pete Doherty's tedious slow-motion self-destruction on 'Can't Stand Me Now' are more *Heat* than light, soundtracking tabloid outrage rather than exploring altered states. Or maybe it's me getting older, and drugs not offering what they used to. As PJ O'Rourke once observed, getting out of it may give the callow youth a sense of identity or a new breadth of imagination, but name me the drug that will get a thirtysomething man out of debt.

1997. I'm walking home from the night before in a leafy suburb of south London. Alone, coming down. The beats from the club are still ringing in my ears, but the melody in my head is the Velvet Underground's bittersweet 'Sunday Morning', with all its baggage of wasted years and loneliness. I've never touched heroin or waited for The Man, but this hits home. Drugs come and go, but payback is perennial.

Good
God

Black gospel music's golden age, like all so-called golden ages, was brief: perhaps 1945 to 1960. The greatest quartets recorded sporadically in inferior studios. Roughly two thirds of the recordings they made are no longer commercially available. And during the groups' heyday, neither the white nor the black press deigned to interview the singers or review their releases. But what remains to us – *good God a'mighty, people* – will flat out move you.

This was, after all, the birthing ground of the greatest of American soul and R&B singers. And thus, by definition, it's here that we find the origins of some of the greatest American music. Before you can reach Solomon Burke, Levi Stubbs, Don Covay, Arthur Conley, Otis Redding and the incomparable Wilson Pickett, you have to go through the church. But not the wimpy, flowers-in-your-hair, Easter-dress, words-on-an-overhead-projector church. *Church* church. This is muscular, sinewy Christianity, sung exclusively by raspy-voiced, barrel-chested men who roar and strut and sweat in shiny gabardine suits that are just a tad too tight. The quartet singer is a man's man – in the words of the Wicked Pickett, 'A man and a half'.

This is 'hard gospel' to differentiate it from jubilee, its predecessor, which saw polite quartets singing arrangements of old spirituals in perfect harmony. Jubilee itself was a hybrid form, a mixture of old spirituals, barbershop harmonies and, thrown in for good measure, a little minstrel-show sensibility. Some jubilee groups, such as the Golden Gate Quartet, were astounding, every bit the equal of the Ink Spots or the Mills Brothers. But it was a different kind of religious music. Catchy. Cute. *Safe*. Hard gospel was never safe.

Cramped four or five to a Cadillac – many of the so-called 'quartets' actually had five singers, often a bass, two baritones, a tenor and a 'lead' – the post-war gospel groups were the world's greatest road warriors. The troupes routinely travelled 100,000 miles and performed 300 or more dates each year, sometimes delivering several complete shows in a single day. If their voices weren't hoarse and raspy before…

The singers that inhabited this universe couldn't help but influence each other, and be influenced by each other, as they went about their business. The circuit was tight-knit: the groups regularly toured together, performing as part of heavily billed 'programs' in black churches and auditoriums. If one singer's voice or dance-step moved Sister Flute, the stereotypical yet archetypal middle-aged doyenne who ruled the roost at most churches, then the other groups quickly took notice.

Emerging from South Carolina in the late 1920s, the Dixie Hummingbirds – or, as they were affectionately called, the Birds – were led by the flamboyant Ira Tucker, whose on-stage and in-pulpit dances, splits and 'clowning' (initially a pejorative term in gospel) defined the break between the flat-footed jubilee groups and gospel. In doing so, he foreshadowed virtually every R&B and rock 'n' roll band yet to come. The Birds may have been gospel's most influential quartet: the first to play a secular New York club in 1942, the first to add a guitarist. But claiming to be first at anything is a dicey business in the narrow world of black gospel quartets.

Aged just 13, Tucker joined the Birds a year before they began recording in 1939. The group went on to amass an unmatched catalogue of hits, among them 'Trouble in My Way', 'Let's Go Out to the Programs' (on which Tucker perfectly imitates several of the other lead singers of the day) and 'Christian's Automobile'. Fast-forward to 1973, and that's the Birds

backing Paul Simon on 'Loves Me Like a Rock'. But their own high-energy performances would have left rhymin' Simon winded and worn.

The Birds' greatest rivals on the gospel highway, the Soul Stirrers (first organised under a different name around 1926) and the Pilgrim Travelers (established a decade later), were both founded in Texas, but neither stayed long and there's little Texas twang in their voices. The Stirrers didn't hit their stride until a decade or so after they formed with the addition of Rebert H Harris (dates are notoriously fluid in gospel music), who claimed to have taught

The Dixie Hummingbirds...

himself to sing while listening to birdsong and the blues of Blind Lemon Jefferson, and who employed a falsetto 'yodel' that was a marvel of control and drama. But it was quite a stride when they eventually hit it. Adding vocal improvisation and preaching to the quartet repertoire, the Stirrers went on to rule Chicago, gospel's most competitive town. When Harris left in 1950, a young man named Sam Cooke joined the Stirrers for a six-year stint, adding his smooth, supple high tenor to an intriguing legacy of well-crafted gospel songs that are closer to pop than gospel.

Having moved from Texas to Los Angeles, the Pilgrim Travelers were widely credited with adding a danceable beat to gospel, after astute producer Art Rupe mic-ed their pounding foot-tapping during sessions and called it 'walking rhythm'. Until Cooke joined the Stirrers in late 1950, the Travelers' dual leads, cousins Kylo Turner and Keith Barber, were the most charismatic singers on the road. Sadly, despite their talents, the group are barely remembered today, although hits such as 'Jesus Hits Like the Atom Bomb', 'Standing on the Highway' and 'Mother Bowed' are well worth investigating.

... and the **Spirit of Memphis Quartet**.

(To digress for a moment: songs about the singer's saintly mother have long been a gospel staple, virtually all of them slow and melancholy. As well as 'Mother Bowed', the Travelers dipped into this well repeatedly with such songs as 'Angels Tell Mother' and 'I've Got a Mother Gone Home', while the Soul Stirrers cut a track entitled 'I'm Still Living on Mother's Prayer'. The Five Blind Boys of Alabama offered 'I Can See Everybody's Mother But Mine', 'Livin' on Mother's Prayers' and 'When I Lost My Mother'; Swan's Silvertone Singers delivered 'I Got a Mother Done Gone'; and, in the early '60s, the Consolers recorded 'Every Christian Mother Surely Prayed for Her Child' and 'I'm Waiting for My Child to Come Home'. Other singers have responded to the listeners' need to beat themselves up over how they'd neglected their grey-haired mamas: take Dorothy Norwood's 1966 epic 'The Denied Mother', for example. But the undisputed mistress of mother songs these days is Shirley Caesar, whose biggest hit was the half-spoken – actually, half-preached – and half-sung six-minute opus 'I Remember Mama', and who still mentions her mother in every concert she gives.)

Less polished but more unpredictable than the Pilgrim Travelers, the Five Blind Boys of Mississippi were founded at a school for the blind in 1937 and featured the ferocious Archie Brownlee, whom even Cooke feared on stage. His voice a force of nature, Brownlee was prone to making Spirit-filled leaps from stages but – somehow, some way – unerringly landed in the aisles. Indeed, so overpowering were Brownlee's performances that he's widely said to have sung himself to death in 1960 at the age of just 35.

Gospel's other greatest shouter, the Reverend Julius 'June' Cheeks, led the Sensational Nightingales, though the group's relationship was often stormy. The illiterate Cheeks, who left school in the second grade and picked cotton by day, sang in regional quartets until tabbed to join the Nightingales in 1946 at the age of 17. A fearless, deeply religious man who became one of the most visible gospel singers of the Civil Rights Movement, Cheeks boasted a growling, menacing baritone so powerful that it routinely over-drove studio microphones, at least until constant use shredded his vocal chords. You can hear that throaty howl best on 'Somewhere to Lay My Head' from 1955.

As if to complete this tight-knit circle, Cheeks briefly left the Nightingales in 1954 and joined the Soul Stirrers. He wasn't with them for long, soon returning to the 'Gales, but the Spirit-filled rendition of 'All Right Now' he recorded with the Soul Stirrers is still discussed in awed whispers in gospel circles. Cheeks has been credited with teaching a young Sam Cooke the intricacies of stagecraft and audience presence; two years after they were briefly in the same group, Cooke left the Soul Stirrers and embarked on a hugely successful pop and soul career.

Like Cooke, the members of the Spirit of Memphis Quartet could sing just about anything, from spirituals to hard gospel. However, for many years, they didn't (or couldn't) travel as much as their more famous counterparts, recorded only erratically and changed personnel constantly. Their ever-changing roster was led by Jet Bledsoe and usually featured tenor Robert Reed and bass Earl Malone, but at one point, the group included Bledsoe, William 'Little Ax' Broadnax and the well-travelled Silas Steele, each a dynamic lead vocalist in his own right.

The group's unreliability undoubtedly contributed to their relative lack of success and, eventually, to the fact that very few of their recordings are available today. However, there is one transcendent track that epitomises all that's good and scary and sublime about this music: 'Lord Jesus', recorded at the vast Mason Temple in Memphis in 1952 and issued in two parts over both sides of a 45 the same year.

The audience is already having church when Bledsoe's eerie laughter suddenly sends the music into some kind of mystical chanted ring-shout, with the group repeating the word 'Jesus' over and over like a mantra. For a frightening, exhilarating couple of minutes, the song reflects what a hidden, forbidden Brush Arbor meeting might have sounded like during the darkest days of slavery. This is a stripped-down version of the Spirit, the group relying only on their vocal prowess to cast a spell on an entire auditorium.

On 'Lord Jesus', gospel completes a circle that began with the first nameless spirituals on America's shores nearly 400 years ago, when the music were still infused with echoes of timeless African possession rituals. And brother, when you hear music this potent, it's chilling and cleansing at once.

Talking Book

1000 SONGS TO CHANGE YOUR LIFE

Sound
and vision

Stephen Troussé on pop in the movies.

It's an infernally hot Parisian night and Denis Lavant is trying manfully, boyishly, to seduce Juliette Binoche. There's other stuff going on: a sci-fi plague that afflicts loveless lovers; Halley's Comet messing with the weather; a planned heist. But the heart of the story is this night and the way Lavant swoons for Binoche.

He switches on the radio and twirls the dial three times, as though it was a roulette wheel or the combination of a safe; he is, after all, on this night, in this story, a teenage thief and *prestidigitateur*. 'Let us listen to the music and let it guide our feelings,' he drawls, in a way you can only get away with in Paris in the dark in the movies, hoping to unlock her heart. But the tune that crackles through is a dud: some quavery old-timer crooning of murder and regret. Lavant sucks a pensive Gitane and prays for something more inspiring and up to date. And tonight, God is a DJ who takes requests. The next song is called 'L'Amour moderne'. From the first revs of guitar, the gated crash of the drums, the matter-of-fact opening lines, we know this number. 'I know when to go out…'

From the moment they're recorded, pop songs roam the airwaves like restless ghosts waiting for the perfect moment to seize, a living body or two to possess. For this song, this is that moment. Lavant tries to resist, but the song drags him out on to the scalding streets. He's losing his cool, but he's overpowered, intoxicated, enchanted. Soon, he's barrelling down the boulevards, as though Iggy Pop had somehow landed the Gene Kelly role in *An American in Paris*.

Don't you wonder, sometimes, about sound and vision? The song is 'Modern Love' by David Bowie. The film is *Mauvais Sang*, directed by Leos Carax. And the scene, for my money, is one of the most magnificent pop moments in the movies. A great part of the wonder is that 'Modern Love' isn't really one of Bowie's finest moments (Carax has a very French sense of the singer's oeuvre: in his debut feature, *Boy Meets Girl*, he conjured strange magic with the early, Newley-ish 'When I Live My Dream'). Yet at this moment, in this film, it sounds like the greatest thing he ever recorded. The combination of scene

EXIT

A very modern love: Denis Lavant and
Juliette Binoche in **Mauvais Sang**.

and song is a marriage made in pop heaven.
What strange magic is at work?

Since the technologies for recording sound
and light were pioneered in parallel in the 19th
century, they've seemed destined to come
together in moments like this. Jean-Luc Godard
famously defined the movies as a simple matter
of a girl and a gun. But these days, that maybe
doesn't go far enough. A girl, a gun and a pop
song: why, now you've got a picture. It's an
equation that might have been formulated

by Quentin Tarantino. 'If a song in a movie
is used really well,' he's said, 'as far as I'm
concerned, that movie owns that song. It can
never be used again. You know, they used "Be
My Baby" in *Dirty Dancing* and it's like, that's
Mean Streets' song! How *dare* you use "Be My
Baby"! If you use a song in a movie, and it's
right, then, you know, you've got a *marriage*.'

Marriages again: it's no coincidence.
Traditionally, the final stage in film production
is called the 'married print': the moment when

'The models for modern movie soundtracks seem to be less the psychotic jukebox and more the diffident mixtape or the quirky iTunes playlist.'

dire adaptation of *The History Boys* for some typically dismal attempts to make a stage play cinematic by adding a soundtrack.) Let's steer clear of Quentin's assertion and insist, instead, that while all unhappy marriages are alike, happy marriages of pop and film are each happy in their own peculiar ways.

Most are marriages of convenience. Even before sound, songs were press-ganged into Hollywood service by house pianists and organists who could vamp up a soundtrack from out-of-copyright classics. DW Griffith's epic *The Birth of a Nation* even came with sheets of recommended tunes, from 'The Ride of the Valkyries' to 'The Star-Spangled Banner'. These days, pop is often similarly stock. James Brown's 'I Got You (I Feel Good)' made its screen debut in *Ski Party!* (1965), a desperate spin on the surf movie that also featured Lesley Gore trilling 'Sunshine and Lollipops', and in the subsequent four decades has practically become a piece of library music, a jingle for Robin Williams cracking wise or Eddie Murphy getting down in latex. At the other end of the mood palette, think of how the ominous opening bars of Coldplay's 'Trouble', or even Kate Bush's 'This Woman's Work', now boldly signpost WARNING: INTENSE EMOTION AHEAD!

Of course, shotgun marriages, born of desperation or necessity, can work. Plotting the dawning dream of *Donnie Darko*, Richard Kelly had originally planned on using 'Never Tear Us Apart' by INXS. But the licensing proved beyond his budget and he had to opt instead for Echo & the Bunnymen's 'The Killing Moon', which serendipitously proved a perfect match. (Kelly, however, disagreed, and reinstated his first choice on the director's cut DVD, daftly diminishing his own movie.) And increasingly in the age of synergy (another word, as David

the soundtrack is grafted to the final cut, after which no further edits are possible. Yet Tarantino's idea of ownership, of the director dominating the pop song, is perhaps a little too typical of the nerdy machismo of his movies. More often, surely, the song owns the film. Every time a director reaches for 'Gimme Shelter' or 'I Heard It Through the Grapevine', 'Lust for Life' or 'How Soon Is Now?', they're hoping, usually vainly, that the song might lend some lustre to their story. (Check out the

Thomson puts it, for the industry 'screwing the audience in every orifice it can find'), the marriages are arranged: hooked up between different arms of the entertainment complex to ensure MTV moments and marketing opportunities, where Céline will always go on, Bryan does everything for you and Whitney will always love you...

Just as it seems that the most watchable of all screen romances are those screwball pairings of the 1930s (Grant and Russell, Tracy and Hepburn), maybe one key to the great marriages of pop and film is a certain tension or incompatibility, an unresolveable argument always on the brink of divorce, a sense that you never really know which partner is going to end up on top. If so, then the first great setting of a pop song in the movies was by director William Wellman: *The Public Enemy*, his 1931 feature, matched James Cagney's beautiful bastard with 'I'm Forever Blowing Bubbles', the dreamy refrain haunting the gangster to the end, still crackling from a Victrola as he crashes to his death on his mother's doorstep. Does the music sweeten the brutality of the movie, turning Cagney's demise into a sweet little homily? Or does the film curdle the cock-eyed dreaming of the song?

If that match of the savage and the sentimental now seems too pat, by now an honourable tradition that leads all the way to David Fincher's use of Donovan's 'Hurdy Gurdy Man' in *Zodiac*, how about Kenneth Anger, the Hollywood phantom who programmatically worked out his alchemy of sound and vision in a series of shorts that culminated in 1964's *Scorpio Rising*? Less a film and more a pop-cult black mass, the short summons up a lurid iconography of biker boys and Nazis, and cuts them to the sound of the Crystals' 'He's a Rebel', Elvis's '(You're the) Devil in Disguise', and, unforgettably, Little Peggy March's 'I Will Follow Him'.

Wellman and Anger, mainstream director and avant-garde ritualist, could be the twin fathers of the modern soundtrack, formulating, a radical alternative to the classically composed Hollywood score from either end of the studio era. Ardent student Martin Scorsese has acknowledged their examples, and it's hard to imagine the soundtrack of *Mean Streets* without the precedent set by either: the tough-guy sentiment is intimately wedded to the dark iconographic magic. If the New York Dolls, formulating their own equation of the Shangri-Las, the Rolling Stones and Manhattan low life, lit the fuse that would blow up into punk, then Scorsese's own equation (the Ronettes' 'Be My Baby' never more glorious than on that 8mm opening sequence, 'Jumpin' Jack Flash' the theme tune to Johnny Boy's own private psychosis) has proved similarly, outrageously influential.

Most notably, of course, with Quentin Tarantino, who worked his own geek magic on the forgotten sounds of the 1970s in *Reservoir Dogs*: 'Little Green Bag' and 'Stuck in the Middle with You' will certainly never sound the same again. 'If I start to seriously consider the idea of doing a movie, I immediately try to find out what would be the right song to be the opening credit sequence, even before I write the script,' Tarantino has said. 'When I find the right one, it's like, "OK, boom, I got that." It's not that the personality of the movie is in that song, but it really gives me a handle on it.' But with Tarantino, it's hard to

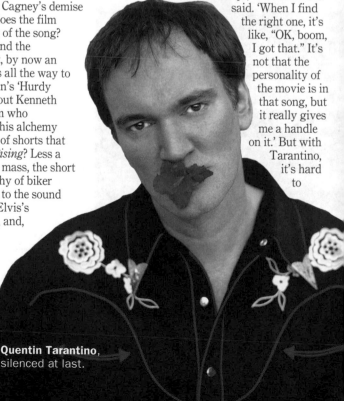

Quentin Tarantino, silenced at last.

De Niro having a gas in **Mean Streets**.

shake the feeling of conceptual cuteness: his musical marriages, no matter how bloody, often feel like droll comedies of manners rather than startlingly original equations.

The other great inheritor of Wellman and Anger is David Lynch, whose equations are arguably too original for his own good. *Blue Velvet* takes the darkness Anger divined in Bobby Vinton's croon and constructs an entirely strange universe around it, as plush and twisted as 1950s suburbia. Is Dennis Hopper's Frank, calling for 'the candy-coloured clown' between puffs on his gas mask, a sinister defiler of Roy Orbison's 'In Dreams', or just its biggest fan? It may be an abusive marriage of scene and song, but it's not entirely clear who the victim is or who's possessing who. In his Martian Jimmy Stewart way, Lynch may

be the last sincere romantic in modern cinema, and his rapt surrender to song is increasingly rare. By comparison, even Pedro Almodóvar, who planted Caetano Veloso's gorgeous rendition of 'Cucurrucucu Paloma' right at the heart of *Talk to Her*, is something of a cynic.

The models for modern movie soundtracks seems to be less the psychotic jukebox and more the diffident mixtape or the quirky iTunes playlist. That is, not Scorsese and Lynch's twisted singles obsessions but the soundtracks of Mike Nichols' *The Graduate* and Robert Altman's *McCabe & Mrs Miller*. Altman cut his film using songs from Leonard Cohen's debut album, a perfect match for the brown studies of the cinematography, and was amazed to find that Cohen was happy for him to use 'Sisters of Mercy', 'Winter Lady' and 'The Stranger Song'.

Nichols famously commissioned Paul Simon to compose original songs for his score, and even persuaded him to retitle his song dedicated to Eleanor Roosevelt as 'Mrs Robinson'.

You can trace this tendency through to Wes Anderson's winsome way with autumnal British psych-pop: the Kinks, the Who and the Stones all over *Rushmore*, the Bowie songs rendered more wistful and translated into Brazilian bossa nova sea shanties for *The Life Aquatic*. However, perhaps the definitive pop image from Anderson's films is Jason Schwartzman dragging his iPod speakers halfway around the world, from New York to rural India, hoping to find another moment to match the time that he staged his own sex scene in the Parisian Hotel Chevalier to the soundtrack of Peter Sarstedt's absurdly affecting 'Where Do You Go to (My Lovely)'.

Paul Thomas Anderson is arguably the ultimate modern director as mixtape composer, his films working less as linear narrative and more as a bridge between scenes with the strange logic of a compilation from song to song. His technique has been most successful in *Magnolia*, which was practically written as an adaptation of the songs of Aimee Mann. The suburban sprawl of the movie leads up to the moment when all the lost parents and children of Los Angeles find some communion or solace singing along to 'Wise Up'. It's as though Anderson's proving the point that if a pop song is large enough and good enough, it will be able to find room for a dying TV exec, a screwed-up cokehead, an anguished cop and even Tom Cruise.

Sofia Coppola may be less profound but more audacious. She's always had a fine fashionista's sense of a stylish soundtrack, commissioning Air to provide the Mogadon mood Moogs to *The Virgin Suicides* and single-handedly resurrecting the career of the Jesus & Mary Chain by crashing 'Just Like Honey' into the Tokyo street scene tears at the end of *Lost in Translation*. But her finest decision was to soundtrack *Marie Antoinette* with English post-punk and new pop. The laziest use of pop in the movies has always been as historical wallpaper, from the 1962 rock 'n' roll cavalcade of George Lucas's *American Graffiti* through to the early '80s Sta-Prest scene-setting of Shane Meadows' *This Is England*, tapping into easy automatic nostalgia. How much more

'Mrs Robinson, you're trying to seduce me.'

uncanny and provocative to begin a film about the decadent end of the French aristocracy with Gang of Four's 'Natural's Not in It'. The spirit of Wellmann and Anger is alive right here.

And maybe it's out on the internet. Almost all the scenes and songs I've discussed here can be found with a few taps of a laptop on YouTube, and you can have a fruitful afternoon clicking from Denis Lavant to De Niro to Dennis Hopper and beyond. But you can also note the way in which music and movies are becoming polyamorous and perverse. The marriage, the ownership on which Tarantino insisted, is increasingly, fantastically adulterous. You can find home-made montages replaying westerns as musicals, imagining Cary Grant as James Bond with a little John Barry, or reworking *Back to the Future* as a tender gay love story via the soundtrack to *Brokeback Mountain*. You can even find hip hop repaying its debt to the original gangster, with a clip of Cagney in *The Public Enemy* that cuts from the scratched disc of 'I'm Forever Blowing Bubbles' to the sound of the Herbaliser's 'Real Killer Pt.2'.

The re-editing and recomposition can be funny, surprising and sometimes even great pop criticism. But is there anything to match the inspired marriage of scene and song? No doubt it will soon be campily re-edited with something out of Napalm Death or Ween or Fall Out Boy, and maybe they'd work just as well, but I think my favourite pop moment in film might still be that scene in Richard Linklater's *Before Sunrise* in which Julie Delpy and Ethan Hawke scurry into some old-fashioned Viennese record store, the kind that still has listening booths. Delpy picks up, of all things, a copy of the profoundly obscure Kath Bloom's 'Come Here' and insists that they listen together. It's a broad folk number, and the scene is nothing more than the faces of Delpy and Hawke caught in the embarrassment of listening to someone's favourite song and not knowing where to look. The moment at which Bloom's glorious warble comes in is priceless in itself, but the whole two-minute scene, the duration of the song, is a reminder, as David Thomson says, that the greatest special effect the movies still has to offer is the shot 'of a face as its mind is being changed'. And what changes our minds, or our hearts, as casually and profoundly as a pop song?

Pop in the movies in 20 songs

'Sweet Emotion' Aerosmith
from *Dazed and Confused*

When Richard Linklater was refused permission to use the Led Zeppelin song of the film's title, he decided to open it with this Aerosmith hit instead. It works a treat, its mix of easy boogie swagger and dreamy vocal harmonies helping to establish the setting as pre-punk, post-hippy Texas.

'Playground Love' Air
from *The Virgin Suicides*

Sofia Coppola's debut feature has some great moments of woozy music/visuals synchronicity (Gilbert O'Sullivan, Todd Rundgren, the Hollies, Styx), but Air's romantic, wistful and dreamlike theme

single kicks in at exactly the right point. Coppola later pulled off the same trick in *Lost in Translation*, with Kevin Shields providing the Air role.

'Stayin' Alive' The Bee Gees
from *Saturday Night Fever*

Used in the opening reel of John Badham's movie, 'Stayin' Alive' brilliantly establishes the film's mix of gritty kitchen-sink realism, desperate escapism and sexual intrigue. As John Travolta's working-class hero struts down the street, his steps are synchronised with a swaggering disco beat that's seditiously undercut by sensuous horns, queasy strings and the Gibb brothers' eerily androgynous, sexually panicked falsetto voices.

'Hallelujah' John Cale
from *Shrek*

This version of Leonard Cohen's much-covered classic can reduce small children to tears, even after the tenth viewing. Who better than canonic rock miserablists Cohen and Cale to introduce pathos to the world's youth?

'The End' The Doors
from *Apocalypse Now*

Okay, so the use of this trippy, Indo-tinged stoner classic to accompany an attack on a Vietnamese village soon became one of cinema's defining sonic clichés, but it works brilliantly, as Jim Morrison's baleful baritone and devastatingly bleak lyrics fit perfectly with the images.

'He Needs Me' Shelley Duvall
from *Popeye* and *Punch-Drunk Love*

Written by Harry Nilsson for Robert Altman's 1980 film version of *Popeye*, in which it soundtracked the *Some Mothers Do Have 'Em*-style love affair between Olive Oyl (Duvall) and Popeye (Robin Williams), this woozy, wonky tune was successfully recontextualised in *Punch-Drunk Love* to lead audiences to believe that they were entering the brain of a demented, lovestruck woman.

'Rhapsody in Blue' George Gershwin
from *Manhattan*

Woody Allen's use of this majestic theme, set to images of a floodlit Yankee Stadium, commuters pouring off the Staten Island Ferry and couples canoodling on the roof of the Metropolitan Museum, set the tone for this defiant hymn of praise to the Big Apple at a time when the city was bankrupt and knee-deep in garbage. It's not, strictly speaking, pop, but the rest of the soundtrack was a compendium of Gershwin's finest showtunes.

'Tiny Dancer' Elton John
from *Almost Famous*

When a young journalist follows a dreary '70s band through a debauched rock 'n' roll tour, the pivotal moment comes when Elton John's song is played on the tour bus. The ensuing singalong reminds us of pop music's healing power, but it also of the fact that Elton wrote some cracking tunes back in the day.

'Down to the River to Pray' Alison Krauss
from *O Brother, Where Art Thou?*

'The cinema is kind of like a big radio these days,' said the film's music director, T Bone Burnett. 'You've got people in the dark for a couple of hours and they're susceptible to new experiences.' Burnett used his cinematic radio to showcase Depression-era pop, white gospel, country blues and haunting Appalachian harmonies, and traditional songs such as this helped kick-start a revival of interest in what became known as Americana.

'Hip to Be Square' Huey Lewis & the News
from *American Psycho*

One of the more hilarious examples of sonic casting against cinematic type. 'Their early work was a little too "new wave" for my taste,' says Patrick Bateman (Christian Bale), strolling around his apartment. 'But when *Sports* came out in '83, I think they really came into their own, commercially and artistically.' Whereupon he dons a raincoat, pops a pill, sticks 'Hip to Be Square' on the stereo and buries an axe into the head of the gentleman sitting quietly on his sofa, all the while holding forth on the band's 'consummate professionalism'.

'Singin' in the Rain' Malcolm McDowell
from *A Clockwork Orange*

Stanley Kubrick specialised in using music counter-intuitively: think Johann Strauss's waltzes in *2001: A Space Odyssey*. However, he never juxtaposed screen action with unlikely soundtrack more perfectly than here, as Alex and his droogs balletically kick a man within an inch of his life while singing this cheery showtune. In the light of what's gone before, Gene Kelly's version, which accompanies the end credits, takes on a horribly discomfiting tone.

'All by Myself' Jamie O'Neal
from *Bridget Jones's Diary*

This genre-defining chick-flick begins with a scene-setting, character-establishing vignette in which Renée Zellweger, with a crushing, gauche literalism, mimes and plays air drums along to Eric Carmen's mournful power ballad. She reprises the trick later to Harry Nilsson's 'Without You'.

'Where Is My Mind?' Pixies
from *Fight Club*

The final reel of *Fight Club* finds director David Fincher using Frank Black's wailing vocal to soundtrack the horror in the eyes of Edward Norton as he surveys the tumbling skyscrapers.

'Lust for Life' Iggy Pop
from *Trainspotting*

Danny Boyle, the film's producer, famously blew a large chunk of the production budget on the rights to use 'Lust for Life' in the opening reel of *Trainspotting*, but it was worth it. The track branded the film as edgy, timeless and rebellious yet oddly familiar, and made the accompanying album an iconic best-seller in its own right.

'Fight the Power' Public Enemy
from *Do the Right Thing*

Rosie Perez's half crumping, half shadow-boxing dance workout during the opening credits of Spike Lee's third full-length feature is one of the defining moments in African American cinema. The extended version of Public Enemy's song, featuring Branford Marsalis's Coltrane-inspired tenor sax solo, is much, much better than the original.

'Monkey Man' The Rolling Stones
from *GoodFellas*

The whole of *GoodFellas* could be seen as a trawl through Martin Scorsese's collection of classic rock vinyl (the Who's 'Magic Bus', Mick Jagger's 'Memo from Turner', Harry Nilsson's 'Jump into the Fire', Donovan's 'Atlantis'), but one particular highlight is this debauched classic, accompanying a scene in which a paranoid, coke-addled Ray Liotta is (rightly) convinced that he's being tailed by a police helicopter.

'Born to Be Wild' Steppenwolf
from *Easy Rider*

Perhaps the first jukebox film, and one that spawned a phenomenally successful synergistic soundtrack album, this turns a rock cliché into pure realism.

'Head Over Heels' Tears for Fears
from *Donnie Darko*

Gary Jules's spartan version of 'Mad World' got all the kudos and hogged the number one spot in the UK charts, but *Donnie Darko* really jumps to life when this exquisite slice of studio rock thumps out from the speakers.

'As Time Goes By' Dooley Wilson
from *Casablanca*

'Play it, Sam,' she says. And so, after a little prompting, he does.

'Across 110th Street' Bobby Womack
from *Jackie Brown*

If Quentin Tarantino pioneered the film soundtrack as a personal mixtape, *Jackie Brown* is possibly his best. Played as Pam Grier strides elegantly to the check-in desk, this song sounds particularly good.

Stage fright

Mark Shenton charts the troubled relationship between pop and musical theatre.

Is it too bold to state, as American critic Martin Gottfried does in his book *Broadway Musicals*, that 'the musical is America's most significant contribution to world theatre'? Although it had European antecedents in works such as John Gay's 1728 *The Beggar's Opera* and the comic operettas of Gilbert and Sullivan, the musical as a distinct genre first emerged on Broadway. 'Unlike our dramas,' writes Gottfried, 'musicals are purely American as a stage form.'

But even as Gottfried speaks up for the importance of Broadway musicals, he's careful to sound a note of caution. 'There have not yet been any musicals to rank with the great classics of the dramatic literature,' he warns. 'There are many beloved shows – even great ones – but they are not works of art; their period qualities are obvious in revivals. We actually love them for their marvellous and timeless songs, not for their plots and productions.'

It's those marvellous and timeless songs, the rich pedigree of great material that was originally written for stage and screen musicals, that provide the anchor for what's commonly known as the Great American Songbook. Between the 1920s and the early '60s, generally regarded as Broadway's 40-year golden age, the songs that emerged from musicals were a major cultural force, supplying a soundrack for the American national identity through the likes of 'White Christmas', penned by Irving Berlin for the 1942 movie musical *Holiday Inn*, and 'God Bless America', written for but discarded from a 1918 revue called *Yip Yip Yaphank* and now the country's favourite rallying cry.

Broadway songs were the pop music of their day until, in the late '50s and early '60s, they were largely eclipsed by the emergence of pop music itself. Elvis Presley and then the Beatles arrived; as rock 'n' roll began to speak to young people, so musicals were quickly cast into its shadow. A generation gap emerged, effectively defined by this shift in tastes. Broadway belonged to the world of yesterday, looking backwards rather than forwards. Rock 'n' roll, though, was about what was happening today.

Broadway took a while to catch up with this culture shock, this invasion of the territory it had occupied for decades. But in 1967, it sought to take on this changed world with *Hair*, and all its promises to usher in the Age of Aquarius. Through the vibrant music of Galt MacDermot and the lyrics of Gerome Ragni and James Rado, the modern pop musical was born, and audiences flocked to it: after a successful opening on Broadway, the show transferred to the West End for a run of more than four years at the Shaftesbury Theatre. However, in the long run, the success of *Hair* proved to be the exception rather than the rule.

Pop figures started dabbling with the notion of working with musical theatre in the late 1960s. However, the music and the theatres were often kept apart. The Who's so-called 'rock opera' *Tommy* was released as an album in 1969, but it didn't reach Broadway for a further 23 years. Des McAnuff, the director of the eventual stage version, remembered the impact that the album had on him in 1969. 'I was 17, in high school and in love with both

Wig out! The original London cast of **Hair**.

the theatre and rock 'n' roll. *Tommy* struck me right away with its inherent theatricality and story, even though the story was a bit sketchy. Moreover, the music was far more exciting to me than any of the rock 'n' roll music in theatre up to that time. When *Hair* came along and *Tommy* was issued, I realised that I could have everything I loved in the theatre.'

McAnuff had to wait until 1992 to see his passions truly married, by which time *Tommy* belonged not to the here and now of rock music but to the nostalgia of musical theatre. In the interim, Broadway musicals had become still more rarefied and specialised, particularly through the advances made to the form by Stephen Sondheim. In his hands, a show no longer had to be defined by its story: his revolutionary and evolutionary 'concept musicals' such as *Company* and *Follies* revolved around an idea rather than a plot. Occasionally, a song broke free from its concept and achieved a wider contemporary resonance; 'Send in the Clowns', from Sondheim's 1973 show *A Little Night Music*, became a pop hit for Judy Collins. But these, too, were not rules but exceptions.

It was the same story across the Atlantic. First staged in 1971, Andrew Lloyd Webber and Tim Rice's early rock opera *Jesus Christ Superstar* seemed to some listeners to be more accessible than Sondheim; it even features a heartfelt love song from Mary Magdalene to Christ in the shape of 'I Don't Know How to Love Him'. But while Lloyd Webber has had occasional chart success, with 'Don't Cry for Me, Argentina' (from *Evita*) reaching number one in 1978 and 'Memory' (from *Cats*) following it into the top ten three years later, even he has failed to integrate fully the worlds of pop and theatre.

Indeed, rather than musical theatre once more wielding an influence over pop music, pop came into the theatre: first by stealth but then by design, as pop's back catalogue became fair if lazy game for producers who sought to make new shows out of old songs. Often, these were merely revues, a counter-evolutionary development that harked back to the revue-based shows of the 1920s – you could call them revuesicals – in which unrelated songs, sketches and dance were stitched together to make a whole. At the height of the format's popularity, producers engaged the services of major Broadway composers and lyricists such as Richard Rodgers and Lorenz Hart, Jerome Kern, Irving Berlin, George Gershwin and George M Cohan to write for their shows. In Britain, meanwhile, the likes of Noël Coward, Sandy Wilson and Flanders & Swann made revue-writing an honourable end in itself, in much the same way that today's pantos have attracted their younger British counterparts.

As a new breed of musical revues emerged from this tradition in the late '70s, the repertoires of Elvis and the Beatles were keenly exploited for multimedia tribute shows. The appetite for these jukebox productions has continued more or less unabated ever since the success of *Beatlemania*, a Broadway hit in 1977. The songs of Jerry Leiber and Mike Stoller, one of the pre-eminent New York songwriting teams of the late '50s and early '60s, have been reworked into at least three revues: *Only in America* and *Yakety Yak* in London, and *Smokey Joe's Café* on Broadway and then the West End. Meanwhile, Buddy Holly, the subject of a show that ran for more than 12 years in the West End before returning in a scaled-down revival, and Frankie Valli and the Four Seasons, on whose lives and careers the Broadway hit *Jersey Boys* was based, are among the artists to have been given the bio-musical treatment, a format that seeks to tell audiences something about the lives (and sometimes deaths) of the performers while also presenting them with the hits they remember so well.

This desire for narrative structure can be traced back to a tradition initiated in 1927 by Jerome Kern and Oscar Hammerstein II when they defiantly broke from the revue template with *Show Boat*, a musical that dared to tell a serious story by using songs not as mere decoration but as dramatic tools with which to advance character and plot. *Show Boat* set musicals on a modern course that lyricist Hammerstein, working with Richard Rodgers on a series of now-legendary musicals that started with *Oklahoma!* in 1943, eventually came to perfect.

In Rodgers and Hammerstein's shows, the songs typically take over where mere words aren't enough; they arrive in order to articulate and elevate the characters' feelings. Take 'If I Loved You' from *Carousel*, in which

'The imitators spawned by *Mamma Mia!* have taken the jukebox musical into the realm of self-parody, as a series of utterly unrelated pop songs are lassoed into padding out ever more ridiculous storylines.'

Hammerstein sets out a cleverly tentative exploration of two characters circling around the possibility of making a romantic connection. Sondheim, a protégé of Hammerstein, used similar devices in 'Too Many Mornings' from *Follies*, in which a character meets a former lover and keenly articulates the notion that they could happily have wasted the intervening years together, and 'Send in the Clowns', which outlines a similar realisation: that the perfect match was there all along, but the singer realised it too late.

One of the few jukebox musicals to rely on techniques such as these has been *Mamma Mia!*. The show sees old Abba songs folded into a new plot, with the familiarity of the tunes creating ripples of recognition while the story gives audiences something fresh to enjoy. Judy Craymer, the producer who helped steer the show into a worldwide hit, believed in the music from the start. 'I always thought there was tremendous potential in the songs,' she has said. 'They have great emotional tension, and each one has a subtext.'

The songs of Benny Andersson and Björn Ulvaeus come complete with some of the defining features found in the best Sondheim and Hammerstein showtunes. The likes of 'Dancing Queen' and 'SOS' are narrative psychodramas in which the characters bare their souls while simultaneously revealing a complex backstory. And in Catherine Johnson's book for the show, they're used to enhance character and propel the plot; take the point

George Gershwin.
Nice work if you can get it.

at which Donna, a single mother, reveals the extent of her emotional losses by singing 'The Winner Takes It All', using a lost card game as a metaphor for a relationship that's ended. In the theatre, as in all music, a great song needs a melody that's both beautiful and memorable, linked to a lyric that speaks directly to the listener.

The success of *Mamma Mia!* has spawned any number of imitators. These new shows have, in turn, taken the jukebox musical into the realm of self-parody, as a series of utterly unrelated pop songs are lassoed into padding out ever more ridiculous storylines. For *We Will Rock You,* writer Ben Elton wedged Queen songs into an excuse for a plot that imagined a dystopian futuristic world where pop music had been banned, but within which a band of loyal underground followers (literally – inhabiting the shell of Tottenham Court Road tube station) kept the flame of Freddie Mercury alive. And for the 2003 show *Tonight's the*

Night, Elton laboured to squeeze Rod Stewart songs into the story of a man who makes a Faustian pact with the Devil in order to become more like Rod, which would then allow him to win the woman of his dreams.

Not all jukebox shows are as bad as that. In 2002, *Our House* adventurously married Madness songs to a new story by Tim Firth that told a *Sliding Doors*-type story of parallel paths: one a life of crime, the other a life of honesty. But some are just misguided. The 2007 West End stage version of the 1985 Madonna film *Desperately Seeking Susan* blended the movie's plot with songs from Blondie's back catalogue, thereby combining the trend for adapting popular films for the stage with the fashion for importing old pop songs into new musicals. However, the producers fatally missed one of the points of relying on such familiarity by combining two different artists under one roof. Audiences arrived expecting to hear Madonna songs, but instead were confronted with the hits of Blondie. The show lasted barely a month.

Old pop songs have been successfully repurposed for the theatre, but can the old pop writers behind them be put to the new purpose of creating original musicals? While unknown writers of new musicals face a near-unwinnable battle to have their voices heard, pop stars already have name recognition with the general public. Harnessing that commercial potential to their undoubted and proven skills as songwriters, an increasing number have been exploring the possibility of writing entire shows for the stage.

Elton John's success co-scoring Disney's *Beauty and the Beast* and *The Lion King* led to him inadvertently becoming a theatrical force when both those movies were translated to the stage. Since then, he's created original work for the stage musicals *Aida*, *Billy Elliot* and *Lestat*, two of them big hits. However, for every Elton success, there's a flop to stand against it. Take the equally instructive experience of Paul Simon, whose hugely expensive production *The Capeman* was both a mess and a miss when it premiered on Broadway in 1998. Similarly, not even the producing might of Disney could turn the Phil Collins-scored *Tarzan* into a hit on Broadway in 2006.

Great songs are never enough on their own: musical theatre is a highly collaborative art form, and the songs need to be skilfully integrated into the shows that house them. That's the challenge with which pop stars from Boy George and the Pet Shop Boys to Barry Manilow and Melissa Manchester have all been grappling in a bid to help the fusion of pop and theatre finally make good on the promise of *Hair*. The success of singer-songwriter Duncan Sheik's *Spring Awakening* on Broadway proves that it can be done. And with Rufus Wainwright writing a commission for the Metropolitan Opera in New York, Luke Haines working on a musical for London's Royal Court Theatre and Damon Albarn looking to follow up his critically acclaimed opera *Monkey: Journey to the West*, it's not time to give up on the format just yet.

Still making money money money: the West End cast of **Mamma Mia!**.

Better
the devil

Martin Hoyle recalls some of opera's great anti-heroes.

Never mind the best tunes: in opera, the devil also has the best figure, part of nature's baffling plan to keep the romantic voice (the tenor) housed in a rotund frame while the villainous (baritone and bass) are almost invariably tall, athletic and good-looking. As a distinguished Australian example of the breed once told me, 'The baritone is Jack the lad. He thinks with his dick.' I'm not sure whether he was characterising the average baritone stage role (jealous lover, vile seducer, envious schemer) or a singer's private life. Better not go there, perhaps.

Either way, there's no doubt that the horned devil in red tights in Gounod's *Faust*, that adored war-horse of the Second Empire, visually sums up plush, melodramatic mid 19th century grand opera in a way no recognisable tenor image does. (Or soprano, come to that, until we come to Valkyries with horned helmets; but Wagner is a one-off.) And musically, the devil has worn just as well; the sardonic and the cynical are, after all, the essence of modernity, more so than languishing romantic love or bellicose patriotism. In *Faust*, you get not only leering innuendo in Méphistophélès' mocking serenade to the sleeping Marguerite, but also a hymn to money: the famous 'Le veau d'or' (or the 'Song of the Golden Calf'), a rollicking ode to materialism and the good times, doubtless rather daring in the 1850s but now the stuff of singalong.

Another Gallic devil, this time in Berlioz's *Damnation of Faust*, sings an even catchier and more lilting serenade, while Boito's Italian Mefistofele has an exuberant bout of whistling written into the score for the opera that takes his name. The most recent interpreter of the role in London, performing at the English National Opera, disappointingly chickened out of the whistle in the face of competition from the Voice of God and sundry angelic choruses; the rest of the opera falls flat after this OTT opening scene.

But if a post-Dawkins world finds even the supernatural hard to take, let alone the divine, then at least the merely human provides plenty of examples of vice singing rings round virtue. Verdi even wanted to call his penultimate Shakespearian opera *Iago*, since the baritone plotter leapt to life so much more vividly than the noble Otello (the eventual title character). Perhaps no more explicable than the Bard's original, the operatic Iago at least is given his own creed, the spine-tingling, declamatory 'Credo in un Dio crudel' – 'I believe in a cruel God who has created me like Himself… From vileness in a germ or atom I was born, and I feel the original slime in me.'

And afterwards? '*La morte è nulla!*' Death is nothingness, he snarls, both defiant and self-loathing over the orchestra's jeering climax. Strong, nihilistic stuff for a fashionable 1887 audience, and, national pride aside, an improvement on Shakespeare. But however thrilling Iago's 'Credo' is to listen to, even in his or her most private fantasies I suspect the operagoer would find unremitting evil a trifle exhausting to maintain. Besides which, Iago's scheming doesn't seem to make him particularly happy.

How different from *Don Giovanni*. Modern directors can point out that, from what we see of the last two days of his life as depicted in Mozart's opera, Giovanni never actually gets the girl, being interrupted, thwarted and generally frustrated every time he comes on to a potential victim. Some psychologists cast doubt on his virility, even his sexual orientation. But we've no reason to doubt his track record as detailed by Leporello, his loyal sidekick, in the 'Catalogue Aria': 640 Italian women, 231 Germans, 100 Frenchwomen, 91 Turks… and in Spain? *'Ma in Ispagna son già mille e tre'* – 1,003.

'The baritone has a nice line in flawed heroes, reflecting the fact that besides being good-looking, he's usually a better actor than the tenor.'

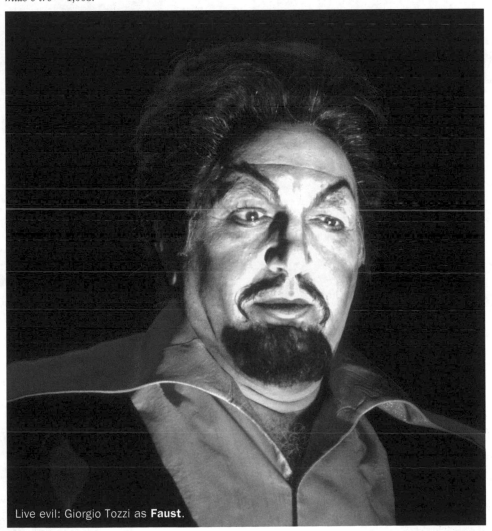

Live evil: Giorgio Tozzi as **Faust**.

Wolfgang Brendel toasts **Don Giovanni**.

No wonder, if the wheedling, caressing 'Là ci darem la mano' is typical of his approach. This duet of seduction with the peasant girl Zerlina is one of Mozart's loveliest, simplest tunes, full of such wistful tenderness that you suspect the composer forgot the dramatic situation and psychological implications and just wrote beautiful music. (And not for the last time: 'Soave sia il vento', the famously melting trio of farewell from *Così fan tutte*, is based on the heartless hoaxing of two of the singers and the mischievous scheming of the third, but it's still a favourite, tear-inducing Desert Island Disc.)

Giovanni's best when relating to others: 'Deh, vieni alla finestra', his delicately-scored serenade, is a textbook example of seduction. But his ebullient let's-have-a-party solo, nicknamed the 'Champagne Aria', is oddly hollow, bearing out the suspicion that alone of Mozart's great operatic figures, Giovanni has nothing to tell us about himself. Incapable of learning or even remembering, he lives entirely for the minute with no past and no future. When he's dragged down to flames and a devilish chorus, you suspect he may have been in hell all along, in a way that even an audience of the Enlightenment may not have grasped.

So, tenor good, baritone bad, bass diabolical. But as with all rules, there are exceptions. You do get good baritones: Mozart's Figaro is the hero of his opera (Rossini's version of the same character is simply the comic) and has subtly varied arias to prove it, culminating in the final-act outburst when, believing himself deceived by Susanna on their wedding night, he pours out his anger, grief and outraged pride, mocked by the horns in the orchestra (that old cuckoldry pun, as international as it was timeless). It all ends happily, of course, as it does for another virtuous baritone, Hoël in Meyerbeer's *Dinorah*, though he has to save the demented heroine's pet goat from drowning, thus restoring her (the heroine's) sanity.

The baritone has a nice line in flawed heroes, reflecting the fact that besides being good-looking, he's usually a better actor than the tenor. Wagner's Flying Dutchman, condemned to sail the world until he finds a woman prepared to love him unto death (as opposed to simply loving him to death), is a haunting, tragic figure. Less noble, and with a flaw that's all too human, is one of the great baritone creations: Billy Budd, the stammering golden

boy, left hideously vulnerable by his innocence. Herman Melville's novella of the Royal Navy during the Napoleonic wars inspired both EM Forster (co-librettist) and Benjamin Britten (composer) in this confrontation of good and evil. It's epitomised by Claggart: ship's master-of-arms, Iago with a bass voice, resentful of beauty that must be destroyed...

On the record
Rufus Wainwright

'O patria mia'

Maria Callas

If I wanted to convey to someone why I love opera, I'd sit them down and play them this to see what happens. And if they're not moved, I'd give up on them, frankly. This is from the second act of Verdi's *Aida*, and it's quite simple and spartan and bold. It's the pitching, the breath control and the emotion that amazes me every time. Opera has been an inspiration to me in that it's something that requires craft and beauty. It's something you get better at as you get older. It's a useful corrective to pop music, which is all about celebrating youth.
Rufus Wainwright's most recent album is Release the Stars *(Universal)*

Moving pictures

Geoff Carter speaks up for the almost-lost art of the cinematic soundtrack.

Bernard Herrmann made eight films with Alfred Hitchcock. The partnership of a Juilliard-trained composer and the larger-than-life 'Master of Suspense' might have looked unusual on paper, but in reality, it was a perfect fit. 'From the moment Hitchcock started using Herrmann,' said lifelong Hitchcock fan François Truffaut, 'something in his films was intensified.'

Unfortunately, Hitchcock and Herrmann had a falling-out in 1966 over the scoring of *Torn Curtain*, and the two men never worked together again. Truffaut blamed their acrimony on studio interference. '[In] Hollywood and elsewhere,' he said, 'it was the practice of the film industry to favour scores that would sell as popular records – the kind of film music that could be danced to in discotheques.'

I can't help but wonder what Truffaut would have made of the state of film music today, an era in which most films are scored with pop songs and loud, club-ready techno. If a modern-day director wants the kind of classic score that Truffaut loved, he has to find a composer who's willing to recapture the sound of the golden age of filmmaking. Or, alternatively, he has to reach back into that bygone age, find a cue he likes, dust it off and simply reuse it.

Case in point: nearly four decades after Herrmann composed the theme to Roy Boulting's schlock thriller *Twisted Nerve*, Quentin Tarantino borrowed it for his own schlock thriller *Kill Bill*, using Herrmann's dramatic music to quickly establish a mood

he might otherwise have taken minutes to build. As the tremulous whistle that begins *Twisted Nerve* gives way to a tangle of swirling, dissonant strings, you get a firm idea of exactly what the characters – in this case, a female assassin – are thinking and feeling, without a word being spoken. The music sounds like anxiety feels: the tightening muscles, the shallow breathing, the fearful thoughts stumbling over each other in their determination to scald your nerves.

Herrmann, like so many great film composers before and after him, didn't write a score to what the audience was seeing, but to what he imagined the characters were feeling. His score for Hitchcock's *Psycho* – controversial for its time, in that it was played on strings alone – is a series of tight, curt movements that scarcely allow the characters or the audience a chance to breathe. Even the film's main titles are scored in such a manner as to render the names of cast and crew as potential weapons, while the score's tour de force – the music for the infamous shower scene, fittingly titled 'The Murder' – is scarcely music at all. The violins make an angry, klaxon-like racket that reacts to the stabbing taking place on screen; with each *vreet! vreet! vreet!* of the strings, the music bores a hole in the listener just as Anthony Perkins drills into Janet Leigh.

If Truffaut was moved by the plight of Hitchcock and Herrmann's association, it's largely because he was fortunate enough to work repeatedly with composer Georges

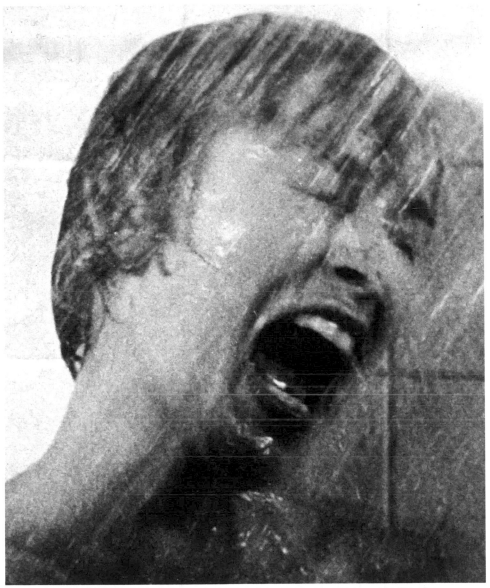

Vreet! Vreet! Vreet! Herrmann scores Leigh's grisly demise in Hitchcock's **Psycho**.

Delerue. Indeed, the director so loved Delerue's work that he once removed the dialogue from a scene in order to let the music speak for the characters. What Herrmann did for terror in *Psycho*, Delerue routinely did for love and longing. 'Holidays', the baroque waltz he wrote for the hopeful but ultimately doomed lovers of *Jules et Jim*, wanders carefree through your head as you might stroll over rolling green fields. There's a sad, sentimental tinge to the whole affair, which Delerue may have laid on to tip viewers that the story wouldn't end happily. However, I prefer to think that he may simply have been expressing his own quiet regret that all holidays have to end, even holidays held immobile in celluloid.

John Barry, 007's constant shadow.

Manipulating emotions through symphonic music sometimes seems a fairly easy trick: sweet melodies evoke good feelings and tense melodies anxiety, right? However, the art is taken to a richer level by Ennio Morricone, who's scored literally hundreds of films and created themes that evoke everything from piety (*The Mission*) to mischievousness (*Ad ogni costo*). He wrote two of his most evocative cues for Sergio Leone's spaghetti western *The Good, the Bad and the Ugly*: the deathless main theme and 'The Ecstasy of Gold'. The main title is filled with sounds you might expect to hear in the American

West – distant drums that could double as the sound of a passing train, whistles that sound like the howl of a coyote – and it's relatively easy for the listener to pick up its vibe of cowboy cool. 'The Ecstasy of Gold', however, is another story. How do you get an orchestra to play the sound of avarice?

Morricone uses several tricks. The piece begins with the sonorous ring of a bell, a rolling set of piano notes and a single oboe playing a plaintive, searching melody. Gradually, the composer adds strings, a soprano vocal and drums that build in intensity as the theme casts wildly about in search

Rewind
Ennio Morricone

Ennio Morricone doesn't speak a word of English. The fact that he's Italian might explain this. But given that Morricone has collaborated with some of Hollywood's biggest directors (De Palma, Beatty, Huston, Levinson, Stone, Nichols, Joffé), it's possible to view his lack of language skills as a slightly truculent act of rebellion.

'They've offered me houses in America,' Morricone tells me through his interpreter. 'They've offered me lots of money to leave Italy. Why would I want to do that?'

I suggest to him that not speaking English must have saved him from lots of Hollywood bullshit. A rare smile. 'I don't speak English but, if I'm working with English-speakers, I sometimes understand every word they say. They don't realise. And that's quite helpful!'

Morricone, a short, dapper and slightly irritable 74-year-old who's called 'the maestro' by everybody he meets, is holding court in his regular recording studio in northern Rome. A vast series of underground chambers built under a huge 1920s art deco church, the Forum Music Village is where he's recorded all but two of his 400 music soundtracks. The bulk of them have been for Italian movies, including a huge canon of loungey pop exotica written in the late 1960s and early 1970s.

Morricone has worked closely with Giuseppe Tornatore ever since 1988's *Cinema Paradiso*, and has collaborated in the past with other Italian heavyweights (Pasolini, Bertolucci and Zeffirelli, to name a few). However, he's still best known for his work with the late Sergio Leone, who was born in the same area of Rome within six months of the composer. Morricone had already scored two spaghetti westerns before Leone approached him to score *A Fistful of Dollars* in 1964.

For his 'Dollars' trilogy, and especially with *Once Upon a Time in the West*, Morricone would compose on seeing the script, with Leone playing the demos to his actors throughout the shooting schedule. 'They would act with the music, follow its rhythms,' Leone has said. 'They would suffer its aggravating qualities which grind the nerves.' Leone's 'horse operas' were often choreographed to Morricone's riotous soundscapes, which were filled with leitmotifs for each character that mirror the extreme close-ups and marathon tracking shots. His scores don't so much illustrate the action as expand and comment on it.

For more than four decades, Morricone's work has inhabited a kind of sonic democracy in which raucous surf guitars and bubblegum pop inhabit the same space as Stravinsky-style modernism and the avant-garde experimentation of Anton Webern, Luciano Berio and John Cage.

'When I first listened to Cage, I thought it was mad. But, thinking about his work and what he did, it started to make sense. Cage would compose by throwing dice, which suggested that you could get to write very complex music without approaching it in a scientific way. When he was silent for a minute in front of a piano, for instance, and then played one note or two notes together, and then there was another minute of silence, you had to think about what that meant. The breaking of a silence was a traumatic and shocking experience. It had a very strong emotion.

'You can see the influence of that in *Once Upon a Time in the West*. Not just the music, but the noises, the sounds of the desert, the train, the machines, the dripping pipes. That was very influenced by John Cage. But the avant-garde can become a trap. The only way forward is to be more avant garde, which can be restrictive.'

Is it true that you don't notice good film music? 'There's an element of truth in that, but it's a superficial judgment. Good film music must be intelligible and easy to listen to. Each theme cannot be too long. And it mustn't distract the viewer – too many sudden key changes can put the viewer off. But that still leaves a huge palette from which to work. You can use different textures, different instruments, different approaches to melody. Film scores must be symphony music, chamber music, pop music, opera music, jazz music. They must be all of them and none of them at the same time.

'Nowadays, lots of big Hollywood films don't use film scores. They use pop songs. I don't like that. They're under an illusion that a mere song can give a film success. And that would be too easy. Too easy. First of all, they should think about doing good films. And maybe then they should think about doing some nice songs.'

John Lewis; from Time Out, *5 November 2003*

TALKING BOOK

On the record AR Rahman

Brandenburg Concerto No.3, movts 2 & 3

Walter Carlos (now Wendy Carlos)

This is from a record called *Switched-On Bach*, released in 1968. It's a series of Bach themes played on the Moog synthesizer. My father, before he died, used to listen to it, and it's one album that he left for me. I must have listened to it maybe 3,000 times, but it still fascinates me and I still listen to it today. It had a profound influence on me – all the intellectual, logical beauty of Johann Sebastian Bach but played with this space-age electronic energy. It convinced me that the synthesizer was the perfect combination of music and technology, of art and science.

AR Rahman has written the scores for dozens of movies in his native India and has sold more than 100 million records worldwide

TALKING BOOK

of resolution. A full choir and a shrill trumpet are added and the tension builds to a giddy crescendo, but the melody remains unchanged, and what started out as a search for something becomes a search for *everything*. Morricone allows the track to peak, die down and rebuild before it ends abruptly, as if to say that your search for riches will go on forever and there's no sense in repeating a cautionary note that first went unheeded.

John Barry, a contemporary of Morricone, did for espionage movies what Morricone did for westerns: he created for them a vernacular. Barry's work on producer Albert 'Cubby' Broccoli's James Bond films is so distinctive that it spawned a sub-strain of trip hop – so-called 'crime jazz' – that kept the likes of Portishead and the Sneaker Pimps in business for a few years. As familiar as the Bond sound may seem today, the urgent guitar riffs and strident horns giving way to lush and romantic strings, there was a time when spy yarns sounded entirely different. Barry was so successful in creating a motif for James Bond that his cues, particularly '007' and 'Space March', became characters unto themselves: Bond's Greek chorus, his not-so-silent partner.

That's not the only way to do things, of course. Where Barry wrote music of personality, guitarist and musicologist Ry Cooder composes to a sense of place; where Morricone owned a West that never was, Cooder reflects and even mimics a truer, more tangible American landscape. Through the light use of electronics and guitar notes that seem to trail off towards infinity, Cooder's

expansive themes to Wim Wenders' movies *Paris, Texas* and *The End of Violence* evoke such a vivid picture of abandoned towns and sun-bleached highways that you can practically feel the high desert wind issuing from the speakers.

Cooder is one of very few composers working today who tries to expand what film music is, and what it's capable of being. There are others – Mychael Danna, Thomas Newman and Carter Burwell spring immediately to mind – but the most inspiring of the current crop is former Oingo Boingo frontman Danny Elfman, who started as a Herrmann clone but has expanded his repertoire in leaps and bounds. He's written scores that take in demented circus music (*Beetlejuice*), epic romance (*Edward Scissorhands*) and even dirty funk (*Dead Presidents*), and each time he improves and transforms his work without losing the distinctive touches – the *Psycho*-like jagged strings, the *la-la-la* choruses – that make it so immediately recognisable.

Elfman's finest score, for Gus van Sant's *Good Will Hunting*, was nominated for an Academy Award that it should have won. The main theme opens with a penny whistle playing a forlorn Celtic melody, but it soon disappears into a thicket of dissonant strings – Elfman's way of getting inside the troubled mind of the title character. The movie also featured songs by Elliott Smith, but as lovely as they sound on the radio, they do little for the film. The most peculiar thing happens when Elfman's music meets Van Sant's direction: the latter's work is intensified in a way that no pop song could hope to match.

The Real McCoy

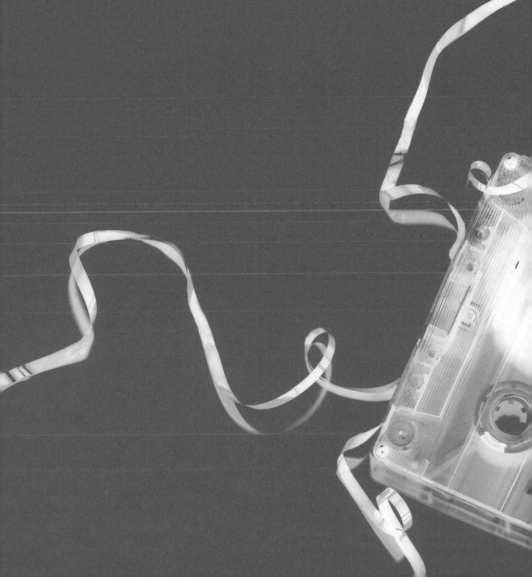

Wrong
notes

Hugh Barker and **Yuval Taylor** on how to make a great record without trying.

Is it possible that the history of rock music can be boiled down to deliberately playing the wrong notes?

… But let's not start there. Instead, let's begin by asking what it takes to write a great rock song. In general, songwriters are faced with a strange task: to create a song that sounds so simple and obvious that one can't imagine it ever having been written. Great songs sound as if they've always existed and have simply been plucked from the ether by the songwriter; anyone could have harvested them. But, of course, thousands of songs are written every year. So how do the best ones come about, and what makes them different?

Songwriters subject themselves to all sorts of regimes, rules and tricks in pursuit of that special song: the hit, the classic, the personal favourite. Some use found material or reportage, while others try to write only from personal experience or use songwriting as de facto therapy. Some plunder musical styles of the past, while others try to work only with unfamiliar or unexpected sounds and structures. And still others rely only on pure

inspiration, trying anything from drugs to exhaustion in order to get themselves into a suitably creative state.

One common theme among songwriters is that no matter how hard they work on their creations, the songs they consider to be their best are usually the ones they wrote in 15 minutes when they weren't even trying. Discussing 'Everybody Hurts', Michael Stipe once said: 'I don't even remember writing it. I'm really proud of that song.' Similarly, Anthony Kiedis has recounted making up the lyrics to 'By the Way' on the spot: 'It was one of those moments when the words were being beamed into me from outer space.' But why do so many songwriters say that this is how their best songs came to life? And are they telling the truth?

One possible answer has been suggested by Iggy Pop, who claimed that, 'When there is a clear-cut, simply understood basis to the lyric, those songs tend to hold up over time.' Great rock songs can be very basic things: there's often not much more to them than a brilliant title or chorus and a memorable riff, and the

rest might as well be clutter. The initial idea for a song often contains a large part of the end result. As Iggy says, 'It's not gonna be any good if it took more than five minutes.'

But there's something else at work here: specifically, the feeling that when one writes a song very quickly, it's almost an unconscious creation. Somehow, one has managed to bypass the conscious thought processes that make songs too ponderous or too crafted and write a song that's come straight from the heart. In short, it's the idea that a song one writes off the top of one's head feels more 'natural' or 'authentic' than a song that was carefully crafted. As Neil Young puts it, 'Songwriting, for me, is like a *release*. It's not a craft… If I can do it without thinking about it, I'm doing it great.'

Young's attitude is comparable to the way in which 1970s bands such as the Grateful Dead and Can treated jamming as a more authentic creative process than playing straightforward songs, or the reason why jazz musicians venerate improvisation as an ideal for personal expression. It's not the simplicity of the song per se that strikes the songwriter as significant, merely the fact that it arrived as if by divine inspiration.

This is an old Romantic ideal. Coleridge played upon it in his preface to 'Kubla Khan'; Shelley wrote of the skylark's 'profuse strains of unpremeditated art'; and according to Keats, 'If Poetry comes not as naturally as the Leaves to a tree, it had better not come at all.' The idea was later taken up by Walt Whitman, Baudelaire, the surrealists, the existentialists and the beats; no wonder it's also infected pop music, the last refuge of Romantic notions.

Even so, there's plenty of truth to it. As a songwriter, one regards a song on which one has worked extensively in a different way from one that came from 'inspiration'. One remembers all the alterations that were painfully made, and the difficult choices between alternative options. When a song comes from 'somewhere else', it can often seem superior because one is in a different relation to it: a recipient of a gift, or even a fan of the song, rather than a craftsman frustrated by its flaws.

This is presumably one reason why Brian Wilson, in a 1988 interview, called 'Surfer Girl' his best song. 'Believe it or not, after I'm dead and gone, that one's gonna be just great… It may not be the best "record" we ever made, but if you consider the song, if you think of it as a song, it's so *simple*.' It is indeed, and everything fits together perfectly. But it's also highly derivative, and pretty stupid to boot. It's likely that Wilson's perceptions of the works more widely recognised as products of his genius, such as 'Good Vibrations' or 'God Only Knows', are distorted by the memories of the compromises, the lyrical struggles and the studio battles that went into their creation.

Listeners often hear songs such as 'Good Vibrations' or Radiohead's 'Paranoid Android' as awesome creations, built up to the heavens from the foundations of rock. But we react very differently to songs that sound more spontaneous and simple. We hear the Troggs' 'Wild Thing' and the Stooges' 'I Wanna Be Your Dog' (co-written by Iggy Pop) as primal and authentic, expressing the pure heart of rock 'n' roll. We make the same distinctions as songwriters, between songs that are inspired and songs that are crafted. And we tend to believe that a simpler song is more likely to be divinely inspired and less crafted than a complex one.

This is the aesthetic behind Sly & the Family Stone's 'Sing a Simple Song' and the Stooges' 'Loose', among others. But even the most basic songs come about only because songwriters have previously learned their craft. They have, at their fingertips or in the backs of their minds, chord progressions, melodic habits and lyrical ideas; they've learned them from tradition, from other songs and from their own hard work in the past. Sophisticated songwriters such as Paul Simon, Randy Newman and Cole Porter could knock out a song in 15 minutes that contained significant musical sophistication and didn't strike listeners as spontaneous. The aforementioned 'Wild Thing' was written not by the Troggs but by professional Brill Building songwriter Chip Taylor. Indeed, Taylor even reused the I-IV-V-IV chord progression of 'Wild Thing' on Merilee Rush's wretched soft-rock standby 'Angel of the Morning' (later a hit for Juice Newton). For all we know, Taylor may even have laboured long and hard over 'Wild Thing' but composed 'Angel of the Morning' in his sleep.

When one tries to let the unconscious flow, to create from inspiration, one falls back on habits, tricks and craft. Jazz and rock improvisation, for example, are shaped by

The wonderfully wayward
Thelonious Monk.

a basic understanding of scales, modes and chord progressions; it follows that the more complex one's musical training, the more likely one is to be able to improvise a complex piece of music. A jazz teacher once gave us some amusing advice about improvisation: 'If you play a terrible, wrong note,' he said, 'make sure you play it again, so the audience thinks you did it on purpose.' He was talking about how to cover up a mistake, but the root of his advice was a recognition that it's the unexpected notes that often mark a jazz solo as especially inspired. In Thelonious Monk's semitone-packed version of 'Body and Soul' (from *Monk's Dream*) or the deliberately out-of-tune opening of Jimi Hendrix's 'Crosstown Traffic', the notes that no one else would have thought of playing are the ones that really grab our attention.

When a musician plays a wrong or unexpected note, it tends to sound more 'real', or at least more inspired, because it's clearly

unedited: it smacks of a first take. Similarly, a ragged vocal performance sounds more authentic than a pure, smooth one, and rough musical edges can result in a more atmospheric recording than a pristine pop confection. So-called wrong notes provoke the same reaction in the listener as a basic, primal song: the sense that this is a spontaneous and passionate piece of music. Of course, inspiration and apparent spontaneity don't always overlap, and truly inspired works can also appear painstakingly crafted. But as listeners, we often take apparent spontaneity as a signifier of authentic inspiration, a sign that this is music that's come from the heart.

Going back to where we started, rock music has, from its origins in blues, been dependent on 'wrong' notes. The blue notes that came to define blues may not sound shocking to a modern ear, but the use of a minor third or a minor seventh over a major chord, or that

Rewind
Brian Eno

Brian Eno and his brother play a game. One of them lowers the needle of his stereo into the grooves of an unspecified record for the shortest possible time – *parp!* – and the other one has to guess what the record is.

'You'd be surprised how often you get it right. You see, this is the unrecognised breakthrough of pop music: that it's a music about *sound*. Pop hasn't made any innovations in terms of harmonic and melodic structure, apart from odd borrowings from Africa, but it constantly experiments with sound palette. It's something that can never be achieved in classical music.'

He grabs a guitar from its position against the legs of a DX-7 in his studio and strums it at a flat angle across his lap, moving up and down the strings with hooked fingers as if absently tickling a small child. You wonder whether all of pop is reducible to one tiny soundbite: *parp!*

'Sometimes I come in here of a morning and sit fiddling around with things; and sometimes, for a long time, nothing happens. Nothing. I could've been sitting in the sun all that time for all the good it did me. Well, if there's another person here, there's a much greater likelihood of something happening. Another person can override your own pessimism or your own sense of taste. There are two jobs, *doing* it and *attending* to it, and it's hard sometimes to fulfil both roles on your own.'

I ask him if working like this wasn't rather like children playing. He looked hard at the chewed stick that he uses to prod distant sliders, or beat in frustration on the side of the console.

'I'm very keen on anything that involves me to the level where I can get incredibly angry about it or incredibly excited. For instance, a couple of weeks ago, I was working here alone and I had the most blissful week I've had in maybe five years. It was the week of the World Cup, plus I was working on these songs and singing in a way I'd never done before. And if you spend a whole day singing, really opening your lungs and not censoring anything, and then you go and watch Gazza weeping on the box... You know, plus I've just had this little girl... So I was in an emotionally open condition.'

For the first time, there's a hint of disorganisation in his syntax.

'So these three things, the singing, the World Cup and my daughter, all combined to create this situation in which I was working very, very hard and was terribly involved with everything. That was really a kind of playing, I suppose.'

He rolls the stick thoughtfully.

'But another part of playing is making up the rules. When you're really playing, you don't know what the game is. It's never quite clear where the boundaries are and so they're always being extended. And I guess that's what happens when you're working with someone else. Most of the time is spent not on generating a result but on getting yourself into a postition that will *then* generate a result. Results are easy to get once you've worked the first bit out. That's the first 98 floors of the building. Then you only have to put the roof on.

'In rock music, what you're really interested in is putting together new feelings in combinations that you've never heard before. And that can have some analogue to the combinations of the feelings you get in real life: two ideas that sit together in the strangest way and create a new synthesis you can't put a name to. It's like the experience of looking at a strong colour and then looking at another one, where you have the after-image of the first superimposed on it in such a way that you can't name the new colour. It's a new feeling, and it doesn't last very long.

'One of the great bugbears about lyrics again is that everyone's going to ask me what they mean for the next ten years. But lyrics don't need to *mean* any more than music does. I mean, no one ever asks you what you *mean* by a D-minor chord, do they? You wouldn't say to a person who's just cooked a pizza, "What does this pizza *mean*?" You'd just eat it, wouldn't you?

'Now, since you're using language you're obviously playing a game of some kind *with* meaning, but it seems to me that the most important thing is to create a credible picture. I like to work on the border where it feels like something's being said, so that one is drawn into the game of interpretation. The game of discovering meaning isn't very interesting; but the game of *interpretation* is very interesting, I think. I'll abandon any word if it doesn't work. Any word.'

He indicates a loose-leaf file, resting in the sunlight on the window sill.

'See that folder? It's got maybe 40 sheets of paper in it, some of them fairly closely written. It's all for one song.'

Nick Coleman; from Time Out, *10 October 1990*

THE REAL MCCOY

strange undulation between major and minor notes that defines a true blue note, sounded extraordinary, abrasive and wrong to listeners raised on traditional or classical music. From childhood, we're able to identify the traditional harmonic intervals used in classical music as being 'right'; to a child's untrained ear, blue notes definitely fall into the 'wrong' category.

Of course, it's a simplification to call these notes 'wrong'. Singing or playing blue notes is a genuine skill; it simply wasn't often exercised before the 20th century, except in music influenced by African and Arab traditions. The blue third is not a pure tone on the Western chromatic scale, but somewhere between a minor and major third (for example, between E flat and E when played over a root of C), often with a slide that appears to be reaching for the latter. When playing 'New Orleans Blues' for musicologist Alan Lomax in 1938, pianist Jelly Roll Morton deliberately played both the major and minor third at the same time in order to approximate the blue note that lies in between.

Rock 'n' roll singers later adopted the blue note with varying degrees of success. Elvis was particularly skilled at it: check out 'Heartbreak Hotel'. Conversely, though, Bill Haley barely managed the flattened sevenths on 'Rock Around the Clock' and struggled painfully with the blue thirds, ending up sounding to posterity like a nightclub singer imitating this newfangled rock 'n' roll thing.

Ever since, blue notes have been a huge part of rock 'n' roll. If you can, try to sing a song such as Chuck Berry's 'Sweet Little Sixteen' (or 'Surfing USA', its bastard offspring), but with the initial minor third converted to a major third. The change makes the melody sound completely anodyne, more like something delivered by a Blackpool organist than a piece of rebellious rock 'n' roll. Later songs such as the Rolling Stones' '(I Can't Get No) Satisfaction' were completely constructed around blues progressions with the blue note as the grit in the oyster, one of the elements that added a feeling of freshness and immediacy to the performance.

Many older listeners found rock 'n' roll to be an unlistenable racket, an accusation that was later levelled at subsequent musical styles from garage to hip hop. Blue notes are merely one example of musical elements that sounded wrong simply because they were shocking

when they were first introduced; others include distortion (Jimmy Page playing the guitar with a violin bow on 'Dazed and Confused') and feedback (the opening of the Beatles' 'I Feel Fine'). One might even say that the perennial goal for those creating popular music has been to find a way to create something that is catchy, melodic and interesting enough to appeal widely to its intended audience, while still sounding like an unlistenable racket to the audience's parents. In songs such as 'The Black Parade', My Chemical Romance achieved this ambition by using the kind of speed-metal guitar work and melodramatic self-obsession that's guaranteed to irritate most people over the age of 18 as a Trojan Horse for catchy, engaging songs.

Still, all shock tactics rapidly lose their effect as listeners grow accustomed to wrong notes, crude lyrics and deliberately rough production values. Guitar distortion moved from Dave Davies taking a razor blade to his amp on 'You Really Got Me' via Jimi Hendrix's version of 'The Star-Spangled Banner' to a bland Richard Carpenter solo in 'Calling Occupants of Interplanetary Craft'. The machine noises, samples and drum loops that were so startling on Public Enemy's 'Bring the Noise' are remarkably similar to the techniques used as hooks by the slick professional songwriting and production teams who created Britney Spears' 'Toxic'. And the smooth soft-rock of the 1980s used many of the same techniques as heavy metal pioneers, but without anything like the same impact.

Songwriters, performers and producers are forever trying to recapture this abrasiveness, this feeling of 'wrongness' or unexpectedness, in a multitude of ways. Assonance, imperfect scanning, incomplete lines and shocking content or language can achieve it from a lyrical perspective, while musical strategies include dischords, extra bars, unexpected key shifts and unresolved suspensions.

The fact that there's never been a magic recipe for writing or recording great rock music is one reason why songwriters treasure their moments of inspiration, but simultaneously wonder how they happened and how to re-create them when the muse fails to visit. Jimmy Webb has written that 'creativity as a concept is perhaps not well understood by the people who practise it most successfully'.

In those dark hours during which songwriters can't create anything that feels fresh or interesting, they often look back at those instant songs or accidental moments and break them down into component pieces, driven to mimic elements of their own (or others') past glories in an attempt to create something that good again. This might mean reiterating harmonic and melodic tricks that have worked before, or attempting to emulate the simplicity and directness that once came naturally.

On the other hand, songwriters often find themselves having to work hard on their creations at times when divine inspiration is lacking. Some even write songs about writer's block: in 'These Words', Natasha Bedingfield evokes Byron, Shelley and Keats while pronouncing 'hyperbole' as 'hyperbowl'; Fatlip blames the failure of his hip hop career on 'Writer's Block'; and Gillian Welch confesses how unoriginal most of her songs are in 'One Little Song'. But attempts like these can occasionally appear too clever, and are therefore rarely judged authentic or soulful.

Because songwriters can't summon great songs at will, the arts of songwriting and recording present problems as to how to merge simulation and conscious creation with an appearance of non-simulation and unconscious flow. The ways in which one might achieve this shift constantly over time. Brian Wilson's most complex music is regarded as inspired because its composer is widely perceived to be a musical genius, whereas the prog-rock musicians who've created similarly complicated soundscapes are seen as merely workmanlike. There's no guaranteed way of being, or appearing to be, inspired, but simplicity and spontaneity often seem to be ingredients in a recipe that leads to great rock music.

One goal among musicians has long been to achieve a natural flow in which the rough edges don't matter: the quickfire song, the atmospheric first take or the accidental recording glitch that gets left in the final mix. A common fallback option has been to simulate these kinds of guarantees of authenticity by deliberately including 'mistakes' or other kinds

It happened in Monterey: **Jimi Hendrix** in 1967.

of rough edges. Neil Young asked his musicians to play instruments they couldn't play on the sessions for *Tonight's the Night*; Dylan did the same thing for 'Rainy Day Women #12 & 35', which sounds improvised on the spot. The Police and the Stranglers were basically prog-rock musicians who, on songs such as 'Roxanne' and 'Peaches', temporarily downplayed their virtuosity in order to simulate the freshness of punk. And other musicians have used lo-fi equipment and horrible guitars to enhance their authenticity: Sebadoh's first few records are great examples of this, especially 'I Can't See', 'Kath' and 'Spoiled'.

At its most extreme, this reliance on spontaneity can become a kind of superstition. Blues producer Willie Dixon used to drive his musicians to distraction by insisting on take after take and waiting for a version in which there was an error; he believed that if the take was 'perfect', it wouldn't be a hit. In other cases, it can become the basis for an entire aesthetic, as with the modern unplugged recordings that revitalised the careers of such musicians as Johnny Cash. On 'Delia's Gone' and 'I See a Darkness' from Cash's *American Recordings* series, the 'wrong' elements – the mistakes, the string buzz, the flawed vocals, the room noise or whatever – work as a guarantee of honesty.

In the end, it's impossible to explain where brilliant music comes from. Great songs can be as simple as 'Johnny B Goode' or as elaborate as 'Strawberry Fields Forever', as mellifluous as the Carpenters' 'Close to You' or as outrageously abrasive as Captain Beefheart's 'Moonlight on Vermont'. Any theory that attempts to explain why certain songs touch us and others don't will inevitably be fallacious. If it weren't, music would be reducible to a formula; and yet there's always someone who comes along and breaks the formula by playing the 'wrong way', changing the way we hear music once again.

The poet Adrian Mitchell wrote of Charlie Parker that 'he breathed in air, he breathed out light'. It's a beautiful description of the alchemy of inspiration that we find in all the music we love. As listeners, we tend to trust in inspiration, believing that when we're touched by a song, it's because the performer or creator has opened a window on their soul just for us. It's not the whole truth, but at least it's something to believe in.

Inspiration versus perspiration in 20 songs

'Prelude & Fugue No.4 in C# Minor' JS Bach
The Well-Tempered Clavier, wrote Bach on the title page, contains 'Preludes and fugues in all tones and semitones, in both the major and the minor modes, for the benefit and use of musical youth desirous of knowledge as well as those already advanced in their learning.' In other words, one of the most important works in the western classical canon is basically a book of studies designed as a practice aid.

'Don't Worry Baby' The Beach Boys
Perhaps the pivotal Beach Boys song, 'Don't Worry Baby' is the point at which Brian Wilson's early reliance on hurry-up inspiration meets the ambition that drove the creation of *Pet Sounds*. Interesting, then, that it's essentially a tribute to another record: the Ronettes' 'Be My Baby'.

'Tomorrow Never Knows' The Beatles
Beatles scholar Ian MacDonald describes the sound world of *Revolver*'s closing track as 'a riveting blend of anarchy and awe'. For all the multi-layered, time-consuming complexity of McCartney's tape loops, which provide the track with its colour, the song itself – what there is of it, anyway – was written in minutes by Lennon after he'd popped some LSD in a bid to tap into some primal creative wellspring.

'Ashé' Terence Blanchard
Found on the soundtrack to Spike Lee's documentary about Hurricane Katrina, 'Ashé' is a beautiful, fragile and perfectly pitched piece of orchestral jazz. Or, at least, it is until Blanchard completely loses his footing as his trumpet solo escalates in intensity, and proceeds to honk out several of the most flat-out hideous notes you'll ever hear. This being jazz, where capturing the moment is at least part of the point, he left them in.

'Jesus' Blood Never Failed Me Yet' Gavin Bryars
Amateur, meet professional. Bryars took a 1971 field recording of a London tramp idly singing an old hymn and elevated it to the status of art by lending the street singer a fully scored orchestra.

'Neon Meate Dream of a Octafish' Captain Beefheart & His Magic Band
Few albums have toed the line separating design from accident more precariously than the still-bewildering *Trout Mask Replica*. There's a fearsomely complex arrangement here, though it's easily mistaken for the sound of five one-armed men playing instruments

they picked up for the first time about 90 seconds before the red light went on. And don't even get started on the lyrics.

'Rufford Park Poachers' Martin Carthy
Carthy is fond of saying that all English folk music has but one beat to a bar, which is a tidy way of explaining or excusing the juddering, emphasis-shifting 5/4 meter he lends to this outwardly straightforward piece of 19th-century story-song.

'On the Corner/New York Girl/ Thinkin' of One Thing and Doin' Another/ Vote for Miles' Miles Davis
With producer Teo Macero, Davis rewired the very nature of jazz in the late '60s and early '70s. The music was no longer about photographing a single snapshot of inspiration: folded together from a multitude of different recordings, On the Corner went against the very nature of jazz by elevating the studio to the status of an instrument equal to anything played by a member of Davis's band.

'Köln, January 24 1975: Part II b' Keith Jarrett
An incredibly versatile pianist, Jarrett has had plenty of creative and commercial success with his reinterpretations of both jazz standards and the works of Bach. However, he remains most renowned for his solo excursions, wholly improvised but built on decades of practice. The soaring, rambling but harmonically approachable extemporisations that make up The Köln Concert invented the clichés that blight much of the so-called New Age music that followed in its wake.

'Louie Louie' The Kingsmen
This archetypally dumb three-chord thump was written and recorded in 1957 by Los Angeles R&B singer Richard Berry, but it's the Kingsmen's chaotic version from '63 that's passed into folklore.

'Up the Bracket' The Libertines
It took the release of the genuinely messy Libertines' second album – and, for that matter, the appalling Babyshambles catalogue – to reveal that although Up the Bracket initially and deliberately sounded like a one-take din, it's actually a highly disciplined piece of alt-rock engineering.

'Tutti Frutti' Little Richard
Pretty much all Little Richard's fabulously unvarnished early singles sound as if they were written in the time it took to record them, none more so than this raucous fusion of wacked-out inspiration and pedal-to-the-metal perspiration. See also his recording of 'Keep A-Knockin'', so basic that its two-and-a-quarter-minute running time was apparently pieced together from a 57-second demo.

'Drive By' The Necks
Much of the music made by this Australian trio depends on free improvisation, but it remains firmly reliant on western tonality and on the virtuosity of the musicians playing it. As keyboardist Chris Abrahams treads gently across the shifting sands provided by drummer Tony Buck and bassist Lloyd Swanton, 'Drive By' might be their finest hour. Literally – like much of their repertoire, it's a single track lasting roughly 60 minutes.

'Got Your Money' Ol' Dirty Bastard featuring Kelis
The sessions for Dirty's album Nigga Please were reputedly anarchic, the rapper strung out on all manner of substances, and it was left to the producers to stitch a little coherence into his shambling freeform rhymes. In the case of 'Got Your Money', it was the Neptunes who added musical order to ODB's lyrical chaos.

'Roadrunner' The Modern Lovers
'Roadrunner' is as much a product of Jonathan Richman's inspirations – the Velvet Underground, golden-age rock 'n' roll – as his imagination. 'The most obvious song in the world,' wrote Greil Marcus, 'and the strangest.'

'Wooly Bully' Sam the Sham & the Pharaohs
Essentially a reworking of Big Bo & the Arrows' proto-ska 'Hully Gully, Now', America's biggest-selling single of 1965 was recorded in one take and apparently named after the singer's cat.

'Peg' Steely Dan
Donald Fagen and Walter Becker were such exacting taskmasters that the seven tracks on Aja were anchored by six different drummers. From Michael McDonald's Lyrca-tight harmonies to the guitar break by Jay Graydon (reputedly the sixth or seventh guitarist to tape a solo for the track), 'Peg' sounds absolutely immaculate.

'The Good Son' David Sylvian
Sylvian forewent his usual place-for-everything precision on Blemish, painstakingly building something approaching pop music from several taped improvisations by legendary free-jazz guitarist Derek Bailey. The results are undeniably interesting, albeit not exactly a roaring success.

'Surfin' Bird' The Trashmen
Songs? Who needs 'em?

'Farmer John' Neil Young
Young's pounding, wayward cover of this nugget, a hit in 1964 for the Premiers, is found on the album Ragged Glory, one of those albums with a title that effectively serves as its own review.

System error

*'Ninety per cent of pop music is about
copying something and getting it wrong'*
Elvis Costello

In 1956, the British jazz trumpeter Humphrey Lyttelton went into the studio to record a number called 'Bad Penny Blues'. It was his attempt at recreating a slice of authentic New Orleans traditional jazz, his own take on Louis Armstrong's 'St Louis Blues'. Unfortunately, the trombone and clarinet players didn't turn up to the session, so producer Joe Meek was forced to foreground the clunky piano line, turn up the drums and generally make the best he could from Lyttelton's spartan quartet. Far from sounding like a jazz record, 'Bad Penny Blues' became the key document in the birth of British rock 'n' roll, a thrillingly rough and ready track that proved to be a seminal influence on musicians from Paul McCartney to Pete Townshend.

It's possible to trace rock 'n' roll as a history of glorious mistakes along the lines of 'Bad Penny Blues'. It's the story of British kids in the 1950s trying to copy American blues, being laughed out of the folk clubs by purists like Peggy Seeger and going on to create their own lo-fi take on the blues called skiffle. It's the story of Jamaicans in the 1950s attempting to mimic the big band jazz they heard on American radio, recreating those swing rhythms with a slightly wonky Caribbean accent and accidentally giving birth to ska and reggae. It's the story of the Beatles trying to sound like a Motown band and the Rolling Stones trying to sound like Muddy Waters, failing miserably, but somehow stumbling across something far more interesting. It's the story, in other words, of Getting It Wrong.

Getting It Wrong has a particular resonance in the history of African American music, which has a long background of using mistakes creatively. After their drums were banned by slave owners, for example, generations of North American slaves learned to make do and mend, syncretically adapting African music for Western instruments. After all, what is a banjo if not a drum disguised as a guitar? Similar developments continued well into the 20th century. Legend has it that slide guitar technique was created by a drunk musician using his beer bottle to fret his instrument. BB King admitted that after he tried and failed to learn slide guitar, he ending up using it as a way of trilling and sustaining notes, a technique that other blues guitarists quickly tried to copy. Albert King, another bluesman, has talked about bending notes as a way of compensating for his inability to play proper scales.

By the early 1970s, some visionaries had started to realise that Getting It Wrong was how music evolved, and started to use it as a guiding principle. Miles Davis, always a believer in prioritising error, instructed John McLaughlin to 'play the guitar like you don't know how to play the guitar' when soloing on the title track of the 1969 album *In a Silent Way*. Jazz drummer John Stevens started working with non-musicians both in and out of the Spontaneous Music Ensemble, believing that he and his bandmates could learn from each other. And in 1970, together with waggish students from Portsmouth School of Art, composer and double bassist Gavin Bryars founded the Portsmouth Sinfonia, an orchestra that recruited non-musicians or musicians playing instruments of which they had no experience. One of the early members of this proudly amateurish experiment in expressionism was an art student called Brian Eno, who chose to play the clarinet.

Around the same time, Eno joined Roxy Music, continuing proudly to proclaim himself a 'non-musician'. Ignoring such petty concerns as tonality and rhythm, he used electronic instruments and mixing desks to sculpt texture and sonic shapes. 'Pop music is about creating imaginary worlds,' he theorised, 'and inviting people to try them out.' Eno left Roxy Music after just one album, citing friction with lead singer Bryan Ferry ('there wasn't room for two non-musicians in the band,' he said, only half-jokingly), but not before he had created the blueprint for Getting It Wrong.

'Virginia Plain', Roxy's 1972 debut single, is a morass of Motown drums, jabbering piano, Morse-code oboe, squalling sax, squeaky synths and histrionic heavy metal guitar. It has no verse-chorus structure, no discernible melody that you can whistle. Bryan Ferry barely sings in tune, instead declaiming his gibberish lyrics like Dadaist poetry. It should, by rights, be a painful bloody mess, but it stands up as a thrilling piece of music. It's also perhaps the most self-aware slice of Getting It Wrong, an ethos that Eno went on to develop into a credo. Alongside artist Peter Wright, he even developed a set of cards called Oblique Strategies, designed to be pulled out and used at random as a way of escaping creative cul-de-sacs; Eno used them himself when producing the likes of Devo, Talking Heads, David Bowie, U2 and Coldplay. Each card contained a single phrase: among them were such instructions as 'Try faking it!', 'Emphasise repetition' and 'Honour thy error as a hidden intention'.

This last one could be seen as a guiding light for punk rock. Eno's anti-musician stance became a dictum that punks, with their DIY attitude and their prioritising of ideas over musical competency, started to take up with great enthusiasm. 'Punk destroyed the skills base of pop music in the UK,' wrote Ian MacDonald in *The People's Music*, a lament to what he regards as pop's mid '60s 'golden age'. In a way, he's right: the carefully crafted techniques that came from the folk clubs and the trad jazz venues were ditched and replaced by a three-chord thrash. But what this lack of skills facilitated was a huge growth in Getting It Wrong.

In a way, punk's approach to Getting It Wrong was a product of the same white-on-black appropriation that had been a staple of rock music since Elvis. It was all about white kids (usually English) falling in love with black music (usually American), trying to copy it slavishly, making a terrible hash of it and, unintentionally, creating something brilliant quite by accident. But while the likes of Jagger, Clapton, Townshend, Davies and McCartney had taken their cues from blues, soul and 'Bad Penny Blues', the punks and post-punks were inspired by funk, disco, reggae and 'Virginia Plain'.

Cover versions provide many of the best examples of Getting It Wrong in punk's catalogue, and there are none better than

On the record
John Lydon

'Reason for Living'

Dr Alimantado

I'm only saying it's my favourite song because I played it last night. But all reggae from that period had a stunning, *stunning* vibe. This has got that skippy, dub beat and a lovely trumpet phrase that keeps recurring, and Dr Alimantado's voice is very pretty, very soulful. The important thing with stuff like this is that you should never, ever try and copy it note for note. That's stealing another man's culture. There's nothing wrong with white kids playing reggae, but don't go and sing in fake Jamaican accents. Do it with your own accent and with your own sensibility, like we did in PiL, or like Smith & Mighty did in Bristol.
John Lydon was, and occasionally still is, the singer with the Sex Pistols

Brian Eno.

Rewind
Robert Wyatt

It's been evident from the first Soft Machine album that Robert Wyatt is the possessor of the most notched, rusty and unfailingly emphatic vocal chords in the entire area of music in which the group operates. Wyatt sang for about nine months in one version of the Wild Flowers, while Richard Coughlan did the drumming. And it's Wyatt's voice that overshadows the early Soft Machine demos. But when the time came to record the first Soft Machine album, Wyatt's voice had extended itself, a multilaterally *true* voice in an arid soundscape of *good* voices. The influence of Daevid Allen, who used to lodge with Wyatt's parents and was an original member of the group, was probably quite substantial.

'Daevid, not by preaching but by example, was living out all the things he was thinking about. To me, activity was reading, looking at paintings and listening to records. Meanwhile, he was writing, painting and playing guitar. What you could do consisted of what you *wanted* to do. He made tapes with people who could play and tapes with people who couldn't play, and there was no difference in quality between them. Things like that shattered the kind of rubbish I'd been thinking until then.'

Despite his beautiful treatment of Hugh Hopper's 'A Certain Kind' on *The Soft Machine*, the lengthy lyrical passages of 'Moon in June' on *Third*, and the extent to which much of the commercial success of Matching Mole's album can be attributed to 'O Caroline' and 'Signed Curtain', it's surprising Wyatt isn't really all that keen on songs, or at least song situations.

'Usually they're just props for making noises. I think that if [you're] going to use words, [you] should use them as carefully as possible. You're talking to somebody, and if you're trying to say something then be careful what you say.

'But the thing I really like about music is way outside intelligible conversation: much deeper, stronger and more moving than stringing sentences together. So I've generally played in bands that were essentially instrumental. I've never played with polite, subservient, accompanist-type musicians, and this creates a situation where if you're going to make your voice fit into the context of a set or an album, you're just throwing your voice into the elements. You're dealing with pure music rather than conveying some cute impression of yourself to strangers.'
Al Clark; from Time Out, *16 June 1972*

the Slits' version of Marvin Gaye's 'I Heard It Through the Grapevine'. The recording starts with organised humming (almost like a Monty Python song), continues with a clumsy, shuffling reggae beat (put through a dub chamber by producer Dennis Bovell), and then starts studiously to extract any vestiges of swing and soul from the song, as lead singer Ari Up sings Norman Whitfield and Barrett Strong's baleful, lovelorn lyrics with a studied indifference and a declamatory, theatrical accent that suggests she's quite happy to be rid of her useless partner. It's utterly *wrong*, but it's also a hypnotic, funny, joyous voodoo chant that completely reinvents the original.

The same process occurred with A Certain Ratio's 'Shack Up'. The 1975 original by Washington, DC funk band Banbarra was a loose-limbed, soulful celebration of living in sin. ACR's version is the exact opposite. Everything is slightly out of tune: the stiff, unfunky guitar sounds like a high-pitched washing board, Martin Moscrop's trumpet resembles a psychotic, discordant melodica, and the call-and-response vocals are droned out by Simon Topping's dolorous, bored, Manc-accented mumble. It is, of course, brilliant.

Sometimes, bands Got It Wrong so magnificently that they bypassed the very genres they were trying to emulate. Take the Clash's version of Junior Murvin's 'Police and Thieves', on which drummer Terry Chimes and bassist Paul Simonon crunch the beat so hamfistedly that it's barely a reggae record any more – instead, it's a kind of brutalised two-step stomp. There's the Pet Shop Boys' 'West End Girls', on which, in a thin, effete, gentrified Geordie brogue, Neil Tennant raps so casually that no one noticed he was reinventing hip hop in an English accent, something that everyone else seemed too scared to try for nearly 20 years. And Soft Cell's 1981 version of Gloria Jones's 1964 single 'Tainted Love' takes a bouncy northern soul favourite and turns it into something cold, clinical and metallic. The snare drum sounds like an aerosol spray and the bassline is unfunky and metrical, yet Marc Almond manages to exude a very different kind of soul, successfully realigning both the singer's gender and the sexuality to reinvent the song.

Of course, Getting It Wrong wasn't just a white-on-black phenomenon: black British

'Boffins in Japan invented technology with a certain intention, but hooligans in Munich, Sheffield and Detroit threw out the manuals and started prodding at the buttons.'

funk groups of the late '70s and early '80s were prone to the same fabulous errors when they tried to copy African American music. In the early 1970s, Brit funkers such as Cymande consciously incorporated Caribbean elements into their music: 'The Message' and 'Bra' contain an unsettling mixture of loping, low-slung funk and Rastafarian *nyabinghi* drumming. But by the end of the decade, British groups were desperately trying to sound American and unwittingly creating something else entirely. The more they tried to emulate the jazz-funk of Herbie Hancock and Donald Byrd or the funkier disco of War and Parliament, the more they betrayed their roots in British punk and Jamaican reggae. Check the military tattoo of the Real Thing's 'Children of the Ghetto', the eerie Sakamoto synths of Freeez's 'Southern Freeez', the Joy Division-goes-to-Africa sound of Gonzalez's 'Saoco' or the clunky punk-funk of Beggar & Co's '(Somebody) Help Me Out'.

By the early 1980s, post-punk bands weren't just Getting It Wrong with funk, disco, ska and reggae: groups such as Talking Heads were starting to bastardise more obviously alien and exotic forms of global music. The New York quartet were prone to getting lost during lengthy studio jam sessions, beating out unrelated rhythmic figures and failing to locate the 'one' of the bar. 'Essentially, we ended up with music that had several different centres of gravity,' said producer Brian Eno, 'and that confusion often made the music rhythmically richer.' The result: the likes of 'Born Under Punches' and 'Once in a Lifetime'.

THE REAL MCCOY

Similarly emboldened, other post-punk bands started to explore different types of music. A Certain Ratio tackled salsa on 'Don't You Worry 'Bout a Thing', Pigbag experimented with free jazz on 'Papa's Got a Brand New Pigbag', Bow Wow Wow's 'I Want Candy' and Adam & the Ants' 'Kings of the Wild Frontier' both borrowed Burundi drumming, the Pop Group's '3:38' tackled Lee 'Scratch' Perry's dub, and 23 Skidoo's 1983 album *The Culling Is Coming* even looked as far as Indonesian gamelan music. Few of these groups researched any of their source material on an ethnological level, but that lack of fidelity bred a certain sonic wildness, as the musicians used those superficially 'alien' sounds and merrily decontextualised them. Malcolm McLaren's 1983 album *Duck Rock* (working title: 'Folk Dances of the World') was perhaps the most gleeful celebration of post-punk inauthenticity, mangling hip hop with Tennessee jug bands ('Buffalo Gals'), NuYorican salsa ('Merengue') and South African township jive ('Double Dutch', 'Jive My Baby').

The wonderful irony is that Getting It Wrong then started to become a two-way process, influencing the very people it imitated. The South Bronx outfit ESG began to take their inspiration from post-punk, getting Joy Division's producer Martin Hannett to produce 'Moody', 'UFO' and 'You're No Good' on their first studio EP. The result sounded like Public Image Ltd with bongos. Furthermore, the clumsy, electronic attempts of British acts such as Depeche Mode, Gary Numan and New Order to ape African American funk started to feed back into American music and became, in turn, hugely influential on a generation of Detroit techno pioneers and R&B producers. Malcolm McLaren was thrilled to discover that 'Buffalo Gals' became an underground hip hop hit in the Bronx.

What's often ignored is that musicians from around the world had been Getting It Wrong for years by making clumsy versions of Western pop, a sound that was just as alien and exotic to them as gamelan music must have been to 23 Skidoo. Spurred on by the Beatles' 1965 tour of Japan, Japanese bands started to copy *Rubber Soul*-era material with an eerie efficiency, right down to the physicalities of the line-up – all had a John Lennon figure who'd double up on organ and rhythm guitar. The music they made became known as 'group sounds': some of the delightfully awkward parodies that emerged from the scene stand up among the most thrilling garage rock of the period.

In late '60s Brazil, meanwhile, a generation of arty bossa nova fans – Gilberto Gil, Caetano Veloso, Os Mutantes – started to copy what they called the 'neo-rock' of the Beatles and ended up creating tropicália. In West Africa during the early 1970s, young kids thrilled by the music of James Brown and the Rolling Stones started to play Africanised versions of funk and rock: Fela Kuti's Afrobeat orchestras remain the best known, but hundreds of smaller outfits emerged in Kinshasa, Lagos, Benin and Togo. And in India, successive generations of Bollywood music directors copied Western trends: C Ramachandra and Cuban rhythms in the '40s; SD Burman and jazz in the '50s; RD Burman (SD's son) and garage rock in the '60s; Kalyanji-Anandji and funk in the '70s; and Bappi Lahiri and disco in the '80s. They all Got It Wrong, often with laughable consequences, but in doing so mashed up Western dance music with Indian folk and classical music in a pioneering way.

However, as the '80s wore on, Getting It Wrong began to be frowned on in both the UK and the US. 'At the start of the 1980s, we were all playing funk in that kinda clumsy way,' said David Byrne from Talking Heads. 'Not just us but the likes of Gang of Four, A Certain Ratio, Cabaret Voltaire, the Clash. The appeal was in the clumsiness. The problem came when everyone started to get too good at it.'

By the middle of the decade, the same bands who were once so brilliant at Getting It Wrong were desperately trying to Get It Right, often with disastrous consequences. Spandau Ballet, who kicked off their career with the itchy, wayward funk of 'To Cut a Long Story Short' and 'Chant No.1 (I Don't Need This Pressure On)', took the same route towards smooth, bland sophistication that afflicted post-Eno Roxy Music. Meanwhile, Heaven 17, who had previously created the brutal electro-punk of 'Penthouse and Pavement' and '(We Don't Need This) Fascist Groove Thang', transformed themselves into a smug corporate soul outfit.

Aphex Twin wonders where he left the instructions.

It was around this time that black soul and white rock started to merge into what music journalist Julie Burchill described as 'beige pop'. Old punks began to buy into the notion of black music as noble, dignified and improving, and started to aim for politicised authenticity: the militant brand of soul music produced by Style Council, the Redskins and the Kane Gang was quickly dubbed 'soulcialism'. There are some great songs from this period that Got It Right: the blue-eyed lovers rock of Culture Club's 'Do You Really Want To Hurt Me', the languid electro soul of the Style Council's 'Long Hot Summer', the classic Muscle Shoals balladry of Simply Red's 'Holding Back the Years'. But, for the most part, Getting It Right was the death of innovation.

At around this time, the transatlantic ping-pong between white rock and black R&B started to break down. White musicians were

On the record
David Byrne

'Work It'
Missy Elliott

THE REAL MCCOY

There are huge blind spots in my musical education. I don't think I've every heard anything by the White Stripes, for instance. But I do own pretty much everything that Missy Elliott has ever recorded. First of all, her beats are really innovative: she does a lot of the production herself but usually you get her and Timbaland putting together a few handclaps, finger-clicks, foot-stomps, weird synthesizer squiggles and stray samples, and they'll make it sound like nothing on earth. She's very innovative: on this track, you can hear her playing the whole chorus backwards, and there's a whole backing track of her hollering which serves as part of the rhythm track. And she's very funny, too – whenever she curses or says something a little outré, it's censored by the hilarious noise of a monkey or an elephant.

I like the way Missy Elliott fits into hip hop. She's simultaneously the archetypal hip hop artist, the most advanced figure in that field, but she's also completely outside the whole genre, constantly telling all these MCs not to take things so seriously.

Formerly the singer and guitarist with Talking Heads, David Byrne now records solo; his most recent album is Grown Backwards *(Nonesuch)*

explore Getting It Wrong. In 1986, a group of amateur musicians in Chicago masquerading under the name Phuture dug out a near-obsolete, fiendishly-difficult-to-programme Roland mini-sequencer called the TB-303 and started mucking about with it. As they did so, they haphazardly created the random sequences of squelchy arpeggios that gave birth to acid house. Phuture's 1987 single 'Acid Tracks' established a familiar pattern for Getting It Wrong: boffins in Japan would invent studio technology with a certain intention, and hooligans in Munich, Sheffield and Detroit would throw out the instruction manuals and start prodding at the buttons. Sampling, sequencing and quantising were used gleefully and amateurishly: rave acts exploited the artificiality of certain lo-tech forms of sampling, while the likes of Autechre, Aphex Twin, Pole and Mouse on Mars started to use the glitches and errors in programming as essential compoments in their music.

Soon, the 'proper' musicians started to leave dance music and, figuratively speaking, the lunatics took over the asylum. Renegade producers such as Dizzee Rascal began doing things that no 'proper' musician would dream of doing – taking drum patterns and revoicing them for instruments, for instance, or using synthesised bass sounds to render melody lines. The results, heard on tracks such as 'Stop Dat' and 'I Luv U', have ended up becoming experimental landmarks in electronic music.

Dance music's barbarian sensibility has ensured that Getting It Wrong remains an essential component of pop, and you don't have to search hard to find noble examples over the past two decades. On 'Mad Cyril' and '24 Hour Party People', the Happy Mondays come off like a drunken working men's club band trying to play jazz-funk. And on 'Down with Prince' and 'The Warning', Hot Chip sound like they're trying to recreate big-budget American R&B on children's toys held together by rubber bands.

Effectively, pop music is an example of what the evolutionary biologist Richard Dawkins might describe as 'the blind watchmaker' in action. While classical composers compose like gods, a top-down process where an all-seeing creator imposes His superiority upon His art, pop is a more chaotic, 'bottom-up' creative process that proceeds through trial and error. Sometimes, a little knowledge can be a wonderful thing.

happy to pay careful and respectful homage to black music without making any of the crucial mistakes that made earlier rip-offs interesting, something that continues today with the 'authentic' neo-soul of Joss Stone, Amy Winehouse and Duffy. The more strenuously artists tried to create authentic soul music, the more inauthentic and ultimately redundant they sounded. Faced with this cruel dilemma at the start of the 1990s, grunge and Britpop acts started to practise a strange form of self-segregation, as if rock bands were so scared of Getting It Wrong that they never strayed from their comfort zones.

By the late 1980s, it was studio-based electronic dance music that really started to

Continental drift

Elisabeth Vincentelli asks if mainland Europe is now top of the pops.

For nearly 60 years, popular music made in the UK and the US has had such an influence on both the charts and the imaginations of the rest of the world that it often feels as if it's the standard by which all modern sounds are judged. Whether rock, pop, rap or R&B, the two countries determine what people listen to and play, right down to the de facto choice of English as lingua franca. It's become an accepted truism that, say, the French can't rock, or the Poles can't do club anthems.

But perhaps Brits and Americans shouldn't be so gung-ho about that whole we-came-up-with-it-and-so-we're-the-only-ones-who-know-how-to-do-it-right thing. It'd allow them to notice that the rest of the world is happily crafting fabulous, idiosyncratic takes on modern pop that more than rival their own. Asian countries are twisting their traditions into new shapes through hugely successful styles such as Cantopop (sung in Cantonese and originating mostly in Hong Kong), K-pop or gayo (aka Korean pop) and Hindi-pop. And back in Europe, musicians from various nations are being incredibly creative as they twist the latest pop formulas from the UK and America, mix them with their own musical heritages and come up with new strains that feel both absolutely right and a little bit off.

This isn't new, of course. In the past, we've had everything from Krautrock to Italo disco and lyric-driven French *chanson* to German *schlager*, just as in 2008, we've got Polish electro and Estonian pop, Moldovan ethnic punk and Portuguese girl groups. These latter movements might not end up having the same level of lasting influence as their precursors. But for now, they sound just great.

The vitality of Eastern European pop never ceases to amaze some and frustrate others, at least if you go on results at recent Eurovision Song Contests. According to common wisdom, Abba redefined European pop in 1974. In truth, though, it did so mostly in Western Europe. While the band was proving that little Sweden could compete on the world stage, political and cultural isolation led musicians in Eastern European countries to experiment with odder combinations of influences, like mad scientists locked up in labs soundproofed from the latest sonic innovations.

When the floodgates opened after 1989 and satellite dishes became as ubiquitous as bowls of borscht, American and British groups at last made it through the barricades, but their influence was filtered through decades of hardened listening habits. This goes some way towards explaining the enduring popularity of ballads and ethnic vibes in the former communist countries, where they remain as potent as any wacky attempts at rap or R&B.

In recent years, Eastern Europe has created extraordinary sui generis stars who both reflect and deflect the musical cultures that spawned them. In Poland, for instance, there's Eurodancey Edyta Górniak and Kasia Stankiewicz, an intriguing singer who started her career in the TV-spawned hit band Varius Manx in the mid 1990s before turning to swanky electro on her 2003 solo album

Extrapop ('Francuzeczka', 'Saint Etienne') and moving on to moody, *Mitteleuropa* electronica on *Mimikra* three years later ('Marzec', 'Mokre Ulice'). From Estonia, there's Eda-Ines Etti and her fab 2004 album *15 magamata ööd* (released under the name Ines); it's kind of like KT Tunstall, only better and with more umlauts. And on tunes such as 'My Story' (aka 'Visionary Dream') and 'On Adjarian Motives', Sopho Khalvashi comes across like a Georgian version of Björk, but a lot less annoying.

Meanwhile, Russia has been confirming that its yen for exuberant sexuality brushed with a healthy veneer of vulgarity extends to pop. One of the biggest male stars in the country is sweet, hunky Dima Bilan, who recorded 'Number One Fan' with Timbaland, while the group Diskoteka Avariya has been offering super-fun club-friendly fusion: try the thumping Slav-disco of 'Opa!' or the Eurodance-rap collaboration with singer Zhanne Friske, 'Malinki'. But the over-the-top approach works best with women, and particularly leggy girl groups such as Propaganda ('Superdetka'), Fabrika ('Zagigaut ogonki', 'Lelik') and Reflex ('Zhestkoe Disko').

That said, some members of Reflex are from Ukraine, a country that gives Mother Russia a run in the outrageousness department. It's has spawned Verka Serduchka, the drag creation of comedian Andriy Danylko and an unlikely runner-up at Eurovision 2007 with the eye-popping 'Dancing Lasha Tumbai'. But the country is also fertile terrain for bright, sassy and crazily entertaining pop, from Tina Karol ('Vishe Oblakov', for example) to a Ukrainian-Russian girl group fortuitously called VIA Gra ('LML'). VIA Gra is only one of myriad girl groups, many of which emerged from reality TV shows, that emulate but also often surpass the template laid down by the likes of the Spice Girls and the Sugababes: check out, for instance, Portugal's Nonstop ('Ao Limite Eu Vou'), Germany's Monrose, whose 'Hot Summer' goes for a brassy Girls Aloud vibe, or France's sadly defunct L5.

Indeed, France has managed to sustain a formidable pool of homegrown talent, with many of its acts singing in their native language. A decisive factor in this trend came in 1992, with the arrival of a law instituting

Mylène Farmer in full flight.

Top ten
Dance crazes

'The Twist' Hank Ballard &
the Midnighters

Building a 50-year career on his cover version
of Ballard's more raucous 1959 original,
Chubby Checker has described the twist as
like putting out a cigarette with both feet while
wiping off your bottom with a towel.

'Charleston' Arthur Gibbs
& His Orchestra

This wide-grinned, loose-
limbed Jazz Age trend
swept the US in the
1920s, despite the
fact that the dance
itself generally
resembles nothing
so much as half a
dozen brooms falling
down an escalator.

'The Loco-Motion'
Little Eva

Bafflingly, co-writer
Carole King passed over
this daffy little thing when
choosing which of her own
Brill Building-era hits to record
for her *Tapestry* album in the early
'70s, so we'll have to make do with the
original hit version, recorded in 1962 by her
18-year-old babysitter.

'The Hustle' Van McCoy & the Soul
City Symphony

Line-dancing hasn't always been limited to
honky-tonks, as this slinky disco hit continues
to prove at weddings around the world.

'Double Dutch' Malcolm McLaren

What the similarly peerless 'Buffalo Gals' did
for breakdance, this unlikely but irresistible
mix of doo-wop, hip hop and Township jive
did for rope-jumping. Hey, Ebo! Ebonettes!

'Vogue' Madonna

This outlandishly peculiar but oddly compelling
dance, equally redolent of the hand jive, the
jitterbug and the tango, was popularised by
Madonna back when she helped set trends
rather than simply followed them.

'The Lambeth Walk'
Ambrose & His Orchestra

From *Ballroom Dancing* by Alex Brown:
'Man walks two steps towards the centre.
Lady walks two steps towards the wall. *Count
one, two.* Both man and lady turn to face each
other and close feet together. *Count three.*
Slap both hands on the legs, just above
the knees, and at the same
time bend slightly forward.
Count four.
'Both man and lady
walk two steps towards
each other. *Count
one, two.* Close feet
together, facing
partner and about
three feet apart.
Count three. Raise
the hands (right)
about level with the
head and give the
Cockney salute,
shouting "Oi".'

'Willie and the Hand
Jive' Johnnie Otis

Predating big-fish-little-fish-
cardboard-box rave culture by
about 30 years, this is perhaps the
only dance craze in pop history that you can do
sitting down. The distinctive beat was nicked
wholesale from Bo Diddley.

'An der schönen blauen Donau'
Johann Strauss (the younger)

It was by no means the first of the Viennese
waltzes, but the 'Blue Danube', written in
the 1860s, helped take the dance far beyond
its Austrian origins. Later used to quite
beautiful effect by Stanley Kubrick in *2001:
A Space Odyssey*.

'Do the Funky Chicken' Rufus Thomas

The 55-year-old Thomas pretty much stole
the show at the fabled Wattstax festival in
1972 – and, for that matter, the subsequent
movie – with this groovesome one-chord
wonder. Not altogether dissimilar follow-ups
'Do the Funky Penguin' and 'The Funky Robot'
sadly proved less successful.

DO THE
FUNKY PENGUIN – Part I
(Jo Bridges-Rufus Thomas-Mack Rice-Tom Nixon)

stax
RECORDS

STA-0112
Stripe Music,
East/Memphis
Music (BMI)
Time: 3:08
(Intro. :14)
(SM-00819)

RUFUS THOMAS
Rhythm by The Movement
Produced by Tom Nixon
11-71
Stax Records Inc. op Nash. Fusion, Memphis, USA

On the record
Björk

'Billie Jean'

Michael Jackson

I don't spend all my time listening to African kora players and avant-garde classical composers and stuff. Honestly! I also listen to a huge amount of pure, shiny pop music – I find it cleansing and life-affirming. And I'm Michael Jackson's biggest fan: I find myself returning to his music again and again, particularly *Off the Wall* and *Thriller*. 'Billie Jean' is a perfect pop song: the bassline digs deep, the strings are dramatic and his singing is perfect, it just glides over the top. It's like a geometric puzzle where all the elements – synth pop, hip hop, rock, Motown – all slot together perfectly. It's also my karaoke song of choice, but I need a few drinks to do it justice.
Björk's most recent album is Volta
(One Little Indian)

THE REAL MCCOY

quotas for radio play: on average, 40 per cent of all playlists on French stations must be performed in French. The law has made for a relatively strong, diversified domestic industry that helps sustain long careers. Véronique Sanson, Michel Polnareff, Michel Sardou or Johnny Hallyday may not sell outside French-speaking countries, but they don't care: they've had a huge audience at home for decades.

Since 1985, one of the biggest French pop stars has been Mylène Farmer, an eccentric redhead who comes out of seclusion every few years to deliver an album of goth-disco doom and put on live shows so outrageous that they make the latest American extravaganzas look like cheap pantos. At the same time, France also produces its own styles of rap, R&B and club music – and, yes, rock (listen to Deportivo or Luke) – along with intriguing new syntheses of North African sounds mixed with R&B (Nâdiya's 'Parle-moi' and 'Tous ces mots') or eccentric pop (Najoua Belyzel's 'Quand revient l'été').

Sweden remains a creative and commercial powerhouse. Although many mark the beginning of its reign with Abba, it should be noted that Abba's singer Agnetha Fältskog had a thriving career before the band, establishing herself as a Scandinavian answer to France's Françoise Hardy. Indeed, both were writing their own material at a time when it was relatively rare for women to do so: Agnetha wrote all but one of the tracks on her fourth album, 1971's *När en vacker tanke blir en sång* (the Beach Boys-esque 'Många gånger än', a totally pre-Abba vibe on 'Nya ord'), before moving into a Carole King vein for her last Swedish-language album, 1975's introspective *Elva kvinnor i ett hus*.

Even countries in which the local language disappeared from the charts for a while are now offering their own takes on familiar styles. Tokio Hotel, for example, are huge in France and Eastern Europe despite singing in German. And rushing behind them are the bossa-inflected Kitty Hoff und Forêt-Noire ('Ewigkeit' off 2005's *Rauschen*, 'Blaue Stunde' off 2007's *Blick ins Tal*); 2raumwohnung, a Berlin duo that offers a stylish take on mainstream club music; and the ultra-poppy Wir Sind Helden ('Die Konkurrenz' from 2007's *Soundso*). Truly, it's time for the US and the UK to realise that they no longer set the rules.

Eternal fame

Justin Lewis is waiting for a star to fall.

Singer-songwriters, teen idols and rock icons don't, on the surface, have much in common. But one subject that generally unites them, with a nodding unanimity, is the concept of celebrity. It's a rare lyricist who, trapped in an anonymous orange-walled motel in Akron, Ohio, or quivering backstage at Chippenham Golddiggers, hasn't felt tempted to pen a haunted hymn to the idea that the price of fame is astronomical and I want a refund; that critics are bitter, impotent, tin-eared soaks; or that the fan base completely misunderstood the ethos of that top-25 smash from last summer, and I was actually being *ironic*.

Certainly, pop stars face a dilemma. Having had 20-plus years in which to create the songs for their debut album, only a few songwriters find much water left in their well of inspiration after signing the eight-record deal that follows its success. The only topic left for the rest of them is life in the public eye. In the case of the Streets' Mike Skinner, the wheels fell off with remarkable gracelessness on his third album's 'When You Wasn't Famous', which expected paying customers to somehow sympathise with the pain and pressure of getting off with another pop star. The following year, the risible Just Jack, basically the Legoland version of Skinner, opened only his second long-player with the cobbled-together ramblings of 'Writer's Block', in which he found no solution to his plight but nonetheless seemed happy to put his name to his own discussion of it.

Conversely, what if you write a song about your struggle and then suddenly find you've achieved unimaginable riches? If you're Sade, you quietly drop second hit 'When Am I Going to Make a Living' and its implications of borderline starvation from your set list on the understanding that it's inappropriate for the greatest hits pension scheme. But if you're Wham!-for-toddlers Bros, you're either unwilling or unable to let go of your literally desperate 'When Will I Be Famous?' when your wish comes true. Oasis, who courted stardom with an admirable absence of self-consciousness, were no less shameless about their aspirations in 'Rock 'n' Roll Star', written before the glare from the spotlight began to *sheeeee*-ine on them. However, they possessed a lorry-load more self-belief than the Goss brothers ever seemed to retain. They were already rock 'n' roll stars; it's just that the public hadn't yet realised.

Few groups or artists have been as explicit on record as Oasis about their hunger for superstardom, particularly after acclaim has arrived and

Jarvis Cocker, no longer one of the common people.

Rewind
Morrissey

Morrissey's media forays thus far have coupled a charming, winning eloquence with a seemingly endless list of controversial statements, and have ensured that his interviews have probably sold more records than his lyrics. 'I'm not so shallow that I'd be happy hiding behind slogans,' he says, half-uneasy at the way he's become not only the group's spokesman, but also that of yet another lost generation of British youth. As the Smiths' records charted ever higher (last month, *Meat Is Murder* went to number one), the often petty controversies surrounding the band grew in stature. 'No more scandals!' said Morrissey when the worst seemed over. But the tabloids didn't believe him.

'They hound me,' he says, 'and it gets very sticky. What makes me more dangerous to them than anyone else is the fact that I lead somewhat of a religious lifestyle. I'm not a rock 'n' roll character. I despise drugs, I despise cigarettes, I'm celibate and I live a very serene lifestyle. But I'm also making very strong statements lyrically, and this is worrying to authoritarian figures. The main reason I'm dangerous is because I'm not afraid to say how I feel.

'They can't say that I'm in a druggy haze or soaked in alcohol. They probably think I'm some sort of sex-crazed monster. But that's okay. They can think what they like. I'm only interested in evidence, and they can't produce any evidence to spoil my character.'

Dangerous? This 25-year-old man in black blazer, lime-green cotton shirt, heavily creased beige pegs and brown shoes? In truth, there is something unsettling about being in his presence. He's almost too soft, too gentle, too nervous, not a million miles from that pathetic archetypal Monty Python accountant. He even bows when he shakes your hand.

'You have to hold on to what you want to stay very tightly, because there are so many people in this industry trying to trip you up and push you over. The industry is just rife with jealousy and hatred. Everybody in it is a failed bassist. Everybody wants to be on stage. It doesn't matter what they do – they all want to be you. But the mere fact that you have that, and that nobody can take it away from you, is your ultimate weapon.'
Simon Garfield; from Time Out, *7 March 1985*

they then have to maintain their standing in the public eye. For Jarvis Cocker, who had spent a decade striving to turn getting noticed into a creative act, the success of Pulp resulted in unexpected celebrity. Yet Cocker's sour experiences of his time spent in the headlines had as much to do with the boredom and emptiness it entailed as it did with being spotted in the street.

Underpinned by epic swooping strings and a queasy, distant sample, Pulp's magnificent 'This Is Hardcore' paralleled the dead-eyed excesses of pornography with the struggle to construct a public image, but it was less an attack on circumstance than a shrug of resignation. Was Cocker an icon because of instantly loveable songs such as 'Common People' and 'Disco 2000', or because he clambered on stage at the Brit Awards in front of Michael Jackson's unhinged sideshow and, to all intents and purposes, said 'knickers'?

Unlike the majority of his cardboard Britpop contemporaries, Cocker had something insightful to say about how he was perceived by his public. It may be that his relative maturity (he was 31 when 'Common People' stormed the charts) prepared him for his retreat from celebrity, if not for celebrity itself. Kirsty MacColl's '15 Minutes' carries an equally detached and acidic air of ennui, but Morrissey, whose rumblings on the nature of his own persona have been rather too widely documented, is richer when commenting on others who've left the spotlight. While 'We Hate It When Our Friends Become Successful' (apparently about fellow Mancunians James) offers spiteful solipsism and little else, 'Little Man, What Now?' captures perfectly the fleeting career of an unidentified child actor, revived but unlamented during a turn on a TV panel show. It's a scenario that seems to have been imported wholesale to the unpleasant identity parade on *Never Mind the Buzzcocks*.

Sometimes, a pop star's privileged position on the inside track offers listeners an insight into situations that they'll never experience at first hand. 'Hello', a B-side from 1985, relates Prince's part-involvement in the USA for Africa charity song 'We Are the World' (he refused to sing on it, instead donating a song to the accompanying album), but turns into a critique of how charity relies on and survives by over-simplifying the issues. De La Soul's 'Ring Ring

Ring (Ha Ha Hey)' is a witty, pithy comment about hangers-on who expect to get more than their foot in the door, while PiL's 'Public Image' adds a sense of humour to its righteous fury over the received notion that the Sex Pistols were solely Malcolm McLaren's brainchild.

Neither 'Ring Ring Ring' nor 'Public Image' bothered to be bothered by the critics, but other bands have proven rather more insecure on record. On Guns n' Roses' 'Get in the Ring', Axl Rose calls out a handful of hacks who, it transpires, didn't like the group's last album. It's idiotic, but it's at least got a little more oomph than the Stereophonics' 'Mr Writer'. Painfully slow (which, in rock shorthand, translates to 'meaning it'), it's also oddly half-hearted in its toy-throwing. During it, singer Kelly Jones even protests that he once treated the press well, a baffling, cart-before-horse moment that seems to suggest the trio thought they were doing the media machine a favour rather than the other way around.

> '**Some of the finest songs about fame aren't whinges or rants: they're about acknowledging both the platitudes and the pitfalls of stardom, the euphoria and the self-disgust.**'

On a very different note, Nick Cave & the Bad Seeds' searing, withering 'Scum' contains an ocean of scorn and might, which may be the reason that it ultimately so impressed its target, *NME* writer Mat Snow. But the last word belongs to Birkenhead's finest and pop's

Mike Skinner of the Streets: gambling on success.

Half Man Half Biscuit,
live at the Deptford Abyss.

funniest, Half Man Half Biscuit. 'Bad Review' is written from the perspective of a band member, suddenly on the defensive after a poor press notice for a recent gig at the (fictional) Deptford Abyss. The listener can't help but side with the review's (fictional) author Jeff Dreadnought despite the fact that not a word of his article is mentioned in the song, as singer Nigel Blackwell demonstrates that you don't have to have tasted fame to realise its hollowness.

Some of the finest songs about fame aren't whinges or rants: they're simply about acknowledging both the platitudes and the pitfalls of stardom, the euphoria and the self-disgust. An entire book could be filled on the subject, and that book is *Feel*, Chris Heath's excellent gaze into the world of Robbie Williams. Appropriate, perhaps, that Williams later went on to work with the Pet Shop Boys, who themselves documented the trials of celebrity in the waspish 'Yesterday, When I Was Mad'. First indignant, then amused and ultimately reflective, Neil Tennant runs through

a dossier of patronising and downright asinine notices from withering critics over the duo's trademark whirling technopop.

Slade's earlier and very different 'How Does It Feel?', an under-appreciated 1975 single that featured in the group's film *Flame*, is the very essence of bittersweet. However, like 'Yesterday, When I Was Mad', it refrains from over-agonising: instead, it simply tries to remember the expectations the group held ten years earlier when they were just getting started, and readily admits that it's a struggle to turn back the clock.

Ambivalence also looms large in Ben Folds Five's heartbreaking 'Boxing'. It's ostensibly an imaginary speech from Muhammad Ali to commentator Howard Cosell, delivered while a devastating balletic arrangement floats, stings and punches in all the right places, but the song was apparently inspired by Folds chewing over his own career options. Maybe writing that resignation letter but never sending it is the very essence of life in the pop spotlight.

Further reference

All About Jazz
www.allaboutjazz.com
Useful for its 20,000 album reviews, which'll suffice until someone sees fit to put Richard Cook and Brian Morton's peerless *Penguin Guide to Jazz Recordings* online.

Allmusic
www.allmusic.com
The net's largest music database contains discographies and reviews for innumerable artists: it's great for pop, rock and jazz, less so for classical music and electronica. The search technology can be cranky and it's not without errors, but this is still an invaluable resource.

Billboard
www.billboard.com
The American music charts, weekly since the '40s and still the industry standard.

Both Sides Now Discographies
www.bsnpubs.com
A staggering net of discographies covering American record labels, from A&M to Zephyr. The majority of stuff featured here is from the '50s and '60s, but the site also covers a number of later labels.

Chart Stats
www.chartstats.com
Several sites offer data on UK charts past and present: see also Everyhit (www.everyhit.com) and Polyhex (www.polyhex.com). However, this is the best of the lot.

Classical Net
www.classical.net
Classical Net effectively serves as a massive bluffer's guide to classical music, complete with repertoire lists for all the major composers (and a lot of minor ones), reviews and a variety of other features.

Commercial Breaks & Beats
www.commercialbreaksandbeats. co.uk
Heard something you like on a UK advert but didn't clock the artist or track? Someone here will know.

Discogs
www.discogs.com
Set up by Kevin Lewandowski as a catalogue of his personal record collection, Discogs has grown into a vast resource that does what it says on the tin: discographies, chiefly organised by artist and cross-referenced in a number of ways. It's expanded across the genres of late, but it's particularly useful for electronica and hip hop.

Grove Online
www.grovemusic.com
The daddy of music encyclopaedias, *The New Grove Dictionary of Music and Musicians* is spread over 29 volumes and contains a perfectly ridiculous 29,000 articles, the vast majority devoted to classical music. The printed version costs a cool £750 ($1,500): the entire thing is also online, though an annual subscription costs £195 ($295).

Jazz Discography Project
www.jazzdisco.org
This tidy site does what Discogs does for electronica and Both Sides Now does does for vintage pop and rock. However, it also includes full sessionographies that track the recording careers of more than 50 jazz notables.

Last.fm
www.last.fm
One of two major websites (the other is the very popular Pandora, online at www.pandora.com) that automatically recommends music to surfers by comparing their tastes with those of other listeners around the world. It shouldn't work but, at least sometimes, it does.

Reel Soundtrack
www.reelsoundtrack.com
Soundtrack listings for movies (see also the Internet Movie Database at www.imdb.com), TV shows, video games and ads. It's not comprehensive enough yet, but it's getting there.

Robert Christgau
www.robertchristgau.com
The self-described 'Dean of American Rock Critics' has been writing regular Consumer Guide columns, covering new and newish releases, for almost 40 years. This archive collates every one of his 13,500-and-counting incisive reviews, alongside reams of equally savvy long-form criticism. Indispensable, in its way.

Rock's Backpages
www.rocksbackpages.com
Edited by Barney Hoskyns, this is a fantastic online library of some 12,000 features, interviews and reviews that first appeared in the UK or US music press. A 12-month subscription costs £30 or $60.

Rocklist.net
www.rocklist.net
Ever wondered what *Kerrang!* voted as the eighth best album of 1986 (the eponymous debut album from the Vinnie Vincent Invastion), or where Freiwilige Selbskontrolle's 'I Wish I Could Sprechen Sie Deutsch' finished in John Peel's Festive 50 of the same year (33rd, just behind The The's 'Heartland' but two places above 'Cemetry Gates' by the Smiths)? Try here.

Ubuweb
www.ubu.com
The strangest corners of the musical world are mapped at this fabulous jumble sale of a website. The files available for free download are either out of print or out of copyright, but they're usually way out there.

Vaughan Williams Memorial Library
http://library.efdss.org
The website of the English Folk Dance & Song Society's library is very much a work in progress, but it does already contain Steve Roud's invaluable database of traditional songs and their origins.

Contributors

Hugh Barker and **Yuval Taylor** are the authors of *Faking it: The Quest for Authenticity in Popular Music* (Faber & Faber). Barker is an ex-musician and publisher. Taylor has edited collections of slave narratives and music writing; his writing has appeared in *The Guardian* and *The Antioch Review*.

Ian Bostridge is one of Britain's leading tenors, appearing regularly in opera and in recital at venues around the world. His own recording of Schubert's *Winterreise*, on which he's accompanied by pianist Leif Ove Andsnes, is available on EMI Classics.

Glasgow-born, Oxford-educated fortysomething NHS pen-pusher **Marcello Carlin** is the author of music blogs The Church of Me and The Blue in the Air. He has also written for *Time Out*, *The Wire*, *Uncut* and Stylus in other people's time. He lives in Fulham and is happily married.

Geoff Carter writes a regular column for NWsource.com, *The Seattle Times*' website, and has contributed to the *Las Vegas Weekly*, the *Las Vegas Sun* and Playboy.com. (Occasionally, he invokes the latter distinction to get free drinks.) He lives in Seattle with a roller derby queen and a novel he expects to be revising for the next decade.

Garth Cartwright was born in New Zealand, lives in south London and is oft' wandering. He writes for *The Guardian*, *The Sunday Times*, *fRoots* and many other publications, and is the author of *Princes Amongst Men: Journeys with Gypsy Musicians* (Serpents Tail).

David Cavanagh was born in Ireland in 1964. He is the author of *My Magpie Eyes Are Hungry for the Prize: The Creation Records Story* (Virgin), and he has written for most of the major music monthlies. He currently writes for *Uncut*.

Kimberly Chun is the senior arts and entertainment editor and a music columnist at the *San Francisco Bay Guardian*. She played, badly, in Hawaii's first all-female punk band, and once go-go danced in a panda suit on stage at the Fillmore alongside XBXRX.

Stevie Chick has written about music for *Mojo*, *The Guardian*, *Kerrang!*, *Plan B*, *NME*, *The Times* and *Sleazenation*, edits *Loose Lips Sink Ships* with photographer Steve Gullick, and is the author of *Psychic Confusion: The Sonic Youth Story* (Omnibus). His favourite song ever, depending on when you ask him, is 'How Low Can a Punk Get' by Bad Brains, or possibly Margo Guryan's 'Someone I Know', or perhaps something off Stevie Wonder's *Talking Book*.

Nick Coleman was *Time Out*'s music editor for nearly seven years, then arts/features editor at *The Independent* and *The Independent on Sunday* for another 12. He then collapsed in a heap and now does a little light writing and broadcasting in between cooking meals for his children.

Californian, *Scram* editrix and bubblegum scholar, **Kim Cooper** spent her formative years flipping through thrift-store vinyl with the peculiar avidity of the record raccoon. Give her a tank of gas, a pocketful of Handi-Wipes and a map of the high desert, and she is content.

Robert Darden is an associate professor of journalism at Baylor University and the author of more than two dozen books, including *People Get Ready: A New History of Black Gospel Music* (Continuum). He is the former gospel music editor for *Billboard* and the co-founder of the Black Gospel Music Restoration Project.

Chuck Eddy is the author of the books *Stairway to Hell* and *The Accidental Evolution of Rock 'n' Roll* (both Da Capo), and has served as music editor at *The Village Voice* and as a senior editor at *Billboard*. He has written thousands of pieces over the years for *Creem*, *Rolling Stone*, *Spin* and other publications. He lives in Queens, New York.

Elliot Elam lives in London. He illustrated this book while listening to Harry Nilsson, Lord Finesse and the rattle of his washing machine.

Dan Epstein is an award-winning music journalist who long ago lost count of how many American, British and Japanese rags for which he's written. He lives and works in Southern California, but even when the weather turns cold, it's always summer in his heart.

Will Fulford-Jones is a staff editor at Time Out Guides and an occasional freelancer on music. He lives in London.

Sophie Harris is a music journalist who writes for *Time Out*, *Mojo* and *The Times*, broadcasts for the BBC World Service, Radio 4 and Sky News, and devised and co-hosted a series for BBC6 Music called *A Guide to the Genres*. She fell in love with music the moment she saw Eddy Grant playing 'I Don't Wanna Dance' on *Top of the Pops*.

Born in Karachi and educated on three continents, **Martin Hoyle** was classical music and opera editor of *Time Out* from 1989 to 2007, and currently writes on radio, TV and film for *The Financial Times*.

David Hutcheon has investigated music in places as far-flung as Ratanakkiri, Sana'a, Faaa and Kyzyl, which you might imagine would make him better than he is at Scrabble. His thoughts on such matters, which appear in *Mojo*, *The Sunday Times* and *The Times*, have led to him being described as 'the Boris Johnson of world music'.

Colin Irwin has been writing about folk music for 30 years and contributes regularly to *Mojo*, *fRoots* and *The Independent*. Previously, he was assistant editor of *Melody Maker* and editor of *Number One* magazine. His music-related books include *In Search of the Craic*, *In Search of Albion*, *Sing When You're Winning* (all Andre Deutsch) and *Legendary Sessions: Bob Dylan – Highway 61 Revisited* (Billboard)

John Lewis was born in Southall and spent some time playing the piano in pubs, working men's clubs and a transvestite karaoke bar. He was a *Time Out* music critic for eight years and now writes about music, film, comedy and theatre for publications including *Uncut*, *The Guardian*, *The Times*, *The Financial Times*, *GQ* and *Metro*.

Justin Lewis is a writer and researcher on music and broadcasting. His credits include *The Rough Guide to Rock*, where he also served as contributing editor, and *Guinness Hit Singles*. He is the co-author of *Prime Minister, You Wanted to See Me?*, a history of BBC Radio 4's comedy series *Week Ending*. He lives in London.

Jack Massarik first heard jazz at 13, then took up the piano at 14 and the sax at 16. A psychology degree at Manchester somehow led to five years spent touring with jazz and R&B bands, two children and 30 years covering news, sport and the arts for weekly papers, the Press Association, Agence France-Presse in Paris, *The Guardian* and London's *Evening Standard*. Discovering John Mayall is nevertheless considered his sole claim to fame.

Michaelangelo Matos is a freelance writer in Seattle and the author of *Sign 'O' the Times* (Continuum).

Kate Mossman is reviews editor for *The Word*. A love of country and bluegrass, and a willingness to travel long distances to hear them,

brought her to music journalism, since when she has contributed to *Classic Rock*, *Rock 'n' Reel*, Guardian Unlimited and Time Out's *1,000 Things to Do in Britain*.

Garry Mulholland began his career in music journalism in 1993, became music editor of *Time Out* in 1997, and has written two books: *This Is Uncool: The 500 Greatest Singles Since Punk and Disco* (Cassell Illustrated) and *Fear of Music: The 261 Greatest Albums Since Punk and Disco* (Orion). His third book, *Popcorn: 50 Years of Rock & Roll Movies,* is due to be published in spring 2009.

Dave Rimmer has contributed to a variety of publications in Britain and abroad, among them *Smash Hits*, *The Face* and *Q*, and is the author of *Like Punk Never Happened: Culture Club and the New Pop* (Faber & Faber) and *New Romantics: The Look* (Omnibus).

Mike Shallcross is the deputy editor of *Men's Health*, and has written about music for *Melody Maker*, *The Wire*, *Mixmag* and *GQ*. He doesn't advocate mixing drugs and music, but thinks the Stooges' *Raw Power* sounds better when you have flu.

Peter Shapiro is the author of *Turn the Beat Around: The Secret History of Disco* (Faber & Faber), and has also written for publications including *Time Out*, *The Times*, *The Wire*, *Spin* and *Vibe*. He is currently selling his soul by becoming a lawyer.

Mark Shenton is the theatre critic for *The Sunday Express* and BBC London, and writes a daily blog for *The Stage*'s website (www.thestage.co.uk/shenton). He's hosted regular events at the National Theatre, and has written liner notes for a number of original cast albums, among them the West End recording of *Chicago*.

Philip Sherburne's columns appear regularly in *The Wire*, Pitchfork and eMusic.com; he has also written for *The New York Times*, Slate.com, *Interview*, *Frieze*, *XLR8R* and the book *Audio Culture: Readings in Modern Music* (Continuum), edited by Christoph

Cox and Daniel Warner. Born in the US but now based in Barcelona, Sherburne is also a respected house and techno DJ; his debut recording appeared on Lan Muzic in 2007.

Sylvie Simmons was born in London and lives in San Francisco, where she writes and plays ukulele. She's been a rock journalist since 1977, first as UK weekly *Sounds*' LA correspondent, these days as contributing editor and Americana columnist for Mojo. Her own books include biographies – *Serge Gainsbourg: A Fistful of Gitanes* (Helter Skelter), *Neil Young: Reflections in Broken Glass* (Mojo) – and cult fiction – *Too Weird for Ziggy* (Black Cat).

Bob Stanley was born in Horsham and grew up in Surrey. He wrote a fanzine called *Caff* in the mid '80s with lifelong pal Pete Wiggs; they formed Saint Etienne in 1990. Since his life peaked with a *Top of the Pops* appearance in 1993, he has made do with writing for *The Times*, *The Guardian* and *Mojo*.

Stephen Troussé was born in Liverpool in the week of Altamont with the Archies at number one, and so had no choice but to become obsessed with pop. He writes regularly for *Uncut* and Pitchfork and is the co-editor of *The Message* (Poetry Society), a book about pop lyrics.

Elisabeth Vincentelli is arts & entertainment editor at *Time Out New York* and the author of *Abba Gold* (Continuum).

Peter Watts has written about music for a number of publications, including *Uncut*, *Time Out London* and *1,001 Albums You Must Hear Before You Die*. He is currently features writer at *Time Out London*.

Douglas Wolk is the author of *Reading Comics: How Graphic Novels Work and What They Mean* (Da Capo) and *Live at the Apollo* (Continuum), and writes about pop music, comics and politics for *Blender*, *Publishers Weekly*, *The Believer*, *The New York Times* and elsewhere. He lives in Portland, Oregon.

Song credits

'You Broke My Heart' – Steven Gregoropoulos/Ronald Rege/ Jeffrey Rosenberg/Rebecca Stark. © Discombobulated Vent Publishing/ Jeffrey Rosenberg Music/Lavender Diamond Music (ASCAP)/Temple Bells (BMI).

'It's My Party' – John Gluck/Wally Gold/Seymour Gottlieb/Herbert Wiener. © World Song Publishing Inc (ASCAP).

'Where Did Our Love Go' – Brian Holland/Lamont Dozier/Edward Holland, Jr. © Stone Agate Music (a division of Jobete Music Co, Inc), admin by EMI Blackwood Music Inc (BMI).

'Hippychick' – Timothy London. © PolyGram Music Publishing.

'You're Breakin' My Heart' – Harry Nilsson. © EMI Blackwood Music Inc/ Golden Syrup Music (BMI).

'Bloodshot Eyes' – Harold Hensley/ Hank Penny. © Bienstock Publishing Company/Quartet Music (ASCAP).

'You Should All Be Murdered' – Harvey Williams. © Copyright control.

'Our Happiness Is Guaranteed' – Sam Coomes. © Filthy Gondola Music (BMI).

'For Shame of Doing Wrong' – Richard Thompson. © Beeswing Music (BMI), administered by Bug Music.

'Divorce Song' – Liz Phair. © Civil War Days/Sony/ATV Tunes LLC.

'I Hope You're Happy Now' – Elvis Costello. © Plangent Visions Music Ltd.

'The Stops' – Elbow, lyrics by Guy Garvey. © Salvation Music.

'I'm 49' – Paddy McAloon. © EMI Music.

'My Young Man' – Kate Rusby. © Copyright control.

'Closing Time' – Lyle Lovett. © Polygram Music Publishing Ltd.

'Smoke Rings' – Gene Gifford/Ned Washington. © Music Sales Corp/EMI Music Inc/Old Acct (ASCAP).

'Legalise It' – Peter Tosh. © ATV Music Ltd.

'Smoke! Smoke! Smoke! (That Cigarette)' – Merle Travis/Tex Williams. © Merle's Girls Music/Unichappell Music Inc (BMI).

'Mairzy Doats' – Milton Drake/ Al Hoffman/Jerry Livingston. © Al Hoffman Songs Inc/Hallmark Music Co/Sony/ATV Tunes LLC.

'A Road is Just a Road' – Mary Chapin Carpenter/John Jennings. © EMI April Music Inc/Getarealjob Music (ASCAP)/ Obie Diner Music (BMI).

'He Thinks He'll Keep Her' – Mary Chapin Carpenter/Don Schlitz. © EMI April Music Inc/Getarealjob Music/Don Schlitz Music/Almo Music Corp (ASCAP).

'Our House' – Cathal Smyth/Chris Foreman. © Nutty Sounds Ltd.

'Wand'rin' Star' – Alan Lerner/ Frederick Loewe. © Chappell & Co Inc (ASCAP).

'America' – Paul Simon. © Paul Simon Music (BMI).

'Driving Away from Home (Jim's Tune)' – John Campbell/Jarvis Whitehead. © Virgin Music Ltd.

'Mexican Minutes' – James M Messina/ Kent Marshall Robbins. © Irving Music Inc/Jasperilla Music Co (BMI).

'New Spanish Two-Step' – Tommy Duncan/Bob Wills. © Anne-Rachel Music Corporation/Bourne Co.

'Adobe Walls' Roger Brown/Luke Reed. © Golden Hook Music (BMI)/ Roger Brown Publishing Designee/ WBM Music Corp.

'All I Know About Mexico' – Jeffrey Steele/Chris Wallin. © Gottahaveable Music/Songs of Windswept Pacific (BMI)/Wallerin Music (ASCAP).

'Stays in Mexico' – Toby Keith. © Tokeco Tunes (BMI).

'Good to Go to Mexico' – Chuck Cannon/ Toby Keith. © Tokeco Tunes/Wacissa River Music Inc (BMI).

'Wooly Bully' – Domingo Samudio. © Sony/ATV Songs dba Tree Publishing Co (BMI)/Three Wise Boys Music LLC (BMI).

'Juimonos (Let's Went)' – Domingo Samudio. © Three Wise Boys Music (BMI).

'Mexican Blackbird' – Frank Beard/ Billy Gibbons/Dusty Hill. © Stage Three Songs (ASCAP).

'Carmelita' – Warren Zevon. © Darkroom Music/Warner-Tamerlane Publishing Corp (BMI).

'Border Radio' – Dave Alvin. © Twin Duck Music (BMI).

'Mexican Radio' – Charles Gray/ Marc Moreland/Joe Nanini/Stan Ridgway. © Big Talk Music/Illegal Songs Inc (BMI).

'I Don't Know What She Said' Cory Batten/Kent Blazy/Lane Turner. © Big Red Toe Music/I Want to Hold Your Songs (BMI)/Major Bob Music Co (ASCAP).

'Rodeo or Mexico' – Garth Brooks/ Bryan Kennedy/Paul Kennerley. © Cowboy Hat Trick Music/Major Bob Music Co/No Fences Music (ASCAP).

'Rum and Coca Cola' – Morey Amsterdam/Paul Baron/Jeri Sullivan. © EMI Feist Catalogue Inc (ASCAP).

'The Seashores of Old Mexico' – Merle Haggard. © Sony/ATV Songs dba Tree Publishing Co (BMI).

'Running Drugs Out of Mexico' – Billy Don Burns. © Burns & Grigsby Music (BMI).

'Wanted Man' – Bob Dylan. © Sony/ATV Music Publishing Ltd.

'El Paso' – Marty Robbins. © Mariposa Music Inc/Unichappell Music Inc (BMI).

'I'm Headed Your Way, Jose' – Dallas Davidson/James T Slater. © Big Borassa Music LLC/Diversion Music/Hope n Cal Music/Pick Them Maters Music (BMI).

'The Gnu Song' – Michael Flanders/ Donald Swann. © Copyright control.

'Jollity Farm' – Leslie Sarony. © Lawrence Wright/EMI Songs Ltd.

'On Again! On Again!' – Jake Thackray. © Plantagenet Music Co Ltd.

'Jump' – Cook/Moore. © Copyright control.

'Tighten Up' – Archie Bell/Billy Buttier. © Cotillion Music Inc/Orellia Publishing (BMI).

'Dunkin' Bagel' – Slim Gaillard. © Optissimo Publishing (ASCAP).

'Eatin' with the Boogie' – Slim Gaillard. © Copyright control.

"Potato Chips" – Bundora. © Embassy Music Corp/Marvelle Music Company (BMI).

'I Belong to Glasgow' – Will Fyffe. © Francis, Day & Hunter Ltd.

'Lay Something on the Bar (Besides Your Elbow)' – Austin/Smith. © Copyright control.

'Sport' – Lightnin' Rod. © On the One Publishing.

'La-Di-Da-Di' – Douglas Davis/ Ricky Walters. © Entertaining Music/Slick Rick Music Corp.

'Rhymin' and Stealin'' – Beastie Boys/Rick Rubin. © Brooklyn Dust Music/Universal Polygram International Publishing Inc/Sony/ATV Tunes LLC/American Def Tunes (ASCAP).

'The New Style' – Beastie Boys/Rick Rubin. © Brooklyn Dust Music/ Universal Polygram International Publishing Inc/Sony/ATV Tunes LLC/American Def Tunes (ASCAP).

'Girls' – Beastie Boys/Rick Rubin. © Brooklyn Dust Music/Universal Polygram International Publishing Inc/Sony/ATV Tunes LLC/American Def Tunes (ASCAP).

'Signifying Rapper' – Jesse Weaver. © Artmann Music/Universal Music Songs (BMI).

'Remix for P Is Free' – Chris Martin/ Lawrence Parker. © Rock Candy Music (ASCAP).

'Straight Outta Compton' – O Jackson/ L Patterson/E Wright/A Young. © Priority Records LLC.

'Express Yourself' – O Jackson/C Wright. © Priority Records LLC.

'Bitches Ain't Shit' – Broadus/Curry/ Wolfe/Young. © Notting Dale Songs Inc/Sony/ATV Songs LLC.

'Let a Ho Be a Ho' – Willie Dee/DJ Akshen/Lil J. © N The Water Music, Inc (ASCAP).

'Da Bichez' – KJ Davis/DJ Premier. © EMI April Music Inc/Gifted Pearl Music (ASCAP).

'Simon Says' – Troy Jamerson. © EMI Blackwood Music Inc/ Trescadecaphobia Music (BMI).

'The What' – Harvey/Smith/Wallace. © Bee Mo Easy Music/Big Poppa Music/ EMI April Music Inc/Justin Combs Publishing (ASCAP)/Universal Music Careers/Wu Tang Publishing Inc (BMI)

'Lola' – Ray Davies. © Carlin Music Corp.

'Anger' – Marvin Gaye/Ed Townsend/ Delta Ashby/Lana Ashby Anderson. © Jobete Music Co, Inc/Stone Diamond Music Corp.

'Kick Out the Jams' – MC5. © Paradox Music (BMI).

'Screaming at a Wall' – Ian Mackaye/ Minor Threat. © Copyright control.

'Loadsamoney (Doin' Up the House)' – Enfield/Higson/Whitehouse/Orbit. © Copyright control/Illegal Music.

'American Girl' – Tom Petty. © Skyhill Pub Co Inc, admin by Almo Music Corp.

'Sunday Mornin' Comin' Down' – Kris Kristofferson. © EMI Songs Ltd.

'Me and Bobby McGee' – Fred Foster/ Kris Kristofferson. © EMI Songs Ltd.

'Shiver Me Timbers' – Tom Waits. © Fifth Floor Music Inc (ASCAP).

'Born to Run' – Bruce Springsteen. © Bruce Springsteen (ASCAP).

'Thunder Road' – Bruce Springsteen. © Bruce Springsteen (ASCAP).

'Nebraska' – Bruce Springsteen. © Bruce Springsteen (ASCAP).

'Icky Thump' – Jack White. © Peppermint Stripe Music (BMI).

'Things Are Worse in Russia' – Sam Mayo. © Copyright control.

'Autumn Almanac' – Ray Davies. © Carlin Music Corp.

'Anarchy in the UK' – Jones/Cook/ Matlock/Rotten. © Stephen Philip Jones/ Warner Chappell Music Ltd/Rotten Music Ltd.

'Stand and Deliver' – Stuart Goddard/ Marco Pirroni. © BMG Music Publishing Ltd.

'Slates, Slags Etc' – The Fall. © Minder Music Ltd.

'Repetition' – Baines/Bramah/Burns/ Friel/Smith. © Minder Music Ltd.

'English Scheme' – Mark E Smith/ Marc Riley/Craig Scanlon. © Minder Music Ltd

'Come Taste My Mind' – Fry/Sanderson/ Marche/King.

'Up the Junction' – Chris Difford/Glen Tilbrook. © Javeberry Ltd (PRS) (trading as Deptford Songs)/Rondor Music (London) Ltd.

'Ticket Collector' – Simon Warner. © Copyright control.

'Marrakesh Express' – Graham Nash. © Nash Notes (BMI).

'Different Trains' – Steve Reich. © Hendon Music Inc, a Boosey & Hawkes Company (BMI).

'Eight Men, Four Women' – Deadric Malone. © Universal/MCA Music Ltd (BMI).

'I Never Loved a Man (The Way I Love You)' – Ronny Shannon. © EMI Songs Ltd.

'The Girls on the Beach' – Mike Love/ Brian Wilson. © Rondor Music (London) Ltd.

'My Sharona' Berton Averre/Doug Fieger. © Chappell Music Ltd.

'Roses' – Andre Benjamin/Matt Boykin/Antwan Patton. © Gnat Booty/ Chrysalis Music (ASCAP).

'Jeepster' – Marc Bolan. © Westminster Music Ltd.

'Dr Kitch' – Lord Kitchener. © Copyright control.

'Sheffield: Sex City' – Pulp/Jarvis Cocker. © Island Music Ltd.

'The Body Breaks' – Devendra Banhart. © Golden Negress Publishing (BMI).

'Ayo Technology' – C Jackson/A Young/ J Harris/T Lewis. © 50 Cent Music Publishing, admin by Universal Music Publishing (ASCAP)/Virginia Beach Music, admin by Warner Chappell Music Publishing (ASCAP)/Danjahandz Music/ WB Music Corp (SESAC)/Tennman Tunes, admin by Zomba Music (ASCAP).

'40 Hours' – Sarah Dougher. © Candid Music Publishing.

'Going Underground' – Paul Weller. © Stylist Music Ltd/Notting Hill Music Ltd.

'Who Put the Bomp (In the Bomp, Bomp, Bomp)' – Gerry Goffin/Barry Mann. © Screen Gems-EMI Music Inc (BMI).

'Sad Songs and Waltzes' – Willie Nelson. © Sony/ATV Songs dba Tree Publishing Co (BMI).

'I Miss You' – Randy Newman. © Randy Newman Music (ASCAP).

'Bad Bad Boy' – McCafferty/Agnew/ Charlton/Sweet. © Carlin Music Corp.

'Our Captain Calls All Hands' – Traditional.

'Barbara Allen' – Traditional.

'Matty Groves' – Traditional.

'Surfin' Bird' Alfred Frazier/John Harris/Carl White/Wilson Turner. © Atlantic Music Corp/Beechwood Music Corp (BMI).

'Ain't No Stoppin' Us Now' – Jerry Cohen/Gene McFadden/John Whitehead. © Warner Chappell Music Ltd.

'Weekend' – Leroy Burgess/James Calloway. © Calebur Compositions/PAP Music/Universal Music Corp (ASCAP).

'Lost in Music' – Bernard Edwards/ Nile Rodgers. © Bernard's Other Music/ Sony/ATV Songs LLC.

'Disco Inferno' – Leroy Green/Ron Kersey. © Famous Chappell Ltd.

'Independent Women Pt.II' – Comstock/ Donaldson/Knowles/Seats/Stewart. © Beyonce Publishing/Sony/ATV Tunes LLC/Criterion Music Corporation/ E Beats Music/Rap Tracks Publishing/ WB Music Corp (ASCAP).

'Modern Love' – David Bowie. © Jones Music America/RZO Music Ltd.

Index of songs

Notes on the indexes

We've included two indexes here, each of which covers all 1,577 recordings mentioned in the book. The first index, which starts below, is ordered alphabetically by title; each track is listed with details of its artist, the album on which it first appeared and its year of release. The second index, which begins on page 272, is ordered alphabetically by artist.

For consistency's sake, the album listed for each track is the album on which it originally featured. A number of these albums have long since been deleted, but many of the

tracks are still available on other albums (and, of course, as single-track downloads from the online music retailer of your choice). For songs that were not originally released as part of an album (single-only releases, 78s and so on), we've instead endeavoured to list currently available compilations on which they're included.

The years given are, for the most part, the years in which the tracks (*not* the albums) were first made commercially available. However, there are a few exceptions. For songs

that were not released until a number of years after they were recorded, we've listed the year of their original recording. For classical works, we've generally listed the date of the work's first performance. And for songs from stage shows, we've used the date of the show's premiere.

Finally, a handful of songs are mentioned in the various essays without the writer referencing a particular recording (jazz standards, for example). For these, we've chosen a representative or otherwise noteworthy recording for this index.

INDEX OF SONGS

Interviews & lists

INDEX OF SONGS

Index of artists

INDEX OF ARTISTS

INDEX OF ARTISTS

3190104754 0044

INDEX OF ARTISTS